PROPORTIONALITY IN INTERNATIONAL HUMANITARIAN LAW

This book seeks to clarify the legal concept of proportionality in international humanitarian law, as it applies during armed conflict. It is argued in the book that a refocus of the interpretation of the proportionality rule is warranted to enhance the protection of civilians. More precisely, this book seeks to dissect the origins of the rule, determine how its components must be interpreted and how it is to be applied in practice. The book considers practical situations that may arise in the conduct of military operations and searches for the limits international humanitarian law sets to commanders' assessments of proportionality during armed conflict. The book concludes that proportionality is an inherently subjective and imprecise yardstick that nonetheless serves to protect civilians during armed conflict.

Jeroen van den Boogaard is legal counsel for international law at the Ministry of Foreign Affairs of the Netherlands and lecturer in international humanitarian law at the University of Amsterdam. He holds an LLM from the Erasmus University Rotterdam and a PhD from the University of Amsterdam.

Proportionality in International Humanitarian Law

REFOCUSING THE BALANCE IN PRACTICE

JEROEN VAN DEN BOOGAARD

CAMBRIDGE
UNIVERSITY PRESS

CAMBRIDGE
UNIVERSITY PRESS

Shaftesbury Road, Cambridge CB2 8EA, United Kingdom

One Liberty Plaza, 20th Floor, New York, NY 10006, USA

477 Williamstown Road, Port Melbourne, VIC 3207, Australia

314–321, 3rd Floor, Plot 3, Splendor Forum, Jasola District Centre, New Delhi – 110025, India

103 Penang Road, #05–06/07, Visioncrest Commercial, Singapore 238467

Cambridge University Press is part of Cambridge University Press & Assessment, a department of the University of Cambridge.

We share the University's mission to contribute to society through the pursuit of education, learning and research at the highest international levels of excellence.

www.cambridge.org
Information on this title: www.cambridge.org/9781108845137

DOI: 10.1017/9781108954648

First published 2023

A catalogue record for this publication is available from the British Library.

Library of Congress Cataloging-in-Publication Data
NAMES: Boogaard, Jeroen van den, author.
TITLE: Proportionality in international humanitarian law : refocusing the balance in practice / Jeroen van den Boogaard, University of Amsterdam.
DESCRIPTION: Cambridge, United Kingdom ; New York, NY : Cambridge University Press, 2023. | Includes bibliographical references and index.
IDENTIFIERS: LCCN 2022039239 (print) | LCCN 2022039240 (ebook) | ISBN 9781108845137 (hardback) | ISBN 9781108949583 (paperback) | ISBN 9781108954648 (epub)
SUBJECTS: LCSH: Humanitarian law. | Proportionality in law.
CLASSIFICATION: LCC KZ6471 .B63 2023 (print) | LCC KZ6471 (ebook) | DDC 341.6/7–dc23/eng/20221201
LC record available at https://lccn.loc.gov/2022039239
LC ebook record available at https://lccn.loc.gov/2022039240

ISBN 978-1-108-84513-7 Hardback

Contents

Preface

This book is based on a PhD thesis in international law, submitted at the University of Amsterdam and written under the supervision of Professor Terry Gill. The thesis was publicly defended on 2 October 2019.[1] This book is an updated and shortened version of that thesis.

The target audience of this book consists, primarily, of academics in the fields of international law, the philosophy of war, international relations theory, military theory, military doctrine and military history. The subject matter – proportionality – is frequently addressed in other disciplines of international law, as well as in military ethics. Beyond the scholarly audience it is believed that the book will be of interest to practitioners in the field, including military legal advisers and civilian legal advisers in the Ministries of Defence and Foreign Affairs, as well as others working closely with military operations, governmental representatives and military officers.

1 The assessment committee consisted of Professor Andre Nollkaemper (Dean of the Law Faculty of the University of Amsterdam), Professor Robin Geiss (University of Glasgow), Professor Liesbeth Lijnzaad (University of Maastricht, Judge of the ITLOS), Brigadier General Professor Paul Ducheine (University of Amsterdam and Netherlands Defence Academy) and Professor Harmen van der Wilt (University of Amsterdam).

Table of Cases

PCIJ/ICJ

S.S. Lotus Case, (France *v.* Turkey), Judgment, 7 September 1927, PCIJ Series A, No. 10 (1927).

Factory at Chorzow, (Germany *v.* Poland), Merits, Judgment, 13 September 1928, No. 13, PCIJ Series A, No. 17 (1928).

Corfu Channel Case, (United Kingdom *v.* Albania) Judgment, 9 April 1949, ICJ Reports 1949, p. 4.

Fisheries Case (United Kingdom *v.* Norway), Judgment, 18 December 1951, ICJ Reports 1951, p. 116.

North Sea Continental Shelf, Judgment, 20 February 1969, ICJ Reports 1969, p. 3.

Barcelona Traction Case, ICJ Reports 1970, p. 3.

Military and Paramilitary Activities in and against Nicaragua (Nicaragua *v.* United States of America), Merits, Judgment, ICJ Reports 1986, p. 14.

Legality of the Threat or Use of Nuclear Weapons, Advisory Opinion, ICJ Reports 1996, p. 257.

Case Concerning Oil Platforms (Islamic Republic of Iran *v.* United States of America), 2003, Judgment, ICJ Reports 2003, p. 161.

Legal Consequences of the Construction of a Wall in the Occupied Palestinian Territory, Advisory Opinion, ICJ Reports 2004, p. 136.

ICTY

Prosecutor *v.* Tadić, (Decision on the Defence Motion for Interlocutory Appeal on Jurisdiction), Case no. IT-94-1-AR72, Appeals Chamber, 2 October 1995.

Prosecutor *v.* Tadić, (Judgment), Case no. IT-94-1-A, Appeals Chamber, 15 July 1999.

Prosecutor *v.* Kupreškić et al., (Judgment), Case no. IT-95-16-T, Trial Chamber, 14 January 2000.

Prosecutor *v.* Blaškić, (Judgment), Case no. IT-95-14-T, Trial Chamber, 3 March 2000.

Prosecutor *v.* Kordić and Čerkez, (Judgment), Case no. IT-95-14/2-T, Trial Chamber, 16 February 2001.

Prosecutor *v.* Galić, (Judgment), Case no. IT-98-29-T, Trial Chamber, 5 December 2003.

Prosecutor *v.* Blaškić, (Judgment), Case no. IT-95-14-A, Appeals Chamber, 29 July 2004.

Prosecutor *v.* Kordić and Čerkez, (Judgment), Case no. IT-95-14/2-A, Appeals Chamber, 17 December 2004.

Prosecutor *v.* Galić, (Judgment), Case no. IT-98-29-A, Appeals Chamber, 30 November 2006.

Prosecutor *v.* Martić, (Judgment), Case no. IT-95-11-T, Trial Chamber I, 12 June 2007.

Prosecutor *v.* Dragomir Milošević, (Judgment), Case no. IT-98-29/1-T, Trial Chamber, 12 December 2007.

Prosecutor *v.* Martić, (Judgment), Case no. IT-95-11-A, Appeals Chamber, 8 October 2008.

Prosecutor *v.* Gotovina et al., (Judgment), Case no. IT-06-90-T, Trial Chamber I, 15 April 2011.

Prosecutor *v.* Gotovina et al., (Judgment), Case no. IT-06-90-A, Appeals Chamber, 16 November 2012.

Prosecutor *v.* Prlić et al., (Judgment), Case no. IT-04-74-T, Trial Chamber, 29 May 2013.

Prosecutor *v.* Prlić et al., (Judgment), Case no. IT-04-74-A, Appeals Chamber, 29 November 2017.

Prosecutor *v.* Karadzić, (Judgment), Case no. IT-95-5/18-T, Trial Chamber, 24 March 2016.

EECC

Eritrea–Ethiopia Claims Commission, Partial Award Western Front, Aerial Bombardment and Related Claims, Eritrea's Claim 25, 19 December 2005.

Eritrea–Ethiopia Claims Commission, Partial Award Western Front, Aerial Bombardment and Related Claims, Eritrea's Claim 26, 19 December 2005.

ICC

ICC, Prosecutor Report on Korea Incidents: Situation in the Republic of Korea, Article 5 Report (ICC Korea Report), 5 June 2014.

Arbitral Tribunals and Awards

Greco-German Mixed Arbitral Tribunal, Kiriadolou *v.* Germany, 1930, *Annual Digest of Public International Law Cases*, 1929–1930, pp. 516–517.

Greco-German Mixed Arbitral Tribunal, Coena *v.* Germany, 1927, *Annual Digest of Public International Law Cases.*

Post-World War II Cases

United States *v.* Otto Ohlendorf et al., 4 Trials of War Criminals before the Nuremberg Military Tribunals under Control Council Law No. 10, pp. 1 et seq., p. 467 (1947).

Ardeatine Caves Case (also known as the *Kappler Case*), 15, *Annual Digest & Reports of Public International Cases*, 1948, p. 471.

Hostage Case of the American Military Tribunal in Nuremberg in 1948, USA *v.* List et al., 11 NMT 757, pp. 1230–1253.

Other International Courts and National Courts

Caroline Case Note of US Secretary of State Daniel Webster, 24 April 1841, Caroline Case, 29 British and Foreign State papers (1841), pp. 1137–1138.

R *v.* Goldstein (1983) 1 WLR 151 at 155.

Shimoda Case, International Legal Materials (ILM), no. 32, p. 626. T.

The Israeli Supreme Court sitting as the High Court of Justice, The Public Committee against Torture in Israel et al. *v.* The Government of Israel et al., HCJ 769/02, 11 December 2005.

HCJ 769/02 Public Committee against Torture in Israel and Palestinian Society for the Protection of Human Rights and the Environment *v.* Israel and Others ILDC 597 (IL 2006) [2006] ('Public Committee against Torture').

Supreme Court in Jerusalem Sitting as the High Court of Justice, Petition 8794/03 submitted by Yoav Hass, Ruling on 23 December 2008, para. 11, available at www.geneva-academy.ch/RULAC/pdf_state/HCJ-decision-8794-03-1-.pdf

Beit Sourik Case (HCJ 2056/04, Beit Sourik Village Council et al. *v.* Government of Israel et al., 58(5) PD, or the English translation in 43 ILM 1099 (2004)), and the case of *Alfei Menashe* (HCJ 7957/04, Mara'abe et al. *v.* Prime Minister of Israel et al. or the English translation in 45 ILM 202 (2006)).

Germany, Federal Court of Justice, Federal Prosecutor General, *Fuel Tankers Case*, Decision, 16 April 2010, para. 2 on p. 63.

Christiansen and *Zuhlke* in the Dutch courts that also followed World War II, where the courts observed the equal application of IHL. See Dinstein 2017, p. 182 and accompanying notes.

Table of Treaties

1856 Paris Declaration Respecting Maritime Law
1868 St. Petersburg Declaration Renouncing the Use, in Time of War, of Explosive Projectiles under 400 Grammes Weight
1899 Declaration IV.1 to Prohibit, for the Term of Five Years, the Launching of Projectiles and Explosive from Balloons, and Other Methods of a Similar Nature
1907 Hague Convention IV Respecting the Laws and Customs of War on Land and Its Annex: Regulations Respecting the Laws and Customs of War on Land
1907 Declaration XIV Prohibiting the Discharge of Projectiles and Explosives from Balloons
1907 Hague Convention IX, Concerning Bombardment by Naval Forces in Time of War
1929 Geneva Convention Relative to the Treatment of Prisoners of War
1945 Statute of the International Court of Justice
1948 United Nations Convention on the Prevention and Punishment of the Crime of Genocide
1949 Geneva Convention (I) for the Amelioration of the Condition of Wounded and Sick in Armed Forces in the Field (GCI)
1949 Geneva Convention (II) for the Amelioration of the Condition of Wounded, Sick and Shipwrecked Members of Armed Forces at Sea (GCII)
1949 Geneva Convention (III) Relative to the Protection of Prisoners of War (GCIII)
1949 Geneva Convention (IV) Relative to the Protection of Civilian Persons in Time of War (GCIV)
1950 European Convention on Human Rights (ECHR)
1954 Hague Convention for the Protection of Cultural Property in the Event of Armed Conflict (UNESCO Convention)

1966 International Covenant on Civil and Political Rights (ICCPR)
1966 International Covenant on Economic, Social and Cultural Rights (ICESCR)
1969 American Convention on Human Rights (ACHR)
1969 Vienna Convention on the Law of Treaties
1976 United Nations Convention on the Prohibition of Military or Any Other Hostile Use of Environmental Modification Techniques (ENMOD Convention)
1977 Protocol Additional to the Geneva Conventions of 12 August 1949, and Relating to the Protection of Victims of International Armed Conflicts (Additional Protocol I or API)
1977 Protocol Additional to the Geneva Conventions of 12 August 1949, and Relating to the Protection of Victims of Non-International Armed Conflicts (Additional Protocol II or APII)
1980 United Nations Convention on Prohibitions or Restrictions on the Use of Certain Conventional Weapons Which May be Deemed to be Excessively Injurious or to Have Indiscriminate Effects
1980 Protocol II on Prohibitions or Restrictions on the Use of Mines, Booby-Traps and Other Devices
1984 Convention against Torture and Other Cruel, Inhuman or Degrading Treatment or Punishment (CAT)
1989 United Nations Convention on the Rights of the Child
1995 Protocol IV on Blinding Laser Weapons
1996 Amended Protocol II on Prohibitions or Restrictions on the Use of Mines, Booby-Traps and Other Devices UN Charter
1997 Ottawa Convention on the Prohibition of the Use, Stockpiling, Production and Transfer of Anti-Personnel Mines and on their Destruction
1998 Rome Statute of the International Criminal Court
2005 Protocol Additional to the Geneva Conventions of 12 August 1949, and Relating to the Adoption of an Additional Distinctive Emblem and (APIII)

Other Instruments

1923 Hague Rules on Air Warfare
1938 Protection of Civilian Populations against Bombing from the Air in Case of War, Resolution of the League of Nations Assembly on 30 September 1938
1948 United Nations Universal Declaration of Human Rights

Abbreviations

API	Additional Protocol I to the Geneva Conventions
DPiH	Direct Participation in Hostilities
DPRK	Democratic People's Republic of Korea (North Korea)
HVO	Croatian Defence Council of Bosnia and Herzegovina (Hrvatsko vijeće obrane)
ICG	International Crisis Group
ICRC	International Committee of the Red Cross
ICTY	International Criminal Tribunal for the former Yugoslavia
IHL	international humanitarian law
ILA	International Law Association
JAG	judge advocate general
KPA	Korean People's Army
MLRS	Multiple launch rocket system
NSAG	non-State armed group
OTP	Office of the Prosecutor
PGM	precision-guided munition
PTSD	Post-traumatic stress disorder
ROK	Republic of Korea
RTS	Radio Television of Serbia
SIC	Special Investigatory Commission
SIRUS	Superfluous injury or unnecessary suffering
UK	United Kingdom
US DoD	United States Department of Defense

1

Introduction

Le principe de proportionnalité occupe donc une place enviable en droit international humanitaire et sous-tend l'ensemble du droit des conflits armés. On peut toutefois se demander si cette présence affirmée n'est pas précisément trop idéale pour être efficace! Ne serait-il pas paradoxal que l'une des branches du droit international où ce principe est le plus nettement affirmé soit également celle où sa mise en œuvre soit l'une des plus difficiles?[1]

1.1 THE TOPIC OF THIS BOOK

In war, people die. But that does not mean that war is totally stripped of humanity. International humanitarian law (IHL) provides the legal framework for those who are fighting for one of the parties to an armed conflict, and for the protection of those affected by the hostilities. The aim of IHL is to regulate the way the war is fought and to protect those who are not taking part in the hostilities.

When military forces attack a legitimate military objective during armed conflict, they may be expected to cause civilian harm, even after feasible precautions to avoid or minimise any collateral damage have been taken. But how many civilians may die when a legitimate military objective is attacked during an armed conflict? Or, how many civilian objects may be destroyed for what type of military advantage? To determine the answer to these vexing questions, military commanders must apply the proportionality

[1] Philippe, p. 1187: [the principle of proportionality thus plays a central role in international humanitarian law and underpins the system of the law during armed conflict. Isn't it paradoxical that in the branch of international law in which the principle is most clearly articulated, is also the branch of law where it is one of the most difficult principles to apply?] (translation by the author).

rule which is part of IHL. The IHL proportionality rule acknowledges that both the law needs to provide sufficient leeway for the military to effectively defeat their enemy and the civilian population must be protected. This rule is the topic of this book.

This book seeks to clarify the legal concept of proportionality as it applies during armed conflict and argues that a refocus of the interpretation of the IHL proportionality rule is warranted to enhance the protection of civilians. More precisely, this book seeks to dissect the origins of the rule, determine how its components must be interpreted and how it is to be applied in practice. The book considers practical situations that may arise in the conduct of military operations and searches for the limits IHL sets to commanders' assessments of proportionality during armed conflict.

1.2 INTERNATIONAL HUMANITARIAN LAW

International humanitarian law is a branch of international law that aims to mitigate the horrors of war by preserving some humanity during armed conflict. The provisions of IHL are applicable whenever there are ongoing military operations during which the armed violence that is used amounts to an armed conflict and in situations of occupation. The provisions of IHL bind the parties to the armed conflict and the members of their forces.

The objective of IHL is twofold. Firstly, it is to prevent suffering of those people who are not, or no longer, taking direct part in the hostilities taking into account the circumstances as they occur in times of armed conflict. Protected are inter alia captured, wounded, sick and even dead soldiers; medical personnel, vehicles and installations; civilians and civilian objects. Secondly, IHL restricts the effect of means and methods of combat used by those who do participate in the armed conflict. Prohibited methods of combat include attacks against civilians and attacks that misuse the protection that has been awarded to others, such as misuse of the protected emblems of the Red Cross, Red Crescent or Red Crystal. Prohibited means of warfare include weapons that cause serious injury or unnecessary suffering, such as bullets that are designed to explode inside the human body, rendering the death of the victim inevitable.

A unique characteristic of IHL is that it is a preventive framework. Although States remain the main addressees of IHL, individuals are bound by it as well as representatives of those States. IHL has been drafted to influence behaviour on the battlefield, during the armed conflict, and not necessarily to make it possible to prosecute people for violations of IHL. In other words: the rules of IHL are drafted for soldiers, not lawyers. Of course, many lawyers were present during the negotiations of the main instruments of international law, but also military practitioners, with a view to keeping IHL workable for the military.

An important factor in IHL is that different legal regimes are applicable to different types of armed conflict. The classical interstate armed conflict, labelled an 'international armed conflict', is regulated through extensive rules of treaty law, including the Geneva Conventions of 1949[2] and the First Additional Protocol of 1977,[3] as well as a number of other treaties pertaining mostly to weapons, but also treaties that provide protection for cultural property and the environment. The other category is that of a non-international armed conflict, which is regulated mainly by common article 3 of the Geneva Conventions. Common article 3 applies to armed conflicts within the territory of one State between the government armed forces and a dissident armed group, armed conflicts between such groups, and arguably a residual group of other types of armed conflicts.[4] The Second Additional Protocol applies to certain types of non-international armed conflicts, in addition to common article 3.[5] Of course, apart from the IHL treaties, customary IHL applies as well.

Much has been written on the history of IHL.[6] Depending on the background of the writer and purpose of the book, a description of the history of IHL may commence by referring to the Bible,[7] the Koran,[8] ancient Hindi texts[9] or texts from other civilisations, including the Maori,[10] the work of Hugo

[2] The Geneva Conventions of 12 August 1949: Geneva Convention (I) for the Amelioration of the Condition of Wounded and Sick in Armed Forces in the Field (GCI); Geneva Convention (II) for the Amelioration of the Condition of Wounded, Sick and Shipwrecked Members of Armed Forces at Sea (GCII); Geneva Convention (III) relative to the Protection of Prisoners of War (GCIII); Geneva Convention (IV) relative to the Protection of Civilian Persons in Time of War (GCIV).

[3] Protocol Additional to the Geneva Conventions of 12 August 1949, and Relating to the Protection of Victims of International Armed Conflicts, 9 June 1977 (hereinafter: Additional Protocol I or API).

[4] See generally Bartels 2009a.

[5] Protocol Additional to the Geneva Conventions of 12 August 1949, and Relating to the Protection of Victims of Non-International Armed Conflicts, 9 June 1977 (hereinafter: Additional Protocol II or APII).

[6] For an overview of the historical development of IHL, see, for example, Best, Kalshoven and Zegveld, Greenwood 2008, pp. 15–27, Green, pp. 20–53 and Amerasinghe, pp. 263–287.

[7] See, for example, Deuteronomy 20: even though this chapter contains a provision stating that all male inhabitants of a conquered city may be killed, it also contains a provision stating that only trees that do not bear eatable fruit may be used to build fortification during a siege.

[8] See, for example, van Engeland, pp. 155–156.

[9] Amerasinghe, pp. 264–267. See also Nirmal, pp. 25–38.

[10] Judge Kenneth Keith presented the Maori 'Solemn rules for governing the fighting', during his lecture 'Tutti Fratelli?' as delivered on 10 February 2009 in the lecture series of The Hague

Grotius,[11] the Lieber Code[12] or a description of the Battle of Solferino in 1859. All these texts prove that the idea that warfare must not be unrestricted is universal, and has existed throughout history. Sadly, many atrocities violating these rules have taken place in history. However, at the same time, there have always been examples of commanders who attached value to a sense of humanity. The famous Sultan Saladin was a highly respected commander throughout the region because of his chivalrous behaviour towards his adversaries during and after combat.[13]

The influence of Henri Dunant cannot be overlooked as an important factor in the development of IHL. In 1862, Dunant published his account of the battle of Solferino, describing the suffering of thousands of soldiers during and after battle. His book A *Memory of Solferino* is a detailed description of courageous acts of war by mostly generals, dukes and princes. But Dunant also describes the suffering of those left *hors de combat* after the battle, with nobody there to care for them. And it is the suffering of these soldiers that motivated Dunant to propose in his book that there should be written rules to protect – in particular – sick and wounded soldiers. This proposal was successful in the sense that the first Geneva Convention was concluded in 1864, providing basic rules aiming to protect wounded and sick soldiers. The almost simultaneous founding of the International Committee of the Red Cross (ICRC), as it is called today, provided the basis for the leading role that this private organisation played, and still plays, in the development and implementation of IHL. The first Geneva Convention of 1864 has since regularly been updated, mostly after major armed conflicts.[14] The result of the Geneva branch of IHL are the four Geneva Conventions of 1949 and its three Additional Protocols.

This so-called Geneva law was in essence just one of the two main lines of development of IHL. The other one consists of rules regulating the means and methods of warfare to be used during the conduct of hostilities. The first modern multilateral effort to regulate affairs during armed conflict was the

Initiative for Law and Armed Conflict (HILAC). The rules were used during the Battle of Gate Pa, New Zealand, in April 1864.

[11] See Grotius' seminal work *de jure ac bella pacis*.

[12] Instructions for the Government of Armies of the United States in the Field, promulgated as General Orders No. 100 by President Lincoln on 24 April 1863, but prepared by Francis Lieber (hereinafter: the Lieber code). See Schindler and Toman, p. 3.

[13] Greenwood 2008, p. 17.

[14] The Geneva Conventions were updated in 1906 and 1929 before they became the applicable four Geneva Conventions of 1949, which have achieved universal ratification, and supplemented by the two Additional Protocols of 1977 and the Third Additional Protocol on the Red Crystal in 2006.

Declaration of Paris of 1856.[15] A more important founding document is the famous Lieber Code of 1863, which served as an early handbook on IHL for commanders during the American Civil War. The Lieber Code was the main inspiration for the Brussels Conference of 1874[16] and has been the basis for the other main line of development of IHL. This current is usually referred to as Hague law, because the founding treaty in which the main rules for the conduct of hostilities have been laid down, the Hague Regulations, was the result of the two Peace Conferences that took place in The Hague in 1899 and 1907.[17] With regard to the use of certain means of warfare, treaties have been concluded on chemical, biological and conventional weapons. The conclusion of treaties prohibiting or restricting the use of a number of specific weapons have proved the direct impact that IHL continues to have on the battlefield.[18]

Today, the distinction between Hague law and Geneva law is used mainly for historical and didactic reasons.[19] For example, API contains provisions on both the protection of persons during armed conflict and the conduct of hostilities. In other words, both Hague and Geneva law. The International Court of Justice notes in this regard that,

> these two branches of law applicable in armed conflict have become so closely interrelated that they are considered to have gradually formed one single complex system, known today as IHL. The provisions of the Additional Protocols of 1977 give expression and attest to the unity and complexity of that law.[20]

International humanitarian law has today become one of the best developed systems of law on the international plane, consisting of an impressive body of treaty law and a number of rules of customary IHL. Paradoxically, the humanitarian ideals behind the rules of IHL, clearly stemming from

15 Declaration respecting Maritime Law, signed in Paris, 16 April 1856 (Declaration of Paris). The Declaration of Paris contains provisions on neutrality such as the neutral flag, blockade and contraband of war. Parties were Austria, France, Great Britain, Prussia, Russia, Sardinia and Turkey. See Schindler and Toman, p. 1053. See also Amerasinghe, p. 269.

16 The result of the Brussels Conference, in which representatives of fifteen European States took part, is generally referred to as the Brussels Declaration. For the text of the adopted documents, see Schindler and Toman, p. 21. See Amerasinghe, p. 270 and Kalshoven 2006, p. 49.

17 Kalshoven and Zegveld, pp. 10–14.

18 One example is the use of anti-personnel landmines because its use has decreased significantly after the conclusion of the Ottawa Convention of 1997.

19 Chetail, p. 238.

20 *Legality of the Threat or Use of Nuclear Weapons*, Advisory Opinion, ICJ Reports 1996 (hereinafter: the Nuclear Weapons Advisory Opinion), para. 75, p. 257.

natural law sources, have succeeded in being codified in positive law. As Draper puts it:

> It is a strange reflection that the humanitarian movement of the mid-19th century appeared in the noon-tide of positivist theories of international law. When the claims of sovereignty of states were at their highest, when the last relics of moral restraint in the old theories of natural law and its corollary, the 'just war' idea, were receding, the full spate of the humanitarian ideal appeared.[21]

As far as customary IHL is concerned, there is still an ongoing debate on this subject, sparked by developments such as the publication of the ICRC Customary Law Study in 2005; the judgments of the Eritrea–Ethiopia Claims Tribunal; the ad hoc international criminal tribunals such as those for the former Yugoslavia and Rwanda, and the emerging jurisprudence of the International Criminal Court. These latter institutions are part of a major development in international relations that has resulted in significant progress in international criminal law (ICL). The developments in this field of law since 1993 are remarkable. It provides the procedural rules necessary for a part of the implementation of IHL: the criminal prosecution of individual violators of IHL outside national jurisdictions. However, ICL only enters the scene after hostilities have ended. The application of IHL by soldiers during combat is where the potential of international law to protect against the horrors of war is exercised to the fullest extent possible. However, ICL judgments undoubtedly provide a valuable source for interpretation of IHL rules and concepts.

1.3 PROPORTIONALITY IN IHL

The subject of this book is proportionality in IHL. This rule, often referred to as a 'principle', acknowledges that civilians and civilian objects may legitimately be affected by warfare. It is a myth that civilian casualties can be entirely avoided during contemporary armed conflicts, not necessarily because the law is violated, but because collateral damage can be caused by other factors. For example, unexpected collateral damage may be the result of imperfect or incomplete information, malfunction or inherent imprecision of weapon systems or damage caused by the activities of other forces. Even though civilians and civilian objects may not be directly targeted, the IHL principle of proportionality allows for civilian casualties and damage to civilian objects, under the restriction that these are not excessive to the military advantage

[21] Draper, p. 131.

anticipated. The IHL proportionality rule is commonly understood to be codified in article 51 (5) (b) of Additional Protocol I (1977) to the Geneva Conventions:

> [Prohibited are attacks] . . . which may be expected to cause incidental loss of civilian life, injury to civilians, damage to civilian objects, or a combination thereof, which would be excessive in relation to the concrete and direct military advantage anticipated.

The principle of proportionality is often cited as one of the principles of IHL.[22] International humanitarian law, or *ius in bello*, is only one of the many branches of public international law.[23] The principle of proportionality in the context of an armed conflict also exists in other branches of international law, such as international human rights law and the law on the use of force by States, or *ius ad bellum*, as it is more generally referred to.[24] These two proportionality standards are discussed in Chapter 2 of this book in order to distinguish them from the IHL proportionality rule.

This book aims to provide more clarity on the concept of proportionality in IHL and the balance it requires between anticipated military advantage and expected collateral damage. The textbook answer to the question of when an attack is conducted in accordance with the IHL proportionality rule is: 'it depends on the circumstances of each specific case'. This seems to be the inevitable outcome of a rule that is phrased as a comparison between the rather generic terms of 'military advantage' and 'civilian casualties and damage'. This makes sense: every attack is different, and for each different military objective, or available type of weapon, the proportionality test will have a different outcome. But still, this textbook answer seems highly unsatisfactory. The goal of this study is therefore to get a more precise answer than that. This goal is important for a number of reasons.

Firstly, it is important for the conductors of an attack to receive more guidance on how to balance military advantage and collateral damage. Members of the armed forces of the parties to the conflict, both military commanders and soldiers, are the people that have been authorised by

[22] See, for example, Rogers 2004, p. 3, and the discussion in Section 2.2.3.

[23] Other names for this branch of law include the Law of Armed Conflict or the Law of War. For example, the United States prefer the term 'Law of War, or Laws and Customs of War', see Bellinger and Haynes, p. 443; Gardam 2004, p. 1. For an explanation of the term *ius in bello*, see Kolb 1997, pp. 553–562.

[24] This study uses the term 'international law' as short for 'public international law', although the term 'international private law' is technically also part of international law. International private law is not the object of this study.

States to take the lives of the members of opposing forces. While they are conducting their operations, IHL applies to their actions. If they violate the provisions of IHL, they may face criminal prosecution. In fact, due to the developments in ICL in the past decades, it is likely that the probability for this to actually occur has increased. Therefore, these fighters are entitled to receive clear guidance about what they can and what they cannot do during hostilities. They deserve this, given the fact that they are the ones putting their lives on the line in combat for the sake of the political goals of their leaders. In turn, States have a responsibility towards their military forces to provide clear guidance on how to conduct the military operations within the boundaries of IHL.

Secondly, clear guidance for members of armed forces participating in armed conflicts is important for reasons of post-conflict reconciliation. The built-in reciprocity of the rules of IHL offers the potential to prevent total escalation of hostilities. Observance of IHL on one side of the conflict can be very important for observance of the same rules by the opposing side. If the IHL proportionality rule is not clear, disproportionate attacks by one side of the conflict may be retaliated by disproportionate attacks of the adverse party. Total escalation of an armed conflict resulting in massive violations of IHL is a key obstacle to reconciliation after the conflict. As noted by Pratzner,

> perhaps most importantly, mitigating collateral damage provides for the possibility of a better peace. Warfare in the modern era demands this, perhaps more than conflicts in the past. . . . A vanquished opponent may fight for years and never give up the fight fully, as seen in Afghanistan and Iraq. The indiscriminate use of force does little to weaken this urge; instead, it may even intensify it. Avoiding and mitigating collateral damage contributes to peace by protecting non-combatants, keeping infrastructure intact, and lessening the enemy's desire to fight perpetual war.[25]

Thirdly, and perhaps most importantly, more clarity of the concept of proportionality in armed conflict will also provide better protection for those civilians and civilian objects that find themselves in the midst of the armed conflict. The obligation to apply a legal rule is at odds with a vague and subjective balance, restricted only by the discretion of military commanders. It is not an easy task for members of the armed forces to balance the concepts of military advantage and collateral damage. The two concepts are of a different nature and there is not always enough information available to assess the exact value of the two components of the IHL proportionality rule. The situation needs to

[25] Pratzner, p. 92.

be avoided that the IHL proportionality rule can be abused to justify the outcome of any attack. Because if that were the case, the protective character of the IHL proportionality rule may prove to be an illusion. As a result, the IHL proportionality rule would merely undermine the prohibition to directly attack civilians and civilian objects.

Thus, the main purpose of this study is to provide more clarity on the application of the IHL proportionality rule that applies during armed conflict, for the sake of the conductors of the attack; for the civilians that may be affected by it, as well as for a better peace.

1.4 METHODOLOGY AND STRUCTURE

The central research question of this study is: what is the normative legal content of the principle of proportionality in IHL? The approach in this book to answering this question is based on a modern positivistic approach to international law.[26] Therefore, for answering the central question and sub-questions arising from it, this study explores the sources of international law, citing and interpreting its rules in accordance with the rules for the interpretation of treaty rules as provided for in the Vienna Treaty on the Law of Treaties. Furthermore, there is a significant role for unwritten law, such as customary law, general principles and soft law instruments, although written rules are the starting point of the analysis. Where necessary for answering the research questions, this study uses illustrations based on military doctrine, such as targeting procedures, and descriptions of the moral underpinnings of the rules that are analysed, such as Just War theory.

The study starts in the domain of general public international law by exploring the rather general notion of principles of international law, which is also a source of international law. This is a study of the theory in relation to the applicable treaty law and its *travaux préparatoires*, judicial decisions of international courts and tribunals and the doctrine, or 'the teachings of the most highly qualified publicists of the various nations'.[27] But the study aims to end on a very practical level: the applicability and interpretation of the IHL principle of proportionality to individual members of an armed or military group who are taking part in actual hostilities. That means that the study aims

[26] This study does not seek to address questions of legal philosophy. See, for a general overview of seven different approaches to international law, Slaughter and Ratner, pp. 291–302: '[p]ositivism summarizes a range of theories that focus upon describing the law as it is, backed up by effective sanctions, with reference to formal criteria, independently of moral or ethical considerations.'

[27] Article 38 of the Statute of the International Court of Justice.

at formulating practical recommendations on how the principle of proportionality in IHL must be interpreted and applied. This objective requires interpretation of the legal norms embodied in international law.[28] Especially for the rules of IHL, this interpretation is informed by 'the promotion of humanitarian principles, beyond the purely "written" text'.[29]

The principle of proportionality in IHL is codified as a rule in Additional Protocol I to the Geneva Conventions. The analysis in this study is focussed on the rule as it has been codified in Protocol I, but also subsequent treaty law such as the Rome Statute.[30] Therefore, a closer look to the *travaux préparatoires* of these treaties is part of the analysis. The principle of proportionality has been commented upon by many leading experts in IHL, and their writings will be an important source for the study. In addition, the principle of proportionality has been addressed in a number of cases of, for example, the International Court of Justice[31] and the International Tribunal for the former Yugoslavia.[32]

This book consists of nine chapters. Chapter 1 provides insight into the subject, structure and methodology of this study. IHL as a branch of international law is first introduced, followed by the concept of proportionality during armed conflict. Furthermore, a short description is provided of the reasons why clarity on the IHL proportionality principle is important.

In Chapter 2, proportionality is positioned in the broader context of the 'principles of IHL'. It is determined whether IHL proportionality should be regarded as a principle or as a rule of IHL. Furthermore, to sketch the place of IHL proportionality in international law in other legal frameworks relating to the use of force, manifestations of proportionality in the *ius ad bellum* and international human rights law are analysed.

Chapter 3 notes and describes a number of other standards of moderation in IHL that resemble the proportionality assessment concerning collateral damage and military advantage. In this chapter, moderation standards are assessed in relation to the use of means and methods of warfare against

[28] Article 31 of the Vienna Convention of the Law of Treaties: '[a] treaty shall be interpreted in good faith in accordance with the ordinary meaning to be given to the terms of the treaty in their context and in the light of its object and purpose.'

[29] Lieblich, p. 201.

[30] Rome Statute of the International Criminal Court, 1998, printed in Schindler and Toman, p. 711.

[31] For example, in the Nuclear Weapons Advisory Opinion.

[32] For example, in the *Kupreskić Case* (ICTY, *Prosecutor* v. *Kupreskić*, Case no. IT-95-16-T, Judgment, Trial Chamber, 14 January 2000).

the enemy; the use of armed force against use of blockades; security measures during occupation; the destruction of enemy property and belligerent reprisals.

In Chapter 4, the historical development of the current IHL rule of proportionality is described. In addition, the status of the IHL rule of proportionality as a rule of customary IHL is assessed in this chapter. The questions that need an answer in this chapter include the following: What is the codification history of the IHL proportionality principle? Is the IHL proportionality rule part of customary international law? Is there a difference in the application of the IHL proportionality rule in international armed conflict or in non-international armed conflict?

Chapter 5 contains the description of the operational and legal context of the IHL proportionality rule. The operational context consists of the targeting processes that are used during different types of military operations. This is where the actual proportionality equation, balancing the military advantage and collateral damage, takes place. The legal context concerns the prohibition of launching indiscriminate attacks and the obligation to take precautionary measures protecting the civilian population, because the IHL proportionality rule is codified in that context.

Chapter 6 contains an in-depth analysis of the different components of which the IHL proportionality rule consists. Issues that are addressed include an assessment of who is responsible for conducting the proportionality analysis, the temporal scope and an assessment of both the 'civilian side' and the 'military advantage' side of the proportionality equation.

Chapter 7 contains a number of examples of factual situations in which the IHL proportionality rule was or should have been applied. Describing these examples is complicated because most militaries are not prepared to openly display the way they conduct their proportionality equation. Nonetheless, some governments have conducted their own investigations and published reports of their military operations. Furthermore, the Prosecutors of the International Tribunal for the former Yugoslavia and the International Criminal Court published reports of military operations they investigated. Also, international non-governmental organisations such as Human Rights Watch and Amnesty International publish reports on armed conflicts. The analysis of the examples is intended to increase the understanding of the issue of how the IHL proportionality rule is put into practice in reality, on different levels of authority.

Chapter 8 assesses to what extent the IHL proportionality rule is an objective or a subjective rule and the concept of the 'reasonable military commander' is discussed.

Ultimately, the interpretation of the word 'excessive' is the central issue in applying the IHL proportionality rule in practice. This interpretation is the subject of Chapter 9 and culminates in a plea for refocussing the balance of the interpretation of excessiveness towards humanity, which would entail increased protection of the civilian population during armed conflict.

2

IHL Proportionality in International Law

There is a lot of misunderstanding about the principle of proportionality.[1]

2.1 INTRODUCTION

In this chapter, proportionality is positioned in the broader context of international law. In that context, two relevant issues are discussed: IHL proportionality as a principle of IHL and the manifestations of proportionality in other legal frameworks relating to the use of force.

The relevance of looking into the broader context of the principles of IHL is that proportionality is commonly recognised as one of these IHL principles. This raises the question of what that means. This chapter therefore aims to clarify the consequences, if any, of proportionality being referenced to as a 'principle', more particularly a principle of law.[2] Being part of international law, IHL is based on the same sources as international law.[3] Principles are enumerated as one of these sources of international law, alongside treaty law and customary international law.[4] Insight into the origins and legal status of principles as sources of international law therefore seems relevant for determining the legal substance of principles of international law and for the category of legal norms in which the IHL principle of proportionality must

[1] Rogers 2008, p. 189.

[2] Law, in general, must be understood to consist of both national and international law. International law must be understood particularly as public international law.

[3] Kleffner 2016, p. 71. See for a discussion on whether the theory of sources of IHL is different from that of general public international law: van Steenberghe, pp. 891–911 and Ratner, pp. 912–935.

[4] Article 38 (1) (c) of the Statute of the International Court of Justice: 'The general principles of law recognised by civilised nations'.

be placed. As it turns out, the relevance of this issue is ultimately assessing the category of norm in which IHL proportionality must be placed. These issues are explored in Section 2.2.

The analysis of proportionality in IHL also raises the question of its relation to other manifestations of proportionality found in international law. That is the second issue that is dealt with in this chapter. International humanitarian law applies during armed conflict, but other branches of international law relating to the use of force are also of relevance in that situation. The two relevant manifestations of proportionality that come to mind in that regard are proportionality in the *ius ad bellum* and proportionality in the context of international human rights law (IHRL). Section 2.3 provides a discussion of proportionality as it is encountered in these other relevant branches of international law and how the different manifestations relate to IHL proportionality.

2.2 IS PROPORTIONALITY A PRINCIPLE OF IHL?

This section sets out to describe and analyse the term principles of international law and the particularities of principles of IHL.[5] However, writing about principles of law requires a preliminary remark about law itself. Legal theory advocates different understandings of law in general, and consequently, of international law.[6] These different understandings impact on the roles ascribed to principles in international law. For example, a strict positivist such as Kelsen would argue that the formation of law is contingent on the existence of a procedure that establishes a norm as law.[7] As a result, international law is in Kelsen's view limited to those norms that States have formed through their specific consent, and principles as underlying or more general notions of law may be deemed irrelevant. Dworkin, on the other hand, sees law as a more

5 This part of the study has served as the basis of the book chapter 'Fighting by the Principles: Principles as a Source of International Humanitarian Law', see van den Boogaard 2013. See also van den Boogaard 2020, https://lieber.westpoint.edu/reimagining-ihl-principles-part-i-wrong-principles/ (part I) and https://lieber.westpoint.edu/reimagining-ihl-principles-part-ii-new-framework/ (part II).

6 See for an overview, Orford.

7 See, for example, Kelsen 1960 and Kelsen 1952. See also Slaughter and Ratner: '[p]ositivism summarizes a range of theories that focus upon describing the law as it is, backed up by effective sanctions, with reference to formal criteria, independently of moral or ethical considerations.' For an in-depth analysis of Kelsen's position with regard to law and the theory of sources, particularly the general principles of international law, see Kammerhofer, pp. 105–112.

dynamic system.[8] This book accepts the latter perception of international law, but it is not intended to provide an in-depth analysis of different legal theories and how these may impact the interpretation of principles of international law. Instead, taking the theory of Dworkin as its starting point, this book adopts as its frame of analysis the distinction between three types of different norms as introduced by Dworkin. This distinction is used to refer to different types of legal norms and to explain how principles may be understood. This informs the interpretation of the IHL principle of proportionality in subsequent parts of this study.

According to Dworkin, a distinction must be made between three types of norms: policies, legal principles and legal rules. Policies can be characterised as norms aiming to certain objectives.[9] As such, policies represent values that are not legally binding, but provide a normative quality in political and moral terms. These 'policies' may perhaps better be referred to as foundations or pillars of a certain legal framework.[10] With regard to the difference between legal principles and legal rules, Dworkin maintains that both sets of norms 'point to particular decisions about legal obligation in particular circumstances, but they differ in the character they give. Rules are applicable in an all-or-nothing fashion'.[11] Thus, if the facts to which a rule relates occur, the rule must be applied. Principles seem to be in between policies and rules and have a somewhat different character. Although they are part of the law, and are thus legally binding, they are often more general or broad of character. As a result, principles can be taken into account as a consideration inclining in one direction or another.[12] Dworkin concludes that, 'principles have a

[8] See generally: Dworkin. See also Lachenmann, para. 26,

> Dworkin not only denies that there can be any general theory of the existence and content of law but he also rejects the institutional focus of positivism. Rather than from legislation, Dworkin proceeds from adjudication. According to legal positivism, Dworkin claims, legal rights do not exist prior to legislation; thus, rights can be taken away by the legislator, leaving the individual exposed to legislative arbitrariness. Thus, in court the individual cannot invoke rights that are rooted in human dignity or equality. By concentrating on legal rules, Dworkin says, positivism fails to acknowledge the role of legal principles that come into play in those 'hard cases' that are not clear-cut and not to be solved by mere subsumption. Such principles (eg fairness) may guide the judge's discretion. In Dworkin's opinion, rules and principles together make up the legal system.

[9] Dworkin, p. 22. The term 'policy' is also generally used to indicate actions by a State that are not necessarily motivated by legal concerns, but by, for example, political motives. Dworkin clearly understands the term 'policies' to refer to extra-legal considerations.

[10] See Winter, pp. 1–31 and van den Boogaard 2020.

[11] Dworkin, p. 24. See also Alexy, p. 44 v.; Petersen, pp. 287–291.

[12] Dworkin, p. 26.

dimension that rules do not – the dimension of weight and importance'.[13] This qualitative aspect sets principles apart from rules. This means that it is the objective of principles to obtain a certain goal, which may, or may not, be reached to a certain extent.[14] Rules, on the other hand, are 'norms that are always either fulfilled or not'.[15]

It is submitted that Dworkin's distinction between policies, principles and rules is useful because it discerns extra-legal considerations (policies) from the law (rules and principles). A principle of law is thus a norm, which is not itself a rule but underlies a rule, and explains or provides the rationale for the existence of the rule.[16] Furthermore, principles may be understood as more important norms than rules.[17] Principles of law play an important role in any legal framework. However, the term 'principle' can have a variety of meanings and is very loosely used in many different contexts. This poses additional challenges in analysing doctrine, conventional law and case law for principles of international law, in general, and for principles of IHL.

It may be deduced from the scholarly literature on the subject that the term 'principles' is often used for very general norms.[18] This is the first type of principles. The legal content of these principles is not as narrowly and precisely defined as that of rules. On the other hand, these principles are part of the law, and are not as broad as general political or moral concepts that are the foundation of the law (in Dworkin's typology: policies). A second type of principles consists of those norms that are deemed particularly important.[19] As a result, the term 'principle' may thus signify not only general norms, but may also point to specific norms, or in other words: the most important rules of a certain legal framework.[20] Thirdly, the term 'principle' is used to refer to underlying notions that have helped to shape other norms.[21] These principles are thus formative norms that serve as a basis of other, legally binding norms.

[13] Dworkin, p. 26. The distinction between rules and principles as drawn by Alexy is consistent with the distinction drawn by Dworkin; however, he assimilates policies with principles, stating that any norm 'is either a rule or a principle'. See Alexy, p. 44.

[14] This requirement of degree is crucial to set principles apart from rules according to Alexy. See Alexy, pp. 47–48.

[15] Alexy, p. 48. See also Gillich, p. 12: '[r]ules and principles contain different levels of intensity in which a specific command is set out or in which a specific aim has to be fulfilled.'

[16] Fitzmaurice, p. 7, see also van Hoof, p. 148.

[17] See also van Hoof, p. 149: 'have a wider scope of application and also more far-reaching consequences ... Principles constitute a more important or fundamental standard than rules.'

[18] See, for example, Alexy, p. 45.

[19] van Hoof, p. 149.

[20] Nasser, p. 64.

[21] See *Concise Oxford English Dictionary*, p. 1141: '[principles are] a fundamental source or basis of something'. See also Salmon, p. 877: 'Principe: Cause ou source première des règles'.

It is submitted that many writers use the term principle in this last context, but within the categories of norms as discerned by Dworkin, principles of this type would often constitute policies, because they consist of extra-legal considerations. It must be noted that norms that are referred to as 'principles' often have characteristics of more than one of these three different types: they may thus overlap and are not mutually exclusive. For example, the principle of distinction is referred to in the realm of IHL as a very important principle, but it is also the basis of specific rules of IHL. Furthermore, the principle of distinction provides a general distinction between categories of persons and objects, which is further specified in numerous rules.[22]

2.2.1 *Principles in International Law*

Principles are also referred to as one of the sources of international law.[23] The sources of international law both serve as the place where international norms are found and how these norms are created.[24] Article 38 of the Statute of the International Court of Justice (ICJ) is often taken as the starting point of analysing the sources of international law, because it includes principles as one of the sources of public international law to be used by the ICJ.[25] The text

22 The ICJ referred to the importance of the principle of distinction by referring to it as 'cardinal', see Nuclear Weapons Advisory Opinion, para. 78, p. 257. The principle is, however, also the origin of specific rules, such as article 44 (3) API: '. . . combatants are obliged to distinguish themselves from the civilian population while they are engaged in an attack or in a military operation preparatory to an attack. Recognizing, however, that there are situations in armed conflicts where, owing to the nature of the hostilities an armed combatant cannot so distinguish himself. . .'

23 Scholars writing on the subject of general principles as sources of international law often start by stating that there is controversy on the subject. See, for example, van Hoof, p. 131, stating that 'the general principles as a source of law are probably the most controversial one', and Degan, p. 1, stating that, '[n]o other source of law raises so many doctrinal controversies as the general principles of law "recognized by civilized nations" . . . Writers disagree on the substance and content of general principles of law, as well as their legal scope and relationship with the other main sources, namely treaties and customary law.'

24 Kolb 2006, p. 4.

25 See, for example, Kleffner 2016, p. 71. For a different view, see Besson, p.164, referring to article 38 of the ICJ Statute as 'the now largely obsolete but still venerated triad of sources'. Article 38 of the ICJ Statute reads:

> (1) The Court, whose function it is to decide in accordance with international law such disputes as are submitted to it, shall apply: (a) international conventions, whether general or particular, establishing rules expressly recognised by the contesting States; (b) International custom, as evidence of a general practice accepted as law; (c) The general principles of law recognised by civilised nations; (d) Subject to the provisions of Article 59, judicial decisions and the teachings of the most highly qualified publicists of the various nations, as subsidiary means for the determination of rules of law.. . .

of the article places principles on an equal footing with treaties and customary law, as the primary sources of international law. The category of general principles of law as codified in article 38 (1) (c) of the ICJ Statute was at the time of drafting aimed at principles of domestic legal orders, that could be used in international law, after the 'discussion moved from considering them in naturalistic overtones to thinking of them in a more positivistic manner as principles of national law, applicable by analogy in inter-State relations'.[26]

The Permanent Court of International Justice (PCIJ) and the ICJ have not used the principles of international law extensively,[27] but that does not mean that the principles of international law have played no role at all.[28] The PCIJ applied principles in the *Chorzow Factory Case*[29] and the *Lotus Case*.[30] The ICJ applied principles in, for example, the *Anglo-Norwegian Fisheries Case*, stating that,

> [i]t does not at all follow that in the absence of rules having the technically precise character alleged by the United Kingdom Government [concerning the course and length of straight base lines], the delimitation undertaken by the Norwegian Government in 1935 is not subject to certain principles which make it possible to judge as to its validity under international law.[31]

In these cases, the principles concerned were principles taken from domestic jurisdictions, 'elevated' to international law and applied in specific cases.[32] Courts can use comparative law techniques to identify and apply these principles.[33]

26 Koskenniemi, p. 402. See for descriptions of the codification, Degan, pp. 7–54, van Hoof, pp. 136–139 and Lammers, pp. 59–60.

27 Friedmann explains why the PCIJ and the ICJ have made very little practical use of general principles. Firstly, many cases before the courts dealt with solving disputes concerning diplomatic relations between States in which principles did not play a role. Secondly, international judicial institutions, such as the ICJ, depend for their jurisdiction, as well as for the acceptability of their decisions and opinions, upon the consent of States. The Courts therefore need to be extremely careful in applying principles of international law, in order to avoid being 'accused of unauthorized exercise of international legislation'. See Friedmann, p. 280.

28 For a thorough survey of the practice of the PJIC and the ICJ, see Degan, pp. 41–53.

29 *Factory at Chorzow*, Merits, Judgment No. 13, PCIJ Series A, No. 17 (1928), pp. 47–49.

30 *S.S. Lotus Case*, PCIJ Series A, No. 9 (1927), p. 31.

31 *Fisheries Case* (*United Kingdom* v. *Norway*), Judgment, 18 December 1951, ICJ Reports 1951, p. 132.

32 Many commentators, for example, Bin Cheng, hold the view that the principles as put down in article 38 (1) (c) exclusively refer to principles originating from national law. See for an overview, Lammers, p. 57.

33 Bassiouni, p. 773. See also Lammers, p. 62 and van Hoof, p. 32.

In other cases, particularly the *Corfu Channel Case*, the *Nicaragua Case* and the Nuclear Weapons Advisory Opinion, it is not clear whether the ICJ applies principles originating from national law. In the *Corfu Channel Case* of 1949, the ICJ recognised the existence of 'certain general and well-recognized principles, among which elementary considerations of humanity, even more exacting in peace than in war'.[34] The ICJ based State responsibility for Albania on these principles, but did not explain the exact content and scope of these principles in this judgment. Nonetheless, these principles seem of a different character than those applied in the earlier cases at the PCIJ, because these 'considerations of humanity' seem to inspire rules of international law (in this case IHL) rather than qualifying as firmly established rules of domestic law. The ICJ confirms this in the *Nicaragua Case*, noting that 'principles of humanitarian law [are] underlying the specific provisions [of IHL]'.[35] Furthermore, in the Advisory Opinion concerning nuclear weapons, the ICJ notes that States that have not ratified the Geneva Conventions and its Protocols are nonetheless bound to 'intransgressible principles of international humanitarian customary law'.[36]

It may thus be suggested that the principles that are mentioned in article 38 (1) (c) of the ICJ Statute also include principles of international law that do not originate from domestic, but instead from international law.[37] The question then arises whether these principles, which apply in a particular branch of international law, may be understood as an independent source of that branch of law, or that the ICJ meant these principles to be included into the category

[34] *Corfu Channel Case*, Judgment, 9 April 1949, ICJ Reports 1949, p. 22 (hereinafter referred to as the *Corfu Channel Case*).

[35] Military and Paramilitary Activities in and against Nicaragua (*Nicaragua* v. *United States of America*), Merits, Judgment (hereinafter referred to as the *Nicaragua Case*), ICJ Reports 1986, para. 215 on p. 112.

[36] Nuclear Weapons Advisory Opinion, para. 79, p. 257.

[37] Mosler raises this point, see Mosler, p. 522. Lammers provides an overview of the authors who share this opinion, see Lammers, p. 58. Lammers, writing in 1980 with regard to the mere existence of this category, argues that *a contrario*, there are no indications that the Committee of Jurists that drafted article 38 of the ICJ Statute was opposed to the idea of filling gaps in conventional and customary international law by means of principles of international law. Secondly, as a textual interpretation of the article, he argues that 'law' in the concept 'principles of law' may refer to national law, but also to international law. Thirdly, Lammers uses the teleological argument that the rationale and purpose of the provision was intended to enable the Court to deal with gaps and uncertainties in conventional and customary international law. Therefore, principles of international law may be looked upon as an expression of the legal conviction of States, which is more directly related to inter-State relations than are principles of national law. See Lammers, pp. 66–67.

of customary law.[38] Some commentators[39] as well as at least one State[40] seem to accept principles as a separate source of law within a particular branch of international law. This, however, raises the issue of how principles as a source of international law relate to treaty law and international customary law and which role these principles play within a particular branch of international law. This issue is relevant to assess whether proportionality fits within that category of norms, whether it may be considered to qualify as a principle of IHL and whether it is legally binding.

If principles of international law are perceived as a separate source of international law, this does not mean that they operate independently from customary international law and treaty law. On the contrary, there is a very close relation between these three sources. Many treaty rules have become part of customary law, and the other way around. Thus, it may be argued that some principles of international law have similarly been incorporated in treaties or are recognised as rules of customary law. Clear expressions of *opinio juris* regarding a certain norm without any supportive State practice may evidence an existing principle of international law.[41] Indeed, it is submitted that principles of international law may have developed into rules of customary law because States have based their practice on pre-existing principles. This customary rule may subsequently have been codified in treaty law.

38 For instance, this seems to be the opinion for principles of international environmental law. See generally Dupuy and Beyerlin.

39 Lammers, p. 66. His view is shared by, among others, Anzilotti and Akehurst, see Lammers, p. 57. Cassese accepts principles in international law as norms that apply in a certain branch of international law, but he reserved the 'article 38 (1) (c) principles' for only a limited number of principles. Cassese was of the opinion that the principles as referred to in article 38 of the Statute of the ICJ are not the same principles as the fundamental principles of IHL. In his view, there are a very limited amount of 'article 38 principles', and each of the branches of international law, such as environmental law, the law of State responsibility and IHL, in turn have their own principles. These principles are 'general legal standards overarching a whole body of law governing a specific area'. See Cassese 2005, p. 103.

40 The 2015 US Manual on Law of Armed Conflict (LOAC), updated in 2016, mentions customary international law and treaty law as the main sources of IHL, and doctrine and judgments as subsidiary sources. This does, however, not mean that principles of international law are omitted as a source of IHL. In the chapter on principles of IHL it is mentioned that there are three foundational principles (military necessity, humanity and honour). In addition, under reference to article 38 of the Statute of the ICJ, the Manual states that the IHL principles are 'a recognized part of international law'. According to the Manual, the functions of these principles are '(1) help practitioners interpret and apply specific treaty or customary rules; (2) provide a general guide for conduct during war when no specific treaty or customary rule applies; and (3) work as interdependent and reinforcing parts of a coherent system.' US DoD Manual, pp. 34 and 50–51.

41 Bassiouni, pp. 768–769 and 800–801. See also Simma and Alston, pp. 202–203 and Petersen, p. 277.

The inclusion of such principles in treaty law may be understood as confirming the existence of the norm as a principle and, conversely, the principle as a legal norm. In practice, however, principles of this category are invoked and applied by reference to their codification as a treaty rule for reasons of clarity and certainty of the law. Thus, there is an intertwining relationship between principles, customary and treaty law where the one may be the evidence or the origin of the other. There may perhaps not be much residual value in establishing norms as principles of international law when these have also been codified in treaty law and are recognised as rules of customary international law. However, depending on the type of principle of international law, it is submitted that, for example in light of their gap-filling role, principles of international law may still be relevant in some situations. Also, if the principles are not accepted as an independent source of international law, the ICJ would at least on some occasions be faced with the problem of having to declare a *non liquet*.[42] As a result, it is submitted that in the absence of the principles of international law, the international legal order would also lose its coherence as a system of legal norms.

From the analysis in this section, it occurs that there are different types of principles of international law, playing different roles. Potentially, therefore, proportionality in IHL may be perceived as one or more of the following: firstly, as a principle applied in international law because it is elevated from domestic law. Alternatively, the principle of proportionality may be understood to constitute an independent source of law within a specific branch of international law, such as IHL. Furthermore, it may be that proportionality is referred to as a principle because it merely underlies a specific rule of IHL, and does not apply as a legally binding norm, but as a 'policy'. Lastly, proportionality may be labelled as a principle because it is a particularly important norm within the branch of law in which it occurs, in this case IHL. In order to determine where in these categories the principle of proportionality fits in, it is first necessary to analyse the substance of principles of IHL, their content and how they may be used.

2.2.2 *Principles of IHL*

There are different avenues that may be taken in identifying the norms that qualify as a principle of IHL. One is to look at what States, international courts and doctrine have expressed. However, as noted in the previous section, the

[42] Degan, p. 54.

term 'principle' is used quite loosely in international law. It is therefore doubtful whether a taxonomy of IHL norms should be based on this approach alone. It is submitted that a more systemic approach is more convincing. This book takes the approach that the question of whether a norm qualifies as a principle of IHL must be answered by looking at its character and function.

With regard to the practice of States, international courts and notable writers, it may be noted that they all identify different norms as 'principles of IHL'. In addition, the number of principles identified differs to a large extent. There is thus no universal or 'official list of core principles'[43] of IHL. Nonetheless, as a guideline for behaviour in armed conflict, 'principles' were recognised more than 150 years ago. For example, the 1863 Lieber Code notes that during an occupation, the 'principles of justice, honor and humanity must be applied'.[44] The Martens Clause refers to 'principles of humanity' in its modern codification.[45] The Geneva Conventions note in the articles about dissemination, that the 'principles' of the Geneva Conventions must be instructed to the members of the military as well as to the civilian population.[46] Consequently, as a minimum, it seems that States have a duty to identify which IHL principles must be included in their IHL dissemination programmes. Indeed, Corn rightly points out that although the principles are the foundation of the universally accepted and codified IHL rules, it is 'impossible to transform every soldier into a LOAC expert. Instead, compliance is built upon a foundation of core principles'.[47] Many States have identified a set of principles of IHL in their military manuals. Furthermore, the Statute of the International Criminal Court (ICC) explicitly refers to principles as part of the applicable law that the ICC shall apply.[48] As Pictet

43 Solis, pp. 268–269 and 306.

44 Lieber Code, article 4.

45 Article 1 (2) API.

46 Article 47 GCI, article 48 GCII, article 127 GCIII, article 144 GCIV. Interestingly, the dissemination article in API (article 83) and APIII (article 7) refer to secure knowledge of the 'instruments' rather than 'principles'. Article 19 APII simply states that, '[t]his Protocol shall be disseminated as widely as possible.'

47 Corn et al., p. 110.

48 Article 21 (Applicable law) of the ICC Statute reads:

1. The Court shall apply:
   (a) In the first place, this Statute, Elements of Crimes and its Rules of Procedure and Evidence;
   (b) In the second place, where appropriate, applicable treaties and the principles and rules of international law, *including the established principles of the international law of armed conflict*;
   (c) Failing that, general principles of law derived by the Court from national laws of legal systems of the world including, as appropriate, the national laws of

notes, the principles of IHL are 'of capital importance' because they 'motivate the whole, enable the respective value of the facts to be appreciated and also offer solutions for unexpected cases. They contribute towards filling gaps in the law and help in their future development by indicating the path to be followed.'[49]

In terms of the functions of principles of IHL, three different roles for the IHL principles may be discerned: a coherency function, an educational function and a foundational function.

The coherency function: the principles of IHL are a source of the legal obligations for States, armed groups and the individual arms bearers whenever armed violence is employed in the course of military operations that exceed law enforcement and are qualified as hostilities. These norms complement the norms these actors have already agreed to in treaties or – through their practice and *opinio juris* – customary international law. There are also other notions that are very important for IHL, but nonetheless fail the criteria to be labelled as principles of IHL. Examples of these notions are chivalry, reciprocity, the principle of equal application and neutrality.[50] These notions are part of the framework of IHL and altogether, IHL forms a coherent legal framework that regulates behaviour of the parties to an armed conflict. The role of the principles of IHL as a supplier of coherency in IHL as a whole is crucial, but these norms in themselves do not serve as legally binding norms for members of armed forces. The different types of principles of IHL together safeguard that IHL is a consistent legal framework that provides guidance for any specific situation during armed conflict, assists in the interpretation of the rules and can be used to fill gaps in the law. Thus, for this role,

States that would normally exercise jurisdiction over the crime, provided that those principles are not inconsistent with this Statute and with international law and internationally recognized norms and standards.

2. The Court may apply principles and rules of law as interpreted in its previous decisions.
3. The application and interpretation of law pursuant to this article must be consistent with internationally recognized human rights, and be without any adverse distinction founded on grounds such as gender as defined in article 7, paragraph 3, age, race, colour, language, religion or belief, political or other opinion, national, ethnic or social origin, wealth, birth or other status.

(Emphasis added)

49 Pictet 1966, pp. 25–26.

50 Compare Dinstein 2016, pp. 4–15: Dinstein finds two 'major premises' as 'antecedent' to the study of IHL: the notion that means and methods are restricted and the 'legal equality' of the parties to the conflict. Furthermore, Dinstein qualifies military necessity and humanity as 'the two driving forces' of IHL and distinction and the prohibition of unnecessary suffering as the 'two cardinal principles' of IHL.

the understanding of principles of IHL is broader than only those norms that are legally binding in itself. In this function, principles of IHL 'serve in a sense as the bone structure in a living body, providing guidelines in unforeseen cases'.[51]

The educating role: principles of IHL are indispensable in educating members of the parties to the conflict. Soldiers, as the main users of the rules of IHL, are not lawyers. Complete knowledge of every single rule of IHL by soldiers is both unattainable and undesirable. The Geneva Conventions note in the articles about dissemination, that the 'principles' of the Geneva Conventions must be instructed to the members of the military as well as to the civilian population. In deciding upon different courses of action, the members of military forces must be trained to apply both humanity and military necessity, because these notions guide the members of armed forces in taking decisions on the battlefield. The principles of IHL then constitute 'a complete summary of the whole, easy to understand and indispensable for the purposes for dissemination'.[52]

The foundational role: the principles of IHL form the origin of the specific rules of IHL, and they are applicable to all parties to an armed conflict. The addressee of the norm in general international law may thus be individual soldiers on the battlefield, because ultimately, it is their behaviour, and targeting decisions, that dictate whether the State is acting in conformity with international law, or not. The principles of IHL, particularly the policies of humanity and military necessity, are the basis of the legally binding principles and rules of IHL. According to Draper: '[a]t least since the time of Grotius the law of war has rested on an uneasy balance between military needs, flowing from the nature of the activity to be subjected to law, and those of humanity'.[53] These foundations are important to interpret the rules of IHL; however, the extent to which IHL itself allows these two policies to play a role in the interpretation of its rules differs. The notion of military necessity is restricted to those situations in which the rule itself expressly allows for invocation of reasons of military necessity.[54] Invoking considerations of humanity as an interpretative tool for the rules of IHL is not expressly regulated, but must nonetheless remain in sync with the considerations of military necessity.[55]

[51] Pictet 1985, p. 59.
[52] Ibid.
[53] Draper, p. 141.
[54] Dinstein 2016, p. 10.
[55] See also van den Boogaard 2018a, pp. 205–206.

2.2.3 *IHL Proportionality Is Not an IHL Principle but a Rule*

Traditionally, proportionality in IHL is seen as the equation that is required from 'those who plan or decide upon an attack' to consider before that attack that if it may be expected that there could be damage to civilian objects or injury or death to civilians, a balance exercise needs to be conducted between the expected collateral damage and the expected military advantage. This was first codified in articles 51 and 57 of API and is recognised as a rule of customary IHL.

It follows from the analysis in the previous sections that proportionality may qualify as a principle of IHL if this would follow from its character and function. Therefore, it would need to be sufficiently general; serve as a basis for other norms and it must play a role in providing the coherence to the legal framework of IHL as a whole. The notion of proportionality codified in articles 51 and 57 of API, however, seems quite specific: it serves to balance expected collateral damage against the anticipated concrete and direct military advantage. It only applies in the particular situation of attacks and it is only one of a wider range of obligations to take precautionary measures to protect the civilian population during the conduct of hostilities. Its function is not to serve as an interpretative tool or to fill gaps in the law, because it applies in clearly delineated circumstances, that of planning and conducting attacks. This norm is thus always either fulfilled or is not: the collateral damage expected from a planned attack is either excessive, or it is not.[56] In terms of the educational role of IHL principles, proportionality may be an important part of the IHL rules of targeting, but it does not seem crucial for explaining the framework as a whole. Neither is it a *conditio sine qua non* for the rules concerning attacks, because if no civilian damage or casualties are expected, the proportionality assessment can be omitted. Proportionality thus seems to qualify as an IHL rule rather than as an IHL principle. The reason why many States and commentators refer to it as a 'principle' only seems to be based on the opinion that it is a particular important rule of IHL, or because the rule leaves military commanders wide discretion applying it in practice.

2.3 PROPORTIONALITY IN INTERNATIONAL LAW

The IHL proportionality rule is certainly not the only relevant manifestation of proportionality found in international law that is relevant during armed

[56] Alexy, p. 48.

conflict. Two relevant manifestations of proportionality that come to mind in that regard are proportionality in the *ius ad bellum* and proportionality in the context of IHRL. The relation between the IHL proportionality rule and these other manifestations of proportionality found in international law is analysed in this section.

2.3.1 *Proportionality and the* Ius ad Bellum

In international law, the *ius ad bellum* regulates the recourse to the use of armed force by States.[57] Its starting point is article 2 (4) of the UN Charter, which prohibits the threat or use of force.[58] Exceptions to the prohibition of the use of armed force by States such as the right to self-defence are strictly regulated. States, courts and authors agree that proportionality is one of the regulatory conditions in the *ius ad bellum* that determines the legality of the use of armed force by States in self-defence.[59]

Article 51 of the UN Charter dictates that a State under attack must fulfil a number of conditions for the legitimate use of armed force in self-defence. First, there needs to be an armed attack. Secondly, once an armed attack is underway, the UN Charter sets a procedural condition that the attacked State needs to fulfil: the attacked State needs to inform the UN Security Council that an armed attack has occurred. Thirdly, there is a temporal requirement to halt the use of armed force in self-defence as soon as the Security Council has taken measures necessary to maintain international peace and security. Three more conditions apply, although these are not spelled out in article 51. These are the substantive conditions of immediacy, proportionality and necessity, which are derived from the *Caroline Case*.[60] The ICJ concluded in the *Nicaragua Case* that the customary right of self-defence complements the

[57] Although this branch of international law is normally referred to as the law regulating the use of armed force by States, this book refers to this field as the *ius ad bellum* for reasons of clarity, because the use of armed force by States is also regulated by IHL and IHRL.

[58] Article 2 (4) of the UN Charter is complemented by customary international law. Dinstein calls the prohibition to use force the 'bedrock of the contemporary international legal system'. See Dinstein 2005, p. 326. For a thorough study of the scope and content of article 2 (4) of the UN Charter, see Stürchler. The ICJ has dealt with questions of the *ius ad bellum* in a number of cases, for example, in the Nuclear Weapons Advisory Opinion, the *Oil Platforms Case* between Iran and the USA and the *Armed Activities Case*.

[59] See Article 51, which notes that, '[n]othing in the present Charter shall impair the inherent right of individual or collective self-defence if an armed attack occurs against a Member of the United Nations, until the Security Council has taken measures to maintain international peace and security.'

[60] *Caroline Case*: See Note of US Secretary of State Daniel Webster, 24 April 1841, Caroline Case, 29 British and Foreign State papers (1841) pp. 1137–1138, available at http://avalon.law

right as it is described in article 51 of the UN Charter.[61] Proportionality in this context relates to the qualitative and quantitative elements of the response to halt and repel the initial armed attack. The principle of proportionality in the *ius ad bellum* is closely connected to the notion of necessity, but the two notions are separate nonetheless.[62] Necessity refers to the existence of an armed attack and the lack of feasible alternatives to respond to that armed attack in any other way than by using armed force.

As a minimum, it seems that there is consensus on the proportionality equation in the *ius ad bellum* to mean that the use of armed force necessary to halt and repulse an armed attack that has occurred, is not disproportionate. For example, if as a result of the initial attack territory of the attacked State has been occupied, the 'liberation' of that territory is deemed to be a proportionate response to the attack. However, a more precise answer to the exact content of the principle of proportionality in the *ius ad bellum* depends to a large extent on the circumstances of the situation, such as the military capacity of the aggressor.[63] The assessment of whether the use of force in this context is proportionate thus requires both quantitative and qualitative factors. Relevant factors are the size, duration and effect of both the initial armed attack and of the attack in self-defence. In addition, a proportionate response is the use of armed force against an armed attack that 'is required under the circumstances to repel it and put an end to the threat of further attacks',[64] thus

.yale.edu/19th_century/br-1842d.asp (hereinafter: the *Caroline Case*). See also Gill 2007, pp. 125–128.

61 'The court does not consider that, in the areas of law relevant to the present dispute, it can be claimed that all the customary rules which may be invoked have a content exactly identical to that of the rules contained in the treaties which cannot be applied by virtue of the United States [multilateral treaty] reservation. On a number of points, the areas governed by the two sources of law do not exactly overlap, and the substantive rules in which they are framed are not identical in content. But in addition, even if a treaty norm and a customary norm relevant to the present dispute were to have exactly the same content, this would not be a reason for the Court to take the view that the operation of the treaty process must necessarily deprive the customary norm of its separate applicability. Nor can the multilateral treaty reservation be interpreted as meaning that, once applicable to a given dispute, it would exclude the application of any rule of customary international law the content of which was the same as, or analogous to, that of the treaty-law rule which had caused the reservation to become effective.' The *Nicaragua Case*, para. 175, p. 94. Brownlie, writing in 1963, came to the same conclusion as the ICJ did in 1986. See Brownlie, p. 274

62 See, for example, Gardam 2004.

63 Gardam 2004, p. 160.

64 Gill 2007, p. 124. Gill explains that, '[i]f an attack is simply an isolated incident, restricted in scale, location and time, self-defence will correspondingly be limited to what is necessary to ward off the attack. If, however, an armed attack consists of a series of related incidents over a period of time, proportionality would allow for a larger scale response aimed at putting an end

also the military capacity and expressed intention of the opponent to repeat or sustain its armed attack are relevant factors to the proportionality equation in the *ius ad bellum*.

Before any relationship between the two manifestations of proportionality in IHL and the *ius ad bellum* may be examined, it must be stressed at the outset that one of the basic premises of IHL is that these two legal frameworks must be kept clearly separated. IHL applies during armed conflict regardless of the basis for using armed force leading to the armed conflict under the *ius ad bellum*. This separation entails that all norms of IHL apply equally to all parties to an armed conflict, regardless of 'their respective standing in the eyes of the *ius ad bellum*'.[65] This is one of the most clearly established and crucial underlying foundations of IHL. It is codified in the preamble to Additional Protocol I. Specifically for proportionality, Dinstein warns that 'proportionality in the context of self-defence – and in the sense of the *ius ad bellum* – has little in common with proportionality as applied and understood by IHL. Consequently, any attempt to transplant rules or caveats from one domain to the other is likely to cause confusion.'[66]

It is thus clear that the proportionality requirements in IHL and the *ius ad bellum* must first and foremost be satisfied within those separate legal frameworks themselves. It may, however, be argued that a certain relationship exists on the level of the application of the rule on proportionality in the respective legal frameworks. The question of whether an attack is in accordance with the requirements of *ius in bello* could, for example, be relevant for the legality of an armed attack under the *ius ad bellum*. Conversely, factors of *ius ad bellum* 'must equally be taken into account in determining whether specific types of targets may be attacked'.[67] Since the legality of the selected targets and the type of weapons and tactics that are used is determined on the basis of *ius in bello*, it seems as if there is, at least, a potential interaction here between issues of *ius in bello* and *ius ad bellum*.

In legal terms, it may, firstly, be argued that if a military operation has been initiated with the purpose of defending, or even saving the civilian population,

to what is in effect a phased attack. In the case of a large scale attack, designed to significantly disrupt the target State, or take over (part of) its territory, proportionality would allow waging a full scale war in self-defense to reduce or eliminate the attacker's capacity to conduct military operations, or otherwise continue the attack. This could necessitate, in some cases, the total defeat of an attacking State and the replacement of its government with one which is ready to meet its international obligations.'

65 Dinstein 2016, p. 5. See also, generally, Sassòli 2007, pp. 241–264.

66 Dinstein 2012, p. 233.

67 See, generally, Gill 2016, pp. 101–119.

it seems contrary to the (*ius ad bellum*) purpose of that operation to apply the IHL proportionality rule that permits civilian casualties that are not excessive. A second area where a relationship between IHL and *ius ad bellum* proportionality seems possible is in the hypothetical situation in which a very large operation is launched that leads to huge and extensive civilian damage, which is, however, not excessive compared to the military advantage that is sought with that operation. The expected devastation caused by this attack may, however, lead to the conclusion that the attack is disproportionate under *ius ad bellum*. An example could be a massive counter-attack in response to a rather minimal initial armed attack.[68] A number of legal difficulties are connected to the latter situation, including the fact that there is a different definition of the term 'armed attack' in the two legal frameworks, and also the divergence of opinion among experts of whether the question of proportionality under the rules of the *ius ad bellum* is still relevant after the armed conflict has started.

These situations show that there is not necessarily an integrating relationship between the two rules on proportionality in the frameworks of the *ius ad bellum* and IHL, but that they operate in parallel. The result of this conclusion is that not only the rules of IHL matter for the actual conduct of hostilities, but in addition also considerations of the *ius ad bellum* may impact on the overall legality of actual operations, albeit only under the *ius ad bellum*.[69] This perhaps asks more from decision makers on the strategic level than they may realise.[70] In particular, it may result in a conclusion that they need to realise that it is their responsibility to sometimes prevent their armed forces from executing certain attacks even though these would be perfectly legal under IHL, for example, because they only attack military objectives, and expect to cause no excessive collateral damage to the civilian population. Here, the *ius ad bellum* proportionality rule provides an extra layer of protection to the civilian population, but this protection is not based on IHL, but on the *ius ad bellum*. A last remark that may be relevant to indicate how the two types of

68 Cannizzaro, p. 785.

69 Cannizzaro disagrees with this conclusion, '[t]his conclusion is not entirely persuasive. Indeed, the strict application of the standards of one system may prevent the purposes of the other from being fully realised. This consequence derives from the different historical origins and from the different logical structures of the two systems.' Therefore, Cannizzaro proposes that, '[t]he two groups of rules may be considered as sub-systems of a coherent and complete normative system regulating the use of force. In this context, proportionality must be applied as a unitary standard that takes into account the purpose of the military action as well as countervailing humanitarian interests.' See Cannizzaro, p. 471.

70 For an illustration, see Gardam 2004, p. 21.

proportionality analyses interrelate, is that in IHL, the analysis needs to be conducted not only on a tactical level, but also on a grand strategic level. It could be said that on that latter level, the analysis gets nearer to the *ius ad bellum* proportionality analysis, except for the fact that the *ius ad bellum* takes not only damage to civilian objectives into account, but all damage.[71]

2.3.2 *The Concept of Proportionality in IHRL*

International human rights law applies in both peacetime and during times of armed conflict, while (the by far largest portion of) the rules of IHL only apply in the latter situation. Therefore, both legal frameworks can apply concurrently and both deal with the question of whether lethal armed force may be used in a particular tactical situation. Interaction may thus be possible between the concepts of proportionality as they apply in the legal frameworks of IHRL and IHL, respectively.[72]

A meaningful analysis of the relation between IHL and IHRL proportionality first requires a closer look at the relation between these two legal frameworks in more general terms. A first factor of note here is the fact that historically, the two legal frameworks have developed separately.[73] The first major codifications of the rules of IHL[74] took place in the years 1863–1868 with the adoption of the Lieber Code in 1863, the first Geneva Convention of 1864 and the St. Petersburg Declaration of 1868. IHRL was first codified in the aftermath of World War II with the conclusion of the Universal Declaration of Human Rights. Before its codification, human rights were mostly found exclusively in domestic law, as an exclusively internal affair of States.[75] The first signs of a closer relationship between the two legal frameworks came to the surface during the 1968 Tehran International Conference on Human

[71] See, for example, Bohlander and Rothe, pp. 245–261, for an overview of the history of the targeted killing of leadership, arguing that this would be a situation of 'overlap' between *ius in bello* and *ius ad bellum*. See Bohlander and Rothe, p. 248.

[72] For an extensive study on the relation between IHRL and IHL, see Pouw. See also Sassòli and Olsen, pp. 599–627, Gill 2014, pp. 335–350, Lubell, pp. 648–660, Krieger, pp. 267–293, Hampson 2013, pp. 185–213, Droege 2008, pp. 501–548 and Prud'homme, pp. 356–395.

[73] See, however, van Dijk, unveiling a much closer link between the historic development of IHL and IHRL.

[74] It must be noted that the codification of maritime *ius in bello* had already started earlier, through the adoption of the 1856 Paris Declaration Respecting Maritime Law, see Roberts and Guelff, pp. 47–52.

[75] Droege 2007, p. 313.

Rights.[76] By that time, the majority of the basic rules and principles of both legal frameworks had already been adopted. However, subsequent treaties show the first signs of similar rules crossing over.[77]

The type of legal relationship that IHL and IHRL regulate is inherently different on the conceptual level. The former is based on the basically horizontal situation in which two parties to the conflict acquire rights and obligations towards each other, both on the grand strategic level of States and on the tactical levels of individuals. The rules of IHL thus regulate predominantly the relationship between two equal entities, as is exemplified by the principle of equal application of the rules of IHL to the parties to the conflict. The legal framework of IHRL, on the other hand, regulates the relation between a State and the individuals under its jurisdiction. This relation may be characterised as a vertical relation between unequal entities: the relation between the State and the persons under its jurisdiction.[78] In addition, as mentioned earlier, IHRL is designed to be applicable at all times, whereas IHL, with a few exceptions, only applies during armed conflict. The extraterritorial application of IHRL obligations is, however, not been definitely established. This book is not the place for a discussion on this issue and it is sufficient for the purpose of this book to note that the limitation on the extraterritorial application of IHRL may also limit the number of situations in which IHL and IHRL apply concurrently.

A substantial difference between IHL and IHRL is the stark contrast between the ground rules of the two legal frameworks. IHRL is built on the right to life and tailored to protect individuals, whereas IHL takes the right to kill your opponent as its basic starting point, in a balance between the protection of civilians and the military reality of armed conflict.[79] Another difference is that many IHRL instruments may be derogated from in times of emergencies, including during armed conflict. IHL does not provide for such a possibility: once it is applicable, States cannot disregard the rules through a formal procedure.[80] Even though the differences play a role to define the

[76] Respect for Human Rights in Armed Conflicts. Resolution 2444 (XXIII) of the United Nations General Assembly, 19 December 1968, reprinted in Schindler and Toman, pp. 345–350.

[77] See, for example, the codification of article 75 of API on fundamental guarantees that are inspired by IHRL and the reference to the rules of IHL in article 38 of the 1989 Convention on the Rights of the Child.

[78] Some commentators are in favour of attributing IHRL obligations to non-State entities. See, for example, Clapham, pp. 491–523, Fortin and Pouw, p. 331.

[79] See also Sivakumaran 2010, p. 524, explaining that the IHRL right to life is 'fundamental to international human rights law, the supreme human right on which all others are built'.

[80] Even if States would renounce their treaty-based obligations, rules of customary IHL continue to apply.

relationship between the two legal frameworks, there are clearly also important similarities between IHL and IHRL. The most basic similarity between both legal frameworks is their shared ideal, in the sense that they both aim to enhance the protection of human dignity.[81] For IHRL, this is evidenced in the preambles of the ICCPR and ICESCR.[82] In IHL, both the general Martens Clause and multiple specific provisions demonstrate this basic purpose of IHL.[83]

In case of armed conflict, the IHL proportionality rule applies and dictates that the relation between expected collateral damage, on the one hand, and expected military advantage, on the other hand, must be analysed in order to decide whether a planned attack can be launched or must be cancelled. The IHRL proportionality rule requires an appreciation of the balance between the values that must be attributed to two factors in a given situation, at a given moment in time. These factors are (1) the expected scale of the risk to human life (of the suspect) of the contemplated use of (potentially) lethal force; and (2) the nature and scale of the concrete threat to the law enforcement officer who is planning to use the armed force, and third persons. IHRL 'requires the taking into consideration of the concrete circumstances of a given situation irrespective of any categorical distinction between targetable combatants or fighters and protected civilians'.[84]

An important question is in which situations there could be concurrent application of the proportionality standards in IHL and IHRL.[85] As noted, the rules of IHRL apply at all times, thus this situation only exists during armed conflict, when the rules of IHL apply as well. In case there is concurrent application of the norms, the next question is that of whether the application of the two rules in that situation would lead to different outcomes. If this is the case, the question remains which rule takes precedence.

The first point to be made is that even though the IHL proportionality rule applies during armed conflict, this does not necessarily mean that the IHL proportionality rule is relevant at all times. It has to be reminded that the IHL proportionality rule must be applied to the specific situation of attacks, and not

81 Droege 2007, p. 312. See also Sivakumaran 2010, p. 525.

82 'Considering that, in accordance with the principles proclaimed in the Charter of the United Nations, recognition of the inherent dignity and of the equal and inalienable rights of all members of the human family is the foundation of freedom, justice and peace in the world, Recognizing that these rights derive from the inherent dignity of the human person.'

83 See, for example, common article 3 (1) (a) and (c) of the Geneva Conventions I–IV and article 75 (1) and (2) of API.

84 Geiss 2010, p. 125.

85 See also Watkin 2004.

necessarily to other types of military operations. Furthermore, the IHL proportionality rule is irrelevant for attacks in situations without civilian presence. This leads to the conclusion that when an attack on a person is planned, the status of this person is crucial to the relevance of the IHL rule on proportionality. In cases where no civilians are present, there is thus no interplay, and thus no relation, between the proportionality rules of IHL and IHRL. Similarly, if an attack is planned on a military object where no individuals are expected to be present, the IHRL proportionality rule is irrelevant and the IHL proportionality rule only plays a role to the extent that civilian objects may be affected.

A situation with the potential of interplay between the IHL and IHRL rules is that when an attack is planned on a military objective, be it a person or an object, and civilians may be expected to be affected by the planned attack. In this situation, the IHL proportionality rule must be applied. The question then arises whether the IHRL rule on proportionality places additional restrictions on the attacker to protect these civilians and/or the members of the opposing forces. Thus, in other words, could the IHRL proportionality rule provide an additional restraint on the use of force against persons who are a legitimate target under IHL *and* on civilians who may be affected by a planned attack?

In the situation where the principles of proportionality under IHL and IHRL apply concurrently, the difference is that the IHRL proportionality principle provides restraints to the use of force against both the civilians present at the scene and the combatants or civilians who participate directly in the hostilities. The IHL proportionality rule does not provide further protection to persons who constitute a legitimate military target. There is thus a relation possible between the two proportionality rules only with regard to the civilians who are present at the scene. However, when the situation is concerned with the direct attack of a civilian, IHL contains a clear-cut prohibition to directly attack civilians, provided the civilians are not directly participating in hostilities. Melzer notes in this regard that,

> [p]articularly in small-scale operations, human rights law is not necessarily more protective than IHL [because] human rights law allows the use of lethal force against anyone where this is 'absolutely necessary' for a legitimate purpose. IHL, on the other hand, prohibits direct attacks against certain categories of persons in absolute terms, that is to say, even in case of 'absolute necessity' for a legitimate purpose.[86]

[86] Melzer 2008, p. 384.

It is submitted that it would lead to unworkable situations for members of the armed forces during hostilities to have to apply the IHRL proportionality standard against their opponents. It is a long-standing rule of IHL that the threat posed by the members of the armed forces of the opponent is a given. Whether they pose that threat at the moment they are attacked is irrelevant and they may thus in principle be attacked at all times. Soldiers cannot be required to conduct an additional law enforcement-style assessment in the midst of hostilities, after they have satisfied the already quite difficult requirements of IHL on when an opponent may be attacked. However, the situation may be different in situations where the armed forces have such control over the situation that it cannot reasonably be considered to constitute a situation of hostilities. In that situation, one may ask the question whether the relation is still horizontal between parties to the conflict or that the controlling party is now in a vertical relation that must be equated with the situation of law enforcement. Planners and executors of an attack will then normally have the opportunity to deliberate about the type of operation they will pursue. In cases like this, Melzer's theory on the paradigm of law enforcement and the paradigm of hostilities makes sense.[87] If the planned operation is directed against civilians, it is prohibited under IHL, provided the civilians are not directly participating in hostilities and as far as IHRL is concerned, it can only be planned as an operation to kill the civilian if the stringent IHRL restraints of necessity, proportionality and immediacy are satisfied. Given the fact that in this scenario the applicability of IHRL is assumed, the operation cannot be planned with the a priori purpose to kill the civilians. In situations like this, a direct relation between IHL and IHRL proportionality standards may arise.

2.4 CONCLUDING REMARKS

This chapter has first explored in which category of norms the IHL 'principle' of proportionality must be placed, based on Dworkin's taxonomy of norms and an analysis of the character and function of the IHL proportionality assessment applicable to attacks on military objectives. It is concluded that IHL proportionality is a specific norm and does not fit the more general norm category of principles and is therefore a rule rather than a principle of IHL.

The analysis in this chapter has further shown that a thorough knowledge and training of military commanders in IHL and its proportionality rule is insufficient. Firstly, military commanders must be made aware that IHRL or

[87] See, for example, Melzer's discussion in Melzer 2010a, pp. 33–49.

ius ad bellum proportionality assessments may also apply. Secondly, they must be aware that depending on the factual circumstances, these assessments may have to be applied concurrently with the IHL proportionality rule. The main rule is, however, that the proportionality requirements under IHL, IHRL and the *ius ad bellum* need to be satisfied within their own frameworks. There is no integrating relationship between the proportionality rules in these legal frameworks. Rather, their relationship is that they work in parallel to the same situation. Parties to an armed conflict thus need to realise that it is their responsibility to sometimes prevent their armed forces from executing certain attacks even though these would be perfectly legal under IHL, because the *ius ad bellum* proportionality rule provides an extra layer of protection to the civilian population. Similarly, although the proportionality rules under IHL and IHRL are clearly separate in content and application, there are factual situations possible in which both proportionality rules must be applied cumulatively. Particularly because the applicability of the IHRL proportionality rule is subject to a large number of conditions, these situations do not occur in every military operation during armed conflict.

This being said, proportionality could also be seen in a more broad sense, as a general standard of moderation aiming to mitigate the horrors of war. Then it could apply in not only the case of an attack, but also other situations to which IHL is applicable. The following chapter assesses a number of other rules in IHL in which the rules seem to manifest such a broader notion of proportionality.

3

Other Standards of Moderation in International Humanitarian Law

3.1 INTRODUCTION

As the principle of proportionality is understood traditionally in IHL, it deals with the balancing of military advantage and permissible collateral damage. The same rule is also included in a number of weapons treaties. As such, the IHL proportionality rule is a standard aiming to moderate the effects of attacks for the civilian population, while acknowledging that these attacks are necessary to win the war. In other words, the proportionality rule in IHL safeguards the balance between military necessity and the requirements of humanity, but only in view of the collateral effects for civilians. International humanitarian law also contains a number of other rules that fulfil a similar role as a standard of moderation and with a broader scope, including effects on enemy forces. Sometimes these rules resemble the IHL proportionality rule, although they are mostly strictly distinct. These other standards of moderation may be express or implied and they are often linked to balancing military necessity and humanity in other situations. These standards then appear as a mechanism to limit the permissive scope of explicit references to military necessity in the applicable rules of IHL, or as a requirement to take humanitarian considerations into account during the conduct of hostilities. The ICRC commentary on the Additional Protocols mentions the 'legal obligation on combatants to engage in a balance between military necessity ... and the requirements of humanity'[1] in order to preclude 'a degree of violence which exceeds the level which is strictly necessary to ensure the success of a particular operation in a particular case'.[2] As a result, there are multiple manifestations within IHL of

1 Sandoz et al., para. 1389, p. 392.

2 Sandoz et al., para. 1395, p. 396.

that balance aiming to prevent 'deliberate and pointless extermination of the defending enemy'.[3]

In fact, one of the basic premises of IHL, that 'in any armed conflict, the right of the Parties to the conflict to choose methods or means of warfare is not unlimited',[4] implies a certain moderation, and requires a balance between what a combatant might *want* to do, and what he is *allowed* to do.[5] Nonetheless, there are also authors who maintain that '[t]here is no general requirement under [IHL] to limit the level of force used against the enemy; and accordingly, the military principle of the use of overwhelming force to overcome the enemy is entirely consistent with [IHL].'[6]

In this chapter, standards of moderation are discussed as they appear with regard to the killing of combatants, as a moderation to the destruction of enemy property, with regard to blockades, reprisals and security measures taken during an occupation.

3.2 COMBATANTS AS HUMAN BEINGS

It has been argued that the principle of proportionality in IHL consists of not only the rule on collateral damage to civilians, but also the prohibition on the use of means and methods of warfare that cause serious injury or unnecessary suffering.[7] This latter principle is now codified in article 35 (2) of API and may be seen as separate from the IHL proportionality rule.[8]

Kalshoven raises the question whether

> the human beings who compose the armed forces constitute military objectives in all circumstances. Numerous Iraqi soldiers seem to have been buried alive in the course of the final ground operations [of operation Desert Storm, in the 1990 war in Iraq]. In such a situation, if combatants are not clearly expressing an intention to surrender and cannot be recognized as being *hors de combat* on other grounds either, they are not legally protected from attack. But what if they are in actual fact utterly defenseless; could it not be argued

3 Sandoz et al., para. 1598, p. 477.

4 Article 35 (1) API.

5 According to Blank and Guiora: '[p]roportionality's fundamental premise is that the means and methods of attacking the enemy are not unlimited.' See Blank and Guiora, p. 56.

6 Henderson and Cavanagh, p. 89, referring to the discussion on military necessity in the *Hostages Trial*, p. 646.

7 See for example Gardam 2004, who refers to the principle that prohibits using means and methods of warfare that cause superfluous injury and unnecessary suffering as 'proportionality for combatants' and the article 51 API proportionality as 'proportionality for civilians'. See Gardam 2004, p. 15. See also Bothe et al., p. 195.

8 See also Oeter 2013, p. 122.

> that for want of any military necessity to attack them, they cease to be military objectives? Should this matter be left open, so that no blame will attach to the commander who sticks to the chosen method of attack, while greater praise may be accorded a commander who desists from doing so?[9]

Parks is of the opinion that this understanding of military necessity does apply to killing enemy combatants and denies that the concept of proportionality can be applied in some way, or was 'intended to be applied in combat operations between combatants on a battlefield devoid of civilians'.[10] Indeed, as far as the language of Additional Protocol I is concerned, there is little support for the proposition that combatants may not be killed lawfully wherever they may be found. On the other hand, since the legitimate objective of armed conflict is to win it, and nothing more, its objective is not to simply kill as many members of the opposing military forces as possible. Rather, as was already stipulated in the preamble of the 1868 St. Petersburg Declaration,[11] the use of deadly force IHL allows for is limited to rendering the enemy *hors de combat*. That means that it is not illegal to kill the enemy, but it is certainly not obligatory either and it is limited to those situations where the enemy is not (yet) *hors de combat*.

In the end, the standard of moderation with regard to combatants boils down to a continuous balancing of the notions of military necessity and humanity. After all, combatants are as equally human as the civilian population, with the exception of the belligerent privilege of the former and the legal protection of the latter. The question could therefore reasonably be asked whether humanity would not stand in the way of certain means and methods of warfare because of the inherent fact that human soldiers retain their humanity even when they are targetable on the basis of their status as combatants. This moderation with regard to combatants may be foreseen at two different levels: with regard to the method of attack and with regard to the type of weapon that is used (means). At least for the States that ratified

9 Kalshoven 1992, p. 42.

10 Parks 1990, p. 170.

11 St. Petersburg Declaration Renouncing the Use, in Time of War of Explosive Projectiles Under 400 Grammes Weight, 11 December 1868: '[c]onsidering: That the progress of civilization should have the effect of alleviating as much as possible the calamities of war; That the only legitimate object which States should endeavour to accomplish during war is to weaken the military forces of the enemy; That for this purpose it is sufficient to disable the greatest possible number of men; That this object would be exceeded by the employment of arms which uselessly aggravate the sufferings of disabled men, or render their death inevitable; That the employment of such arms would, therefore, be contrary to the laws of humanity.'

Additional Protocol I, the obligation exists to assess the legality of new means or methods of warfare their armed forces study, develop, adopt or acquire.[12]

3.2.1 *Methods of Warfare*

Combatants may be attacked on the basis of their status. This means that it is irrelevant whether combatants are actively participating in the hostilities or not, for example because they are on leave, asleep or they are geographically dislocated from the battlefield. However, when combatants are unable to pose any threat at that particular time, or any time soon after that, it may be militarily unnecessary to attack them, and humanitarian considerations may put weight on the side of the equation that may make the opposing military commander refrain from attacking. In addition, military necessity may also point in the same direction. By capturing the combatant that poses no direct threat, the commander may be able to acquire valuable information of enemy positions, tactics, weaponry and strength. In addition, for reasons of economy of force, the kinetic assets may be used another day, against an enemy who does pose an active threat. In addition, a prisoner of war may be exchanged against friendly forces captured by the enemy. Of course, the fact that the rules of IHL provide an authority to kill the enemy combatant does not mean that there is a duty to do so. Some would argue that there may also be extra-legal reasons of chivalry that would argue against attacking an adversary who is posing no threat and who may easily be captured.[13] In any case, the prohibition to refuse quarter[14] may be understood as a manifestation of an underlying broad principle of proportionality applicable also to combatants.

It seems possible to construe a proportionality balance with regard to the methods of warfare during hostilities. A number of scenarios could be envisioned where there seems to be an incongruity between the authority IHL provides to lawfully killing combatants on the one hand and humanitarian considerations on the other. An example could be the situation in which other methods of warfare may be used to reach the same – or a similar – result. One is perhaps the following: during the Gulf War in 1991, scores of Iraqi soldiers were killed at the frontline not by kinetic means, but they were simply buried alive in their bunkers by US tanks equipped with bulldozers.[15] Another is the

12 See article 36 API.

13 Gill 2013, pp. 54–56.

14 See, for example, article 23 (d) Hague Regulations 1907, rule 46 of the ICRC Customary Law Study and article 40 API.

15 See, for example, R. J. Schmitt and Sloyan.

killing of fleeing combatants by air power, where there is no possibility for the combatants to surrender, as may have happened on the so-called 'highway of death'.[16] Another example could be the destruction of a sailing boat used to train naval cadets in classic navigation techniques and sailing. Although the ship would qualify as a military target and the cadets are part of the regular armed forces, it is questionable what military advantage would be gained from killing the cadets, especially when it would also be possible to simply order the cadets to surrender.

Of course, in these examples it is assumed that the combatants may be attacked on the basis of their status – not their conduct – and the threat they pose as the result of that conduct. An important factor here, one that is indeed conduct-based, is whether the enemy has had the opportunity to surrender. As soon as the enemy has in fact done so, it becomes simply illegal to attack them.

This type of proportionality, it could be argued, resembles what in military doctrine is called the principle of the economy of the use of force.[17] It seems military practice not to use an overly destructive force when the use of a small amount of armed force will lead to the same result. It could be argued that because of this, a single enemy combatant should not be attacked by an overwhelming amount of armed force such as a large-scale artillery attack. However, provided that there is no collateral damage expected from the attack, there seems to be no legal rule of IHL that prohibits using 'a steam hammer to crack a nut, if a nutcracker would do'.[18] It is the decision of a military commander to assess whether the military advantage of an attack is sufficient to allocate his limited military resources to it, or to save them for another, more militarily advantageous objective. Military commanders will therefore carefully consider the troops, type of weapons and munitions at their disposal before they waste them on a military objective of minor importance. In addition, as noted by Olasolo, there is a danger that if the principle of proportionality and the principle of the economy in the use of force become equated, the former loses its preventive force, and the humanitarian considerations that form the basis of the principle of proportionality become secondary to tactical and logistic considerations.[19]

[16] See BBC News.

[17] The US Department of the Navy recognises the economy of force as one of the 'principles of warfare', together with the military concepts of objective, mass, surprise and security. See, for example, the Annotated Supplement to the Commander's Handbook on the Law of Naval Operations, NWP 9 (REV. A)/FMFM 1-10 (1989) pp. 5–7.

[18] Lord Diplock in *R* v. *Goldstein* (1983) 1 WLR 151 at 155, as quoted in Arancibia, p. 297.

[19] Olasolo, p. 163.

3.2.2 *Means of Warfare*

Another manifestation of a proportionality equation in IHL may be found in the law that applies to means of warfare, or in other words, weapons. The prohibition on the use of means of warfare that cause superfluous injury or unnecessary suffering is one of the two principles that determine the legality of means and methods of warfare, the other being the principle of distinction.

The prohibition on the use of weapons that cause superfluous injury or unnecessary suffering is particularly aimed at the limitation of the effects of weapons to combatants.[20] The principle strikes a balance between the military advantages of the employment of a particular weapon, compared to the military necessity of the human suffering that type of weapon causes to opposing combatants.[21] Oeter states that '[i]njuries can only be "superfluous" either if they are not justified by any requirement of military necessity or if the injuries normally caused by the weapon or projectile are manifestly disproportionate to the military advantage reasonably expected from the use of the weapon.'[22] It is, therefore, important to assess the inherent lawfulness of any type of weapon. This is not necessarily what unnecessary or superfluous harm that type of weapon is ultimately capable of inflicting, but 'what it is actually designed and intended to do'.[23]

[20] According to the ICJ in the Nuclear Weapons Advisory Opinion, 'unnecessary suffering' means 'a harm greater than that unavoidable to achieve legitimate military objectives'. Nuclear Weapons Advisory Opinion, p. 226, para. 78, p. 257.

[21] According to the ICRC Commentary to article 35 API:

> [a]t the beginning of the first session of the Conference of Government Experts in 1971, the ICRC was already quite convinced that, from the point of view of humanitarian law, it would be difficult today to make provisions only with regard to the care to be given to the wounded and the sick, or even only to formulate rules of protection. It has become necessary to deal with the means which are available to the combatants. Article 35, paragraph 2, has this sole aim, although it merely announces the principle without detailing any specific points. *The object of combat is to disarm the enemy. Therefore it is prohibited to use any means or methods which exceed what is necessary for rendering the enemy 'hors de combat.' This rule is the corollary to paragraph 1, which denies an unlimited right to choose the means to harm the enemy. Neither the combatants nor the Parties to the conflict are free to inflict unnecessary damage or injury, or to use violence in an irrational way.* All in all, this is the position adopted by the ICRC.

See Sandoz et al., para. 1411 on pp. 400–401 (emphasis added).

[22] Oeter 2013, p. 125.

[23] S. Haines, 'The Developing Law of Weapons: Humanity, Distinction and the Need for Proportionality', Academy Lecture Series, delivered 14 April 2010, Geneva Academy of International Humanitarian Law and Human Rights, on file with the author. This lecture is published as chapter 11 of the 2014 *Oxford Handbook of International Armed Conflicts*, p. 273.

It is clear that certain types of weapon have been prohibited explicitly because of the suffering they cause to the members of the armed forces, such as the permanently blinding laser weapons that are prohibited by Protocol IV to the Conventional Weapons Convention.[24] They were prohibited because there was sufficient information on the 'horrific effects of blinding laser weapons both on their victims and on society and the fact that such systems, being small arms, would be likely to proliferate widely'.[25]

The prohibition on the use of weapons that cause superfluous injury or unnecessary suffering is also found in a number of express prohibitions of types of weapon, which may be seen as codifications of the general principle. However, according to Oeter,

> [t]he relationship between these two sets of rules is far from clear. How far the definite prohibitions are only specific expressions or materializations of the general prohibiting provision, and to what extent they are, to the contrary, constitutive developments of a merely political programme, . . . is a question which still needs careful consideration.[26]

During the negotiations that led to the adoption in 1995 of Protocol IV on permanently blinding laser weapons, it became clear that universal acceptance by States of the prohibiting force of the principle with regard to these types of weapon was lacking.

3.3 THE DESTRUCTION OF ENEMY PROPERTY

Another standard of moderation can be identified in the obligation to limit the destruction and seizure of enemy property to what is required by the mission. Article 23 (g) of the 1907 Hague Regulations prohibits 'to destroy or seize the enemy's property, unless such destruction or seizure be imperatively demanded by the necessities of war'. This prohibition is repeated in similar words in rule 50 of the ICRC Customary Law Study.[27] In addition, article 147 of the Fourth Geneva Convention asserts that extensive destruction of

On p. 277, Haines notes that '[t]he key to determining the inherent lawfulness of a weapon or a means of warfare is to assess it in relation to its defined and designed purpose.'

24 For a short commentary of the Protocol: see Zöckler, pp. 333–340. See also van den Boogaard 2018b.

25 Doswald-Beck 1996, p. 273.

26 Oeter 2013, p. 124.

27 Henckaerts and Doswald-Beck 2005a, pp. 175–177.

property is a 'grave breach' if 'not justified by military necessity and carried out unlawfully and wantonly'.[28]

Clearly, this rule refers to the restrictive military necessity principle[29] that is deeply rooted in the rules of IHL and that was already enshrined in the Lieber Code of 1863.[30] As has been mentioned earlier, the principles of necessity and proportionality are deeply connected. In this case, the principle manifests itself as a moderation on the general rules in armed conflict with respect to the targeting of lawful military objectives. It dictates the limits on the legality of an attack on, or the seizure of, enemy property, and, when it is not militarily necessary, it must thus be considered excessive. The clearest example of a method of warfare that is illegal for this reason is the 'scorched earth tactic'.

It must be noted that the situation for military objectives is different than it is for combatants. Once individuals qualify as combatants, the military advantage arising from their neutralisation is considered to be a given, unless they surrender or have been rendered *hors de combat*. The language of article 52 (2) API, however, refers to the fact that it is not sufficient only for a military objective to qualify as such on the basis of its nature, location, purpose or use, but adds the additional requirement that the total or partial destruction, capture or neutralisation of that object in the circumstances ruling at the time offers a definite military advantage. Thus, when it does not, the destruction of the enemy property lacks 'a reasonable connection between the destruction of property and the overcoming of enemy forces'.[31] In that case, the destruction would be illegal. As an example, Dinstein points to the setting on fire of hundreds of Kuwaiti oil wells in 1991 by retreating Iraqi armed forces, which did not create any military advantage at that time of the war.[32]

3.4 BLOCKADES

The IHL rule of proportionality has mainly developed in the context of land operations. However, in the law that applies to other types of operation, there are also rules where a balance must be struck between the military utility of a

[28] See also article 8 (2) (b) of the ICC Statute.

[29] See, for example, Rogers 2004, pp. 7–10. See also Hayashi, pp. 113–114.

[30] Lieber Code, article 14: '[m]ilitary necessity, as understood by modern civilized nations, consists in the necessity of those measures which are indispensable for securing the ends of the war, and which are lawful according to the modern law and usages of war.'

[31] Hostage Case of the American Military Tribunal in Nuremberg in 1948, *USA* v. *List et al.*, 11 NMT 757, pp. 1230–1253.

[32] Dinstein 2004, p. 218. It may, of course, be debated whether the oil wells can be characterised as lawful military objectives in the first place.

military operation and the suffering this may cause to the civilian population.[33] One manifestation of this is the rules that apply to blockades. Blockades are among the classic methods of naval warfare applicable in international armed conflicts. A blockade could, for example, be used before a landing operation, in order to surround the enemy or with the purpose of cutting off the supply lines of the enemy.[34] Blockades are mentioned in the Charter of the United Nations as one of the actions the Security Council may authorise to maintain or restore international peace and security.[35] As early as in the 1856 Paris Declaration, naval blockades were established as a method for warships to prevent other vessels from entering or exiting harbours and the coastal area.[36] The result of such a blockade could be starvation among the civilian population. Although according to one writer, 'starvation incidental to a naval blockade is not illegal',[37] it must be remembered that the restrictions on the means and methods of warfare that apply on land warfare apply equally to naval warfare.[38] Thus also for the method of the naval blockade, there is an obligation to minimise collateral civilian damage. The San Remo Manual on Sea Warfare, therefore, prohibits employing methods or means of naval warfare that are indiscriminate.[39] It follows, as far as a naval blockade is concerned, that there is a limit to the suffering endured by the civilian population that is allowed by a blockade. In other words: the military advantage of the blockade needs to be proportionate in relation to its effects on the civilian population. The purpose of this manifestation of a broader proportionality principle is thus equal to the IHL rule on proportionality. The San Remo Manual contains specific obligations implementing the principle. These require the parties to the conflict to prevent excessive effects on the civilian population. Paragraph 102 of the San Remo Manual states that a blockade is prohibited if:

> a. it has the sole purpose of starving the civilian population or denying it other objects essential to its survival;

33 Krüger-Sprengel, pp. 187–188.
34 Heintschel von Heinegg 2000, p. 204.
35 See article 42 UN Charter.
36 1856 Paris Declaration on Respecting Maritime Law, Section 4: 'Blockades, in order to be binding, must be effective, that is to say, maintained by a force sufficient really to prevent access to the coast of the enemy', in Roberts and Guelff, pp. 47–52.
37 Parks 1990, p. 22, note 87.
38 See also Heintschel von Heinegg 2013, pp. 479–480.
39 1994 San Remo Manual on International Law Applicable to Armed Conflicts at Sea, para. 42, in Roberts and Guelff, pp. 573–606.

b. the damage to the civilian population is, or may be expected to be, excessive in relation to the concrete and direct military advantage anticipated from the blockade.[40]

In addition, free passage must be given to humanitarian convoys that provide food and other essential supplies to the civilian population, subject to certain conditions, and medical supplies for the civilian population and wounded or sick members of the armed forces.[41]

The proportionality principle in naval blockades may thus be understood as a balance between the military advantage of that blockade and the damage it causes to the civilian population. Thus, '[t]he gist of this principle is that the greater the military advantage anticipated from the naval blockade, the greater the damage to the civilian population that can be justified.'[42]

A recent incident where the subject of the proportionality of a naval blockade has been under scrutiny was the naval blockade of Gaza by the Israeli armed forces and the boarding of the *Mavi Marmara* (a vessel sailing under the flag of the Comoros) on 31 May 2010 that was part of the so-called Gaza Flotilla.[43] In one of the reports in response to the incident, the proportionality equation mentioned earlier was, referring to the San Remo Manual, dealt with under the heading of the 'principle of humanity'.[44] The so-called Palmer Report concludes that the naval blockade was not disproportionate, because of the fact that there is no commercial port in Gaza, therefore the suffering of the civilian population of Gaza was not the result of the naval blockade (but rather caused by the closed border crossings on land).[45]

With the development of aeroplanes, the possibilities to enforce a blockade became wider than only by naval means. In addition, analogous to the naval blockade, effective aerial blockades became technically possible. According to the HPCR Manual on Air and Missile Warfare, an aerial blockade is 'a belligerent operation to prevent aircraft from entering or exiting specified airfields or coastal areas belonging to, occupied by or under the control of

40 1994 San Remo Manual on International Law Applicable to Armed Conflicts at Sea, para. 102.

41 1994 San Remo Manual on International Law Applicable to Armed Conflicts at Sea, paras. 103–104.

42 Buchan, p. 271.

43 On the legality of the naval blockade of Gaza: see Sanger, pp. 397–446.

44 For the Palmer Report, see United Nations Secretary General 2011a. See also Buchan, pp. 270–273.

45 Palmer Report, p. 43. See also Buchan, p. 273, who disagrees with this conclusion.

the enemy'.[46] Aerial blockades are subject to the same proportionality equation as naval blockades.[47]

3.5 BELLIGERENT REPRISALS

Belligerent reprisals are intentional violations of the rules of IHL with the purpose to stop ongoing violations of these rules by the adversary and with the objective to restore the situation as it was before the initial violations started. Belligerent reprisals are thus measures to enforce IHL.[48] Belligerent reprisals must be set apart from reprisals under the *ius ad bellum*, as an illegal use of armed force as a countermeasure. Belligerent reprisals are an instrument of IHL applicable to an international armed conflict, their applicability during non-international armed conflicts is subject to debate.[49]

There are specific rules governing the legality of reprisals. Firstly, under the rules of IHL, reprisals against many categories of persons are prohibited. These categories include wounded, sick and shipwrecked combatants, as well as medical and religious personnel and prisoners of war. There is no unanimity on the legality of reprisals against the civilian population under customary IHL, but the prohibition of reprisals against civilians does apply to the parties to Additional Protocol I.[50]

Secondly, in order for belligerent reprisals to be legal, they need to meet five requirements,[51] including the requirement that reprisals need to be proportional to the initial violation of IHL or the aim it pursues.[52] The proportionality requirement that applies in the use of reprisals 'entails not only that the reprisals must not be excessive compared to the precedent

46 HPCR Manual on air and missile warfare, rule 147. See Program on Humanitarian Policy and Conflict Research, Harvard University 2009a.

47 HPCR Manual on air and missile warfare, rules 157–159.

48 Kalshoven and Zegveld, p. 156.

49 For an overview of this debate, see Bílková, pp. 31–65.

50 See article 51 (6) API.

51 See generally Bílková, pp. 34–35: (1) there has been a previous violation of IHL to which the reprisal is a response; (2) other measures to stop the violation of IHL have remained unsuccessful and the reprisal is thus a measure of last resort; (3) the reprisals need to be in conformity with the constraints of humanity and morality; (4) the reprisals need to be proportional to the initial violation of IHL or the aim it pursues; and (5) the decision to use the reprisal must be taken by a high level of military or civilian authority of the State. See also the *Kupreškić* Trial Chamber Judgment, para. 535: '[reprisals] may be taken only after a decision to this effect has been made at the highest political or military level; in other words they may not be decided by local commanders'.

52 See Dinstein 2004, p. 221; Greenwood 1989b, pp. 39–48; Mitchell, pp. 158–161; Bílková, pp. 34–35; Darcy, pp. 189–196.

unlawful act of warfare, but also that they must stop as soon as that unlawful act has been discontinued'.[53] It is thus important that the violence applied by way of reprisals does not exceed the initial violation, because this would be the start of a further escalation of the violations of the protective rules of IHL.[54] On the other hand, the violence of the reprisal does not need to be exactly identical.[55] Dinstein explains that '[s]ometimes there is no direct counterpart in State A for the object struck in State B. It is also possible that State B lacks the technical capacity of meting out to State A measure for measure in the same field.'[56] In any case, the comparison of the initial violation and the reprisal that responded to it must be viewed not on a strategic level but rather a more tactical level.[57]

The difficulty is of course in an actual comparison between the initial violation and the reprisal that was executed in response. For example, in the *Ardeatine Caves Case*, the court did not equate the life of one person to another, based on a difference in rank.[58] In addition, the result of the reprisal may be very different than expected beforehand, for example when an attack by way of reprisal with prohibited weapons leads to many more casualties than expected and therefore becomes excessive in comparison to the initial violation of the adversary. McDougal and Feliciano adopt a slightly different position, stating that '[t]he kind and amount of permissible reprisal violence is that which is reasonably designed so as to affect the enemy's expectations about the costs and gains of reiteration or continuation of his lawful act so as to induce the termination of and future abstention from such act.'[59] Although this latter approach is in line with the required objective of the reprisal, it is even more difficult to qualify (and quantify) than the approach that the reprisal must be assessed strictly in comparison with the initial violation that invoked it. It may therefore again cause a further escalation of the ongoing intentional violations of IHL. It is obvious that there must be a degree of

53 *Kupreškić* Trial Chamber Judgment, para. 535.

54 Kalshoven 1971, p. 341. See also Mitchell, p. 160.

55 Hampson 1988, pp. 823–824.

56 Dinstein 2004, p. 221.

57 Greenwood 1989a, p. 282.

58 The *Ardeatine Caves Case* (also known as the *Kappler Case*) concerned the killing of 355 Italian prisoners as a reprisal against the killing of 33 German military policemen in a bomb attack by the Italian resistance. The court found the reprisal to be disproportionate not only on the basis of the quantity of the victims, but also on the basis of their different ranks. The Italian victims included five generals, eleven senior officers, twenty-one subaltern officers and six non-commissioned officers. See 15 *Annual Digest & Reports of Public International Cases*, 1948, p. 471.

59 McDougal and Feliciano, p. 682.

discretion for the State that falls victim of a violation of IHL and that wishes to use a reprisal to stop that violation. Kalshoven notes that the principle of proportionality in this field is not a strict calculation, but must be understood as 'the absence of obvious disproportionality … [and that] there is no alternative but to accept the flexibility and relative vagueness of the requirement of proportionality'.[60] As a result, the proportionality calculation for belligerent reprisals remains always an assessment 'on a very crude scale'.[61]

3.6 SECURITY MEASURES DURING OCCUPATION

Occupation is the situation where a territory is actually placed under the authority of a hostile army.[62] An occupying power is authorised to take measures that enhance its security, such as detaining persons who pose a threat to them[63] or changing the law.[64] However, this authority is limited to the measures that are necessary for military reasons and thus these measures may not be taken excessively by the occupying power.

In case of the internment of persons, for example, article 78 of Geneva Convention IV mentions explicitly that there may be an exception to the general rule. The question may arise as to what happens when the law does not provide for an explicit exception. For example, in the situation that an occupying power wishes to remove public officials from their post, occupation law gives that possibility.[65] But does that count for any official the occupier wishes to remove, or only for some particularly influential ones? Surely an occupied territory may not be left without any public officials, because that would be contrary to the occupier's obligation to 'restore, and ensure, as far as possible, public order and safety, while respecting, unless absolutely prevented, the laws in force in the country'.[66] So absent an explicit mention, one could argue that proportionality must be applied as a general principle, restricting the occupying power to remove officials from office randomly. It would, in the first instance, be more prudent if the occupier only removed those who pose a significant threat to the security of the occupying force.

60 Kalshoven 1971, pp. 341–342. An example of obvious disproportionality is given by Darcy, p. 195: 'in the Einsatzgruppen case, … the Nazis executed 2100 people purportedly in reprisal for the killing of twenty-one German soldiers'.

61 Greenwood 1989b, p. 45.

62 Article 42 Hague Regulations.

63 Article 78 GCIV: 'for imperative reasons of security'.

64 Article 64 GCIV: 'to ensure the security of the Occupying Power'.

65 See article 54 GCIV.

66 Article 43 Hague Regulations.

It may also be argued that article 54 of the Geneva Convention (IV) (GCIV) contains only the exception to the general rule, which is that an occupying power is allowed to remove any person from office the occupier deems necessary. The first sentence of article 54 GCIV then provides a restriction, or merely a warning, to the occupying power to make sure that, in particular, judges are spared from any major clean-up operation among government officials. However, it is unclear whether the source of this restriction is indeed the principle of proportionality, or military necessity. Carcano concludes that the de-Ba'athification of Iraq after the regime of Saddam Hussein was ousted 'does not appear to be proportionate to, and justified by, the security needs of the occupants'.[67]

The relevance of the source of the exception becomes clear when the example of the Israeli security fence is assessed.[68] The Supreme Court of Israel dealt with a number of petitions on concrete demarcations on the ground of the security fence.[69] The Court deemed that the principle of proportionality is a general principle of international law and as such, there must be a proper balance between military necessity and humanitarian considerations to justify the route of the fence that was chosen. Dinstein disagrees with the finding of the court that the principle of proportionality must be seen as a principle applicable to the entire body of international law but he seems nonetheless prepared to accept that proportionality is central in this case.[70] In the subsequent case of *Alfei Menashe*, the Supreme Court of Israel stated that security reasons must be counterweighed against humanitarian considerations, and this balance must be struck through the principle of proportionality.[71] This proportionality equation was further defined as a three-step analysis: '(1) a rational fit between means and ends; (2) a demonstration that Israel has chosen the least harmful means to secure its security objective; and

67 Carcano, p. 217. As a result, Carcano finds the process violates the 'principles of fairness and proportionality'. See Carcano, p. 221.

68 See, for example, Dinstein 2009, pp. 247–259, A. M. Gross 2006, pp. 393–440 and Pertile, pp. 678–734. See also the Wall Advisory Opinion, which concluded quite rigorously that the construction of the barrier *in* occupied territory was illegal.

69 See the *Beit Sourik Case* (HCJ 2056/04, *Beit Sourik Village Council et al.* v. *Government of Israel et al.* 58(5) PD, or the English translation in 43 ILM 1099 (2004)) and the case of *Alfei Menashe* (HCJ 7957/04, *Mara'abe et al.* v. *Prime Minister of Israel et al.* or the English translation in 45 ILM 202 (2006)). See also the case note by Watson.

70 Dinstein 2009, pp. 249–250.

71 *Alfei Menashe Case*: The Supreme Court Sitting as the High Court of Justice, HCJ 7957/04 *Mara'abe* v. *The Prime Minister of Israel*, paras. 28–30, pp. 20–21.

(3) a showing that damage caused to the individual must be of appropriate proportion to the benefit stemming from it'.[72]

The point here is that it is generally agreed under international humanitarian law that military necessity may not be invoked as 'an exception to prohibitive norms'[73] by a party to an armed conflict unless it is explicitly mentioned in the applicable rule. This restriction does not apply similarly to proportionality, which is used here as a mechanism to assess the proper balance between military necessity and humanitarian considerations, but only in those instances where there is a specific reference to military necessity in the relevant prohibitory norm. If there is no such reference, the proportionality equation is between the effect of a security measure (which is not prohibited) and humanitarian considerations.

3.7 CONCLUSION

As has been demonstrated in this chapter, IHL contains a number of standards of moderation that fulfil a similar role as the traditional IHL rule on proportionality that concerns the calculation of the expected collateral damage and the anticipated military advantage with regard to a planned attack during armed conflict. Some of these resemble a restrictive interpretation of military necessity, others seem to refer to mitigating superfluous injury or unnecessary suffering or may be construed as extra-legal moderations based on notions of chivalry.

72 Watson, p. 898.
73 Pertile, p. 713.

4

The Concept of Proportionality in International Humanitarian Law

As a rule of international humanitarian law, proportionality features a number of design flaws and remains extremely vague.[1]

4.1 INTRODUCTION

The focus of this chapter is the principle of proportionality in IHL, or, more precisely, the IHL rule on proportionality.

Today, with the Hague Conventions of 1907 still in force, the applicable treaty law of targeting is codified in particular, but not exclusively, in the 1977 Additional Protocol to the Geneva Convention. The definition of the IHL rule on proportionality as it stands today in treaty law reads that an attack is indiscriminate if it 'may be expected to cause incidental loss of civilian life, injury to civilians, damage to civilian objects, or a combination thereof, which would be excessive in relation to the concrete and direct military advantage anticipated'.[2]

The IHL rule on proportionality is a typical component of IHL, in the sense that it requires participants in an armed conflict to strike a balance between humanity and military necessity.[3] It is a crucial factor in any targeting decision taken during armed conflict. The IHL proportionality rule does not stand on its own, but is part of a larger framework, particularly the principles of distinction and precautionary measures.

1 Dill, p. 2.
2 See article 51 (5) (b), article 57 (2) (a) (iii) and article 85 (3) (b) API.
3 The United Kingdom Manual of the Law of Armed Conflict, p. 25. See, however, Greenwood 1989a, note 22 on p. 278: Greenwood states that the principle as codified in API is 'based on purely humanitarian considerations'.

The IHL rule on proportionality is meant 'as a last line of defence'[4] for civilians and objects that do not qualify as military objectives. The rule is also included in the law pertaining to the use of landmines: article 3 of Protocol II, as well as Amended Protocol II, to the 1980 Certain Conventional Weapons Convention, expressly prohibits the use of landmines, booby-traps and other devices laid outside military zones that are used indiscriminately because they may be expected to be disproportional. For the purpose of understanding the origin of the provision in the Mines Protocol, it may be noted that the wording of the IHL rule on proportionality in the three articles of API and the wording used in Protocol II to the CCW 1980 is 'deliberately identical'.[5] Finally, the rule is also included in article 8 (2) (b) (iv) of the Statute of the International Criminal Court (ICC), in a slightly different wording, as discussed subsequently.

The existence of the IHL rule on proportionality is without debate. But its content and application in practice is not straightforward.[6] This chapter contains an overview of the development of the IHL rule on proportionality that led to its present codification in treaty law. In addition, the existence of the IHL rule on proportionality in customary law is discussed.

4.2 THE DEVELOPMENT OF INTERNATIONAL HUMANITARIAN LAW PROPORTIONALITY

4.2.1 *The First Codifications of International Humanitarian Law*

The Lieber Code of 1863 is the first attempt to codify modern IHL rules for land warfare. It notes the fact that collateral injury and death to civilians may be the effect of hostilities. Article 15 reads that '[m]ilitary necessity admits of all direct destruction of life and limb of armed enemies, and of other persons whose destruction is incidentally unavoidable in the armed contests of war'. In the following articles, the citizens of the opponent are first defined as enemies, and as such, it is considered lawful that they are 'subjected to the hardships of the war'.[7] These articles, however, recognise that it is 'more and more acknowledged that the unarmed citizen is to be spared in person, property,

4 Kalshoven 1992, p. 42.

5 Sandoz et al., para. 2205, p. 684.

6 In the words of Fenrick: 'The main problem with the principle of proportionality is not whether or not it exists but what it means and how it is to be applied.' See Fenrick 2000, p. 58 and the ICTY OTP Kosovo Report, para. 48.

7 Article 21 Lieber Code.

and honor as much as the exigencies of war will admit',[8] but this protection 'was, and still is with uncivilized people, the exception'.[9]

The first multilateral treaty law concerned with the way parties to an armed conflict are to conduct their operations on land is the 1899/1907 Hague Conventions.[10] There is no specific rule on proportionality contained in this document, but there are a number of provisions, particularly articles 22–28, that contain the basis of the presently applicable provisions on targeting. In turn, these provisions are based on articles 12–18 of the 1874 Brussels Declaration.[11] In these articles, the protection of the civilian population and civilian objects is clearly not a priority for the belligerents. In the words of Kalshoven: 'not a word is spent on the inhabitants of a defended place and their homes'.[12] *The War Book of the German General Staff*, published in 1902, which is based on the 1899 Hague Convention, states on the subject of sieges and bombardments that '[w]ar is waged not merely with the hostile combatants, but also with the inanimate military resources of the enemy. This includes not only the fortresses but also every town and every village which is an obstacle to military progress.'[13] It may well be argued that this is a manifestation of the 'Kriegsraison geht vor Kriegsmanier' doctrine that has been defended at some point in time, but that doctrine 'has never had a place in international law'.[14] Yet, in 1926, McNair wrote with regard to land warfare that 'the fact that non-combatants are besieged together with the combatants, and have to endure the same hardships, may, and very often does, exercise pressure upon the authorities to surrender'[15] and thus perceived as a military advantage. The responsibility for collateral damage was generally placed on the defending side of the conflict, for locating military objectives too close to the civilian population.[16] The reason for the absence of a rule devoted to the protection of incidental casualties and damage may also be explained by the

8 Article 22 Lieber Code.

9 Article 24 Lieber Code.

10 The 1907 IV Hague Convention and the annexed Regulations on the Laws and Customs of War on Land is slightly different from the 1899 Hague Convention II Respecting the Laws and Customs of War on Land. See Scott, pp. 529–532, for a juxtaposition of the articles of the two Conventions.

11 Scott, p. 145. For the text of the articles of the Brussels Declaration, see Schindler and Toman, pp. 24–25.

12 See Kalshoven 2007, p. 434.

13 Grossgeneralstab of the Kingdom of Prussia, p. 34.

14 Garraway 2010, p. 215.

15 McNair, p. 283.

16 Parks 1990, p. 21.

way Western armies fought their battles at close range in open fields, with a limited civilian presence.

The IHL rules on the subject of the protection of the civilian population have made huge strides since then, following technological developments that have increased the distance from which enemies engage each other. One major cause for increasing attention to this subject is the rise of air warfare.[17] The expected development of air warfare was the reason for a five-year prohibition on the use of bombing from the air at the 1899 Hague Peace Conference.[18] At the 1907 Hague Conference, the development of air warfare had already progressed so much that, although a new moratorium was adopted, it was not ratified by all States that had been a party to the 1899 Declaration, which had expired.[19] There were attempts though to replace the 1899 Declaration with a permanent prohibition, but these were unsuccessful.[20] Agreement could be reached on placing some restrictions on air warfare, and these were incorporated in article 25 of the 1907 Hague Convention on Land Warfare, by adding the words 'by whatever means' to the existing text which prohibits the attack or bombardment on undefended towns. There can be no doubt, therefore, that this article also applies to air warfare.[21]

Simultaneous to the law on aerial warfare, the law pertaining to bombardment from the sea developed. The 1907 Convention on naval bombardment also contains a prohibition on attacking undefended ports and towns.[22] Additionally, article 2 of the Convention provides that the commander 'incurs no responsibility for any unavoidable damage which may be caused by a bombardment' of both military and civilian naval installations that are present in undefended ports and towns, but that may be used for military purposes.

An early reference to the proportionality rule as it is today is included in the Hague Rules on Air Warfare of 1923. Article 23 (4) reads: '[i]n the immediate

[17] See McNair, pp. 368–370 and Lauterpacht in consecutive editions of *Oppenheim's International Law*, for example Lauterpacht 1935, pp. 414–420. For an overview of the development of the law, see Ronzitti, pp. 3–15; Rogers 2008, p. 190. For an overview of the use of air warfare until 1920, see Garner, pp. 458–465.

[18] Declaration IV.1 (signed 29 July 1899) to Prohibit, for the Term of Five Years, the Launching of Projectiles and Explosive form Balloons, and Other Methods of a Similar Nature. See Schindler and Toman, p. 309.

[19] Declaration XIV (signed 18 October 1907) Prohibiting the Discharge of Projectiles and Explosives from Balloons. See Schindler and Toman, p. 309. See also Garner, p. 466, and Ronzitti, pp. 4–5.

[20] Although the 1907 Declaration XIV remains in force today, it is regarded as 'having no legal significance'. See Parks 1990, p. 17.

[21] Garner, p. 467.

[22] Convention IX (signed 18 October 1907), Concerning Bombardment by Naval Forces in Time of War. See Schindler and Toman, p. 1079.

vicinity of the operations of the land forces, the bombardment of cities, towns, villages habitations and buildings is legitimate, provided there is a reasonable presumption that the military concentration is important enough to justify the bombardment, taking into account the danger to which the civil population will thus be exposed.'[23] The Hague Rules on Air Warfare never entered into force, but the content may still be seen as part of the development of the law on targeting. At the time, however, the provisions were criticised, even labelled 'unrealistic'.[24] Parks notes that the proposed article 24, which requires care for collateral civilian casualties, was a '180-degree change of course in then-existing bombardment philosophy'.[25]

Another reference to proportionality before World War II started can be found in a resolution adopted by the League of Nations Assembly on aerial warfare in 1938.[26] It prohibits the 'intentional bombing of civilians' and reiterates that '[a]ny attack on legitimate military objectives must be carried out in such a way that civilian populations in the neighbourhood are not bombed through negligence.'[27]

In summary, the codification efforts of the Hague Peace Conferences and other developments before World War II reflect an increased acceptance of distinction. A rule on proportionality increasing the protection of the civilian population was, however, still far off, although an awareness that some care had to be taken for the civilian population against the effects of the hostilities was emerging.

4.2.2 *Legal Doctrine before World War II*

Still, the principle of proportionality had in the meantime also surfaced in legal doctrine. Spaight emphasises the principle of distinction, but he goes further than that. He comments in 1930 that,

23 For the text of the Hague Rules on Air Warfare, see Schindler and Toman, pp. 315–325.

24 Rogers 2008, p. 194. Rogers also notes that if the Hague Rules on Air Warfare would have been binding law, the area bombing practice during World War II would have been illegal. Parks labels the Hague Rules as 'an immediate and total failure'. See Parks 1990, pp. 31–36.

25 Parks 1990, p. 32.

26 Protection of Civilian Populations against Bombing from the Air in Case of War, Resolution of the League of Nations Assembly on 30 September 1938. Reprinted in Schindler and Toman, pp. 329–330.

27 See Fenrick 1982, p. 96. Fenrick points to the fact that the resolution could also be read as an absolute ban on casualties among the civilian population. For the text of the resolution, see Schindler and Toman, p. 1079.

> [e]ven a *military* objective in an urban area may not lawfully be bombed if, by reason of its restricted area or its situation in a densely populated district, the natural and reasonable probable result of an attempt to bomb it will be widespread and wholly disproportionate loss of non-combatant life throughout the district. Subject to this reservation … the bombing of military objectives must be held to be lawful even if the incidental result is loss of innocent life.[28]

Spaight is less concerned about civilian property, and argues in favour of a new rule that would allow the bombing of civilian property, subject to some restrictions.[29]

Royse was of the opinion that the civilian population was already normally a lawful military target. He concludes in 1928 that, '[i]n the realm of war, populations whether actively engaged in combat or whether remote from all hostilities are subject to whatever force the enemy can apply.'[30] Harm done to civilians when legitimate military objectives are attacked he regards as 'an unavoidable incident of warfare'.[31] The general attitude towards air warfare in the period between the two World Wars paid little consideration to the effects of air warfare on the civilian population.[32] The development of air warfare was feared, and its potential devastation effects to civilians were recognised, even anticipated as soon as the next war broke out.[33]

Hall is very clear about the protection of civilians under the law of air warfare. According to him, the civilian population of a country engaged in armed conflict is 'exposed to all the injuries to person and property resulting from military or naval operations directed against the armed forces of their State'.[34] That does not mean, however, that direct attack of the civilian population is permitted. Hall discusses the possible bombardment of London and concludes that the indiscriminate bombardment of the city as

28 Spaight 1930, p. 201. Emphasis in original.

29 Spaight 1924, pp. 257–259; Spaight 1933, pp. 239–259.

30 Royse, p. v.

31 Royse, p. 241.

32 One commentator on air warfare notes in 1930: '[h]itherto the non-combatants' part has been to pay up, work hard at what is given them to do, try to keep smiling, draw their belts, disbelieve enemy propaganda, and replace casualties. But now, and in the future, the non-combatants' role is quite different, for the avowed object of each contestant is to cripple the economic life of each other.' See Charlton, p. 168. Mumford notes that 'Europe had progressed beyond civilian massacre for many centuries before the invention of the aeroplane; that invention, used nationally, has restored the curse.'

33 Mumford, p. 66. Writing in 1936, Mumford anticipated 'diabolic death and disastrous destruction undreamed of by Ghengis Khan or Alexander the Great'.

34 Hall, p. 77.

such is prohibited, but adds that there are certainly military objectives present in London that could be legally targeted. However, the 'difficulty is to get sufficiently close to such objectives to obtain any reasonable chance of hitting them, but the difficulty of this and the consequent danger to innocent people in the neighbourhood does not make such attacks illegal'.[35]

The general feeling towards air warfare was that, at the time, the rules of international law regulating it were inadequate.[36] The application of the principles of the law of warfare on land to air warfare was contemplated, but there was no unanimity on the subject.[37] The situation had apparently changed in 1940, when according to Lauterpacht, '[a]lthough the Hague Rules on Air Warfare have not been ratified ..., air warfare, while calling for rules of its own regulating in detail the specific situations to which it gives rise, is subject to the general principles of a customary or conventional character which underlie alike the law of war on land and at sea.'[38]

When World War II started, there were certainly a number of rules of customary IHL applicable that protected civilians. However, the rule of proportionality was not among them, considering the practice of aerial bombardment during World War II. As for the reason why this was so, Rogers concludes that there was no balance between military necessity and humanitarian considerations, because the latter were not contemplated at all during World War II.[39] Spaight writes in 1944 that 'nothing was done [to regulate air warfare], and the omission was, in part at least, the result of a determination that nothing should be done'.[40] The applicable rules of IHL with regard to the regulation of the conduct of hostilities could be summarised as a prohibition to attack the civilian population directly, and an obligation to take some care to spare the civilian population when military objectives were attacked.[41]

Nonetheless, the heated debate between Churchill and Eisenhower with regard to the choice between two separate bombing plans aimed at paralysing the movements of German troops in Belgium and Northern France just

35 Hall, p. 80. The issue was discussed in *The Times* newspaper in the early part of 1914.

36 See the overview in Rogers 2008, pp. 195–202. See also Royse, p. 237.

37 There had, however, been cases, such as *Coena Brothers* v. *Germany*, decided in 1927 and *Kiriadolou* v. *Germany*, decided in 1930, both by the Greco-German Mixed Arbitral Tribunal, that had applied article 26 of the 1907 Hague Convention on Land Warfare to German air operations in Greece. See Lauterpacht 1935, p. 417. Royse, however, argues that there cannot be such an extension to air warfare. See Royse, p. 241.

38 Lauterpacht 1944, p. 410.

39 Rogers 2008, p. 203.

40 Spaight 1944, p. 19.

41 See Rogers 2008, pp. 202–203; Parks 1990, p. 31.

before D-Day shows that there was at least some sensitivity towards preventing civilian damage and civilian casualties in the conduct of air operations.[42]

4.2.3 *After World War II: The Red Cross Draft Rules*

After World War II, the principle of proportionality entered the scene in the Red Cross Draft Rules for the Limitation of the Dangers incurred by the Civilian Population in Time of War.[43] The Red Cross Draft Rules, including a commentary, were drawn up by the ICRC with the help of experts of national Red Cross and Red Crescent societies, after a number of expert meetings held in Geneva in 1954.[44] The Red Cross Draft Rules were published in 1956, with a view to being discussed at the XIXth International Red Cross Conference to be held in New Delhi in 1957.[45] The incentive to draft these rules was 'the fact that recourse has been had very generally to the system of indiscriminate bombing [which] seems to have led to its becoming, as it were, an accepted practice, and given right to a kind of fatalism'.[46] The Red Cross Draft Rules were meant not to replace the rules already codified in the Hague Conventions, but to bring detail to the existing rules.[47]

Article 8 of the Red Cross Draft Rules, which deals with precautions in the planning of an attack, states: 'The person responsible for ordering or launching an attack shall, first of all: … take into account the loss and destruction which the attack … is liable to inflict upon the civilian population. He is required to refrain from the attack if, after due consideration, it is apparent that the loss and destruction would be disproportionate to the military advantage anticipated.'

The commentary to article 8 states that the experts drafting the Rules sought to underline the general principle found in doctrine that there must be a balance between the anticipated military advantage and the risks for the civilian population.[48] It adds that what is new in this proposed article is the

[42] See generally Gaughan, pp. 229–285.
[43] Hereinafter: The Red Cross Draft Rules.
[44] See Rogers 2008, p. 203 and *International Review of the Red Cross*, Supplement IX, 1956, p. 164. For the commentary, see *International Review of the Red Cross*, 1956, pp. 623–650 and 695–710.
[45] ICRC 1956, Supplement IX, p. 164.
[46] Ibid.
[47] ICRC 1956, p. 558.
[48] 'La proportion dans l'attaque entre l'avantage militaire recherché et les risques pour la population est un principe généralement admis en doctrine et que les "Experts de 1954" ont tenu à souligner' (translation by the author). See *International Review of the Red Cross*, 1956, p. 700.

obligation to conduct the proportionality calculation in all circumstances.[49] It therefore seems that the principle of proportionality was already seen as a 'general doctrinal principle' which was also underlined by the experts who had prepared the Red Cross Draft Rules.[50] The Commentary to the Red Cross Draft Rules makes it clear that the drafters viewed the calculation between the military advantage on the one hand and the harm to civilians and damage to civilian objects on the other hand to constitute 'the principle of proportionality in the laws of war'.[51]

The resolution containing the Red Cross Draft Rules that was discussed during the International Red Cross Conference in New Delhi 'does not call for a formal approval of the Draft Rules'.[52] There was extensive discussion on the Draft Rules themselves during the Conference; however, much of that debate was allocated to issues that were of particular importance at that time, such as nuclear weapons.[53] The reaction of the major powers to the Draft Rules was 'adverse'.[54] As a result, there was simply no reaction to the Draft Rules from States.[55] Sandoz noted later that this was because the Draft Rules 'directly addressed the question of nuclear weapons'.[56]

But at least as far as the proposed article on the proportionality rule was concerned, that does not mean that the Red Cross Draft Rules were a pointless effort. On the contrary, its inclusion in the Draft Rules was noted.[57] Even though the text of the proportionality rule as it would later be adopted in Additional Protocol I has a different wording than the one proposed in the Red Cross Draft Rules, the basic significance of the provisions on the proportionality principle is not fundamentally different. Both require a balance between the expected military advantage and civilian costs of the planned attack. The text of the article on proportionality and its commentary in the

49 *International Review of the Red Cross*, 1956, p. 701.

50 See also Rogers 2008, p. 203.

51 'Le principe de la proportionnalité dans les lois de la guerre'. See ICRC 1956, p. 702.

52 ICRC 1957, p. 10.

53 For the report of these discussions, see ICRC 1957.

54 Aldrich 1984, p. 130.

55 See the introductory note in Schindler and Toman: 'As there was virtually no response from governments, no further action was taken with a view to adopting a convention on the basis of this draft.' Schindler and Toman, p. 339. See also Parks 1990, p. 66.

56 Sandoz 1997, p. 7. During the negotiations leading to the adoption of Additional Protocols I and II, discussion of nuclear weapons was deliberately avoided, by restricting the deliberations to conventional weapons.

57 For example, by Kunz, p. 324.

Red Cross Draft Rules may be seen as the first explicit reference to the IHL rule on proportionality as it would be adopted about twenty years later.[58]

4.2.4 *Additional Protocol I*

The IHL rule on proportionality is mentioned in three separate, yet closely related, articles in Additional Protocol I: firstly, article 51 (5) (b); secondly, article 57 (2) (a) (iii) and 57 (2) (b); and thirdly, article 85 (3) (b), which refers to the violation of the rule of article 57 (2) (a) (iii) as a grave breach when committed wilfully and causing death or serious injury to body or health.

During the international conference that led to the adoption of API, '[i]t was a widely held view that a general affirmative obligation on the part of combatants to consider in advance the relationship between incidental civilian losses and expected military advantage, would inure to the benefit of civilians and provide increased protection.'[59]

Some authors seem to be of the opinion that a broader principle of proportionality was already part of existing law at the time of the negotiations leading to the 1977 Additional Protocols. Brown, for example, notes that, '[a]lthough proportionality has yet to be codified as a principle of civilian protection, the idea that military means should be proportionate to their anticipated ends is widely recognized as a basic norm of the law of warfare.'[60] However, some delegations to the international conference that led to the adoption of API had their doubts about including the IHL rule on proportionality in the treaty. They feared it could lead to abuse and that it would blur the clear and unambiguous principle of distinction. However, given the fact that the conduct of hostilities inevitably cause injury, loss of life and damage to civilians and civilian objects, '[t]he view prevailed that it was preferable that the law should reflect this reality and be used to enjoin constraint, rather than be silent on the matter and leave it entirely to the practice of the belligerents.'[61]

58 Rogers notes that the official US Army manual on the law of land warfare of 1956 also includes an explicit rule of proportionality (see section IV, para. 41 at p. 14 of FM 27-10 (1956)), and suggests that this may be a result of the attendance by the American representative in the meetings that drafted the Red Cross Draft Rules. See Rogers 2008, p. 203.

59 Reed, p. 26.

60 Brown, p. 136.

61 Blix, p. 148.

4.2.4.1 Draft Article 46 (the Present Article 51 API)

The text of article 46 of the draft Protocol I, as proposed by the ICRC, has a different wording than the text that is now codified in article 51 API. The formulation of the draft article was clearly derived from the Red Cross Draft Rules, promulgated by the Red Cross Movement in 1956.[62] Draft article 46 (3) (b) provides that in particular it is forbidden 'to launch attacks which may be expected to entail incidental losses among the civilian population and cause the destruction of civilian objects to an extent disproportionate to the direct and substantial military advantage anticipated'.[63]

In the draft version of Protocol II, the IHL rule on proportionality was embodied in draft article 26, which dealt with the protection of the civilian population. Draft article 26 (3) (b) provided that it is forbidden in particular 'to launch attacks which may be expected to entail incidental losses among the civilian population and cause the destruction of civilian objects to an extent disproportionate to the direct and substantial military advantage anticipated'.[64]

In the General Discussions in the Plenary Meetings in 1974, the discussions were hardly concerned with the principle of proportionality. A number of delegates mentioned the need to enhance the protection of the civilian population, but the focus was in this regard on the enhancement of the principle of distinction. See, for example, the statement of the Government of Sweden, who mentioned the increasing civilian casualties caused by war, ranging from 5 per cent in World War I, 50 per cent in World War II, 60 per cent in the Korean War and 70 per cent in the Vietnam War. Additionally, the statement mentioned the 'heavy casualties' caused by air warfare.[65]

The draft provisions containing the proportionality principle were discussed in Committee III. Explaining the proposed article, the representative of the ICRC said that '[t]he Red Cross was conscious of the fact that the rule of proportionality contained a subjective element, and was thus liable to abuse.

[62] Best, p. 325. For details, see ICRC, Final Record Concerning the Draft Rules, ICRC, April 1958, see www.loc.gov/rr/frd/Military_Law/pdf/RC_Final-record-rules-limitation.pdf

[63] See the Official Records of the Diplomatic Conference on the Reaffirmation and Development of International Humanitarian Law Applicable in Armed Conflicts, Volume I, Part Three, p. 16.

[64] See the Official Records of the Diplomatic Conference on the Reaffirmation and Development of International Humanitarian Law Applicable in Armed Conflicts, Volume I, Part Three, p. 40.

[65] See statement by Mr Lidbom, on 7 March 1974, Official Records of the Diplomatic Conference on the Reaffirmation and Development of International Humanitarian Law Applicable in Armed Conflicts, Volume V, Plenary Meetings, First Session, on p. 143.

The aim was, however, to avoid or in any case restrict the incidental effects of attacks against military objectives.'[66]

In the subsequent discussions on the matter, there was a clear difference between the opinions of the ICRC and a number of Western States[67] on one side, and some Eastern European States[68] and a number of States from the Middle East (Egypt, Iraq, Syria) on the other side. The former supported the inclusion of a rule of proportionality in the new Protocol I, the latter were opposed to that idea. In the words of the representative of the German Democratic Republic:

> [b]ecause it considered that protection of the civilian population could not be improved if the concept of proportionality was retained. To permit attacks against the civilian population and civilian objects if such attacks had military advantages was tantamount to making civilian protection dependent on subjective decisions taken by a single person, namely, the military commander concerned.[69]

To illustrate the substance of the debate, the interventions of the representatives of the United States and of Hungary may be compared. According to the representative of the United States of America, the

> rule of proportionality [as proposed] was based on existing international law.... Collateral damage to civilians and civilian objects was often unavoidable and it was unrealistic to attempt to make all such damage unlawful: the rule of proportionality was as far as the law could reasonably go.[70]

On the other hand, the representative of Hungary said that:

> [a] rule well established in international law should be reflected in practice and should produce the intended effects. Yet the number of civilian victims had increased alarmingly over the past few years: accordingly, either the rule was not well established and hence not binding; or it existed and could not be

66 Official Records of the Diplomatic Conference on the Reaffirmation and Development of International Humanitarian Law Applicable in Armed Conflicts, Volume XIV, CDDH/III/SR.5, 14 March 1974, para. 12, p. 37.

67 Canada, Federal Republic of Germany, the United Kingdom, France and others.

68 Romania, Hungary, Czechoslovakia and the Democratic Republic of Germany.

69 Official Records of the Diplomatic Conference on the Reaffirmation and Development of International Humanitarian Law Applicable in Armed Conflicts, Volume XIV, p. 56.

70 Official Records of the Diplomatic Conference on the Reaffirmation and Development of International Humanitarian Law Applicable in Armed Conflicts, Volume XIV, p. 67.

applied in armed conflicts; or it was applied, but the results of its application provided the best argument against it.[71]

Being unable to reach consensus on the article, the matter was thus referred to the Working Group, which discussed article 46 of draft Protocol I. The Report to Committee III of the Working Group summarised the issue of article 46 (3) (b) as follows:

> The principle of proportionality ... received a mixed reaction. Some delegations considered it a necessary means of regulating the conduct of warfare and of protecting the civilian population. Other delegations rejected that principle as a criterion and asserted that in humanitarian law there should be no condonation of casualties among civilians. Some who took the latter view considered that it would be desirable to delete subparagraph 3 (b) as a whole, while others of the latter view proposed the deletion of the words 'to an extent disproportionate to the direct and substantial military advantage anticipated'.

Eventually, paragraph 3 (b), containing the IHL rule on proportionality, was 'drafted only after article 50 [of draft Protocol I, on the subject of precautions in attack] had been settled, since both concerned the same issue'.[72] Eventually, article 46, as amended, was agreed upon, and adopted by consensus during the Second Session of Committee III, on 14 March 1975.[73] Subparagraph 3 (b) of article 46 only referred to article 50. The question of whether there would be a cross-reference between the two articles, in which of the articles the text of the IHL rule on proportionality would appear (or indeed in both as it is today), was referred to the Drafting Committee.

4.2.4.2 Draft Article 50 (the Present Article 57 API)

The proposed article on precautions in attack contained a number of references to proportionality. Article 50 of the draft Protocol I reads:

> 1. Constant care shall be taken, when conducting military operations, to spare the civilian population, civilians and civilian objects. In the planning, deciding or launching of an attack the following precautions shall be taken:

[71] Official Records of the Diplomatic Conference on the Reaffirmation and Development of International Humanitarian Law Applicable in Armed Conflicts, Volume XIV, p. 68.

[72] Official Records of the Diplomatic Conference on the Reaffirmation and Development of International Humanitarian Law Applicable in Armed Conflicts, Volume XV, p. 275.

[73] Official Records of the Diplomatic Conference on the Reaffirmation and Development of International Humanitarian Law Applicable in Armed Conflicts, Volume XIV, p. 301.

(a) (Proposal I) those who plan or decide upon an attack shall (Proposal II: those who plan or decide upon an attack shall take all reasonable steps to ...) ensure that the objectives to be attacked are duly identified as military objectives within the meaning of paragraph 1 of Article 47 and may be attacked without incidental losses in civilian lives and damage to civilian objects in their vicinity being caused or that at all events those losses or damage are not disproportionate to the direct and substantial military advantage anticipated;
(b) those who launch an attack shall, if possible, cancel or suspend it if it becomes apparent that the objective is not a military one or that incidental losses in civilian lives and damage to civilian objects would be disproportionate to the direct and substantial advantage anticipated; ...

2. All necessary precautions shall be taken in the choice of weapons and methods of attack so as no cause losses in civilian lives and damage to civilian objects in the immediate vicinity of military objectives to be attacked.[74]

In explaining the draft of article 50 of draft Protocol I, on precautions in attack, the representative of the ICRC held that,

> [t]here was always a risk that any attack, even when directed against a clearly determined military objective, might affect the civilian population: it could arise from such factors as the configuration of the terrain (danger of landslide, or of ricocheting); the relative accuracy of the weapons used (relative dispersion according to trajectory, firing range, ammunition used, condition of the equipment); meteorological conditions (the effect of the wind, of atmospheric pressure, of cloud); the specific nature of the military objectives (ammunition stores, fuel tanks, army nuclear stations); or the combatants' mastery of techniques (the standard of technical training and technical ability in handling weapons).[75]

This article repeats the formula of proportionality that was proposed in article 46 of draft API. The ICRC proposed the article with the ideal in mind of the 'complete elimination, in all circumstances, of losses among the civilian

[74] See the Official Records of the Diplomatic Conference on the Reaffirmation and Development of International Humanitarian Law Applicable in Armed Conflicts, Volume I, Part Three, p. 17.

[75] Official Records of the Diplomatic Conference on the Reaffirmation and Development of International Humanitarian Law Applicable in Armed Conflicts, Volume XIV, p. 181.

population'.[76] However, the ICRC recognised that an explicit rule to that extent would be impracticable and it was unrealistic to expect it to be credible or effective. Therefore, the ICRC proposed a limited rule to formulate that ideal, 'offering a balance of the various factors involved' and with 'the advantage that it could be observed'.[77]

It took the Working Group to Committee III many heated discussions to work out paragraph 2 (a) of draft article 50 of draft Protocol I.[78] It was eventually agreed upon after inserting two paragraphs containing additional precautions and after the term 'disproportionate' was deleted from the text. In the new draft of the article, the rule referred to 'excessive in relation to the concrete and direct military advantage anticipated'. According to Frits Kalshoven, it was his proposal to use the word 'excessive' which eventually solved the deadlock and therefore became the standard that is now applied as the IHL rule on proportionality.[79] Additionally it was supplemented by paragraph 50 (5) of the draft article 'to make clear that it may not be construed as authorization for attacks against civilians'.[80] Article 50 was adopted by Committee III on 14 March 1975.

In the end, it appears that in the Working Group report there is nothing more about the reasons why the principle is phrased as we know it today than the remark that it 'required much time and effort'.[81] At the time the codification of the IHL rule on proportionality was indeed seen as important, because it filled the gap[82] between the prohibitions to attack civilians directly[83] and the prohibition to attack military objectives without distinction.[84]

76 Official Records of the Diplomatic Conference on the Reaffirmation and Development of International Humanitarian Law Applicable in Armed Conflicts, Volume XIV, p. 183.

77 Ibid.

78 See also Brown, p. 138.

79 As Frits Kalshoven claimed during a meeting of the Kalshoven-Gieskes Forum on International Humanitarian Law on 27 November 2012, following a presentation on the principle of proportionality of the present author.

80 Official Records of the Diplomatic Conference on the Reaffirmation and Development of International Humanitarian Law Applicable in Armed Conflicts, Volume XV, p. 285.

81 Official Records of the Diplomatic Conference on the Reaffirmation and Development of International Humanitarian Law Applicable in Armed Conflicts, Volume XIV, p. 183. Reminiscing about the Diplomatic Conference, the Rapporteur of the Working Group notes that essential to the resolution of a number of problems, such as the codification of the principle of proportionality, was the fact that he had established personal relations with the Soviet and Vietnamese delegations during the Vietnam peace negotiations and several agreements concluded with the Soviet Union. See Aldrich 1984, p. 134.

82 Brown, p. 155.

83 As prohibited in article 51 (2) API.

84 As prohibited in article 51 (4) (a), (b) and (c) and article 51 (5) (a) API.

4.2.5 *The Rome Statute of the International Criminal Court*

There is a small difference in the wording of the war crime of violating the IHL rule on proportionality as it is codified in the ICC Statute and the wording in the other treaty provisions mentioned earlier. The prohibition in the ICC Statute prohibits during international armed conflict: 'intentionally launching an attack in the knowledge that such an attack will cause incidental loss of life or injury to civilians or damage to civilian objects ... which would be *clearly* excessive in relation to the anticipated direct overall military advantage anticipated'.[85]

It has been debated whether the IHL rule on proportionality as it is codified in Additional Protocol I is exactly identical to the IHL rule on proportionality as it is recognised in customary international law, or that the formulation in the ICC Statute should prevail.[86] Rogers reaches the conclusion that the formulation of article 8, paragraph 2 (b) (iv) of the ICC Statute is the correct formulation of the IHL rule on proportionality, because that article

> was drafted with states not party to Protocol I very much in mind and involved in the negotiations ... and the drafters of this article took into account the various statements made on ratification of Protocol I and, by adopting a middle way, have tried to accommodate the requirements of military necessity without abandoning humanity, by allowing one to look at the bigger operational picture.[87]

According to Dörmann, the different formulation in the ICC Statute was caused by a general feeling during the negotiations of the ICC Statute that the wording as included in that Statute was the state of affairs in international customary law at the time.[88] McCormack and Mtharu, however, call the addition of the word 'clearly' an 'additional requirement' for the prohibition of disproportionate attacks in order to constitute a war crime under the ICC Statute.[89] The question of whether the adjective 'clearly' must be deemed to be part of the IHL proportionality rule is discussed in Chapter 8.

[85] Article 8 (2) (b) (iv) ICC Statute (emphasis added). It should be noted that the principle is only included in the ICC Statute as a war crime in international armed conflicts.
[86] For example by Watkin 2007, p. 19 and Rogers 2008, p. 208.
[87] Rogers 2008, p. 208.
[88] Dörmann 2003a, pp. 169–170.
[89] McCormack and Mtharu, p. 196. See also Olasolo, pp. 83–84 and R. J. Barber, p. 479.

4.3 IHL PROPORTIONALITY IN INTERNATIONAL CUSTOMARY LAW

If the 1977 Additional Protocol I to the Geneva Conventions would have been universally ratified instantly after their conclusion, there would be no discussion about the question whether the IHL rule on proportionality is applicable during armed conflict. However, a number of States did not, or not immediately, ratify the protocol. The universal acceptance of the 1949 Geneva Conventions therefore has not (yet) been achieved for its three Additional Protocols. Also, although the existence of the principle of proportionality was not challenged, a number of States accompanied their ratification of Protocol I by reservations or declarations that also concerned the application of the IHL rule on proportionality.[90] The customary status of the rule is particularly relevant for the rules regulating non-international armed conflicts (NIACs). There is no specific reference to 'the principle of proportionality' in the Geneva Conventions and its Protocol applicable to NIACs. More generally, there are only a few treaty rules applicable during NIACs. As a result, the rules of customary IHL applicable during an NIAC are the prevalent source of law for the parties to those types of conflicts. Therefore, the question whether the IHL rule on proportionality has achieved the status of customary international law remains relevant.[91]

The representative of the United Kingdom during the negotiations of Additional Protocol I and II, Sir John Freeland, stated with regard to the status of the IHL rule on proportionality at the moment of its codification in the Additional Protocols, that it 'was a useful codification of a concept that was rapidly becoming accepted by all States as an important principle of international law relating to armed conflict'.[92] One commentator notes that the result in the applicable provisions of API 'probably combines elements of codification and progressive development',[93] while others conclude that the IHL rule on proportionality was already part of customary international law in 1977.[94] On the other hand, Parks writes in 1990 that in the view of the US Department of Defense, the text of the draft article of API, presented to the

90 See Schindler and Toman, pp. 792–818. See, for example, the declarations of Australia, Canada, the Netherlands and others made at the time of ratification.

91 For the relevance of customary IHL in general, see Henckaerts 2005, pp. 177–178.

92 Rogers quotes Aldrich with regard to the status of the principle of proportionality as a rule of customary IHL during the negotiations of the Additional Protocols to the Geneva Conventions as holding the view in 2006 that 'John Freeland stated it best'. See Rogers 2008, note 103, pp. 214–215.

93 Greenwood 1989a, p. 278, in note 23.

94 Bothe 1982, p. 276; Penna, p. 220.

diplomatic conference was not a reflection of customary international law.[95] In any case, it seems clear from the records of the diplomatic conference, as discussed earlier, that when Additional Protocol I was concluded, there was no universal agreement on the exact content of the IHL rule on proportionality.[96] The question remains today whether it may be considered as a part of customary international law.

4.3.1 *Challenges in Establishing a Customary IHL Proportionality Rule*

The existence of rules of customary IHL is sometimes not straightforward.[97] This is because there is no unanimity among scholars, courts and States about the method to identify rules of customary international law.[98] As a result, it is unclear what the exact required level and character of the State practice and *opinio juris* is to conclusively determine the customary status of a rule of IHL.[99] Even though these two components of customary law are widely acknowledged, the importance of the one factor over the other is subject to debate.[100] The authors of the ICRC Study on customary IHL had to deal with this issue when they compiled the collection of 161 rules of customary IHL. Although the Study is an impressive piece of work, its methodology has received both criticism and acclaim.[101] The experience of its drafting process illustrates the difficulties that are encountered in the identification of

95 Parks 1990, p. 174. Fellmeth states that, '[i]nternational practice has proven impervious so far not only to all attempts to identify the content of the rule of proportionality in any detail, but to assessing the status of the principle itself as a binding custom.' See Fellmeth 2010, p. 2.

96 Fenrick notes that 'there was some debate' on the customary status of the principle of proportionality at the time of the conclusion of API. See Fenrick 1982, p. 125. Greenwood regards the principle of proportionality part of customary IHL prior to 1977, but feels that the principle is 'expressed in the Protocol in more precise language than that was used hitherto'. He concludes 'that Article 51 (5) (b) should be treated as an authoritative statement of the modern customary rule'. See Greenwood 1991, p. 109. Meron, writing in 1989, affirms the customary status of the principle and adds that it is 'perhaps also a general principle of law'. See Meron 1989, note 178 on p. 65.

97 Part of the discussion in this section was published in the book chapter 'Fighting by the principles: principles as a source of international humanitarian law', see van den Boogaard 2013, pp. 13–16.

98 See, for example, Shaw 2014, pp. 51–66 and the accompanying notes.

99 See for an overview, Ronen, pp. 482–495. See also generally Wood, pp. 727–736.

100 See article 38 (1) (b) of the ICJ Statute: 'international custom, as evidence of a general practice accepted as law'. See also Shaw 2014, pp. 53–54.

101 This subject has been debated, for instance, during the launching events of the ICRC Humanitarian Law Study that have taken place worldwide. A summary of the proceedings of a number of these events is available: www.icrc.org/Web/Eng/siteengo.nsf/htmlall/section_ihl_customary_humanitarian_law?OpenDocument.

customary rules of IHL.[102] The methodology that the International Tribunal for the former Yugoslavia has used to identify rules of customary international law was similarly criticised.[103] The specific character of IHL makes the methodological problems even more prominent. International humanitarian law is a preventive framework, meant to regulate the hostilities as soon as they begin. The rules of IHL are the user's manual for the use of the arms that the parties to the conflict deploy in their operations, as well as for the methods they may use. The problem in terms of the creation of State practice is that it is difficult to get access to the practice during the operations for reasons of operational security. Also in terms of the creation of *opinio juris*, there is no reason to pay attention to those instances when nothing at all happens since an attack has been cancelled. Therefore, States will normally only express their opinion if something has gone wrong. The State that is under attack, however, for propaganda reasons, will be likely to declare an attack during which there has been damage to civilian objects or death or injury to civilians as grossly disproportionate.

The existence of State practice can be determined on the basis of the 'duration, consistency, repetition and generality'[104] of State behaviour. However, this leaves uncertainty concerning the question of which behaviour constitutes State practice. Legal scholarship concerning the methodology to establish customary international law revolves around the question whether actual State practice applying a rule is required to constitute a customary rule, or that other types of practice could suffice to satisfy the requirement of State

[102] See Henckaerts and Doswald-Beck 2005a, vol. I, pp. XXXI–XLV; the contributions of Bethlehem 2007, Scobbie 2007 and Hampson 2007 to the book by Wilmshurst and Breau; Bellinger and Haynes; and Henckaerts 2007 for a discussion on the various aspects of the methodology used in the ICRC Customary International Humanitarian Law Study.

[103] For example, Kalshoven and Zegveld 2011 extend criticism to the way the ad hoc tribunals for Rwanda and the former Yugoslavia have identified customary international law and conclude that the tribunals should actually have been referring to principles:

> In particular, this more recent extension of the scope of customary law of armed conflict appears to rest on the assumption that for this type of armed conflict, general opinion about preferred behaviour outweighs the requirement of demonstrable practice seen as law. To the extent that this 'general opinion of preferred behaviour' reflects accepted principle, we would prefer to call it that.

And with regard to the ICRC Customary Law Study: 'in particular with respect to internal armed conflict not all of these rules may rest on the type of actual field practice traditionally required of rules of customary law. Yet they may well reflect existing principles and thus deserve to be promoted under that heading'. See Kalshoven and Zegveld 2011, p. 5; see also Baker, Ratner and Stahn.

[104] Shaw, p. 54.

practice. According to some writers, only actual physical acts, through the agents of a State, count as State practice.[105]

The State practice one would therefore typically search for in order to identify a rule of customary law is battlefield practice, such as the actual targeting behaviour of States during armed conflict.[106] This practice could, for example, be derived from After Action Reports containing the deliberations of the military commanders demonstrating their argumentation before the attack, including both the reasons for proceeding with and cancelling an attack. Conclusive proof of the practice should draw from a large collection of these types of report from various States and conflicts, providing proof as to how various factors were weighed in the decision-making process and the subsequent behaviour of operational planners and commanders. Preferably, the After Action Reports should also include Collateral Damage Assessments of those planning, ordering and executing the attack and how the different factors under the specific circumstances of the attack were evaluated, before a decision to attack was taken. Unfortunately, in practice, these assessments are not always publicly available, if they are made in written form at all.[107] There are a number of reasons for this,[108] the most important reason being that those who would be best placed to conduct a thorough assessment of targeting decisions are not among those with a particular interest in the outcomes of the assessment.[109] With regard to the application of the IHL proportionality rule, it has been suggested that on every occasion civilian casualties occur as a result of a specific attack, an inquiry should always be conducted into the

105 See, for example, D'Amato, p. 88.

106 See, for example, Bellinger and Haynes, p. 445, Maxwell and Meyer, pp. 10–11, Fellmeth 2010, p. 4.

107 That does not mean, of course, that there is no oversight at all. For example, there was a practice of relatively independent oversight in the armed forces of the Kingdom of the Netherlands by the Royal Military Constabulary (Koninklijke Marechaussee) and the office of the Public Prosecutor of the Arnhem District Court with regard to instances where the members of the military used armed force during the deployment of Dutch troops in the Afghan province of Uruzgan from 2006 to 2011. Another example is the investigation into the bombing of two stolen fuel tankers on 4 September 2009 in Kunduz, Afghanistan. It was investigated by the German prosecutor and by the German Bundestag. For the report see Deutscher Bundestag.

108 Fellmeth mentions four reasons: the fact that the concept of sparing the civilian population in armed conflict emerged only rather recently; the fact that the way military operations are conducted is usually contingent on confidentiality restrictions; the fact that 'few states are eager to publicize their own crimes'; and, finally, the fact that most armed conflicts nowadays have a non-international character, and States regard the treatment of their own civilians as a 'matter of sovereign internal control'. See Fellmeth 2010, pp. 2–3.

109 Shamash, p. 146.

possible disproportionate use of force.[110] These inquiries could be helpful, if published in full, to assess whether, and how, the proportionality rule is applied in practice. However, this does not seem to be an obligation which would be welcomed by the parties to an armed conflict. Parties to an armed conflict are generally reluctant to 'expose the decision process to public view [because] it could enable current or future adversaries to predict the military organization's strategy and tactics, undermining its effectiveness and exposing its personnel to danger'.[111] Other authors however claim that actual behaviour is not necessary to identify State practice, and that 'it is artificial to distinguish between what a State does and what it says'.[112]

The second component of customary law is that of *opinio juris sive necessitates*, which is also known as the psychological component of customary law. It may be defined as the 'belief by a state that behaved in a certain way that it was under a legal obligation to act that way'.[113] Different indications of State practice or *opinio juris* have to be used in determining the customary character of rules of IHL, for example military manuals.[114] Of course, how States instruct their military is certainly relevant for the practice in the context of the conducting of hostilities in armed conflict. It seems to be more logical, however, to classify the way States have phrased the obligations for their militaries in their military manuals as an expression of *opinio juris* rather than State practice. Military manuals indicate how States would *want* their armed forces to conduct their operations, or what they regard as legal behaviour. But often, military manuals express no opinion at all, but merely restate the States' treaty obligations, and should be considered as nothing more than that.[115] This is particularly the case for the military manuals of States that have not been involved in armed conflict for a long time. In case of incidents involving

[110] See Cohen 2010, pp. 29–36.

[111] Fellmeth 2010, p. 3.

[112] Akehurst, p. 3. See, however, van Steenberghe 2017, p. 897: '[t]he material or verbal nature of any State manifestation does not impact its description as State practice; it may only influence the weight to be attributed. Moreover, although one normally must be more cautious when grounding a customary rule on State speeches rather than on State material behaviours, some declarations, particularly those taking the form of international or internal legal acts, carry more weight because States commit themselves to abide by what they said. In addition, material acts are often deprived of much weight unless they are associated with a legal explanation, usually in the form of a declaration which enables an understanding to be had of the legal significance of the conduct.'

[113] Shaw, p. 53. See also the ICJ in the *Nicaragua Case*, pp. 108–109, and the *Continental Shelf Cases*, ICJ Reports 1969, p. 44.

[114] Particularly in the ICRC Customary Law Study, see Henckaerts and Doswald-Beck 2005b, Volume II, Practice.

[115] See, for example, Schmitt 2007, p. 133.

(alleged) violations of the rules, the reaction of States to that incident may also be regarded as *opinio juris*.[116] But then many factors are still unclear, such as the question whether the practice of non-State actors should be taken into account.[117]

In the author's view, a variety of indicators and methods may be considered to assess the customary status of a rule of customary IHL.[118] The following sections assess the customary status of the IHL rule on proportionality through a number of sources. As a starting point, the outcome of the updated ICRC Customary Law Study will be discussed. Next, a selection of cases is discussed in which the customary character of the IHL rule on proportionality is addressed. Furthermore, it will be assessed how the customary character of the IHL rule on proportionality is regarded in a number of other sources.

4.3.2 *The ICRC Customary Law Study*

The ICRC Customary Law Study, published in 2005, identifies the IHL rule on proportionality as a rule of customary IHL.[119] Rule 14 reads:

> Launching an attack which may be expected to cause incidental loss of civilian life, injury to civilians, damage to civilian objects, or a combination thereof, which would be excessive in relation to the concrete and direct military advantage anticipated, is prohibited.

It may be noted that the rule is formulated identical to the treaty provision in API. The same is true for most of the formulation in Rules 15, 17 and 18, which deal with precautions to be taken before and during attacks in order to respect the IHL rule on proportionality.

The State practice that the ICRC has collected to support the statement that the rule is indeed of a customary nature includes treaty texts and other official instruments, military manuals, national legislation, official statements by States, submissions by States to international courts and the reported

[116] Schmitt 2007, pp. 132–133.

[117] See Fellmeth and Sylvester for a study of the practice during the Colombian civil war, concluding that *opinio juris* that the proportionality rule was upheld during the conflict by the Colombian Army 'has been lacking'. See Fellmeth and Sylvester, p. 556.

[118] See on the methodology to establish rules of customary IHL the discussions that were the result of the first edition of the ICRC Customary Law Study: Henckaerts and Doswald-Beck 2005a, vol. I, pp. xxxi–xlv, Henckaerts 2007, pp. 178–184, Meron 2005, Dinstein 2006, pp. 3–8, Bothe 2007a, pp. 143–178, the critical remarks of the US Government as voiced by Bellinger and Haynes and the response by Henckaerts, see Henckaerts 2007. See also generally Penna, pp. 202–209.

[119] Henckaerts and Doswald-Beck 2005a, Rule 14, pp. 46–50.

practice of States.[120] The collected practice also includes the practice of States not a party to Additional Protocol I, such as India, Israel, Pakistan, the Philippines and the United States. In addition, some other types of practice are mentioned, for example resolutions of international organisations like the United Nations and the Council of Europe.

The list of military manuals containing the IHL rule on proportionality is impressive: thirty military manuals contain the principle. In the military manuals of many of these States, the principle 'has been copied verbatim, or by adopting its essence, according to which civilians are not to be attacked, unless they are taking a (direct) part in the hostilities'.[121] It may, however, be assumed that many, but not all, of these thirty States have incorporated the IHL rule on proportionality in their military manual because the relevant State ratified API. The ICRC Study has been criticised for its methodology and the types of practice that were used, but for the IHL rule on proportionality the amount of State practice and other indicators seem to be quite comprehensive.

4.3.3 *Case Law on the IHL Rule on Proportionality*

Case law is a subsidiary source of international law, but does not constitute State practice by itself.[122] Case law may, however, serve to clarify and assist in the interpretation of the primary sources of international law, such as customary IHL. Especially when rulings of (international) courts receive general agreement by States and in legal doctrine, its findings may provide 'persuasive evidence' of the customary character of a rule.[123] Although case law often mentions the IHL proportionality rule, cases in which the rule is actually applied are sparse. Since the principle was not codified before 1977, jurisprudence on the subject prior to that date is virtually non-existent.[124] Nonetheless,

120 The practice that the ICRC has relied on to identify the customary status of the rules has been published in an updated online database. For Rule 14, see www.icrc.org/customary-ihl/eng/docs/v2_cha_chapter4_rule14.

121 Wells-Greco, p. 411, mentioning the military manuals of Australia, Canada, France, Germany, Italy, New Zealand, the United Kingdom and the United States (Air Force). For another US Manual, see also the US Interservice Field Manual FM 3-06 Aviation Urban Operations, July 2005, pp. I-6.

122 Akehurst, p. 11.

123 Henckaerts 2005, p. 179. See also *Prosecutor* v. *Kupreškić*, Trial Chamber Judgment, ICTY Case nr. IT-95-16, 14 January 2000 (hereinafter the *Kupreškić Case*), para. 542.

124 In 1927, there were judgments by the Greco-German Mixed Arbitral Tribunal on the basis of the Treaty of Versailles with regard to an aerial attack by Germany on Greece (destroying 'certain stores of coffee' in Salonica) and on Bucharest. The Tribunal applied the provision

a number of international and national courts have mentioned the IHL proportionality rule. The following sections provide an overview of those cases, which were adjudicated before both national and international courts. Cases in which the IHL proportionality rule is actually applied are discussed in Chapter 7.

4.3.3.1 The *Shimoda Case* (1963)

In the case of *Shimoda* v. *State*,[125] concerning the bombing of the Japanese cities of Hiroshima and Nagasaki in 1945, the Japanese District Court ruled

applicable to land warfare to the aerial attack, and ruled that '[i]t was one of the generally recognised principles of international law that the belligerent ought to respect, as far as possible, the life and the property of the of the civilian population.' Germany was held liable for the damage, but on the basis that it had not issued a warning, not because the damage to the civilian property had been out of proportion. Proportionality was not considered in this case. See *Coenca Brothers* v. *Germany*, in *Annual Digest of Public International Law Cases*, 1927, pp. 570–572. For the attack on Bucharest, the Tribunal referred to the writings of Spaight in order to grant the claim. See *Annual Digest of Public International Law Cases*, 1929–1930, pp. 516–517. See also Parks 1990, pp. 37–38. After World War II, the Nuremberg Tribunal did have the possibility to prosecute the crime of 'indiscriminate bombing' but because of the fact that indiscriminate bombing was practised extensively by the armed forces of both the Allies and the Germans, the prosecution of this crime was not pursued. Parks mentions that 'The Charter of the Nuremberg International Military Tribunal listed "indiscriminate bombing" as a crime recognizable by the Tribunal, but in practice the United Nations War Crimes Commission routinely rejected cases alleging indiscriminate bombing if the bombarded towns or cities contained military objectives'. See Parks 1990, pp. 37–38. Conot contains a description of the plea by Goering on the legality of the bombardments on Warsaw, Rotterdam and Coventry, where he claims that in all cases there were important military objectives located in these cities. See Conot, p. 334. Olasolo mentions the judgment in the *Einsatzgruppen Case*:

> [a] city is bombed for tactical purposes: communications are to be destroyed, railroads wrecked, ammunition plants demolished, factories razed, all for the purpose of impeding the military. In these operations it inevitably happens that non-military persons are killed. This is an incident, a grave incident to be sure, but an unavoidable corollary of battle action. The civilians are not individualised. The bomb falls, it is aimed at the railroad yards, houses along the tracks are hit and many of their occupants killed. But that is entirely different, both in fact and in law, from an armed force marching up to these same railroad tracks, entering those houses abutting thereon, dragging out the men, women and children and shooting them.
>
> (*United States* v. *Otto Ohlendorf et al.*, 4 Trials of War Criminals before the Nuremberg Military Tribunals under Control Council Law No. 10, pp. 1 et seq, p. 467 (1947)).

See Olasolo, p. 157, note 623.

[125] *Shimoda Case*, International Legal Materials (ILM), nr. 32, p. 626. The case concerned Japanese survivors claiming compensation from the Japanese Government. The claims were denied on the basis of the fact that Japan had waived all its claims against the United States in the 1951 Peace Agreement.

that an indiscriminate attack on an undefended city is prohibited under customary international law, on the basis of the Hague Rules on Air Warfare of 1926.[126] The court acknowledged that the bombardment from the air of a military objective will also lead to destruction of civilian property and casualties to non-combatants, but that this is 'not unlawful as long as it is an inevitable result incidental to the aerial bombardment of a military objective. Nevertheless, … aerial bombardment without distinction between military objectives and non-military objectives (the so-called "blind aerial bombardment of an undefended city") is not permissible … '.[127] The Court held that the aerial bombardment using nuclear weapons was in essence a blind aerial bombardment because of the 'tremendous' destructive power of the atomic bomb and therefore contrary to the applicable rules of IHL in 1945.[128]

As such, the *Shimoda Case* does not contain a specific reference to the IHL rule on proportionality. Of course, at the time, the rule had not then been codified, and the applicable law to the case was the law as it stood in 1945. Yet, the case does seem to make an attempt to strike a balance between the presence of military objectives and the damage to civilians and civilian objects that could be expected from bombardment by atomic bombs on the two cities. The Court concludes, basing its ruling on customary law, that the attacks were indiscriminate, but it does not express whether this conclusion is based on excessive civilian casualties and damage (due to the means of warfare that was used) or on the basis of a lack of distinction.

4.3.3.2 The Nuclear Weapons Advisory Opinion (1996)

The IHL rule on proportionality was considered again in relation to nuclear weapons in the Nuclear Weapons Advisory Opinion of the International Court of Justice (ICJ).[129] This case was instigated by the World Health Organization and the United Nations General Assembly, which asked the ICJ to consider the legality of nuclear weapons. In its Advisory Opinion of 8 July 1996, the Court did not make any direct reference to the IHL rule on proportionality, but a number of judges noted in the explanation of their vote that they considered the IHL rule on proportionality to be a part of customary law.[130]

[126] *Shimoda Case*, ILM 32, p. 631.

[127] *Shimoda Case*, ILM 32, p. 632.

[128] Ibid. See also Brown, p. 141, and Fenrick 1982, p. 113.

[129] For a general description of the case, see, for example, David 1997.

[130] Separate Opinion of Judge Guillaume, para. 5, ICJ Reports (1996), p. 289; Dissenting Opinion of Vice-President Schwebel, ICJ Reports (1996), p. 320; Dissenting Opinion of Judge Higgins, para. 20, ICJ Reports (1996), p. 587. See Doswald-Beck 1997, p. 40.

Additionally, proportionality is addressed by some of the States who intervened in the case.[131] Judge Schwebel provides two examples where nuclear weapons may be used without violating the IHL rule on proportionality, namely when used against military objectives in the middle of the ocean, or the desert.[132] Judges Higgins and Guillaume note that in order to use a nuclear weapon, the military advantage that arises from the attack will necessarily have to be very huge, to outweigh the anticipated collateral damage form the attack.[133]

Judge Higgins also states in a widely quoted statement that,

> [t]he law of armed conflict has been articulated in terms of a broad prohibition – that civilians may not be the object of armed attack – and the question of numbers or suffering (provided always that this primary obligation is met) falls to be considered as part of the 'balancing' or 'equation' between the necessities of war and the requirements of humanity. Articles 23 (g), 25 and 27 of the Annex to the Fourth Hague Convention have relevance here. The principle of proportionality, even if finding no specific mention, is reflected in many provisions of Additional Protocol I to the Geneva Conventions of 1949. Thus even a legitimate target may not be attacked if the collateral civilian casualties would be disproportionate to the specific military gain from the attack.[134]

The Court notes that the use of nuclear weapons would be 'scarcely reconcilable' with the principles of IHL, but it does not draw the conclusion that the use of nuclear weapons would always be disproportionate. Rather, it concludes, though the views of the judges diverge on this point, that under the circumstances of a particular attack, the use of nuclear weapons could be lawful.[135] In conclusion, it is fair to say that the Nuclear Weapons Advisory Opinion underscores the existence of the IHL rule on proportionality as a rule of customary IHL.

[131] For example, by the United Kingdom, as stated during the oral pleadings and quoted in the Dissenting Opinion of Judge Schwebel on p. 321 of the Advisory Opinion. See also the Written Statement of the Netherlands, p. 13, the Written Statement of the United Kingdom, paras. 3.70 and 3.71 on pp. 53 and 54. See also Henckaerts and Doswald-Beck 2005a, note 14 on p. 48, listing also Egypt, India, Iran, Malaysia, New Zealand, Solomon Islands, Sweden, the United States and Zimbabwe.

[132] Dissenting Opinion Judge Schwebel, pp. 320–322 of the Advisory Opinion. These examples are also mentioned in the Written Statement of the United Kingdom, see paras. 3.70 and 3.71 on pp. 53 and 54.

[133] See para. 21 of the Dissenting Opinion of Judge Higgins and the Separate Opinion of Judge Guillaume on p. 289 of the Advisory Opinion.

[134] Nuclear Weapons Advisory Opinion, p. 587.

[135] See Greenwood 1997, p. 70.

4.3.3.3 ICTY Case Law (1995–Present)

It is clear that the International Criminal Tribunal for the former Yugoslavia (ICTY) regards the IHL rule on proportionality as part of international customary IHL.[136] Its Trial and Appeals Chambers have addressed the IHL rule on proportionality in a number of cases.[137] However, as Bartels notes, the ICTY judges would usually mention the rule without actually applying it to the facts of the case.[138] The ICTY Trial Chamber provides 'the first actual application of this principle by the ICTY to date'.[139] In the *Gotovina Case*,[140] however, the decision was overturned by the Appeals Chamber.[141]

Of particular significance is the *Kupreskić Case*.[142] The Trial Chamber held that the rules of API that contain the IHL rule on proportionality, 'it would seem, are now part of customary international law, not only because they specify and flesh out general pre-existing norms, but also because they do not appear to be contested by any State, including those which have not ratified the Protocol'.[143] This statement, which has been characterised as 'sweeping'[144] does not come accompanied by a lengthy analysis detailing the line of argumentation in support of the statement.

In the *Galić Case*, the IHL rule on proportionality is discussed by the Trial Chamber in relation to twenty-three different incidents.[145] The proportionality

[136] See also Rogers 2008, p. 208.

[137] See, for example, *Prosecutor* v. *Blaskic*, ICTY Case nr. IT-95-14, Trial Chamber Judgment, 3 March 2000, paras. 507–510 and Appeals Chamber Judgment, 29 July 2004, paras. 439–441; *Prosecutor* v. *Galic*, ICTY Case nr. IT-98-29, Trial Chamber Judgment, 5 December 2003, paras. 58–61, and Appeals Chamber Judgment, 30 November 2006, paras. 190–194; Also, in the *Martić Case*, the Trial Chamber considered whether the shelling of Zagreb by M-87 Orkan Rockets should be considered a disproportionate attack. The Trial Chamber decided that instead the attacks amounted to a direct attack on the civilian population, even though there were military objectives in Zagreb, due to the nature of the means of warfare that was used. See *Prosecutor* v. *Martic*, ICTY Case nr. IT-95-11, Trial Chamber Judgment, 12 June 2007, paras. 463 and 469 and Appeals Chamber Judgment, 8 October 2008, paras. 245–271.

[138] See Bartels at the EJILTALK blog: www.ejiltalk.org/prlic-et-al-the-destruction-of-the-old-bridge-of-mostar-and-proportionality/: Bartels notes that '[e]xamples of such cases are Kupreškić, Galić, Strugar, Martić, and Dragomir Milošević'.

[139] Bartels 2013, p. 272.

[140] ICTY, *Prosecutor* v. *Gotovina, Cermak and Markac*, Judgment, IT-06-90-T, Trial Chamber 1, 15 April 2011 (Gotovina Trial Judgment).

[141] ICTY, *Prosecutor* v. *Gotovina, Cermak and Markac*, Judgment, IT-06-90-A, Appeals Chamber, 16 November 2012 (Gotovina Appeals Judgment).

[142] *Kupreskić* Trial Chamber Judgment.

[143] *Kupreskić* Trial Chamber Judgment, para. 524.

[144] See Boivin, note 151, p. 41.

[145] Olasolo, p. 179.

principle is also discussed by the Chamber evaluating the attack on a football match in Sarajevo.[146] In these incidents, however, it seems that the Trial Chamber used the incidents to prove that there was an ongoing 'campaign of sniping and shelling against civilians'[147] rather than prosecuting the accused for violation of the IHL rule on proportionality.

The ICTY report on the NATO campaign in Kosovo in 1999 also considers the IHL rule on proportionality. Although the opinion of the Prosecutor can obviously not be equated to a judgment of an international court, the Report is nevertheless significant. The report notes the statement in *Kupreskić*, but regards it as 'a progressive statement of the applicable law with regard to the obligation to protect civilians'.[148] The Report, however, states that there is no doubt about the existence of the IHL rule on proportionality, but that it is difficult to assess how it should be applied.[149] The report reviews a number of incidents, such as the proportionality of the attack by NATO on the Radio and Television Tower in Belgrade on 23 April 1999, killing at least ten people. The Report found that as a part of the overall attack with the objective to disrupt Serbian command, control and communications system, it did not appear to be manifestly excessive in relation to the key military advantage expected from the disruption.[150]

4.3.3.4 The Eritrea–Ethiopia Claims Commission (2000–2005)

In the cases before the Eritrea–Ethiopia Claims Commission (the Commission), a number of cases also dealt with proportionality issues.[151] The claims concerned the armed conflict between Eritrea and Ethiopia in the period from 1998 until 2000. Eritrea maintained that the Ethiopian bombings were, among other things, disproportionate. In these claims,

[146] See the Trial Chamber Judgment in the *Galic Case*, para. 387. See also Kravetz, pp. 532–533 and Olasolo, pp. 180–182.

[147] *Galić* Trial Chamber Judgment, para. 594.

[148] See the Final Report to the Prosecutor by the Committee Established to Review the NATO Bombing Campaign Against the Federal Republic of Yugoslavia (hereinafter: the ICTY OTP Kosovo report), para. 52.

[149] The ICTY OTP Kosovo report, para. 48.

[150] The ICTY OTP Kosovo report, paras. 77–79. See also Olasolo, pp. 129–131. On the subject of the principle of proportionality in the ICTY OTP Kosovo report, see also Benvenuti, pp. 517–519, Bring, pp. 44–45, Murphy, pp. 65–75 and Voon, pp. 6–13. For further analysis, see Chapter 7.

[151] For an overview of the work of the Eritrea–Ethiopia Claims Commission, see Aldrich 2003. See also van Houtte, p. 391, and accompanying notes for a short overview of the cases where the conduct of hostilities of the parties to the conflict was scrutinised. The Awards are available at www.pca-cpa.org/upload/files/FINAL%20ER%20FRONT%20CLAIMS.pdf.

Eritrea relied particularly upon the provisions of API.[152] Since Eritrea is not a party to Additional Protocol I, the Commission assumed the provisions referred to by the parties to be part of customary IHL:

> [a]lthough portions of Geneva Protocol I involve elements of progressive development of the law, both Parties, with one exception, treated key provisions governing the conduct of attacks and other relevant matters in the claims decided by this Partial Award as reflecting customary rules binding between them. The Commission agrees and further holds that, during the armed conflict between the Parties, most of the provisions of Geneva Protocol I were expressions of customary IHL.[153]

The Commission summarised the applicable provisions of API as follows:

> [t]hey emphasize the importance of distinguishing between civilians and combatants and between civilian objects and military objectives; they prohibit targeting civilians or civilian objects; they prohibit indiscriminate attacks, *including attacks that may be expected to produce civilian losses that would be disproportionate to the anticipated military advantage*; and they require both attacker and defender to take all feasible precautions to those ends.[154]

The Commission did 'generally not find indiscriminate or disproportionate bombing where it was foreseeable that civilian losses would be excessive in relation to the military advantage anticipated'.[155] The Commission does not elaborate any specific proportionality calculations it may have reviewed in order to support this conclusion. According to the Award, this is due to the fact that the claimant (in this case: Eritrea) failed to provide the necessary proof to support its statement.[156] Generally, it is concluded, the civilian casualties and damage to civilian objects were in some cases the result of unfortunate

[152] Particularly articles 48, 51, 52 and 57 API. See Eritrea–Ethiopia Claims Commission, Partial Award Western Front, Aerial Bombardment and Related Claims, Eritrea's Claim 26, 19 December 2005, para. 93, p. 27.

[153] Eritrea–Ethiopia Claims Commission, Partial Award Western Front, Aerial Bombardment and Related Claims, Eritrea's Claim 26, 19 December 2005, para. 14, p. 5. Eritrea questioned the customary status of article 54 API, since at the time of the adoption of API, it was considered to be an innovative element of IHL. The claims commission ruled, however, that by 2000, the provision had achieved the status of customary IHL. See para. 105, pp. 29–30.

[154] Eritrea–Ethiopia Claims Commission, Partial Award Western Front, Aerial Bombardment and Related Claims, Eritrea's Claim 26, 19 December 2005, para. 95, p. 27 (emphasis added).

[155] See van Houtte, p. 391, and accompanying notes for a short overview of the cases where the conduct of hostilities of the parties to the conflict was scrutinised.

[156] Eritrea–Ethiopia Claims Commission, Partial Award Western Front, Aerial Bombardment and Related Claims, Eritrea's Claim 26, 19 December 2005, para. 97, p. 28.

targeting mistakes from the side of the Ethiopian armed forces. Other losses could have been avoided if the legitimate military objectives that were under attack would have been located at greater distance from civilian objects.[157]

In one specific case, the attack of the Hirgigo Power Station,[158] there is a reference to proportionality in the separate opinion of President van Houtte.[159] In the text of the claim itself it is held that since Eritrea has not claimed any damages for sustained civilian casualties, and since the object was a legitimate military objective, the extent to which the attack had been proportionate did not have to be considered.[160] In his separate opinion, van Houtte concludes that the power plant was a civilian object, and therefore it had to be considered whether the attack on the Eritrean batteries that were placed there to protect the power station was proportionate.[161]

In summary: the Commission did conclude that '[t]he provisions of Geneva Protocol I relevant to this Claim, which are found in Articles 48, 51, 52, 57 and 58 of that Protocol, expressed customary IHL during the 1998–2000 armed conflict between the Parties.'[162] The only incident in which a proportionality calculation was conducted concerned the damage to a civilian object (the Hirgigo Power Station), which van Houtte found to be excessive in his separate opinion on the basis of a failure of the Ethiopian forces to comply with the obligation to take precautionary measures when attacking a military objective. The Commission did not, regrettably, provide detailed analysis for its conclusion that the bombing efforts of the Ethiopian armed forces were generally not disproportionate.

4.3.3.5 The Supreme Court of Israel Sitting as the High Court of Justice (2005)

In the so-called Targeted Killings Judgment of 11 December 2005, the Israeli Supreme Court treats the principle of proportionality in a more general way,

[157] Eritrea–Ethiopia Claims Commission, Partial Award Western Front, Aerial Bombardment and Related Claims, Eritrea's Claim 26, 19 December 2005, para. 96, p. 27.

[158] Eritrea–Ethiopia Claims Commission, Partial Award Western Front, Aerial Bombardment and Related Claims, Eritrea's Claim 25, 19 December 2005, paras. 106–121, pp. 31–36.

[159] Eritrea–Ethiopia Claims Commission, Partial Award Western Front, Aerial Bombardment and Related Claims Separate Opinion to Claim 25, pp. 1–3.

[160] Eritrea–Ethiopia Claims Commission, Partial Award Western Front, Aerial Bombardment and Related Claims, note 28 on p. 35.

[161] Eritrea–Ethiopia Claims Commission, Partial Award Western Front, Aerial Bombardment and Related Claims Separate Opinion to Claim 25, paras. 10 and 11, p. 3.

[162] Eritrea–Ethiopia Claims Commission, Partial Award Western Front, Aerial Bombardment and Related Claims, Eritrea's Claim 26, 19 December 2005, Award, sub 2 (a), p. 30.

summing up a number of areas of law where proportionality is applicable. As far as IHL is concerned, the Court refers to 'proportionality *strictu senso*', which is defined as 'the requirement that there be a proper proportionate relationship between the military objective and the civilian damage'.[163] The Court acknowledges the customary character of the IHL rule on proportionality, referring to the ICRC Study of customary IHL and the *Kupreskić Case* of the ICTY.[164] The Court adds that it is a 'value based test'[165] and that even though '[p]erforming that balance is difficult ... there's no choice but to perform it'.[166]

4.3.3.6 Sub-conclusion on Case Law

The judgments of the courts, commissions and tribunals that have reviewed the customary character of the IHL rule on proportionality all confirmed the customary status of the IHL rule on proportionality. The Prosecutor of the ICC has referred to a potential prosecution for violations of the criminal law version of the proportionality rule in its Korea Report.[167] For future prosecutions for this crime at the ICC, the ICC Prosecutor would presumably not need to make an assessment of the customary status of the IHL proportionality rule, since these prosecutions would be based on the text of the crime as embodied in article 8 (2) (b) (iv) of the ICC Statute.

[163] The Israeli Supreme Court sitting as the High Court of Justice, *The Public Committee against Torture in Israel et al.* v. *The Government of Israel et al.* HCJ 769/02, 11 December 2005 (hereinafter: *The Targeted Killings Case*), para. 41.

[164] *The Targeted Killings Case*, para. 42:

> The principle of proportionality is a substantial part of international law regarding armed conflict (compare §51 (5) (b) and 57 of The First Protocol [1977 Additional Protocol I] ... That law is of customary character (see ... Prosecutor v. Kupreskic, ICTY Case no. IT-95-16 (2000)). The principle of proportionality arises when the military operation is directed toward combatants and military objectives, or against civilians at such time as they are taking a direct part in hostilities, yet civilians are also harmed. The rule is that the harm to innocent civilians caused by collateral damage during combat operations must be proportionate ... Civilians might be harmed due to their presence inside of a military target, such as civilians working in an army base; civilians might be harmed when they live or work in, or pass by, military targets; at times, due to a mistake, civilians are harmed even if they are far from military targets; at times civilians are forced to serve as 'human shields' from attack upon a military target, and they are harmed as a result. In all those situations, and in other similar ones, the rule is that the harm to the innocent civilians must fulfill, inter alia, the requirements of the principle of proportionality.

[165] *The Targeted Killings Case*, para. 45.

[166] *The Targeted Killings Case*, para. 46.

[167] See International Criminal Court, Office of the Prosecutor, pp. 6–8 (hereafter ICC Korea Report).

It is striking to note that none of the courts or tribunals provides a detailed method for conducting the proportionality calculation in the circumstances put before them, which would have facilitated a more detailed conclusion on the exact content of the principle. As a result, the exact meaning of the components of the principle remains under debate. The interpretation of these components is further explored in Chapter 6.

4.3.4 *Other Indicators*

In addition to the conclusions of the ICRC Customary Law Study and the statements made by (international) courts, other indicators to ascertain the customary status of the IHL rule on proportionality can also be mentioned. Obviously, many expressions of State practice have already been examined by the ICRC Customary Law Study. In this section, a number of additional indicators will be reviewed.

Firstly, it is important to note that States that have not ratified API have expressly acknowledged the customary status of the IHL rule on proportionality, including Israel[168] and the United States.[169] Despite the fact that the exact content of the principle and the interpretation of its components do not seem to be universally agreed upon, this is certainly a clear indication that the rule is indeed part of customary international law.

Secondly, another indicator of the customary character of the principle is the reports of experts, especially if States have been consulted or participated in the process of the drafting of the report. The Manual on Air and Missile Warfare, published in 2010, is a good example.[170] The Manual on Air and Missile Warfare recognises the IHL rule on proportionality as part of the existing legal framework regulating air and missile warfare. It is defined as: '[a]n attack that may be expected to cause collateral damage which would be excessive in relation to the concrete and direct military advantage anticipated is prohibited.' The significance of this report is not only that it has been prepared by a group of prominent experts, including representatives from the ICRC, but also that States have been consulted extensively in order to enhance the acceptability of the rules contained in the Manual. The San

[168] Israel, for example, acknowledges the customary status of the principle in its report on Operation Cast Lead in Gaza, see Israel Ministry of Foreign Affairs 2008, paras. 120–131 on pp. 44–48.

[169] See Matheson, p. 419.

[170] Program on Humanitarian Policy and Conflict Research, Harvard University 2009a (hereinafter: HPCR Manual on air and missile warfare).

Remo Manual on International Humanitarian Law Applicable to Non-International Armed Conflict also confirms the IHL proportionality rule.[171]

Furthermore, the Report of the International Law Association Study Group on the Conduct of Hostilities in the 21st Century, published in 2017, was compiled by a group of notable experts in the field of IHL. The Report refers to the ICRC Customary Law Study, acknowledging the customary status of the IHL proportionality rule: '[b]y virtue of customary international law, parties to an armed conflict are under an obligation to abide by the principle of proportionality in both international as well as non-international armed conflicts.'[172] Some of the experts that were part of this Study Group were also part of the 'Amici' who sent an Amicus Curiae brief to the ICTY Appeals Chamber in the *Gotovina Case* before the ICTY. In this brief, the Amici confirmed that 'commanders who choose to target enemy objectives co-mingled among a civilian population must scrupulously comply with the IHL principles of distinction and proportionality'.[173] Similarly, the Tallinn Manual 2.0,[174] published in 2017, notes the IHL proportionality rule as a rule that is 'generally accepted as customary international law applicable in international and non-international armed conflicts'.[175]

A clear indication of the acceptance of the IHL rule on proportionality as a rule of customary IHL was also evidenced in State practice resulting from the deliberations in the forums of the United Nations with regard to weapons. For example, in the context of the Conventional Weapons Convention 1980, it was established that '[t]he rule on proportionality was identified by 97 percent of Respondent States as relevant to the use of munitions that may result in explosive remnants of war.'[176] McCormack and Mtharu, therefore, conclude that States regard the proportionality equation as a crucial obligation in targeting procedures for their armed forces.[177]

[171] San Remo Manual on the Law of Non-International Armed Conflict, pp. 22–25.

[172] For the report, see the ILA website (www.ila-hq.org/index.php/study-groups?study-groupsID=58), 19 YIHL (2016) pp. 287–336 and http://stockton.usnwc.edu/ils/vol93/iss1/12/, p. 351. This author was part of this process, although the part on the IHL proportionality rule was not specifically drafted by this author.

[173] For the text of the Amicus Curiae brief, see http://icr.icty.org/LegalRef/CMSDocStore/Public/English/Application/NotIndexable/IT-06-90-A/MSC7958R0000353013.pdf

[174] The Tallinn Manual 2.0 on the International Law Applicable to Cyber Operations, second edition, 2017, which was the result of a group of nineteen renowned experts and a large number of other participants and peer reviewers in the field of international law.

[175] Tallinn Manual 2.0, p. 471.

[176] McCormack and Mtharu, p. 193, referring to McCormack et al., p. 17.

[177] McCormack and Mtharu, p. 193.

Other practice originating from the United Nations acknowledging the customary status of the IHL proportionality rule can be derived from the reports of UN fact-finding committees and expert panels, such as the panel of experts that has reviewed the final phase of the conflict between the Government of Sri Lanka and the Liberation Tigers of Tamil Eelam,[178] the United Nations Fact Finding Mission on the Gaza Conflict (the Goldstone Report) that reported on the 2008–2009 Gaza War[179] and the Independent International Commission of Inquiry on the Syrian Arab Republic.[180]

Furthermore, as a subsidiary source of international law, legal doctrine may be mentioned. The opinions of international legal scholars should be reviewed with some reservations, however. Firstly, it could be that a scholar merely echoes the position of a certain government or organisation, or serves to justify that position from an academic point of view. Secondly, the choice of an author to present the opinions of some, and ignoring and disregarding the opinions of others is highly subjective. Thirdly, opinions of scholars often contain not only *lex lata*, but also traces of the way the author would like the law to become. However, with regard to the customary status of the IHL rule on proportionality, the opinions of authors who have written on the subject are uniform in accepting the IHL rule on proportionality as customary IHL.[181]

In addition, organisations such as Human Rights Watch[182] and Amnesty International[183] regard the IHL rule on proportionality as part of the IHL. However, some reports of such non-governmental organisations have received criticism in the past and have been accused of applying the standards

[178] The IHL proportionality rule is mentioned on p. 65, see www.un.org/News/dh/infocus/Sri_Lanka/POE_Report_Full.pdf

[179] See www2.ohchr.org/english/bodies/hrcouncil/docs/12session/A-HRC-12-48.pdf. The reference to the proportionality rule is in para. 362, on p. 92.

[180] See United Nations General Assembly 2017, submitted to the HRC, p. 32: 'the use of cluster munitions in civilian populated, urban areas violates customary IHL principles of distinction and proportionality, due to the wide dispersal pattern and high dud rate noted above'.

[181] See, for example Defendant Ante Gotovina's Submission of Expert Report of Professor Geoffrey Corn pursuant to Rule 94 bis, *ICTY Prosecutor* v. *Gotovina et al.*, IT-06-90-T, 30 June 2009, Appendix A, p. 12; Dinstein 2016, p. 153; Fenrick, 2001, p. 498; Gardam 2004, p. 136; Parks 1990, p. 168; Schmitt 2006a, p. 292; Shamash, p. 109; Watkin 2007, p. 5.

[182] See, for example, Human Rights Watch 2008, p. 4.

[183] See, for example, Amnesty International's Report on the war between Israel and Hezbollah, AI Index MDE 18 July 2006, published in August 2006, p. 5. Amnesty acknowledges the principle, but notes there is a difference of opinion in their interpretation and the interpretation of the Israeli Government.

incorrectly when reviewing the behaviour of parties to an armed conflict in their reports.[184]

4.3.5 *Customary Law in both IAC and NIAC?*

As for the question of whether the IHL rule on proportionality would also be applicable in NIACs, the ICRC Customary Law Study is very clear. It concludes that the principle is indeed part of customary international law in NIACs.[185] Logically, it would be absurd if, in a civil war, the nation's own civilians did not benefit to the same extent from the protection of the IHL rule on proportionality as 'enemy' civilians would in an international armed conflict.[186] However, this logical conclusion is problematic because of 'the primary assumption in international relations, and indeed international law, ... that the relationship between a state and its own citizens is a matter exclusively for the domestic legal order'.[187] On the other hand, since IHL generally applies between the parties to the conflict, this assumption is unpersuasive to discharge applicability of the IHL proportionality rule during NIACs.

The IHL proportionality rule is not included in common article 3 of the Geneva Conventions, nor is it codified in Additional Protocol II.[188] However, in their commentary on the 1977 Additional Protocols, Bothe, Partsch and Solf state that the IHL rule on proportionality was deleted from the draft text of APII by Committee III (of the Steering Committee for Human Rights) before the simplification process that stripped APII of most provisions on the conduct of hostilities. However, in their opinion, '[n]evertheless, ... the principle of proportionality is inherent in the principle of humanity which was explicitly made applicable to Protocol II under the fourth clause of the Preamble.

184 See, for example, the discussion between Michael Schmitt and Human Rights Watch with regard to the report on the 2003 invasion of Iraq, published in the *Yearbook of International Humanitarian Law*, vol. 6. See Schmitt 2006b and PoKempner et al.

185 See generally for the typology of armed conflicts: Vité.

186 As the ICTY noted in the famous *Tadić Case*: 'What is inhumane, and consequently proscribed, in international wars, cannot be inhumane and inadmissible in civil strife.' See ICTY, *Prosecutor* v. *Tadić*, IT-94-1-1, Appeals Chamber Decision, 2 October 1995, para. 119.

187 Wells-Greco, p. 409.

188 There was an article (draft article 26 (3) (b)) containing the principle of proportionality in the draft Protocol II that the ICRC prepared for the diplomatic conference that adopted the Additional Protocols in 1977. The provision was however deleted, together with most other draft articles on the conduct of hostilities. See Official Records of the Diplomatic Conference on the Reaffirmation and Development of International Humanitarian Law Applicable in Armed Conflicts, Volume XV, p. 321.

Thus, the IHL proportionality rule cannot be ignored in applying Protocol II.'[189] The San Remo Manual on International Humanitarian Law Applicable to Non-International Armed Conflict confirms that 'the relative absence of express mention of proportionality in instruments governing NIACs should not be construed as meaning that it is inapplicable in such conflict'.[190] Furthermore, the IHL proportionality rule is included in a number of other treaty rules applicable in NIACs, more particularly in the Amended Protocol II to the Conventional Weapons Convention of 1996 and the Second Hague Protocol for the Protection of Cultural Property in the Event of an Armed Conflict 1999.

State practice of the United States points in the same direction, as evidenced in declaring the principle applicable in all types of conflicts in 'long-standing policy, through directives, instructions, and operational rules of engagement.... Proportionality from the U.S. perspective, among other States, is customary international law regardless of designation of the armed conflict as international'.[191] This conclusion is also supported by a number of authors.[192] For example, Corn states, with regard to the IHL rule on proportionality, that, '[i]t is universally accepted as a customary norm of the *jus in bello*, applicable to all armed conflicts.'[193]

4.3.6 *Sub-conclusion: The Customary Character of the IHL Rule on Proportionality*

Even though the type of practice that was found is not always of the most telling character, it is my conclusion that there can be no doubt about the existence and applicability of the IHL rule on proportionality as a rule of customary international law. It is a rule that is well established in treaty law, State practice, international case law, legal doctrine and other indicators. The quantity and character of the presented practice on Rule 14 of the ICRC Customary Law Study is certainly widespread, and given the additional indications of the existence of the principle, the applicability of the rule in customary IHL in any type of armed conflict today is established with certainty.

[189] Bothe et al., pp. 677–678.
[190] San Remo Manual on the Law of Non-International Armed Conflict, pp. 22–25.
[191] Maxwell and Meyer, p. 10.
[192] See, for example, Byron, p. 208, Turns, p. 145 and Meron 1996, pp. 243–244.
[193] Defendant Ante Gotovina's Submission of Expert Report of Professor Geoffrey Corn pursuant to Rule 94 bis, ICTY *Prosecutor* v. *Gotovina et al.*, IT-06-90-T, 30 June 2009, Appendix A, p. 12. See also Wells-Greco, p. 409.

4.4 CONCLUSION

This chapter demonstrated that the IHL rule on proportionality has known a gradual development, but is currently considered to constitute a rule of customary IHL that applies similarly in international armed conflicts as it does in NIACs. It is remarkable how a rule that was virtually non-existent in 1945 has acquired such a widespread acceptance in IHL today. That being said, the exact content of the IHL rule on proportionality is still not entirely clear. There continues to be much debate about the exact meaning of the different components of the IHL rule on proportionality, and also how these components need to be balanced.[194] An inquiry into actual targeting behaviour in a significant large number of incidents in different armed conflicts by different types of armed forces[195] would possibly increase the understanding of the exact content of the rule. One thing that is clear, however, is that its context matters.

194 Bothe concludes that there remains controversy not about the rule, but about 'the yardstick of proportionality', see Bothe 2007a, p. 167.

195 Fellmeth 2010, p. 5 and see Fellmeth and Sylvester for an analysis of the application of the IHL proportionality rule during the internal armed conflict in Colombia.

5

Proportionality in Context

[T]he law of proportionality, deciding what attacks are permissible, is far too vague to be useful, and leads to experts on different sides talking past each other.[1]

5.1 INTRODUCTION

The focus in this chapter is on providing more insight into the practical and legal context in which the proportionality rule must be applied. For that reason, firstly, the place of the proportionality analysis is explored in the process that is at the heart of IHL: attacking the enemy. Therefore, a short descriptive analysis of the targeting process is provided in this chapter, to provide an introduction of the practical context in which the IHL proportionality rule must be applied. Subsequently, the notion of indiscriminate attacks is briefly explored because the prohibition of disproportionate attacks under IHL is categorised as a subset of that category of attack. In addition, this chapter explores how the IHL proportionality rule, as a precautionary measure in itself, fits in the system of obligations under IHL with regard to precautionary measures protecting civilians during attacks and military operations.

5.2 TARGETING AND PROPORTIONALITY

The IHL proportionality rule applies when an attack is planned and when that attack is subsequently executed during an armed conflict.[2] The activity of planning the use of armed force, even when used in defence, together with

1 Daniel Reisner, former head of the Israel Defense Force's International Law Department, see Yonah (2016).

2 The term 'attack' is defined under international humanitarian law as an act of 'violence against the adversary, whether in offence or in defence'. See article 49 (1) API.

the actual launch of an attack, may be labelled as 'targeting'. Targeting is 'the sine qua non of warfare'.[3] In order to grasp the practical circumstances under which the IHL proportionality rule must be applied, it is relevant to analyse the concept of targeting.

Boothby aptly defines targeting as

> [a] broad process encompassing planning and execution, including the consideration of prospective targets of attack, the accumulation of information to determine whether the attack of a particular object, person, or group of persons will meet military, legal and other requirements, the determination of which weapon and method should be used to prosecute the target, the carrying out of attacks, including those decided upon at short notice and with minimal opportunity for planning, and other associated activities.[4]

Defined as such, targeting covers a wide range of issues, criteria and considerations that play a role in the application of the IHL proportionality rule.

Although 'important discrepancies' do exist between the rules applicable to targeting in international armed conflicts as opposed to targeting in non-international armed conflicts (NIACs),[5] for the purpose of the application of the IHL proportionality rule, this division has mostly become irrelevant. As already established, the IHL proportionality rule applies equally in any type of armed conflict.

Targeting rules applicable during land warfare also apply to attacking targets on land from the air or from the sea.[6] Although the 'fundamental principles of the laws of armed conflict apply equally in naval warfare',[7] additional and specific rules apply to targeting in naval warfare (thus between or among ships at sea and planes in the skies above the sea) as well as in particular types of operation such as peace operations. For the purpose of this chapter, it is important to note that the rules on the protection of the civilian population apply as soon as naval, space or cyberspace warfare affects the civilian population on land.[8]

Targeting comes in a variety of forms. It may be conducted through a carefully pre-planned procedure involving specialised personnel, or ad hoc,

3 Schmitt 2012.
4 Boothby, p. 4.
5 Boothby, p. 5.
6 Article 49 (3) API: 'The provisions of this Section apply to any land, air or sea warfare which may affect the civilian population, individual civilians or civilian objects on land. They further apply to all attacks from the sea or from the air against objectives on land but do not otherwise affect the rules of international law applicable in armed conflict at sea or in the air.'
7 Heintschel von Heinegg 2013, p. 478.
8 For naval warfare, see generally Heintschel von Heinegg 2013, pp. 463–547, in particular p. 479 and Boothby, p. 309. See also Schmitt 2016, p. 269: '[T]he general rules governing targeting

as a small unit or even an individual soldier under attack needs to decide how to respond to a given situation. For the purpose of this chapter, it is assumed that there is a military commander present who is responsible for the decision to launch an attack. This is normally the person who needs to conduct the proportionality assessment before and during the use of mostly kinetic means of striking an opponent.[9] The law has trusted the military commander with the responsibility to conduct the proportionality analysis and make decisions with regard to the excessiveness of civilian casualties and damage to civilian objects. This military commander is present on different levels, ranging from a high-ranking military commander at a headquarters far away from the location where the attack will impact, to an on-scene commander whose personal safety may be on the line. In fact, most of the actual fighting in warfare takes place at the tactical, small unit level and even 'an infantry private deciding to engage an enemy belligerent is implementing [IHL] principles in a real-time targeting process'.[10] These privates have no military lawyers following them to provide them with legal advice. However, IHL requires all types of military commander to assess whether the launch of an attack is lawful. The proportionality analysis is part of this assessment, or targeting process.

While conducting the thinking exercise of the targeting process, the military commander is dependent on many factors. For example, the means and methods available to the military commander may differ to a large extent. A commander of an artillery battery will normally have only one or very few types of artillery shell at his disposal. An aircraft pilot is dependent on the bombs attached to the plane and those cannot be changed while in the air. Therefore, although the commanders may be able to adjust the fuses that detonate the bombs and grenades, the options to adjust the choice of a weapon system in order to limit collateral damage are restricted in these two situations.[11] The same goes for smaller units, using only their rifles, (rocket-propelled) grenades or, at most, smaller types of mortar. These latter commanders may, however, be able to call in airstrikes or close air support. Higher level commanders, on the other hand, may be able to choose between different units (an artillery unit, an armed drone, an attack helicopter, or an

apply equally in land, air, sea, space and cyberspace. Specialized rules may apply in particular types of operations, such as peace operations or naval warfare.'

9 This chapter understands targeting as a kinetic activity involving the use of armed force. For non-kinetic targeting, see Ducheine, pp. 201–230.

10 Corn and Corn, p. 344.

11 Although sometimes the fuse of a certain bomb may be adjusted. Generally, the fuses of grenades and air-delivered munitions may be set to explode on impact, delayed or in the air. See McNeal, p. 22.

armoured infantry unit) to conduct the attack on a certain military objective. To these types of commander therefore, more options may be available when conducting a targeting process.

In addition to the availability of weapons systems, the capability to collect, interpret and compare information is also crucial to conducting a targeting process. Access to information may be very much dependent on the level of sophistication of the military forces of a party to an armed conflict. For example, the joint headquarters of a coalition of Western States may be able to conduct airstrikes through a sophisticated planning process using software systems that provide input into the decision-making process on the expected damage to civilian structures and using real-time footage from unmanned drones.[12] The situation is usually different for non-State armed groups (NSAGs) planning to attack a town or dwelling, or to defend a certain part of a larger city. These soldiers may only be able to rely on the information that is visible to the naked eye, or perhaps some historical information as to where military objectives and concentrations of civilians may be found. Circumstances influencing the targeting process include time pressure and there may be ongoing hostilities that result in a lack of information and a high level of stress. Many different factors matter for the manner in which the targeting process of a specific operation's is carried out: 'the goal itself, the time allotted for planning, the means or capabilities, and the tools available to assess'.[13] Nonetheless, a number of common features are found in any type of targeting process, whether by an NSAG or by regular armed forces of a State and these features are common for all levels on which military commanders are making decisions.[14] An example of a targeting process, to take as the basis for further analysis of the role of the proportionality rule, is the six-step targeting process proposed by Henderson. It is comprised of the following steps:

Planning phase:

1. Locate and observe the potential target and its surrounding area;
2. Assess whether the target is a valid military objective and that it is otherwise unprotected from attack by IHL;

[12] See, for example, the Joint Targeting Toolbox (JTT), which is a system that was developed by the United States: it consists of a 'suite of web-based interoperable targeting tools designed around the Joint Targeting Cycle which are used to support operations and intelligence targeting requirements at the national, theater, operational and tactical levels', see Information Directorate, Wright-Patterson Air Force Base. See also software systems such as Rainstorm, see Northrop Grumman. See also Section 5.2.3.

[13] Pratzner, p. 80.

[14] Ibid.

3. Take all feasible precautions to minimise collateral damage;
4. Assess whether any expected collateral damage is proportional … to the anticipated military advantage to be gained from the attack;

Execution phase:

5. Take such care as is appropriate in the tactical situation to release or fire the weapon to achieve the best possible chance of hitting the selected aim point;
6. Cancel or suspend the attack should it become apparent that any one of the assessments made under steps 2 or 4 is no longer valid.[15]

An additional step may be to assess the result of the attack, which may in turn lead to a next phase in an ongoing operation.

5.2.1 *Specifics of Targeting by Less Sophisticated Armed Forces*

Targeting is as such not different during NIACs compared to international armed conflicts: the objective to affect the military capability of the enemy through attacks is identical. As mentioned previously, the rules applicable to the two types of armed conflict are mostly identical for the purpose of the IHL proportionality rule.[16] The character of the parties to the conflict, however, varies during the different types of armed conflict. By its nature, one of the parties to an NIAC is an NSAG. A major difference that exists between these different parties to the conflict in the context of targeting is often the level of sophistication of those parties, in the sense of the weapons and other capabilities the fighters of these groups possess. This is particularly relevant for the purpose of an analysis of the application of the IHL proportionality rule.

Many different situations may occur during which on-scene commanders or individual soldiers need to decide whether the course of action they want to pursue, or that they are ordered to execute, is proportionate. It may be that the forces that are about to launch an attack, and that are thus obliged to conduct a proportionality analysis, are part of an NSAG that is technologically inferior to its opponent. This could mean that the NSAG has only a very limited capability to focus on preventing civilian casualties, compared to the more sophisticated party to the conflict they face. This may be the case as a result of

[15] Henderson, p. 237 (footnotes omitted).

[16] See, for example, the customary rules as cited by the ICRC Customary Law Study with regard to targeting, such as Rules 5–22. See Henckaerts and Doswald-Beck 2005a, pp. 17–71.

the aerial dominance of the opposing party, including the presence of reconnaissance drones, or the types of weapon the NSAG has at its disposal, usually predominantly light and improvised weapons.[17] The targeting process is therefore not in all situations as sophisticated and well structured as this book may at times suggest. There are, however, no special IHL targeting rules for less sophisticated armed forces. It has to be noted that it is not only NSAGs that use less advanced weaponry during NIACs. For example, the use of 'barrel-bombs' by the armed forces of some States indicates that not all States use strictly precision-guided munitions (PGM) during their operations.[18] If the target of those types of bomb is a large military objective, the use of barrel bombs is not prohibited per se; however, the use of these types of bomb in populated areas may violate the IHL proportionality rule.

Yet, it may be imagined quite easily that NSAGs encounter situations in which collateral civilian damage is possible, and thus the proportionality rule must be applied. For example, if a squad of NSAG fighters is approaching a certain military objective of the opponent, such as a defending firing position of State forces, that they may want to attack through a Rocket Propelled Grenade, it is very possible that civilian objects are located in the near vicinity of the enemy position. Also, it could be that a civilian shelter is located at such a position for the simple reason that civilians feel better protected against the violence of an NSAG if they hide from the hostilities near a defending position. Therefore, in this scenario, the NSAG has to take the possible collateral damage into account when they launch their attack (assuming it is feasible that they are aware of the presence of civilians). Furthermore, an NSAG may have acquired powerful weaponry that they wish to use against their opponent even though the NSAG has no capabilities to reasonably be aware of the whereabouts of the civilian population. In that case, the commander of the NSAG forces needs to reconsider the initial plan of attack once the presence of the civilian population on the scene becomes apparent.

17 The use of lighter types of weapons are also less likely to result in collateral damage than more sophisticated, often heavier weapons systems such as artillery and airstrikes.

18 See, for example, for the use of barrel bombs in the context of the armed conflict in Syria: Roth. Barrel bombs are described by Human Rights Watch as improvised weapons consisting of 'oil drums or similar canisters filled with explosives and metal fragments. They are dropped without guidance from helicopters hovering just above antiaircraft range, typically hitting the ground with huge explosions and the widespread diffusion of deadly shrapnel.' Other governments would drop bombs from the air in primitive ways: '[w]eapons experts told the organizations that the munitions used are unguided and are often rolled out manually from Antonov cargo planes or launched from other aircraft in a manner that does not allow for accurate delivery.' See Human Rights Watch.

Less sophisticated forces may thus not be capable of determining the presence of civilians and civilian objects at the location of attack. This may be caused by the lack of assets such as surveillance drones and satellite images, although this is true for the majority of armed forces in the world. In addition, the lack of advanced communications systems may pose an additional challenge to the commander of an NSAG unit to acquire information about the presence of civilians. This does not mean that the commander is relieved of the obligation to verify that the target is a military objective. Furthermore, commanders must do everything feasible to assess whether the planned attack will comply with the IHL proportionality rule. Although the threshold of the necessary effort is equal to a commander with less sophisticated means at his disposal compared to a commander that does have these capabilities available, the actual options may be very limited. The result of this is that the level of uncertainty of the presence of civilians on the scene may have to be accepted as higher than the level of certainty required from commanders with more feasible options to ascertain the absence of civilians.

5.2.2 *Specifics of Targeting by Sophisticated Armed Forces*

The targeting process is well defined by Western States and alliances of States such as NATO.[19] The United States has defined the targeting process as '[t]he process of selecting and prioritizing targets and matching the appropriate response to them, considering operational requirements and capabilities.'[20] Another definition describes targeting as

> [t]he deliberate application of capabilities against targets to generate effects in order to achieve specific objectives. It is about the application of means (weapons) of warfare to affect addressees (people or objects) using a variety of methods (tactics) that create effects contributing to designated goals. Targeting, accordingly, represents the bridge between the ends and means of warfare.[21]

For sophisticated armed forces, there are two different types of targeting process.[22] Firstly, deliberate targeting focusses on known future targets, which

[19] See, for example, the US Joint Chiefs of Staff, Joint Publication 1-02 2010. NATO's targeting doctrine is the 2008 Allied Joint Publication AJP 3.9. This publication is, however, not generally available. Therefore, references in this research to AJP 3.9 are of a general descriptive nature.

[20] US Joint Chiefs of Staff, Joint Publication 1-02 2010, p. 236.

[21] Ducheine et al., p. 2.

[22] Pratzner, p. 81, see also Jachec-Neale, pp. 200–204.

may be attacked either on call or on a moment previously scheduled.[23] The defining factor of deliberate targeting is thus that there is usually sufficient time to assess whether a certain target is a military objective and what the possible military value of the target is, as well as to gain information about possible collateral damage when it would be attacked. Secondly, dynamic targeting involves the process that needs to be followed before targets may be attacked which have been identified too late to be included in a deliberate targeting process.[24] The targets that are processed through the dynamic targeting process may be previously identified military objectives (e.g., a missile launch installation) or persons, the location of which was previously unknown, but that becomes known to the attacker at a given moment. Dynamic targets may also be previously unknown military objectives that suddenly present themselves. A particular type of dynamic targeting is targeting against time-sensitive targets. Whether these targets can be attacked needs to be addressed as soon as possible in case they endanger friendly operations, or because the military advantage of attacking them is particularly high and the window of opportunity in which the targets can be attacked is limited.[25] For these types of target, NATO has developed a quicker targeting process.

On a tactical level, ground targets can be attacked through two distinct types of air operation, namely air interdiction operations and close air support. The latter consists of airborne assets attacking military objectives in support of ground troops, and can be done by fixed-wing or helicopter assets. Normally, close air support operations are planned and executed through the dynamic targeting process, since the exact support that is needed in a ground operation usually only presents itself when the ground forces are already underway. Nonetheless, it is imaginable that a ground operation has been planned in advance including the deliverance of close air support of air assets, in which case the situation allows for following the process for deliberate targeting.

In a sophisticated targeting process, it is not only the use of explosives or other kinetic means that are considered to achieve a certain objective. Indeed, the targeting process also aims to coordinate the efforts and apply non-military assets such as information operations to achieve a similar result. As such, the

23 Scheduled deliberate targeting may be described as attacking targets that must be attacked at a specific moment in time, whereas in the case of on-call targeting, the actions are not necessarily to be addressed at a specific moment. See NATO 2008, pp. 1–2.

24 NATO 2008, pp. 1–2: the dividing line is the question whether the attack is to take place within a three-day period, or later.

25 NATO 2008, pp. 1–3.

targeting process 'enables targeteers to plan and execute operations and activities comprehensively, efficiently, and effectively. At the same time, it enables commanders to use force (or assets and resources) more economically by providing additional options to them with which to accomplish their mission.'[26]

A wide variety of assets and sensors enable sophisticated forces to conduct an extensive analysis of the situation surrounding a military objective.[27] The identification of possible military objectives that may be targeted during an armed conflict may have taken place already in peacetime. As a result, a target 'folder' or 'package' may be available upon the outbreak of actual hostilities.[28] Sophisticated armed forces may thus have a pre-approved list of military objectives that may be attacked to pursue the objectives of the leadership on the political and strategic level.[29] Once an armed conflict is ongoing, the analysis of the 'pattern of life' at the location of the military objective provides the opportunity to determine exactly which type of weapon may be used to reach an optimal effect, while minimising the risk to civilians, and the optimal time window in which the objective may be best attacked to avoid or at least minimise collateral damage, as well as maximising the military advantage of the attack. Targeteers will also have a software system available that enables them to predict how the use of a certain weapon system or type of bomb will affect the target as well as its immediate surroundings.[30] These software systems are capable of producing collateral damage estimates, which offer contemporary military commanders unprecedented possibilities to match the optimal type of weapon with a view to minimising collateral damage. Especially if there is sufficient time to conduct extensive surveillance, or even a reconnaissance mission on the ground, the deliberate planning process, augmented with good quality intelligence, may present an optimal profile of the target and enable the planners to take all other feasible precautionary measures to limit collateral civilian damage. At the same time, the deliberate planning process provides targeteers with the opportunity to verify thoroughly whether a certain object is a military objective, as well as whether it may be expected to be sufficiently militarily advantageous at that moment to destroy the object. The quality of this process is not only dependent on the factors that were already mentioned: time and available information and intelligence, but

26 Ducheine et al., p. 3.
27 Pratzner, p. 82.
28 Henderson, p. 239.
29 See, for example, the list drawn up by Reynolds, p. 100.
30 Targeteers are persons with a special qualification to predict the effect of certain types of weapon or to analyse the way targets may most effectively be attacked.

in addition, 'competency in the targeting tradecraft; and . . . the mental agility to change the plan as the environment evolves'[31] is required to maximise the effects of the deliberate planning process.

For time-sensitive targeting, the situation is slightly different, because the time factor does not usually allow for such an extensive effort as there is in deliberate planning. The importance of this factor cannot be overstated: '[a]lthough information and communications technology (ICT) has enabled many lower end functions to be automated, there are necessary steps – command direction and course checks, legal reviews, proper vetting of individual targets, etc. – that demand time to properly complete.'[32] Sophisticated armed forces or alliances will normally already have a list available of possible military objectives that may be targeted through time-sensitive targeting. These lists of time-sensitive military objectives enable targeteers to address certain sub-questions in advance. This may shorten the decision process to assess whether the target can be attacked as soon as a time-sensitive target has actually 'popped up'. Even though the time-sensitive targeting process aims to take much less time than the deliberate planning process, it is subject to the same legal obligations. To name just two examples, the positive identification of the target as a military objective as well as the obligation to take feasible precautionary measures remain applicable. The information that is needed to take decisions with regard to the identification of a target as a military objective, or the presence of civilians and civilian objects in the vicinity of the target, may be supplied other than by the attacking force.[33] This may sometimes present a problem as far as time-sensitive targeting is concerned, because there may be no time to verify this information. As far as taking precautionary measures is concerned, Henderson provides a useful example of how this may play out in practice when conducted under time pressure:

> [a]n infantry soldier who is under fire from enemy combatants cannot be expected to take the same steps to improve the accuracy of his or her shot as would be expected of a sniper in a camouflaged position whose presence is unknown to the enemy.[34]

However, when time is available to conduct a deliberate targeting process, it may be possible to apply collateral damage estimate methodology.

[31] Pratzner, p. 82.
[32] Ibid.
[33] Henderson, p. 235.
[34] Henderson, p. 236.

5.2.3 *Targeting and Collateral Damage Estimate Methodology*

Any targeting process involves a number of steps, both in the planning and execution stage of an attack. The IHL proportionality rule applies during both the planning and the execution phase of an attack. Some armed forces or coalitions of armed forces possess procedures and assets that assist in making well-informed proportionality assessments prior to launching attacks. These attacks are primarily conducted by air-to-surface weapons and artillery. Collateral damage estimate (CDE) methodology, used by the United States[35] as well as NATO, allows planners, targeteers and commanders to make rather precise predictions on the impact area of certain types of bomb.[36] This methodology thus enables an assessment of the number of civilians that may be expected to be affected by the planned attack. This concerns the casualties expected to be caused by the damage done by a bomb, consisting of the result of the pressure wave, fragmentation, blast and the crater that will be caused. In other words: '[t]he commander and his subordinates place a point on a map representing the target, draw an effects radius around that target, and assess what known collateral concerns exist within that radius.'[37]

The CDE methodology assists foremost in determining the impact of the weapons to be used, particularly whether damage to civilian objects and civilian casualties may be expected. It therefore also requires a determination of whether the military objective has an additional civilian function, and how close civilian objects are to the intended point of impact of a certain type of weapon. It is therefore the primary function of the computer program integrated in the CDE methodology to assist in assessing the expected collateral

[35] Osinga and Roorda, p. 62:

> [t]he United States introduced a computer program, nicknamed 'BugSplat', to calculate the risk that bomb blast and fragments might affect civilian objects near a pre-planned target. Each potential target could be examined for proximity to civilians or civilian property. Officially named the Fast Assessment Strike Tool – Collateral Damage (FAST-CD), it generated blob-like images resembling squashed insects that precisely modelled the potential damage produced by a particular type and size of bomb, dropped by a particular aircraft flying at a particular altitude. FAST-CD took account of the characteristics of terrain and the objects being struck in order to forecast an often irregular pattern of damage. If the predicted risk of collateral damage was deemed too high, targeting specialists could attempt substituting either a smaller weapon or one with a delayed fuse – which lets a bomb penetrate first and then detonate – or try changing the type of aircraft or its angle of attack.

[36] Werres, pp. 47–50.

[37] McNeal, p. 14.

damage of a planned attack.[38] Despite the name of the CDE methodology, however, the use of this computerised model also makes it possible to predict the extent to which the military objective will be destroyed, killed or disabled. This may assist in assessing the expected military advantage of a certain attack, although the actually expected military advantage may also be dependent on other factors. The computer model is not the only tool that commanders must use when assessing the military advantage; they also need to use their experience, expert advice and common sense and assess other factors such as, in the case of a coordinated attack, the progress reached in other strikes.

According to the CDE planning tool, there are levels one to five of expected collateral damage.[39] These five levels determine who must take the ultimate decision on the execution of the attack. When the CDE methodology calculates that collateral damage may be expected from a planned attack, the CDE methodology can subsequently assist in the commander's duty to do everything feasible to avoid, or at least minimise, collateral civilian damage.[40] The methodology furthermore takes into account the possible risks of causing environmental damage, as well as whether risk exists for causing chemical, biological or radiological harm. Also, when it is clear in the planning stage that an object is a dual-use object, it is always placed in the highest category.[41] When civilian casualties cannot be excluded according to the CDE methodology, the authority to approve the attack moves up the chain of command, at least to the level of a general.[42] The five levels dictate in which cases a further analysis may need to be executed into the effects of using alternative weapons systems to attack the target under scrutiny. That means

38 One tool that is used by US CDE methodology is the Population Density Reference Table. This table 'lists data from the intelligence community and other sources and methods and allows for estimates of the population density per 1,000 square feet per day, night, and special events for any given collateral structure based on its functionality'. See McNeal, pp. 26–27.

39 See, for example, Wright, p. 832.

40 As required by the obligations concerning precautionary measures, see article 57 (2) (a) (ii) API.

41 Werres, p. 49.

42 In the US practice for pre-planned strikes conducted in the context of operation ISAF in Afghanistan, '[t]he President of the United Sates or the Secretary of Defense must approve any pre-planned ISAF strike where 1 civilian casualty or greater is expected.' See McNeal, p. 2. When this is the case, it depends to a large extent on the so-called 'Non-Combatant Casualty Cut-Off Value' (NCV) that has been proclaimed at the outset of the operation. Where the NCV is one, for example, the decision to launch the attack moves up the chain of command as soon as one single civilian casualty is expected from a planned attack. It may, however, also be the case that the NCV is determined to be ten, in which case lower commanders may decide to launch the attack without seeking approval from higher authorities as long as they expect nine or fewer civilian casualties to occur. See McNeal, p. 26. As an example, McNeal notes that during the major combat operation Iraqi Freedom in 2003, the NCV was thirty non-combatant casualties. See McNeal, p. 27.

that in the first CDE level, it is determined whether any collateral damage is expected. If this is not the case, the CDE process is finished, and the attack may proceed. If some collateral damage is expected, the process moves to the second level, where it is assessed whether weaponeering options can mitigate the expected collateral damage. This process repeats itself, while during each CDE level an analysis is conducted whether a particular attack may be launched, or based on failing the parameters for that level, the planned target must be assessed at a higher level in the CDE process before it may be launched.

The software system that is used to make the CDE assessments is 'grounded in scientific evidence derived from research, experiments, history, and battlefield intelligence, and ... designed to adapt to time-critical events'.[43] Furthermore, it is constantly updated with the effects of existing bombs in different conditions, or by new types of weapon. This implies that the accuracy of the predictions of the software is improving constantly, especially when the methodology is used over a longer period within the context of a particular operation, since more accurate information becomes available concerning the effects of the different types of weapon on the ground and on the buildings specific to that particular area.[44] Eventually, according to McNeal, the US practice of collateral damage estimation and mitigation 'is intended to ensure that there will be a less than 10 percent probability of serious or lethal wounds to non-combatants'.[45]

In order to maximise the probability of the calculated and deemed acceptable effects to ultimately occur, the 'worst-case' scenario of a certain attack is often taken as the basis of the calculations. That means that normally the actual collateral effects of an attack are less severe than expected based on the calculation of the CDE methodology.[46] Of course, there may also be factors that impact the proportionality assessment and that cannot be calculated through computer programs. An example is what happens when a target is hit that functions as weapons storage. If precise information is lacking on the quantity of explosive material present at the location, it seems hardly possible to predict the impact of even a small explosive on the target, because of the secondary detonation of the stored explosives that will follow. In addition, in the case of a military objective located next to a busy street, the presence of civilians on that street is also difficult to predict through a computer program.

43 McNeal, p. 5.
44 McNeal, p. 15.
45 McNeal, p. 1.
46 McNeal, p. 20.

Of course, the program may be able to calculate based on general assumptions that there are less people on the streets at night than there would be during the day. But the actual circumstances at the time of the attack may be very different than the situation the computer is programmed to assume. It is therefore important for planners, targeteers and commanders to bear in mind that CDEs must always be interpreted through sound human judgement, in order to prevent inherent flaws of computerised systems from nullifying the obligations posed by the proportionality rule.

It may be concluded from the discussion in this section that the IHL proportionality rule must be integrated in any decision-making process in the context of the planning and execution of armed forces. The legal obligation applies equally to a private firing his weapon as to an attack that is planned in a high joint military headquarters, through an institutionalised procedure conducted by highly trained and skilled targeteers and military commanders. It starts by identifying a military objective and considering whether any incidental collateral damage may be expected. If that is the case, precautionary measures must be taken and subsequently a proportionality assessment needs to be conducted.

5.3 INDISCRIMINATE ATTACKS AND PROPORTIONALITY

Having explored the targeting process of which the proportionality assessment is a part in practical terms, the next step is to assess the place of the IHL proportionality rule in legal terms. According to the definition of a disproportionate attack, it is a subset of the wider category of indiscriminate attacks. Therefore, it is to this category that the analysis now turns.

The principle of distinction is the crucial requirement in IHL protecting civilians and civilian objects. Without distinction, the IHL proportionality rule is pointless. Through the identification of the civilian population and those individuals who participate in the armed conflict, it is possible to set them apart and direct attacks only to the latter category. The IHL rule on proportionality acknowledges that civilians will be affected by armed conflict, but it has to be borne in mind that they may not be directly targeted. The fact that they may be affected is contingent to the obligation that the attacks can only be aimed at military objectives. Or, in other words, the IHL rule on proportionality supplements the principle of distinction in the protection of civilians.[47] The IHL rule on proportionality has logically only been recognised

[47] Reynolds, p. 24.

since the principle of distinction was firmly established. The relevant provisions of the 1907 Hague Convention prohibit the attack of undefended places and encourage commanders of the attacking force to warn the authorities in order to protect civilians.[48] In spite of the existence of the distinction rule, during World War I, numerous land, air and naval bombardments were executed on undefended towns, where sometimes only civilians and civilian objects were hit.[49] The existence of the distinction principle was nonetheless accepted. As Garner wrote in 1920: 'there is a substantial unanimity of opinion that belligerents should, so far as possible, confine their attacks to the fortifications, military works, depots, etc., and do all in their power to spare private houses, hospitals, educational and religious institutions, and the like'.[50] Nonetheless, the civilian population was again heavily affected in World War II. The principle of distinction was reaffirmed in clear terms in the 1977 Additional Protocols, prohibiting the direct attack of civilians.[51]

The starting point for a discussion on the notion of indiscriminate attacks is its definition in treaty law. Article 51 (4) API prohibits as indiscriminate attacks:

(a) Those which are not directed at a specific military objective;
(b) Those which employ a method or means of combat which cannot be directed at a specific military objective; or
(c) Those which employ a method or means of combat the effects of which cannot be limited as required by API.

And consequently, in each such case, are of a nature to strike military objectives and civilians or civilian objects without distinction.

Article 51 (5) API adds as examples of the attacks mentioned in section 4 of the same article:

(a) an attack by bombardment by any methods or means which treats as a single military objective a number of clearly separated and distinct military objectives located in a city, town, village or other area containing a similar concentration of civilians or civilian objects, and
(b) disproportionate attacks.

[48] See articles 25 and 26 of the 1907 Hague Convention IV Respecting the Laws and Customs of War on Land and its Annex: Regulations Respecting the Laws and Customs of War on Land. Reprinted in Schindler and Toman, pp. 55–87.

[49] See Garner, pp. 417–433, discussing among others the attacks by naval bombardment by the German Navy of the English coastal towns of Scarborough, Whitby and Hartlepool on 16 December 1914.

[50] Garner, pp. 424–425.

[51] Article 48 API.

In addition to the definition in API, customary IHL also contains a prohibition on indiscriminate attacks. The ICRC Customary Law Study states that indiscriminate attacks are prohibited under customary IHL in both international and non-international armed conflicts (Rule 11). Rule 12 repeats the definition of indiscriminate attacks found in article 51 (4) (a), (b) and (c) API, with the exception that the scope of subsection (c) (methods and means of combat the effects of which cannot be limited as required by API) is extended under customary IHL to include the entire corpus of IHL, not only API. This latter extension makes sense given the fact that API is not the only treaty that deals with weapons that may be regulated by this prohibition, as well as the fact that international customary law may also contain prohibitions on certain means and methods of warfare.

The temporal scope of the prohibition of indiscriminate attacks is obvious. It applies throughout the targeting process, so the assessment must be made in advance of planned attacks, as well as during the execution phase of the attack. As is the case for the evaluation of the expected collateral damage and military gain from an attack, the circumstances ruling at the time and the information that was reasonably available to the persons planning and executing the attack dictate whether they could foresee the planned attack to be indiscriminate. As a preventive framework, IHL dictates that commanders take due regard before launching an attack, but IHL certainly does not rule out the possibility that an attack that had devastating results for the civilian population was *bona fide* expected to be a discriminate attack when it was planned and ordered to be launched. Therefore, attacks that seem indiscriminate in hindsight may not always have appeared as such when they were planned. This fact makes it very difficult for anybody other than the people who planned and executed the attack to have sufficient information to make a well-founded claim that any attack was indeed indiscriminate. It is therefore very difficult to prove that the prohibition of indiscriminate attacks was violated. Criminal tribunals or fact-finding commissions can only look into what actually happened in hindsight, thus on the basis of the result of the attack.[52] Their main problem therefore is that a violation of this prohibition can only be proven if sufficient information is available about the way the attack was planned in advance and whether it was executed in accordance with a plan that would not violate the prohibition. The ICRC commentary states in relation to criminal law that 'the Protocol requires intent and, moreover, with regard to indiscriminate attacks, the element of prior knowledge of the predictable result'.[53]

52 See, for example, Ponti and Moneta for a discussion of criminal prosecutions of individuals for indiscriminate attacks in the context of the ICTY.

53 See Sandoz et al., para. 1934 on p. 617.

The purpose of the prohibition on indiscriminate attacks is summarised by the ICRC Commentary: 'it confirms the unlawful character of certain regrettable practices during the Second World War and subsequent armed conflicts. Far too often the purpose of attacks was to destroy all life in a particular area or to raze a town to the ground without this resulting, in most cases, in any substantial military advantages.'[54] The indiscriminate attacks prohibited in article 51 (4) (a) and (b) seem to be primarily attacks carried out by attackers who 'just don't care'. These attacks are planned and carried out by persons who seem not primarily interested in trying to hit the military forces of their opponent, but just anything they can hit regardless of its status or protection. This implies that these prohibited indiscriminate attacks violate the distinction obligation because no military advantage can be attained (unless it happens by accident) by attacks that are not directed at military objectives as prohibited in article 51 (4) (a) and (b). The attacks prohibited by article 51 (4) (c) and the examples mentioned in article 51 (5) (a) and (b), on the other hand, are directed at a military objective, but are indiscriminate nonetheless.

The prohibition of indiscriminate attacks thus covers (1) attacks failing to take into account whether the target may have a protected status under IHL; (2) attacks using means and methods that are indiscriminate; (3) attacks using means and methods whose effects cannot be contained (such as water, fire, poisoned wells); (4) attacks failing to treat singular military objectives as separate targets but instead attack an area that also contains civilians and civilian objects; and (5) disproportionate attacks.

Not covered by the prohibition are attacks that have indiscriminate effects, but were not planned or executed in advance with the reasonable expectation that they would have these effects that seem indiscriminate in hindsight. This is an inherent characteristic of the way IHL works to prevent destructive effects of warfare on the civilian population. The fact that an attack may sometimes seem to have been indiscriminate in hindsight, judged by the destruction of civilian objects and injury to civilians it caused, cannot be taken as the only basis to evaluate the (il)legality of an attack. International humanitarian law does not prohibit the launching of an attack that was not reasonably expected to have indiscriminate effects when it was planned. Rather, collateral damage could be the result of an honest mistake or weapons systems malfunction. In practice, it may be difficult to prove whether the attacker indeed had no reason to expect indiscriminate effects to result from the attack. It would,

[54] See Sandoz et al., para. 1946 on p. 619.

however, be impossible for military commanders to conduct attacks if they were held responsible for the effects of an attack on the civilian population when at the time they were planning that attack, they had no reason to believe these effects would occur.

It has been noted that the way the prohibition of indiscriminate attacks has been drafted is 'unsatisfactory' because it 'confuses the distinction and proportionality principles'.[55] This is because a disproportionate attack is explicitly mentioned as an example of an indiscriminate attack. Since the latter category of attack is referred to as attacks that 'consequently, in each such case, are of a nature to strike military objectives and civilians or civilian objects without distinction', this seems to intermingle distinction and proportionality. In the sequence of the planning and execution of an attack, it is indeed illogical to conclude that disproportionate attacks violate the distinction principle. It would have been clearer if the article had recognised that once the attacker has distinguished between military objectives and civilian objects and the civilian population, and the attack has been directed strictly to a military objective, the principle of distinction has been complied with. The issue of the proportionality of the attack would subsequently be assessed without giving rise to the possibility that the distinction rule may be violated.

It seems in a broader sense that the prohibition of indiscriminate attacks basically requires attackers to use the weapons they were entrusted with wisely, and to think before they act. The prohibition serves to remind any attacker that military necessity allows the use of means and methods in armed conflict, but that with the availability of weaponry, there is also a duty to only launch discriminate attacks. In general, military commanders can prevent their attacks from being indiscriminate by taking appropriate precautions in attack. Since the proportionality rule is also a precaution in itself, the following section discusses the place of the proportionality rule in the obligations in the legal context of precautions in attack.

5.4 PRECAUTIONS IN ATTACK AND PROPORTIONALITY

The IHL proportionality rule is included in IHL not only as a prohibition in the context of indiscriminate attacks, but also as an obligation commanders need to take into account in the planning and execution of attacks. The IHL rule on proportionality is by its nature an obligation that needs to be adhered to before an attack is actually executed, or whilst the attack is going on, in

[55] Rogers 2004, p. 26.

order to spare the civilian population. Therefore, the IHL rule on proportionality is a precaution in itself. The obligations with regard to precautions in attack are wider, however, than just the IHL proportionality rule.[56]

This section discusses the place of the IHL proportionality rule in the obligations with regard to precautionary measures. Section 5.4.1 introduces the issue, explaining the relation between the IHL proportionality rule and precautionary measures. In addition, the difference between active and passive precautionary measures is explained. Section 5.4.2 addresses the 'feasibility' standard that is included in a number of precautionary obligations. Section 5.4.3 discusses the personal scope of the obligation to take precautionary measures. Subsequently, the standard to collect information by the persons who have the obligation to take precautionary measures is analysed in Section 5.4.4. In addition, the obligation to take 'constant care' is discussed in Section 5.4.5 and specific precautionary obligations are listed in Section 5.4.6.

5.4.1 *Introduction*

When the rule of proportionality in IHL was codified in the 1977 Additional Protocol I, it was formulated in the context of the precautionary measures, and subsequently copied to the article containing the prohibition of indiscriminate attacks.[57] The proportionality rule is a precautionary measure in itself, in the sense that it is aimed at limiting collateral civilian damage during attacks. The precautions in attack are an important part of the targeting process described previously. The precautionary measures fit in different phases of the targeting process and they guide the sequence of steps of which the targeting process is comprised. As Corn observes: '[t]he precautions obligation will often involve more objective considerations than application of the proportionality obligation: precautions involve a series of concrete steps in a coherent targeting process that can be applied in a systematic manner.'[58] Therefore, the approach of precautionary measures is much more process-driven, resulting in an effective implementation of substantive rules of IHL.[59] The suggestion that proportionality only needs to be assessed in either the precautions phase or at the time an attack is actually launched must be rejected. Proportionality

[56] See generally: Corn 2014; Sassòli and Quintin; Quéguiner; Henderson, pp. 155–196. See also van den Boogaard 2018a and van den Boogaard and Vermeer, which are partly based on this and other chapters of the PhD thesis on which this book in turn is based.

[57] Rogers 2008, p. 191.

[58] Corn 2014, p. 424.

[59] Corn 2014, p. 465.

analysis must be done throughout the targeting process, from planning to the actual pushing of the button,[60] and even beyond, during the execution of the attack.

The rules with regard to precautions in attack are codified in article 57 of API. Article 57 API is placed in part IV of API, which has as its topic the 'Civilian population' and the stated objective of section I of this part of API is the 'General Protection against the Effect of Hostilities'. Thus, without losing sight of considerations of military necessity, the provisions of this part of API must be read with that objective in the back of our heads. In addition, the ICRC has identified the precautionary measures as rules of customary IHL applicable in both international and non-international armed conflicts.[61] The precautions in attack obligations may be generally divided into two parts: a general obligation to take 'constant care' to spare the civilian population in military operations during armed conflict (article 57 (1) API) and a list of specific obligations that operate to implement the general obligation during the specific situation of attacks (article 57 (2) and (3) API).[62] It must be noted in addition that precautionary obligations can also be derived from other rules,

60 Shamash, pp. 112–113.

61 Henckaerts and Doswald-Beck 2005a, Rules 15–21.

62 Article 57 (2) API reads:

> With respect to attacks, the following precautions shall be taken:
>
> (a) those who plan or decide upon an attack shall:
> (i) do everything feasible to verify that the objectives to be attacked are neither civilians nor civilian objects and are not subject to special protection but are military objectives within the meaning of paragraph 2 of Article 52 and that it is not prohibited by the provisions of this Protocol to attack them;
> (ii) take all feasible precautions in the choice of means and methods of attack with a view to avoiding, and in any event to minimizing, incidental loss of civilian life, injury to civilians and damage to civilian objects;
> (iii) refrain from deciding to launch any attack which may be expected to cause incidental loss of civilian life, injury to civilians, damage to civilian objects, or a combination thereof, which would be excessive in relation to the concrete and direct military advantage anticipated;
>
> (b) an attack shall be cancelled or suspended if it becomes apparent that the objective is not a military one or is subject to special protection or that the attack may be expected to cause incidental loss of civilian life, injury to civilians, damage to civilian objects, or a combination thereof, which would be excessive in relation to the concrete and direct military advantage anticipated;
>
> (c) effective advance warning shall be given of attacks which may affect the civilian population, unless circumstances do not permit.

Article 57 (3) API reads, '[w]hen a choice is possible between several military objectives for obtaining a similar military advantage, the objective to be selected shall be that the attack on which may be expected to cause the least danger to civilian lives and to civilian objects.'

such as the specific regulations that apply for attacking works and installations containing dangerous forces 'if such attack may cause the release of dangerous forces and consequent severe losses among the civilian population'.[63] Corn suggests that the obligations to take precautionary measures 'should be understood to include a broad range of measures'[64] that also includes measures such as training military lawyers in IHL and the targeting process.[65]

Armed conflict is a situation during which all parties take turns in launching attacks, conducting a defensive move and executing a counter-attack. For an analysis of the context of the IHL proportionality rule, the focus is on the precautionary measures *attackers* are obliged to take in the conduct of their military operations. That does not take away the fact that defending parties to the conflict have a similar obligation. That obligation, codified in article 58 API, refers to the precautions against the effects of attacks, or 'passive precautions'.[66] It states that the parties to an armed conflict shall, to the maximum extent feasible:

a. Without prejudice to the prohibition of deportation of civilians, endeavour to remove the civilian population, individual civilians and civilian objects under their control from military objectives;
b. Avoid locating military objectives within or near densely populated areas; and
c. Take the other necessary precautions to protect the civilian population, individual civilians and civilian objects under their control against the dangers resulting from military operations.

Article 58 API is complemented by the prohibition of human shields as codified in article 51 (7) API.[67] It has to be noted that although the obligations on precautionary measures against the effects in attack are worded quite

[63] See article 56 API and Henckaerts and Doswald-Beck 2005a, Rule 42.
[64] Corn 2014, p. 465.
[65] Ibid.
[66] See Jensen.
[67] Article 51(7) API reads:

> [t]he presence or movements of the civilian population or individual civilians shall not be used to render certain points or areas immune from military operations, in particular in attempts to shield military objectives from attacks or to shield, favour or impede military operations. The Parties to the conflict shall not direct the movement of the civilian population or individual civilians in order to attempt to shield military objectives from attacks or to shield military objectives from attacks or to shield military operations.

This is also a rule of customary IHL applicable both in international and non-international armed conflicts. See also Quéguiner, pp. 811–812 and Henckaerts and Doswald-Beck 2005a, Rule 22.

clearly, they are also restricted by a specific reference to military necessity and the specific circumstances of the situation. Obligations of the passive precautions of the defender are thus restricted to doing that which is 'to the maximum extent feasible'. Similar wordings appear in the obligations to take precautions in attack, as will be further elaborated later.

The precautions discussed subsequently refer to the precautions to the dangers to the civilians on land. This follows from article 49 (3) API. However, article 57 (4) states that '[i]n the conduct of military operations at sea or in the air, each Party to the conflict shall, in conformity with its rights and duties under the rules of international law applicable in armed conflict, take all reasonable precautions to avoid losses of civilian lives and damage to civilian objects.' This provision serves to underscore that for operations between aircraft, between warships or among aircraft and warships, where collateral civilian damage is normally absent, the effects on the civilian population and civilian objects must nonetheless be taken into account.[68]

5.4.2 *'Feasible' Precautions*

Some of the precautionary obligations of article 57 API are contingent on an element of feasibility. This concerns the specific precautionary measures of article 57 (2) (a) (i) and (ii). According to the treaty text, the other precautionary obligations are not limited by a feasibility requirement, and thus at least in theory, military commanders cannot evade their legal obligations by invoking the excuse that taking these measures was not feasible. The rules on precautions in attack in customary IHL as identified by the ICRC, however, seem to insert the element of feasibility equally in the latter group of obligations.[69]

How the word 'feasible' must be understood is dependent on the respective specific precautionary measure it applies to. In general, however, it may be said that the word feasible must be understood as a reality check: it simply means that the obligation applies to the extent possible under the relevant circumstances. There is no absolute obligation for military commanders to do everything imaginable from the point of view of a larger planning staff with all possible information of the specific circumstances available and plenty of time to deliberate on all imaginable measures that could be taken to minimise

68 Sandoz et al., para. 2230, pp. 687–688.

69 Rule 15 reads: 'In the conduct of military operations, constant care must be taken to spare the civilian population, civilians and civilian objects. *All feasible precautions* must be taken to avoid, and in any event to minimize, incidental loss of civilian life, injury to civilians and damage to civilian objects' (emphasis added). Arguably, that does not apply to the State parties to API for those precautionary measures that contain no specific reference to feasibility.

civilian casualties. Rather, it depends on the circumstances: whether there is time pressure, the availability of personnel to examine different options, the importance of the target, the tempo and moment of the ongoing operation, what the opponent is doing and so forth. There is a specific reference here to a military necessity exception and thus the obligation to take precautionary measures in order to avoid civilian collateral damage 'is not absolute'.[70] However, a genuine and good-faith effort has to be made.[71]

The ICRC proposed two alternatives in their draft article on precautions in 1972: to use the words 'ensure' and 'all reasonable steps' in the text regarding the verification and proportionality obligations. With regard to the obligation on the choice of weapons and methods, the ICRC included the term 'all necessary precautions'. Ultimately, however, the word 'feasible' was accepted by the majority of States and preferred over other words. The feasibility of the precautionary measures was consequently used consistently throughout the obligations for taking precautionary measures of those who plan or decide upon an attack. In particular, it was felt that 'feasible' was preferred over 'reasonable', as it imposed 'a higher positive obligation to take such measures'.[72] On the other hand, it was decided that the word 'ensure' imposed a standard that was too strict. Therefore, the result is that the highest standard with regard to the protection of the civilian population that proved to be possible was that of feasibility. Of course, the protective standard of feasibility satisfies one of the general goals of IHL: to protect civilians. Simultaneously, the word takes military necessity into account, implying that damage to civilians and civilian objects has to be avoided to the extent that it is not necessary to 'weaken the military forces of the enemy'.[73] The general obligation to take precautionary measures to spare the civilian population is thus an expression of restrictive military necessity.[74] In addition, the use of the word 'feasible' recognises that if military considerations do not allow for precautionary measures, the attacker cannot be obliged to do so. The United Kingdom (UK) issued a declaration of understanding of the word feasible in this regard, which states that the word 'feasible' should be understood to mean 'that which

70 Fenrick 2001, p. 501.

71 Quéguiner, pp. 809–810.

72 Sassòli and Quintin, p. 82. See also the commentary to Rule 15, noting that a standard of reasonableness is 'a little less far-reaching' than that of feasibility.

73 St. Petersburg Declaration Renouncing the Use, in Time of War, of Explosive Projectiles under 400 Grammes Weight (1868), para. 3.

74 Sassòli and Quintin note that '[t]he principle of military necessity as a prohibitive rule implies that civilian losses must be avoided whenever possible.' See Sassòli and Quintin, p. 75.

is practicable or practically possible, taking into account all the circumstances ruling at the time, including humanitarian and military considerations'.[75] This explanation of the word feasible is subsequently used consistently by States.[76] Moreover, the UK declaration has been inserted verbatim in article 3 (4) of the 1996 Protocol on Prohibitions or Restrictions on the Use of Mines, Booby-Traps and Other Devices as amended (Protocol II to the 1980 CCW Convention).[77] Examples of the circumstances that must be taken into account according to the UK may be found in the UK Military Manual and that same article of Protocol II to the 1980 CCW Convention. These circumstances include the importance of the target and the accuracy and radius of effect of the available weapons.[78]

It is clear that the rules on precautionary measures oblige the parties to the conflict to prefer the absolute avoidance of civilian losses over the acceptance that some civilian damage will occur and merely strive to minimise its magnitude. The feasibility requirement of the precautionary measures implies that such avoidance is dependent on the available resources during the conduct of the military operation. This may concern the availability of precision weapons, such as GPS- or laser-guided missiles or grenades. Indeed, in some situations the obligations of precaution 'cannot be fulfilled without using precision guided weapons'.[79] Similarly, certain methods of warfare may be unfit to destroy certain military objectives and obtain the military advantage associated with those military objectives. For example, it may be impossible to attack a certain person in an urban area because the proportionality obligations preclude the use of a large artillery projectile in that area, and the only other option may be to send a squad of Special Forces. If such forces are unavailable to the military commander on the scene, the military objective is simply out of reach for the commander to attack, even if the military objective remains in the same place for an extended period of time.

[75] The United Kingdom's declaration of understanding reprinted in Roberts and Guelff, notes 47, 511. See also article 2 of the 1995 Protocol on Blinding Laser Weapons (Protocol IV to the 1980 Conventional Weapons Convention) stipulating that feasible precautions include 'practical measures'.

[76] Henckaerts and Doswald-Beck 2005a, Rule 15.

[77] Article 3 (4) Protocol II to CCW reads: 'All feasible precautions shall be taken to protect civilians from the effects of weapons to which this Article applies. Feasible precautions are those precautions which are practicable or practically possible taking into account all circumstances ruling at the time, including humanitarian and military considerations.'

[78] United Kingdom, Ministry of Defence, pp. 83–84.

[79] HPCR Manual on air and missile warfare, Rule 8. See also Boothby, pp. 124–125 and O. Gross, p. 1.

5.4.3 *Personal Scope*

The next relevant general issue with regard to taking precautionary measures is the personal scope of the obligation, or, in other words: to whom does the obligation apply? Whereas the general assumption is often that the obligations are placed in the hands of the military commander, the character of the precautionary measures is such that they would need to apply to a broader group of persons in order to play a meaningful role. Boothby notes in this regard that 'it may not always be realistic to expect subordinate level commanders to balance factors some of which are unknown to them'.[80] A number of States expressed their reluctance regarding an overly broad application of the precautionary obligations. For example, the Swiss Government made a reservation upon ratification of API to the effect that 'this provision only creates obligations for commanding officers at the level of batallion or group or above'.[81] Furthermore, the UK Government made a statement upon ratification of API that the obligation to cancel or suspend the attack when it is not proportionate, only applies to 'those who have the authority and practical possibility'.[82]

However, it is equally true that subordinate-level commanders may be faced with a situation which was not foreseen by higher level commanders, such as human shields, as may not be uncommon in the dynamics of today's urban warfare. It may thus be that the commanders on the scene are presented with a different picture than the one assumed by their superiors. In such cases, the subordinate-level commanders are not absolved of their own responsibility to comply with the obligation to take feasible precautionary measures, if only to report the situation and to check whether their orders need to be adapted given the new information.

Henderson notes that 'the obligations in article 57 API apply to all personnel who have the authority and practical possibility to affect the course of an attack'.[83] Indeed, it is submitted that 'the obligation to take precautions in attack applies to all forms of attack',[84] that the obligations 'apply where they can be met'[85] and are not dependent on 'the authority under rules, regulations

80 Boothby, p. 120.
81 Sandoz et al., para. 2197 on p. 681. The declaration is now withdrawn.
82 The UK Declaration is available on the website of the ICRC, see www.icrc.org/applic/ihl/ihl.nsf/Notification.xsp?action=openDocument&documentId=0A9E03F0F2EE757CC1256402003FB6D2.
83 Henderson, p. 157.
84 Henderson, p. 159.
85 Henderson, p. 160.

and instructions'.[86] Therefore, taking precautionary measures is required in all military operations and at every level of the military hierarchy[87] and they must be taken by anyone who has the authority or practical possibility to do so.[88]

5.4.4 *Collecting Information*

The civilian population is endangered as much by bad information as it is by bad decisions. An attack that complies with all precautionary measures may result in devastating effects for the civilian population if it is based on incorrect information with regard to the presence of civilians. Therefore, the basic obligations to take constant care and feasible precautions create a continuing duty 'to assign a high priority to the collection, collation, evaluation and dissemination of timely target intelligence'[89] with a view to making a decision pertaining to the planning or execution of further military operations. The intelligence that is gathered in advance of a military operation should therefore not only focus on information regarding the identification of military objectives and the military advantage of attacking these. Information on the context of the military objective must also be gathered, including in particular information on the likelihood of damage to civilian objects and civilian casualties.

It is obvious that responsible military commanders prefer to base their decisions on a complete picture of the situation in the area where they are conducting their operations. It is, however, unrealistic to expect that picture to be complete and a further blurring occurs amid the chaos that is inherent to armed conflict. It is therefore submitted that the available information and decisions following from it must be assessed in accordance with a standard of reasonableness. Commanders must take decisions during their operations and they are not always in the luxurious position that they can rely on information collected, analysed and combined in real time by a variety of sophisticated sensors. For most NSAGs, advanced systems gathering information on the activities of the adversary on the battlefield may be absent in its entirety. Nonetheless, those deciding are obliged to 'make a reasonable effort to discover pertinent information'.[90]

86 Sassòli and Quintin, p. 111.
87 University Centre for International Humanitarian Law
88 See also Section 6.2.
89 Bothe et al., p. 405.
90 P. Barber, p. 689, adding that '[i]t is not possible to determine exactly what "everything feasible" incorporates, but if normal intelligence gathering methods that had proven reliable in the past had been used on this occasion, it is probable that this would meet the required

According to the ICRC Study on Customary IHL, decisions with regard to precautions in attack must be based on 'the information from all sources which is available . . . at the relevant time'.[91] The ICRC has taken the position that the endeavour of acquiring information on which decisions are based 'must be made in good faith and in view of all information that can be said to be reasonably available in the specific situation'.[92]

Ultimately, the collection of information is extremely situation dependent. Even military forces equipped with the most modern weapons and surveillance systems do not always have the assets available to reach absolute certainty on whether an object constitutes a military objective. In fact, the more information is gathered, the more complicated and important the analysis of this information becomes. It must be realised that IHL does not require absolute certainty for those planning and deciding on attacks. But that does not allow commanders to rely only on speculation or assumptions when planning military operations. On the contrary, there is an increased duty to verify information as it becomes available in the course of an operation. The information on which a decision is based must therefore be up to date, which means that it must be as current as can reasonably be expected given the circumstances, which also means that the capacity and capability to verify play an important role. The collection of the information must in particular be aimed at verifying the nature and location of the military objective, the presence of civilians and the likelihood of a meaningful change in these circumstances. This also implies that it is not at all times required to update the information continuously, although drones and other technological developments may be able to provide real-time information in today's conflicts which enhance 'considerably the possibility of gleaning accurate information about the battlefield'.[93] However, military forces equipped with more limited operational capabilities, as far as the available reconnaissance and observation systems are concerned, cannot always be expected to be able to implement their precautionary obligations to the same level of parties to the conflict equipped with more advanced weapons systems.

standard. If normal intelligence methods were ignored or not used when available, then it is likely that liability could ensue.' In support of this position, see Schmitt 2007, p. 163 and Henderson, p. 165. In support of the application of the feasible standard to the commander in the case of a lack of information, see Sassòli and Quintin, pp. 82–83.

91 Henckaerts and Doswald-Beck 2005a, Rule 15, p. 55.

92 Melzer 2009, p. 75.

93 Dinstein 2010, p. 140.

5.4.5 *The Obligation of Constant Care*

The objective of section I of part IV of API is repeated in the body of the text of article 57, in the first paragraph, stating that, '[i]n the conduct of military operations, constant care shall be taken to spare the civilian population, civilians and civilian objects.' Furthermore, with regard to NIAC, note should be taken of article 13(1) APII, which reads: '[t]he civilian population and individual civilians shall enjoy general protection against the dangers arising from military operations.'

The obligation to take constant care is not intended to lead to the conclusion that civilians may not be affected by military operations at all. As Dinstein observed: '[c]ivilians almost always suffer in wartime.... In wartime, there are inevitable scarcities of foodstuffs (indeed food, clothing, petrol and other essentials may be actually be rationed); buses and trains may not run on time, curfews and blackouts may impinge on the quality of life, etc.'[94] In addition, the malfunction of a weapons system, human errors and faulty intelligence may cause tremendous suffering among the civilian population, but is not necessarily caused by a failure of taking precautionary measures.[95]

The general obligation of taking constant care has a broader scope than the remaining specific precautionary measures. According to the text of the article, as well as Rule 15 identified by the ICRC Customary IHL Study, the obligation of constant care applies to the broader concept of 'military operations', whereas the application of the other specific precautionary measures is restricted to the special military operation of 'attacks'. Attacks are specifically defined in article 49 API, whereas the term 'military operations' is not defined in API.[96] In general, however, military operations other than attacks could include sweeping mines or other explosives, detention operations and logistic operations. Some types of military operation, such as simply moving a unit from one location to another, may sometimes be merely a logistical affair, whereas sometimes it may be a manoeuvre in an offensive operation. In the first situation, it may be no problem that a road through a populated area is used, whereas in the latter situation, it may be better to use a route that avoids populated areas. In the latter situation, the 'active' precautionary measures of

94 Dinstein 2010, p. 135.

95 Ibid.

96 The ICRC Commentary states that: 'The term "military operations" should be understood to mean any movements, manoeuvres and other activities whatsoever carried out by the armed forces with a view to combat'. See Sandoz et al., para. 2191 on p. 680.

article 57 may coincide with the obligations of 'passive' precautionary measures of article 58 API.

Quéguiner makes the point that the obligation constitutes an independent legal obligation and cannot be seen as 'merely inspirational'[97] to the other more concrete precautionary measures. Thus, despite its general wording, the obligation to take constant care of the civilian population expresses the obligation for commanders to reconsider, even when an operation would lead to proportionate civilian damage. As such, the rule is meant to provide an additional layer of protection for the civilian population during military operations.

5.4.6 *Specific Precautionary Obligations*

The first and crucial specific precautionary measure is codified in article 57 (2) (a) (i) API. It deals with the obligation to verify whether a planned target is indeed a military objective. It states that with respect to attacks, those who plan or decide upon an attack shall 'do everything feasible to verify that the objectives to be attacked are neither civilians nor civilian objects and are not subject to special protection but are military objectives within the meaning of paragraph 2 of Article 52 and that it is not prohibited by the provisions of this Protocol to attack them'. The rule is also identified as a rule of customary IHL.[98] This precautionary measure works to reinforce more specifically the general obligation to take constant care to spare the civilian population and dictates that attacks must be aimed at military objectives. This obligation is therefore closely associated with the principle of distinction. Furthermore, special protections that apply to persons and objects also need to be taken into account. This concerns, in particular, medical units (article 12 API), cultural objects and places of worship (article 53 API) and works and installations containing dangerous forces (article 56 API).

The second specific precaution prescribes that all feasible precautions need to be taken with a view to avoiding, and in any event minimising, collateral damage, emphasising the overall goal of precautions in attack.[99] It underlines that in the course of planning or deciding on an attack, it must be contemplated whether it is possible to avoid affecting the civilian population in

[97] Quéguiner, pp. 796–797.

[98] See Henckaerts and Doswald-Beck 2005a, Rule 16.

[99] See article 57 (2) (a) (ii) API and Rule 17 (ii), in Henckaerts and Doswald-Beck: 'those who plan or decide upon shall take all feasible precautions in the choice of means and methods of attack with a view to avoiding, and in any event to minimizing, incidental loss of civilian life, injury to civilians and damage to civilian objects'.

achieving the military objective of an attack. The ICRC Customary Law Study states that '[t]his rule must be applied independently of the simultaneous application of the principle of proportionality'[100] as included in Rule 14 of the Study. This means that it is not sufficient to stay within the parameters that the proportionality principle prescribes, but that also a good-faith effort needs to be carried out to avoid collateral damage in the first place. When the military advantage that is sought cannot be achieved without injuring civilians and causing damage to civilian objects, the rule dictates that the choice of means and methods of attack must be adapted, if feasible, in order to minimise the collateral damage. One may question the scope of this obligation. Obviously, as was mentioned earlier, the required standard is that the precautions must be 'feasible'. This means that the feasibility depends on the availability of options with regard to the weapons that can be used (bigger or smaller explosive, detonation before or upon impact or delayed fuse, etc.), or the way the attack is conducted (ground troops or aerial attack; an isolated pinpoint attack or as part of a larger and more encompassing operation; which route is used towards the military objective; etc.).

The third specific precautionary obligation states in subparagraph (2) (b) of article 57 API that an attack shall be cancelled or suspended if it becomes apparent that (1) the objective is not a military one; (2) is subject to special protection; or (3) the effect is expected to be disproportionate.

This obligation imposes a continued obligation to monitor the objective under attack and it tells the military commander that the responsibility to minimise damage to the civilian population does not end once the attack has been initiated. Instead, the commander must also, when the attack has long been underway, continue to consider its effects on (1) the civilian population, and (2) objects and persons under special protection. These persons could also include wounded adversaries. In addition, the military commander needs to continuously monitor that the expected further damage that will be done to civilian infrastructure and the civilian casualties the further execution of the attack may be expected to cause are still not excessive compared to the military advantage of the attack.

In a military headquarters where a large attack is being commanded, there may be a massive amount of information coming in that cannot always be expected to be processed, analysed and re-distributed in time to realistically change the existing plan of attack. The new information may, however, lead to the conclusion that the target of the attack is not a military objective, or

100 Henckaerts and Doswald-Beck 2005a, p. 57.

subject to special protection. This may result in a new obligation for the commander to suspend or cancel the attack, if that is possible, or to abort the attack when it is already (partly) underway. This may be very difficult for certain types of weapons system, such as loitering 'fire-and-forget' systems.

Apart from the availability of new information, a second factor that may invoke the application of this rule is the factual development of an attack. When viewed on the operational level, the success, or lack of success, of other parts of the attack may lead to the conclusion that the proportionality equation has changed so considerably that it may become illegal to further pursue the planned attack. This may be the result of the fact that the military advantage that was expected from the attack has either already been attained or because it became evident that it has become impossible to attain that military advantage at all. When the outcome of the proportionality assessment has shifted to a sufficient extent, the attack must be discontinued.

A fourth specific precautionary obligation is found in article 57 (2) (c) API, which provides that 'effective advance warning shall be given of attacks which may affect the civilian population, unless circumstances do not permit'. This rule is also of a customary nature in both international and non-international armed conflicts according to the ICRC Customary Law Study.[101] The objective of warning the civilian population is 'to give civilians the chance to protect themselves'[102] in situations where an impending attack may put them in danger. Therefore, the obligation extends to situations where it is uncertain whether civilians will be affected by the attack and whether the attack is expected to result in more than just inconvenience. To achieve that objective, it is essential that the duty to give warning is taken into account throughout the different stages of the targeting process, and deliberated continuously as an inherent part of the process of choosing between the available options of attack.

Warnings are potentially most effective during operations against targets that are situated in populated areas. This, however, does not relieve attackers from their duty to warn before attacking a military objective where a small number of civilians is expected to be present. An important element of the duty to warn is that the warning must be 'effective'. Whether a warning may be considered effective depends on the circumstances of the planned attack. It has been stated in this context that: 'effectiveness must be judged from the perspective of the concerned civilians, namely whether the warning enables

[101] Henckaerts and Doswald-Beck 2005a, Rule 20. This section served as the basis of van den Boogaard 2018a.

[102] Sandoz et al., para. 2225 on p. 687.

them to actually take measures enhancing their protection against the danger arising from military operations'.[103] These warnings may be general or, unless circumstances do not permit, specific. The warning must preferably be clear, timely and not consist of misleading or unclear instructions to the civilian population on how they may escape being affected by an impending attack.

An example of circumstances that 'do not permit' the attacker to warn the civilian population is a situation in which the accomplishment of the mission depends on the element of surprise. Of course, although warning the civilian population of an upcoming bombardment allows them to escape from the effects of the attack, the same goes for soldiers of opposing forces. Therefore, the element of surprising the enemy may often be applicable in situations aiming to kill members of enemy forces and is more likely to arise in situations where military objectives are targeted that are not easily relocated. In addition, a warning is not required if issuing the warning would jeopardise the safety of the attacking forces in a situation that leaves no time for the attacker to issue a warning. However, also in situations of a time-sensitive attack, the military advantage of attacking the military objective concerned must be sufficient in order to justify refraining from issuing a warning. Here, the more general rule of article 57 (1) API to take constant care to spare the civilian population comes into play, as well as article 57 (2) (a) (ii) API. A final exception to the obligation to issue an effective warning is the situation in which giving a warning is simply impossible. After all, in some situations there are simply no realistic options to convey a warning to the civilian population.

Warnings give the civilian population the possibility of leaving an area where hostilities are planned to take place. Putting measures in place to warn the civilian population is thus an important component of the process of planning military operations, particularly in urban areas. However, even in a pre-planned operation, the exact location of intense fighting may not always be predictable since it is also dependent on the conduct of the opposing forces. Still, the obligation to warn can only be meaningfully fulfilled if several options to warn the civilian population are taken into account before an operation is launched. It seems therefore mandatory for military commanders or planners to include methods that would enable the civilian population to be warned in the planning process of any future operations.[104]

[103] Presentation of an expert during a meeting of the ILA Expert Group: 'The conduct of hostilities under international humanitarian law: challenges of 21st century warfare' in November 2013, on file with the author.

[104] As Corn notes, '[t]he feasibility for issuing warnings prior to attack, to include when, how, and to whom, should be factored into all courses of action, and not just raised as a consideration after they have been developed.' See Corn 2014, p. 439.

There is a clear relation between the duty to warn and the proportionality rule. Firstly, like the other obligations to take precautions in attack in order to minimise civilian casualties or damage, the obligation to warn civilians is a practical measure that enables military commanders to implement the principles of distinction and proportionality and it thus increases the protection of the civilian population. There is, however, an additional relationship between the obligation to issue an effective warning and the proportionality rule under IHL. It may be that it follows from the proportionality assessment that the civilian collateral damage of a certain attack is excessive compared to the expected military gain. If, however, after a specific warning the civilian population has largely left the area, the residual collateral damage may be deemed to no longer be excessive. This effective warning may thus have made an attack legally possible that would otherwise have been illegal because of excessive collateral damage. An ironic fact is that those civilian casualties that do result from this attack would not have occurred when no warning was given, because then it may have been assumed that the military commander would have cancelled the attack. As such, however, that is certainly within the boundaries of IHL. In fact, assuming that an effective warning has led to the evacuation of the civilian population from an area where subsequently hostilities take place is beneficial from an operational point of view. This is because the fact that the number of civilians present in the area has decreased also increases the attackers' opportunities to conduct attacks on the adversary. The obligation to warn is thus also a 'useful tool in the hands of commanders for gaining more freedom of action'.[105]

The last specific precautionary measure contained in article 57 API refers implicitly to the proportionality rule. Article 57 (3) and Rule 21 of the ICRC's Customary IHL Study reads, '[w]hen a choice is possible between several military objectives for obtaining a similar military advantage, the objective to be selected shall be that the attack on which may be expected to cause the least danger to civilian lives and to civilian objects.' The rule is formulated identically to its conventional and customary IHL version. This rule therefore deals with 'target selection', and is in many ways challenging to apply.

Firstly, for this rule to be applicable, military commanders would need to identify lawful military objectives that have a similar military advantage. This may seem easy if identical military objectives are planned to be attacked, such as two tanks. But even in this simple example, there may be a larger military advantage in attacking the tank in the front of a column, because the military advantage that follows from the attack is both the destruction of the tank and the blockade of the road by that tank. In this context, the focus must be on not

[105] Baruch and Neumann, p. 373.

only the military advantage of destroying the target, but the expected effect of attacking the planned targets. In the example of the tank, the effect of destroying the first tank while a column of military vehicles is crossing a bridge or a dam is much more than the destruction of the one tank, since it may result in halting the column for a considerable time, perhaps even pinning it down, which would make it easy to destroy the other tanks.

5.4.7 *Sub-conclusion*

The precautions in attack consist of a number of coherent legal obligations, which form an extensive framework of checks the commander needs to take into account in order to shield civilians and civilian objects from the effects of hostilities.[106] The proportionality rule is only one of these measures and there is no clear separation. Because of the way targeting procedures work, it is necessary to conduct the proportionality assessment several times during the planning and execution of an attack. If it is already clear at an early stage of the planning process of a certain attack that the attack will be disproportionate, continuation of the planning process would be pointless. This is the precautionary proportionality of article 57 (2) (a) (iii) API. However, at the end of a planning process it is necessary – as the last check before the attack is carried out – to check on the prohibition of article 51 (5) (b) API. When it becomes clear during the execution of an attack that the attack will be disproportionate, article 57 (2) (b) API dictates that it has to be cancelled or suspended.

The difference between the two provisions of articles 51 and 57 API is therefore that the IHL rule on proportionality is phrased as both a prohibition (in article 51 (5) (b) API) and an obligation (in article 57 (2) (a) (iii) API).[107] However, there is no difference in content and components of the rules found in the two provisions. This is supported by the fact that the wording of the principle as codified in the two articles was agreed upon during the deliberations of article 57 API, and then copied to article 51 API. In practice, the precautionary obligations of article 57 API 'support the general prohibition in Article 51 by placing obligations on attackers'.[108] It could also be said that article 57 clarifies in practice the obligations imposed by article 51 and identifies what precautions must be taken and by whom before launching an attack.[109] However, the proportionality assessment is always the final step.

[106] See, for example, Rogers' checklist, Rogers 2004, pp. 113–117.

[107] According to Rogers, the precautionary provisions are 'expressed more as an exhortation'. See Rogers 2008, p. 189.

[108] Rogers 2008, p. 191.

[109] Gardam 2004. p. 96.

Even in the event that all precautionary requirements are complied with, 'there is an additional obligation not to undertake the attack if it is apparent that the civilian losses and damage to civilian objects are likely to be excessive in light of the anticipated military advantage'.[110] Conversely, a planned attack on a military objective that is not expected to be disproportionate may still violate the rules concerning precautions, when civilian casualties and damage could have been avoided or minimised if the attacker had taken feasible precautions.[111] One could say that in this regard the proportionality rule is a secondary rule that only enters the scene when it is impossible to take precautionary measures that are expected to avoid collateral damage completely.

5.5 PROPORTIONALITY IN CONTEXT

The rules concerning targeting, indiscriminate attacks and the duty to take precautions in attack are obviously also rules of common sense for professional soldiers. Minimising civilian casualties and damage to civilian objects is consistent with professional military values simply because it does not bring about any military advantage.[112] Others would argue that this is consistent with a principle of chivalry.[113]

Seen from the viewpoint of a military commander who is engaged in armed conflict, there are a number of courses of action he (or she) could take. Even during armed conflict, a commander may be passive and wait until an attack occurs on their unit and fight back when that happens, or they could be active and plan and subsequently launch an attack themselves. Which course of action is taken obviously also depends on the actions of the opposing force and the orders handed down from the chain of command. These are all operational considerations, but the IHL proportionality rule must be considered in all these situations. However, the question remains of how the proportionality rule may be applied in practice. To shed more light on that question, the next step is to analyse the different components that play a role in the proportionality assessment. Heated debates in the literature concerning the interpretation of these components show that the application of the IHL proportionality rule in practice is no simple task.

110 Gardam 2004, p. 98.

111 Margalit, p. 158.

112 Carnahan, p. 868: A professional member of the military 'will respect the principles underlying articles 51, 52 and 57 [of API] simply as a matter of sound military judgement . . . [and] serve not so much to limit military effectiveness as to provide legal reinforcement for professional military values'.

113 Gill 2013, p. 43.

6

Components of the Equation

Somebody thinking in terms of collateral damage must be a bad guy, a cold technocrat being ready to sacrifice innocent lives on the altar of military efficiency.[1]

6.1 INTRODUCTION

The proportionality rule in IHL requires a balancing act between the anticipated military advantage and the expected incidental damage. As a result, the answer to the question of whether an attack complies with the IHL rule of proportionality is dependent on the interpretation of these two components. For example, there is discussion about civilians who, be it voluntarily or involuntarily, by their presence are shielding a legitimate military objective from attack.[2] On which side of the proportionality equation should they be included? Also, there is disagreement about the issue of whether opponents who are *hors de combat* should be taken into account in the proportionality equation as incidental damage.[3] But the discussion is broader than just that, because of other parts of the definition of the IHL proportionality rule. The disagreement on the components of the IHL proportionality rule is exemplified by the large amount of literature that deals with the subject and the converging opinions therein.[4] Before it is possible to determine how the IHL

[1] Oeter 2010, pp. 167–194.

[2] See, for example, the discussion in Schmitt 2009, pp. 330–332.

[3] See, for example, Henderson, p. 206.

[4] The issue was also mentioned by the ICTY Prosecutor in the ICTY OTP Kosovo report. It stated that there are four unresolved issues that must be addressed for the purpose of the application of the IHL proportionality rule:

(a) What are the relative values to be assigned to the military advantage gained and the injury to non-combatants and or the damage to civilian objects?

proportionality rule may be applied in practice, which is during military operations in armed conflicts, a thorough understanding of all components of the equation is required. Even if it turns out that it is impossible to provide a simple flowchart for applying the IHL proportionality rule, commanders need to know which factors must be taken into account and how these should be valued.[5]

The aim of this chapter is to assess the different factors which comprise the IHL proportionality rule. Recalling the definition as provided for in API, an attack is considered to violate the IHL proportionality rule if it 'may be expected to cause incidental loss of civilian life, injury to civilians, damage to civilian objects or a combination thereof, which would be excessive in relation to the concrete and direct military advantage anticipated'. Therefore, Section 6.2 looks into the personal scope of the rule: who is bound to apply the IHL proportionality rule? Since the IHL proportionality rule applies to attacks, Section 6.3 assesses how the notion of an attack is defined. Section 6.4 analyses why civilian casualties and damage included in the equation are labelled as 'incidental'. Section 6.5 looks into the temporal scope of the IHL proportionality rule, assessing whether only immediate damage may be counted as increasing the military advantage or collateral damage of a planned attack, or whether more distant consequences of an attack must also be taken into account. The civilian side, the first of the two major parts of the IHL proportionality equation, is assessed in Sections 6.6 (persons) and 6.7 (objects). It is assessed in Section 6.8 whether there are objects and persons other than the strict civilian ones that must be included on the civilian side of the proportionality equation. Section 6.9 looks into the question of how a 'combination' of the respective civilian factors must be evaluated. Section 6.10 analyses the other major component of the IHL proportionality rule: the military advantage side of the equation.

(b) What do you include or exclude in totalling your sums?
(c) What is the standard of measurement in time or space? And
(d) To what extent is a military commander obligated to expose his own forces to danger in order to limit civilian casualties or damage to civilian objects?

See International Tribunal for the former Yugoslavia, Office of the Prosecutor for its Kosovo Report. See also Fenrick 2000, p. 75.

5 In the words of Geiss, the proportionality calculation 'requires fixed points of reference. Otherwise it would be impossible to carry out the balancing judgment that the proportionality principle requires'. Geiss 2012, p. 86.

6.2 THE PERSONAL SCOPE

The first question to be answered is the question of who exactly is 'planning', 'deciding on' or 'executing' an attack, because according to the rule, that person is also the one obliged to conduct the proportionality equation. In this context, a distinction can be drawn between the question of *who* is making the assessment and the question of *what* this person needs to take into account. The answer to these questions is very dependent on the type of attack and the level of command. It is first established *who* must conduct a proportionality assessment. Subsequently, it is discussed whether a concerted string of attacks that may result in civilian casualties or damage to civilian objects in different phases and on different locations must be assessed only on an attack-to-attack basis, or whether a more comprehensive proportionality analysis is required. In addition, a short analysis is provided of proportionality calculations on a strategic level.

6.2.1 *Who Conducts the Proportionality Equation?*

States are the primary objects of international law. As such they conclude treaties and are bound by the rules of the treaties they ratify, including the IHL proportionality rule. Furthermore, States are bound by the rules that follow from the other sources of international law, including the customary rule on proportionality in IHL. In reality, of course, the IHL proportionality rule is implemented by State agents, or by members of a non-State party to the conflict. According to article 57 (2) (a) API, the persons who are responsible for conducting the proportionality equation are 'those who plan or decide upon an attack'. At first sight, this seems to exclude the person who actually executes the attack, in situations where this is a different person. However, article 57 (2) (b) API states that the 'attack shall be cancelled or suspended if it becomes apparent that . . . the attack may be expected to cause incidental loss of civilian life, injury to civilians, damage to civilian objects or a combination thereof, which would be excessive in relation to the concrete and direct military advantage anticipated'. This implies that from the moment the attack is actually underway, the responsibility no longer rests with the planner of the attack. Instead, the responsibility to monitor whether the attack continues to comply with the IHL proportionality rule shifts to the commander overseeing the attack or even the executor of the attack in those situations where this is a different individual. This executor may be situated at a lower level than the planner or commander who has ordered the attack.

If an attack is a single airstrike on a pre-planned military objective, military planners assess the components of the IHL proportionality equation before submission of the target to the commander for approval. This can take place long before an attack is actually launched, although information needs to be updated before it is decided if the attack can go ahead. But if the target is a civilian house from which an infantry platoon has unexpectedly come under fire during a foot patrol, the platoon commander, or even a lower commander who is present on the spot, will be responsible for the proportionality calculation if the decision is made to return fire and attack the house. It must thus not be ruled out that in the execution of an attack, the responsibility may rest on one individual soldier,[6] a pilot or a forward air controller.[7] The obligation to conduct the proportionality calculation, preceding the decision to attack, may sometimes for reasons of policy be placed higher in the chain of command: not only up to the level of generals, but some decisions are referred to the Minister of Defence, or a Head of State. As a quite extreme example, it was claimed that some targeting decisions during Operation Allied Force in 1999 'finally ended up on President Clinton's desk for his approval'.[8]

The ICRC Commentary is helpful to interpret this provision of API. It states:

> [s]ome considered that the introductory words ('those who plan or decide upon an attack') could lay a heavy burden of responsibility on subordinate officers who are not always capable of taking such decisions, which should really fall upon higher ranking officers. This view is not without grounds, but it is clear that a very large majority of delegations at the Diplomatic Conference wished to cover all situations with a single provision, including those which may arise during close combat where commanding officers, even those of subordinate rank, may have to take very serious decisions regarding the fate of the civilian population and civilian objects. It clearly follows that the high command of an army has the duty to instruct personnel

6 As an example, picture a situation in which a squad of soldiers tries to attack a man with a gun in his house. After the man returns fire, the room is attacked by two fragmentation hand grenades, killing the man, five children and wounding four women and children. In this situation, which is derived from an actual event involving Australian soldiers and an Afghan man in 2010, the soldiers tossing the grenades are required to conduct a proportionality assessment themselves. See Hyland.

7 The forward air controller (FAC) is also known as a 'JTAC', which stands for a Joint Terminal Attack Controller. Both terms mean a member of the armed forces who is trained to direct aerial attacks from the air from a forward position, for example, to enable close air support to a ground unit.

8 See Clark, p. 203.

adequately so that the latter, even if of low rank, can act correctly in the situations envisaged.[9]

The observation in the ICRC Commentary seems valid. Even though subordinate officers may not always have the authority to execute some types of attack, the other side of the coin is that there is not always time to 'phone home' for any targeting decision that could lead to collateral damage, especially not for those on-scene commanders who are in the midst of a battle. Although Switzerland made a reservation to article 57 (2) API, according to which this provision only creates obligations for commanding officers at the level of battalion or group or above,[10] this reservation was revoked in June 2005.[11]

It seems logical to assume that one can only make decisions with regard to the degree to which a certain attack is proportionate if the person involved has sufficient access to information to make an informed decision. It is therefore also logical that an individual soldier does not have the oversight to be able to identify the role of the attack that he is ordered to execute in a larger framework, as, for example, the battalion commander has. On the other hand, the individual soldier on the scene may be better placed to anticipate the number of civilians that may be affected by an attack than a battalion commander who is situated in his command post. If the information of individual soldiers is different than the information that was briefed by superiors, it is their responsibility to act upon that information. Tension may exist in that situation between the orders the soldiers received and their IHL-based legal obligations. Time is also a crucial factor. Time-sensitive targets, or when a unit is under attack itself, would arguably justify a less elaborate proportionality calculation, because the reasonable options to obtain conclusive information on expected military advantage and potential collateral damage are limited. Nonetheless, it is particularly in the midst of combat that IHL obligations, including the IHL proportionality rule, need to be applied and complied with.

Furthermore, the level of decision-making is very much dependent on the type of military operation, and the level of sophistication of the available weaponry. After all, the weaponry of an infantry unit is very different from

9 Sandoz et al., para. 2197.

10 Sandoz et al., para. 2197, note 5. A similar statement appears in Switzerland's Basic Military Manual (1987), which states, '[d]uring every attack, commanding officers at the battalion or group level, and those of higher ranks, shall see to it that the civilian population … does not suffer any damage.'

11 Switzerland.

that of an artillery unit or an attack helicopter. The proximity to the battlefield is not always relevant: if an attack is executed by an operator who is flying an armed drone, it could be that the person who is executing the attack is physically dislocated from the place of the attack. For the purpose of the IHL obligations, there is, however, little difference between the position of the drone operator and a jet pilot.[12] The level of communication and control that is possible also implies that if the communication is sufficiently sophisticated to enable having actual 'eyes on target' from a distance of thousands of kilometres, it could in theory also be possible that decisions to attack are made at a higher level, possibly even up to the political level. A possibly more problematic scenario is where an autonomous weapons system is capable of attacking without human intervention. In that situation, the case could be made that the person responsible for the proportionality equation is the person who decided that the system would be deployed, or even the person who wrote the software code on which the decisions of the system are based. Technological developments seem to point in the direction that future autonomous weapons systems deployed with artificial intelligence software will be capable of independently conducting a proportionality assessment and deciding to launch an attack. In a complex environment where civilians and military objectives are intermingled and circumstances change quickly, the person who deployed the system is unable to conduct the proportionality assessment. Whether future autonomous weapons systems will be able to conduct a proportionality assessment in accordance with the restraints dictated by IHL under these circumstances is still unclear.[13]

6.2.2 *Levels of Authority*

A general division of the tiers of command or authority in a military organisation is the distinction between the strategic, operational and tactical level. The strategic command is the higher command, overseeing the big picture, whereas the tactical level relates to the lower level of command.[14]

[12] There may be many differences in practical terms, however. The drone operator is not in danger himself, being located elsewhere than the drone. The fighter pilot, however, is sometimes able to get his own eyes on target and look at the bigger picture. But in legal terms, their obligations under the IHL proportionality rule are equal.

[13] See generally van den Boogaard 2015.

[14] NATO defines the levels as follows: The strategic level: The level at which a nation or group of nations determines national or multinational security objectives and deploys national, including military, resources to achieve them. The operational level: The level at which campaigns and major operations are planned, conducted and sustained to accomplish strategic

The operational level is the intermediate level. In simple terms, at the tactical level, a commander needs to take decisions incident by incident. At the operational level, commanders plan and decide on an attack-by-attack basis, involving different types of unit (often both air assets and land units) operating in a concerted manner. At the strategic level, decisions regard the overall military campaign.[15] In addition, a 'grand strategic' or political level could be defined to which may be referred questions regarding the *ius ad bellum*, which is thus outside the scope of IHL. Decisions on the political level are motivated by not only military considerations, but also, if not predominantly, political motives, such as conducting an attack to strengthen the position of a political leader.

Depending on the level on which a proportionality analysis is undertaken, that person also needs to assess the expected military advantage and collateral damage corresponding to that level of authority, which corresponds to 'whatever level the regulated functions are being performed'.[16] The type of military advantage and collateral damage to be taken into account may thus differ on the corresponding levels.[17] However, some States interpret the military advantage expected from a tactical attack rather broadly. According to the 2002 United States Joint Doctrine for Targeting, for example, the military advantage of an attack 'is not restricted to tactical gains, but is linked to the full context of a war strategy'.[18] Already during the diplomatic conference leading to the adoption of API, there was controversy on the level at which the components of the proportionality equation need to be assessed. This controversy led to a number of declarations and reservations made by States ratifying API, such as the declaration of Canada, that it 'is the understanding of the Government of Canada in relation to subparagraph 5(b) of Article 51, paragraph 2 of Article 52, and clause 2(a) (iii) of article 57 that the military advantage anticipated from an attack is intended to refer to the advantage

objectives within theatres or areas of operations. The tactical level: The level at which activities, battles and engagements are planned and executed to accomplish military objectives assigned to tactical formations and units. See NATO Glossary of Terms.

15 Olasolo, pp. 158–159. But compare Henderson, pp. 238–241.

16 Sloane, p. 315.

17 See, for example, the discussion in Else, pp. 200–206.

18 United States Joint Targeting Doctrine, Joint Publication 3-60. See also '[f]or the US military, the expected incidental civilian damage and the anticipated military advantage must be analysed in light of the strategic needs of the relevant armed conflict' (Olasolo, pp. 182–183, quoting Parks 1982 and Carnahan, p. 866). However, Olasolo identifies a trend that the United States is also conducting proportionality analysis at an operational level (Olasolo pp. 186–188).

anticipated from the attack considered as a whole and not from isolated or particular parts of the attack'.[19]

The text of the Canadian declaration seems to imply that the decisions with regard to the proportionality of an attack are reserved to the higher levels of command, corresponding to the operational level. This seems to be based on the premise that a group commander or platoon commander on the tactical level may not have the necessary knowledge to assess whether a particular attack would be (dis-)proportionate given the importance of the military advantage that is sought by the operation as a whole. The declarations are inspired by the historical example of the attacks on the Calais area in June 1944.[20] Nowadays, many of these attacks would probably be labelled as disproportionate, but they were meant as a diversion and as such they were part of the overall invasion plan in Normandy. This seems to imply that a disproportionate attack on a tactical level would be legal as long as the operational or even strategic operation, of which the tactical attack is a part, is not expected to cause excessive collateral civilian damage. It must be noted that the reservations are directed not to the entire proportionality equation, but to the estimation of the expected military advantage, which is only one of the components of the proportionality equation.[21] The declarations and reservations to API, as mentioned earlier, seem to be based on the preference that targeting decisions involving collateral damage (of a certain level) should be made by higher-ranking officers with a certain degree of oversight, for example on the operational level. The declarations make sense from the perspective of a State that wishes to retain the flexibility to conduct a minor disproportionate attack that is linked to a subsequent larger attack with lower collateral damage, thus leaving the attack as a whole (consisting of different phases) proportionate. There is some support for this in doctrine.[22]

[19] Similar declarations were made by Australia, Belgium, Germany, Italy, Ireland, the Netherlands, New Zealand, Spain and the United Kingdom. See Roberts and Guelff, p. 501. The declarations are also available on www.icrc.org.

[20] See Program on Humanitarian Policy and Conflict Research, Harvard University 2009b, p. 255. See also Schmitt 2015.

[21] However, it seems unlikely that the final estimation of the expected military advantage of a certain attack is decided upon by a different person than the proportionality equation as a whole. See also subsequent discussion in this chapter.

[22] Olasolo suggests that proportionality assessments must be carried out in a broader context than a single attack. He points out that military personnel that can carefully conduct the targeting decision-making process is not usually allocated at the platoon- or company-level. He concludes that 'the fact that the position favouring the proportionality analysis at the tactical level has gained support in recent years does not mean that IHL currently requires application of the proportionality rule at this level'. See Olasolo, p. 179.

However, it is submitted that conducting a proportionality assessment on the operational level alone is insufficient to meet the requirements of the IHL rule on proportionality. Instead, it is submitted that the IHL proportionality rule must be applied on all levels of command and the calculation must, therefore, be conducted separately on each of those levels. This is true because restricting the proportionality equation to the operational level is at odds with the conclusion in the previous section that the obligation to conduct a proportionality assessment may rest on very different persons, situated at very different levels of command. Individual soldiers and on-scene commanders may be unable to conduct a proportionality analysis on the strategic or operational level, because there is insufficient information for them at their level. But the same is true vice versa: the tactical situation may look very different from that anticipated at the operational level. The obligation to conduct a proportionality calculation, even a very basic one, must therefore be placed on anyone who approves or takes the ultimate decision to execute the attack.[23] As a result, in terms of responsibility and accountability, it depends on the exact circumstances of the attack to determine who is required to conduct a proportionality assessment of a planned attack.

The ICRC Commentary to API regarding the precautionary measures confirms the validity of the critique against the approach of focussing exclusively on the *overall military advantage* in a proportionality assessment. The Commentary states that '[t]his article [i.e. article 57, (2)(a)(iii)], like Article 51 (Protection of the civilian population), is not concerned with strategic objectives but with the means to be used in a specific tactical operation.'[24] The text of the reservations and declarations on the level to decide on the proportionality of an attack, it is submitted, contradicts the IHL obligations for some types of attack, such as operations of Special Forces, operations of infantry units in close combat in an urban area and of pilots of attack helicopters. Also, many situations may be envisaged in NIACs with small units of a NSAG conducting attacks. It must be clear that the IHL proportionality rule applies throughout all stages of an attack in all types of armed conflicts, from the planning to the execution phases, and that there is a continuous need to carry out the calculation.[25]

[23] Presumably, this is the person who in the words of Henderson has 'effective control over the attack'. See Henderson, p. 235.

[24] Sandoz et al., para. 2207.

[25] Program on Humanitarian Policy and Conflict Research, Harvard University 2009b, para. 15 of Rule 14, p. 94.

It is therefore submitted that as a minimum, proportionality assessments must *also* be conducted on the tactical level. It may be argued that this assessment is redundant when the on-scene commander is certain that the tactical situation corresponds with what was expected on the operational level. It is submitted that amidst situations of hostilities, that is an extremely exceptional situation. Furthermore, especially if the connection between the separate parts of the attack is unclear, it may be expected that the (in itself disproportionate) collateral damage of the tactical attack will be retaliated, leading to counter-attacks with ever increasing levels of collateral damage, spiralling into total disregard for civilian lives.

Therefore, it is suggested, the responsibility for a single attack must instead be on the corresponding level, even when it is part of a concerted attack. Thus, the on-scene commander retains a personal obligation to conduct a proportionality analysis and it is incorrect to dismiss the responsibility of combatants deciding on single attacks to conduct a proportionality equation. Bohrer and Osiel note that denying the tactical level of the obligation to conduct proportionality assessments could lead to 'horrific results'.[26] However, 'the law of tactical proportionality can demand no more in efforts to safeguard civilians than consistent with the measure of discretion that soldiers of lower rank, in those circumstances, actually possess'.[27]

Furthermore, it is submitted that an additional proportionality assessment must be made on the operational level because it is possible that an attack may seem proportionate on a tactical level, but proves excessive based on a lack of military advantage to be attained on the operational level, due to earlier failures or successful results of other parts of the same concerted attack.[28]

Watkin is of the opinion that since military operations are planned on a strategic level, the military advantage that is sought to be achieved should also be viewed on the corresponding strategic level.[29] This seems in line with the commentary to API, which says that it is obvious that 'an attack carried out in a

[26] Bohrer and Osiel, p. 790.

[27] Bohrer and Osiel, p. 792.

[28] An example would be a concerted land operation aimed at killing or detaining a certain commander who is expected to be in a certain area. An attack on a building in that area from which even minor collateral damage is expected becomes excessive when the commander has already been apprehended by another unit. Therefore, the proportionality assessment on the operational level in this example decisively influences the proportionality assessment of the tactical level. See also Neuman, p. 98, providing the example of a single strike against a power station which cannot be attacked based on a cumulative approach if the enemy were able to use another power station.

[29] Watkin 2007, pp. 43–47.

concerted manner in numerous places can only be judged in its entirety'.[30] This approach suggests that even though one particular attack may be expected to cause excessive collateral damage, this attack may nonetheless proceed, provided the attack is part of a larger, concerted military operation, and the overall military advantage of that larger operation is not expected to be disproportionate. A justification that has been put forward for this is the execution of attacks with the object of misleading the enemy. The historic example typically provided to support this interpretation of military advantage is the heavy bombardment on the French shores near Calais, right before the Allied landing in Normandy during World War II.[31] The State practice of the United States is reported to be focussing on the strategic level for the proportionality equation.[32] Also, the Prosecutor of the ICTY has claimed that when discussing integrated attacks, that '[t]he proportionality or otherwise of an attack should not necessarily focus exclusively on a specific incident.'[33]

The question may be valid whether the scope of the overall armed conflict plays a role. As Carnahan notes,

> [i]n weighing military advantages against civilian casualties, a more restrictive standard might be appropriate for operations in a 'limited' conflict, such as Vietnam, than for operations in a 'general' war, such as World War II. Such a distinction, however, finds no basis in [API].. . . If different legal standards are to be applied to the conduct of limited and general wars, then the Vietnamese combatants would have been permitted to conduct themselves and their operations in ways prohibited to their American allies and opponents. Such a double standard for the conduct of 'limited' wars would be militarily impracticable.[34]

This seems to be a fair conclusion. Of course, when an armed conflict has only reached the level of small border incidents, the question may be asked whether there is any 'overall' military advantage of an attack in the first place. However, the law does not exclude larger operations to be launched.

The strategic approach could be criticised because it does not seem to be in conformity with the words 'concrete and direct'. Also, an inherent threat of the strategic approach seems to be that the 'ultimate advantage – the end of the

[30] Sandoz et al., para. 2218.

[31] See, for example, Geiss 2012, p. 77. See also Bothe et al., p. 324.

[32] See the discussion in Olasolo, pp. 182–183, quoting Parks 1982 and Carnahan, p. 866. However, Olasolo identifies a trend that the United States is also conducting proportionality analysis at an operational level (Olasolo, pp. 186–188).

[33] International Tribunal for the former Yugoslavia, Office of the Prosecutor, para. 78.

[34] Carnahan, p. 867.

war – appears to have too remote a connection with any tactical operation. The alternative would be to deprive proportionality of all meaning, as it would appear to sanction a strategic nuclear strike, provided the strike was thought likely to bring the conflict to an end'.[35] It has also been argued that it is not justified to conduct only one calculation of the total expected casualties and the anticipated intensity of the campaign for a series of attacks. This would amount to dismissing the significance – or even legality – of single attacks for the reason that these attacks should be seen in the framework of the effect of the total operation.

Watkin states that 'the use of a strategic approach in considering proportionality need not be viewed as a means by which conflict will get out of control as long as the analytical framework incorporates an assessment of the effects of the attacks at tactical, operational and strategic levels'.[36] In his view, the military advantage of a certain strategic campaign logically also incorporates the calculations of military advantage on the operational and tactical levels. Indeed, the 'overall' military advantage seems to refer not to the war as a whole, but to a finite event.[37] The conclusion may thus be drawn that the 'overall' military objective is meant to refer to the operational level, or the lower strategic level.

The tactical approach does seem less logical when the concept of the targeting of 'systems' is considered. These could be very simple systems: destroying one bridge gives little military advantage if there is another one right next to it. For large networks, such as the communications systems of the armed forces of the opponent, the destruction of a single component leads to no military advantage whatsoever, leading to the conclusion that certain dual-use military objectives may only be attacked as part of a large and comprehensive system attack, because they form a part of that system that is a military objective when viewed as a whole.[38]

It is submitted that in many cases, especially when a more or less concerted attack is being planned, it is most appropriate to include the 'overall' military advantage in the proportionality equation. However, when there is an attack taking place in a situation where a target has suddenly 'popped up', or when an attack is conducted in response to a sudden enemy attack, there can be no 'overall' military advantage to that attack, and the military advantage of the

35 Hampson 1992, p. 47.

36 Watkin 2007, p. 47.

37 Dinstein 2004, p. 87, see also Dörmann 2003a, p. 164.

38 See Henderson, pp. 201–202, and the quotations used there: in particular, the Air Force Pamphlet 14-210 Intelligence, p. 18. See also Watkin 2007, p. 46, on the attack on the petroleum, oil and lubricants stock and refineries during the 1991 Gulf conflict.

attack must be viewed on the tactical level. Also, for pre-planned targets, the emphasis on the 'overall' military advantage should not lead to situations in which a total disregard would emerge for the well-being of civilians. Therefore, it is submitted that in addition to a proportionality calculation on the higher levels of command, there should always also be an evaluation of the military objective to be attained on the tactical level.

In the end, both the strategic and the tactical approach of the military advantage seem at odds with the IHL proportionality rule if they are the only level on which the military advantage of planned military action is analysed. The fact that the individual deciding on the launch of a planned attack is situated at the tactical, operational or strategic level should not make any difference for the question of whether a proportionality assessment needs to be conducted, including the assessment of the expected military advantage.[39] In addition, there is a risk if commanders conduct attacks that are disproportionate when they are assessed in isolation, but that are part of a larger, proportionate, attack. That risk is that commanders feel they are allowed to disregard their obligations under the IHL proportionality rule. If the tactical commander is supposed to assume that the specific attack he is to conduct is part of a larger plan, he may also assume that he has no duty to conduct a proportionality calculation. This would not do justice to the protective scope of the IHL proportionality rule and could lead to catastrophic results.

Thus, it is submitted that the ground rule is that proportionality assessments must be done on both the operational and the tactical level. The exception to this may be a situation in which three conditions are fulfilled: when the tactical operations are (1) part of a pre-existing plan on the operational level, (2) the tactical commander is aware of the fact that he will encounter a certain degree of prima facie excessive collateral damage, and (3) the situation as it becomes apparent to the tactical commander in the course of the execution of the operation is as expected in the planning phase.

6.2.3 *Proportionality on a Strategic Level*

The military advantage sought from operations on a strategic level may be expected to correspond with higher permissible levels of collateral damage. There are diverging opinions in doctrine on this subject. Some writers seem to confuse the IHL proportionality rule on a strategic level with a general

[39] See also Stone, p. 537.

comparison ex post facto between the number of civilian casualties resulting from the operation and the objectives that were achieved.[40] Other authors maintain that to focus only on a strategic level for the calculation of the proportionality of an attack is incorrect.[41] However, simply adding the military advantages at the operational and strategic levels onto the military advantage expected at a tactical level, as proposed by Neuman, seems over-broad.[42] Attaching military advantage at other levels to the expected collateral damage of a single tactical attack would allow for extensive collateral damage of that single attack. Since at that level also, if not primarily, political objectives are pursued, this seems to be at odds with the required concrete and direct military advantage.[43] Although State practice shows that the proportionality assessment is also done on a strategic level,[44] this must, however, not be understood to indicate that the proportionality of the entire conflict must be assessed as part of a single attack. Such a wide interpretation confuses proportionality as understood in the realm of the *ius ad bellum* rules of self-defence with the IHL rule on proportionality.[45]

There may be some confusion in the language used within the military for labelling some military objectives particularly important for an operation on a strategic level. For example, the surface-to-air capabilities of the opponent would be characterised as such, because disabling the air defences would render the attacker air superiority.[46] Nonetheless, attacking one 'strategic'

40 See, for example, the faulty conclusion by Barnidge, p. 181, and the accompanying notes. He, as well as the statements of others he refers to, all refer to the alleged lack of proportionality of Operation Cast Lead as a whole. See also generally Parks' description of the Rolling Thunder and Linebacker operations: see Parks 1982 and 1983, and Fenrick 2001 with regard to the Allied Forces.

41 See also Dörmann 2003a, p. 171.

42 Neuman, p. 100.

43 Arai-Takahashi, p. 357.

44 For an example, see Section 7.2.

45 See International Law Association, note 73 on p. 19 of the Final Report of the ILA Study Group on the conduct of hostilities and IHL:

> [t]he Conduct of the Persian Gulf War: Final Report to Congress, Pursuant to Title V of the Persian Gulf Conflict Supplemental Authorization and Personnel Benefits Act of 1991 (Public Law 102-25) April 1992, at p. 611 seems to reflect such confusion ('An uncodified but similar provision is the principle of proportionality. It prohibits military action in which the negative effects (such as collateral civilian casualties) clearly outweigh the military gain. This balancing may be done on a target-by-target basis, as frequently was the case during Operation Desert Storm, but also may be weighed in overall terms against campaign objectives').

46 See, for example, US Joint Chiefs of Staff, pp. I–3: '[h]ighly sensitive strike missions against longrange strategic targets will generally require a higher level of detailed planning and centralized control.'

objective is an operation on a tactical level, but presumably with a significant expected military advantage. If the single attack is part of a larger operation aiming to disable the air defence capabilities of the opponent, the same attack is also part of an attack at the operational level. It is submitted that, in such a situation, it is unacceptable to conduct a proportionality equation exclusively on the strategic level, because such a test would be too imprecise to lend any protection at all to the civilian population. Of course, a proportionality assessment on the grand strategic level may *also* be necessary to assess the justifiability of the use of force in the *ius ad bellum*, but in IHL it would be incorrect to leave it at that.[47] Thus, it is submitted that the proportionality of an attack should be assessed as a minimum on both the operational and the tactical level.[48]

In sum, if specific attacks seem to be disproportionate on a tactical level, they should be either cancelled altogether or checked with the higher headquarters whether the attacks must be seen as part of an operational plan that would result in such a large military advantage. As a result, the rules pertaining to the proportionality equation apply 'on all levels of military action and at all stages of the planning and execution of attacks'.[49] This is also important since this approach offers a means by which 'military commanders at all levels of the chain of command can be held accountable'.[50] The conclusion is thus that operations consisting of a string of attacks must be assessed not only on an attack-to-attack basis, but a more comprehensive proportionality analysis is required on the respective levels of authority.

6.3 WHAT IS AN 'ATTACK'?

According to article 51 (5) (b) API, a disproportionate attack is prohibited. Article 57 (2) (a) (iii) and (b) API add that both before and during an attack precautions must be taken to prevent disproportionate attacks. Therefore, it is relevant to define what according to IHL constitutes an 'attack'.

47 One method of measuring the proportionality of an attack on the strategic level could be the method that is proposed by Parks 1990. See also table 2 on p. 65 of Fenrick 2000. Fenrick calls this a 'very crude indicator of regard for collateral casualties'. See Fenrick 2000, p. 79.

48 It may be debated whether this means that the reservations and declarations made by a number of States upon ratification of API, that the 'overall' military advantage must be addressed, should be reconsidered.

49 Kalshoven 1992, p. 44.

50 Watkin 2007, p.47.

Attacks are defined in article 49 (1) API as 'acts of violence against the adversary, whether in offence or in defence'.[51] This concept must be interpreted broadly.[52] That means that an attack covers the use of armed force to damage objects or injure or kill persons.[53] According to Kalshoven, this implies the use of weapons, or in other words, the use of armed force through 'violent means'.[54] Rogers adds that the threshold of an attack is already passed by the use of a light weapon by a single soldier.[55] This does not imply that any military operation should be regarded as an attack. Military logistic operations or detention operations during armed conflict do not qualify as an attack, because they can generally not be characterised as 'acts of violence'.[56] Dinstein states that,

> [t]he term attack ... means any act of violence, understood in the widest possible sense (including a non-kinetic attack), as long as it entails loss of life, physical or psychological injury, or damage to property. Attacks do not include non-forcible acts, such as non-injurious psychological warfare. The line of division between what is permissible and what is not, is accentuated by computer network attacks (CNA). These would qualify as attacks within the accepted definition only if they engender – through reverberating effects – human casualties or damage to property (it being understood that a completely disabled computer is also damaged property).[57]

Nonetheless, the notion of 'attack' is not limited to kinetic force: operations involving chemical, biological or radiological means of warfare are also accepted to qualify as attacks. Thus the effects of an operation are decisive.[58]

It must furthermore be noted that an attack may also include acts of violence 'in defence'. This includes shooting back when one is attacked, but also a more concerted counter-attack against an adversary that has attacked first. Outside the ambit of armed hostilities, the military would understand this type of use of armed force as 'self-defence'. The concept of self-defence is,

[51] It is important to note that the concepts 'attack' and 'armed violence' are also important in *ius ad bellum* where these concepts are used to determine whether a certain use of armed force is legitimate under the law on the use of force by States. The definition of an attack under *ius ad bellum* is, however, distinct. See Sandoz et al., para. 1882, p. 603.

[52] Sandoz et al., para. 1880, p. 603.

[53] Dinstein 2010, p. 1.

[54] Kalshoven and Zegveld, p. 100.

[55] Rogers 2004, p. 32.

[56] Rogers 2004, p. 33. See also Oeter 2008, pp. 175–177.

[57] Dinstein 2008, p. 2. As noted in the Tallinn Manual 2.0, Rule 92: '[a] cyber attack is a cyber operation, whether offensive or defensive, that is reasonably expected to cause injury or death to persons or damage or destruction to objects.' See Schmitt et al., p. 415.

[58] Schmitt et al., p. 415.

however, not a useful concept in IHL. The concept of 'self-defence' is used in *ius ad bellum* and could also be a lawful breach of a person's right to life under international human rights law in a law-enforcement paradigm. International humanitarian law is, however, indifferent to the reason why the armed force is used. It simply dictates that during armed conflict, one who defends is, like the attacker, obliged to adhere to the rules of IHL, such as distinction, proportionality and the obligation to take precautionary measures. In addition, the laying of mines is also considered an attack.[59]

According to the next part of the definition of an attack, the armed violence must be directed 'against the adversary'. This implies that the intention of the use of the armed violence is relevant. The idea of this part of the definition is first of all to underline that the use of armed violence may not be directed to the civilian population or civilian objects, but must be directed to the opponent.[60] Conversely, the use of armed violence that is not directed against the enemy would then not be considered part of the definition of an attack. Exceptions to this are indiscriminate attacks, because those fail to distinguish between military objectives and civilian objects or the civilian population. That means that although they are generally not as such 'directed at the adversary', they should still qualify as attacks in the sense of IHL, even as an explicitly prohibited type of attack.[61] On the other hand, armed violence used during military exercises, or firing weapons at a shooting range, may obviously not be labelled as armed violence directed against the adversary, and thus does not constitute an attack. This would also apply to other types of use of weapons, such as celebratory fire.

It is clear that a direct attack on civilians is prohibited. An interesting issue that may be raised is the connection between the definition of an attack and a warning shot that may be fired. Understood in the classical sense, this is an easy question: by definition, a warning shot is never aimed at the actual target. Therefore, a warning shot is not an attack because it is not directed against the adversary. However, in the context of the conflict in Gaza in 2008–2009, the Israeli Defence Forces used the so-called 'knock-on-the-roof' method to warn civilians to leave a certain building. These knocks on the roof would include a minor attack on the building that was to be destroyed, in order to make it clear that an attack on the building was imminent and to persuade the civilians that were present to leave it. It has been argued that these smaller attacks should be

59 Kalshoven and Zegveld, p. 176.
60 See article 51 (2) and (3) API.
61 Article 51 (4) API.

labelled as direct attacks on civilians.[62] However, it seems that the better definition of these 'knocks' were in fact – as warning shots – precautions in attack in the sense of article 57 API, and as such, not violations of IHL, or attacks on the military object as such.[63]

6.4 'INCIDENTAL' DAMAGE: EXPECTATION AND ANTICIPATION

The definition of the IHL proportionality rule states that the collateral damage that is counted in the equation should be 'incidental'. This must be understood as damage that is caused willingly, but not in itself the primary objective of the attack.[64] Furthermore, as a result of the precautionary obligations, it must be minimised as far as that is feasible.[65] Military planners and commanders may be expected to thoroughly assess what may be expected from a certain planned attack, motivated by both operational considerations, because unexpected results may be contrary to their objectives, and the precautionary obligations, including the obligation to apply the IHL proportionality rule.[66] Accordingly, military planners, commanders and operators prefer weapons, munitions and methods of warfare that cause predictable effects.

The military advantage that may be taken into account is limited to the advantage that is 'concrete and direct'. With regard to the collateral damage, such a limitation is not applicable. The use of the word 'incidental' serves merely to underline that there may not be a deliberate attack on the civilian population and civilian property. The term 'incidental' cannot be understood

62 United Nations General Assembly 2009, p. 131.

63 See also Byron, p. 199. See more particularly van den Boogaard 2018a.

64 One could wonder whether this means that there could be a difference between different types of collateral damage. Reynolds notes there could be 'involuntary' and 'voluntary' collateral damage. The former could be described as 'any unintended, unanticipated effect of an attack resulting from system malfunction, human error or other errant cause'. The latter would then be 'any anticipated incidental damage or other effect of an attack that is justified under the principle of proportionality'. See Reynolds, p. 89. However, this distinction is not useful for clarifying the IHL proportionality rule. Involuntary collateral damage is by definition unexpected. Thus, it cannot be taken into account in the proportionality calculation, simply as a matter of logic. The IHL proportionality rule only requires what may be expected to be taken into account.

65 See article 57 (1) API: '[I]n the conduct of military operations, constant care shall be taken to spare the civilian population, civilians and civilian objects' and article 57 (2) (a) (ii): 'take all feasible precautions in the choice of means and methods of attack with a view to avoiding, and in any event to minimizing, incidental loss of civilian life, injury to civilians and damage to civilian objects.'

66 Garraway 2005, p. 3.

as an additional qualifier of the 'loss of civilian life, injury to civilians, damage to civilian objects, or a combination thereof'.[67]

The question then is which factors those who plan, execute or decide upon attacks must take into account when they examine the information available to them. As the ICRC Commentary to API notes,

> [t]he danger incurred by the civilian population and civilian objects depends on various factors: their location (possibly within or in the vicinity of a military objective), the terrain (landslides, floods etc.), accuracy of the weapons used (greater or lesser dispersion, depending on the trajectory, the range, the ammunition used etc.), weather conditions (visibility, wind etc.), the specific nature of the military objectives concerned (ammunition depots, fuel reservoirs, main roads of military importance at or in the vicinity of inhabited areas etc.), technical skill of the combatants (random dropping of bombs when unable to hit the intended target).[68]

Additional factors are the availability of reconnaissance assets by the attacking force (reconnaissance drones, real-time surveillance by Special Forces, helicopters and other aircraft), the availability of effective precautionary measures (both general and specific warnings), time pressure (the place and role of the specific attack in the general war effort). This list is certainly not exhaustive, because the circumstances of every single attack are different.

It is an important feature of the proportionality calculation that it concerns not the *result* of an attack, but what was expected to happen before the attack was launched. A number of States declared specifically upon ratification of API that a decision on proportionality must not be judged with the advantage of hindsight.[69] The ICTY Trial Chamber agreed in its judgment in the *Galic Case* in 2003. It states that '[i]n determining whether an attack was proportionate it is necessary to examine whether a reasonably well-informed person in the circumstances of the actual perpetrator, making reasonable use of the information available to him or her, could have expected excessive civilian casualties to result from the attack.'[70] The applicable standard of the

[67] See Geiss 2012, note 77 on p. 89. Geiss argues that '[t]he word "incidental" is certainly broader than the requirements of being "concrete and direct".'

[68] See Sandoz et al., para. 2212 on p. 684, see also Reed, p. 25.

[69] For example, Germany stated that '[t]he decision taken by the person responsible has to be judged on the basis of all information available to him at the relevant time, and not on the basis of hindsight.' Similar declarations were also made by Switzerland, Italy, Belgium, The Netherlands, New Zealand, Spain, Canada and Australia. See www.icrc.org for the exact texts of the statements.

[70] See the *Galic Case*, para. 58.

commander's knowledge is thus 'that which he reasonably knew under the circumstances'.[71] This is true both for the expected collateral damage and for the military advantage to be obtained. As Canada stated upon ratification of API,

> [i]t is the understanding of the Government of Canada that, in relation to Articles 48, 51 to 60 inclusive, 62 and 67, military commanders and others responsible for planning, deciding upon or executing attacks have to reach decisions on the basis of their assessment of the information reasonably available to them at the relevant time and that such decisions cannot be judged on the basis of information which has subsequently come to light.[72]

The civilian side of the proportionality equation is thus based on a combination of expectations, as assessed by a reasonable military commander. Expectations are subjective by definition, yet an expectation may become more objective when there is sufficient information available on the nature of the target and the presence of civilians and civilian objects surrounding the target. The availability of surveillance assets and other information sources are therefore important in order to be able to obtain a clear picture. Also, other objective factors may play a role, such as the type of weapon that is used or a temporal component.[73] A tragic example of how expectation can be deceiving is the attack on the Al-Firdis bunker in Baghdad on 12 February 1991. The expected collateral damage of the specific attack was zero. The US planners reportedly had no knowledge that the families of the military would hide for safety in the bunker at night. As a result of the attack, a considerable number of civilians died.[74]

The fact that expectation is the decisive factor also means that civilian casualties and damage to civilian structures that have occurred by accident are outside the equation. It is of little comfort to the victims of such attacks that the executors of such an attack never intended for these casualties to happen in the first place. After all, that does not change the damage done, nor does it provide solace for the lives lost. There is a limit to these accidents of course.

[71] Bill, p. 136. Bill calls this the 'Rendulic Rule'. Bill states explicitly that the Rendulic Rule is a rule of customary international law and it applies to the IHL proportionality rule. See Bill, pp. 151 and 140.

[72] See https://ihl-databases.icrc.org/applic/ihl/ihl.nsf/Notification.xsp?action=openDocument&documentId=172FFEC04ADC80F2C1256402003FB314.

[73] For example, a munitions factory may be expected to contain less civilian workers at night than during the day.

[74] See Human Rights Watch 1991.

It is a fact of life that weapons will sometimes malfunction, or that civilians are present in places they were not expected to be. But when it is known that the used weapon malfunctions often, this does impact the proportionality equation. The same goes for the presence of civilians: if the planner and executor of an attack have to act upon the knowledge that they may reasonably be expected to possess, they are required to examine whether their assumptions are correct. When they decide to be reckless, the responsibility of the attack must be attributed to them. If they are not reckless, but have reasonably come to the conclusion that the attack they plan to execute is proportionate, the damage resulting from that attack is caused legitimately because IHL allows for these casualties and damage to occur. Of course, other factors may play a role in the determination of recklessness, such as the question of how much time there is to conduct the planning or an attack, the value of the target and whether the attackers are under fire themselves.

As far as the use of weapons is concerned, the expectation of the effect of that weapon plays a role. This means that knowledge is required of the exact effects of the type of weapon that is planned to be used in an attack, to be able to calculate the amount of military advantage it may be expected to accomplish, but also the amount of collateral damage that may be expected to result from the attack using that particular weapon. In this regard, the question may be asked whether the expected failure rate of a particular type of weapon must be taken into account. On the one hand, it seems apparent that there is always a chance that a certain weapon will malfunction. This seems part of the reality of warfare and not a factor that a military commander must take into account when he uses a type of weapon or munitions. On the other hand, there does seem to be a limit to this. Part of this limit is the scale of the planned attack: if the attack is assessed on an operational level, the failure rate and expected percentage of malfunction of a certain type of weapon used in a significant number of single attacks of that operation can be statistically calculated. Resulting collateral civilian damage is thus foreseeable and must therefore be taken into account. The obligation to take this into account may, however, also present itself on a tactical level. As an example, one could think of some cluster munitions. A considerable percentage of some types of submunitions are well known to malfunction. When this is known to commanders, they are indeed obliged to take this effect of the weapon into account when calculating the proportionality of an attack. This means that when using certain types of cluster munitions, the commander will have to take into account that the expected military advantage is decreased because a large number of bomblets will fail to explode upon impact. This will also increase the likelihood of civilian casualties in the longer term as well.[75] Greenwood and Boothby, however, think that only immediate risks caused by weapons known to result in leaving dangerous explosive remnants of war after their use should be taken into account by the military commander who plans an attack, because 'there are too many factors which are incapable of assessment at the relevant time'.[76] They argue that these effects are only 'immediate' in the first few hours after the attack, and that the commander does not have to include an expectation on the possible return of civilians to the area. Henderson, however, states that since cluster munitions are well known to possess a high dud rate, it can be expected that there will be civilian casualties when cluster munitions are to be used in civilian areas.[77] It is submitted here that it has now been sufficiently established, at least for some types of cluster munitions, that remaining submunitions will pose a threat to the (returning) civilian population, thus increasing expected civilian casualties.[78] Even though the casualties resulting from remaining bomblets may only be substantiated in the longer term and they may be labelled as indirect, these consequences of cluster munitions are nevertheless foreseeable and are thus part of the proportionality equation.[79] The nature of cluster munitions is why these weapons were, and still are, the subject of substantial efforts to prohibit them altogether.[80]

Another issue is the situation when only less-precise bombs are available to an attacker. After all, not all parties to armed conflicts around the world have laser-guided weapons that can be directed to an exact location, thus minimising the collateral damage to civilians and civilian objects. Less-precise bombs may be expected to impact over a larger area, thus the expectation increases that they miss the intended military target at which they were aimed. An example might be the sophisticated weapons that were engaged by the Israeli Defence Force against 'katoesja' and other primitive rockets that were deployed by fighters of Hezbollah and Hamas. The fact that these latter armed groups do not have more sophisticated weapons at their disposal does not

[75] See, for example, McCormack and Mtharu, p. 206: 'Israel's apparent reckless disregard for the rule of proportionality by ignoring the mid to long term civilian damage from unexploded submunitions makes it more difficult for other states to argue that the general rules of international humanitarian law adequately cover the use of cluster munitions and obviate the need for any additional specific prohibition.'

[76] See McCormack and Mtharu, p. 197.

[77] Henderson, p. 210.

[78] See, for example, Human Rights Watch 2007, p. 47.

[79] Garraway notes in 2005 in a brief on the issue of cluster munitions that, '[i]f it is known that there is a likelihood, or even a certainty, that an attack will leave behind some explosive remnants of war, then that must be factored into the equation.' See Garraway 2005, p. 5.

[80] Haines, p. 284.

mean that they are not bound by the same IHL restraints as the Israeli Defence Force. In theory, the protective value of the IHL proportionality rule seems to benefit from the development and use of increasingly sophisticated weapons – at least those that are more precise and with more limited effects. However, assuming both parties to a conflict conduct a thorough proportionality calculation before an attack, the party with more sophisticated weapons may end up having more potential legitimate targets available to attack than the party armed with less sophisticated weapons, because the former may be presumed to have the better capability to limit the expected collateral damage. However, there is a danger here: assuming more targets can be attacked because the weaponry is more sophisticated and thus more precise means that the proportionality analysis must be done on a more detailed scale. These details may not be easily anticipated, however. This may in turn lead to an increase in the expected collateral damage.

As an additional problematic issue in the identification of that which may be anticipated from a certain attack, the question of the probability of success of an attack should be addressed. Sometimes there is only a limited likelihood estimated to exist in advance that the military advantage that is sought by an attack will also be achieved. How must this percentage be factored into the total proportionality equation? Suppose it is possible to identify that a certain high-value target is present in a certain house, with one civilian. The military advantage of killing him would be very high, and although it is equally likely that the civilian will also be killed, suppose for the sake of argument that this would be proportionate. However, what if, given the circumstances, there is only a 10 per cent chance that the target would indeed be killed, because you know that the target is wearing a bulletproof vest, while the civilian is not. Does this alter the proportionality equation? When the expected military advantage of an attack is considered, it is obvious that if a relatively small military advantage is sought, the probability that the operation will actually attain this objective must be larger than in a case where there is much more at stake.[81] Thus, the probability of failure must also be examined, and that includes the failure rate of the means and method that is employed in the operation. It seems logical to conclude that the success of the operation also needs to be taken into account in such a way that the smaller the likelihood of success, the smaller also the amount of collateral damage may be in order for the attack to remain proportional.[82]

[81] McPherson, p. 94.
[82] See also subsequent discussion, Chapter 9.

There is another danger in conducting the proportionality equation: military commanders may intuitively conduct their proportionality equation subjectively. As a result, some components of the equation are not weighed in a sufficiently objective manner, particularly when one of the parties is militarily superior.[83] In the words of McPherson: '[o]ur tendency when we are in a position of considerable advantage will be to identify with the possible benefits to ourselves and others for whom we have special concern and to dissociate from the costs to persons likely to bear the burdens of use of force.'[84] It seems to be a common feature of mankind to become more or less indifferent to the suffering of the adversary. Yet this kind of indifference is in direct contrast with the whole reciprocal spirit that forms the basis of IHL. At the other end of the spectrum, it has also been suggested by the Commentary to the 1956 Red Cross Draft Rules that in cases of doubt of how large the collateral damage will be, it should be estimated as large as possible: *in dubio pro humanitate*.[85] This statement, however, seems to tip the balance too far to the disadvantage of military personnel. A more helpful suggestion, made by a number of writers,[86] is to include in the equation a 'reversed assumption': whether the commander would consider the attack lawful if the expected collateral damage consisted of civilians of his own side. In this rather simple way, the danger may be avoided that the lives of civilians of the adversary are seen as less valuable than the lives of their 'own' civilians.

Another factor that impacts on the expected collateral damage and military advantage are foreseeable secondary explosions. This may, for example, occur when an object is attacked that contains a large amount of explosive material. If secondary explosions are reasonably foreseeable, they also need to be taken into account.

83 See, for example, Fenrick 2000, p. 74 and Rowe, p. 160:

> [i]t is, for instance, common for those who make targeting decisions to exaggerate (albeit unwittingly) the contribution to military action and the military advantage to be gained from a particular bombing mission and, in addition, to expect the 'smart' weapons to produce precision bombing (and thus leave civilians untouched). The reason for this is that Protocol I sets the dividing line between an indiscriminate attack (illegal) and one that is not (legal) on the basis of expectation before the attack is commenced. At this stage of military operations those planning the attack are at their most optimistic and civilians are at most risk. The position has been reached where the well-established principle of distinction between civilian objects and military objectives has been rendered of little practical significance when some military advantage in the destruction of the object is discernible and smart weapons are used.

84 McPherson, p. 94.

85 ICRC 1956, p. 702.

86 Guisández Gómez 1998, pp. 347–363, see also Henderson, p. 229.

It may be concluded that everything that may be expected to occur in terms of incidental civilian damage or casualties as a result of a planned attack must be taken into account. It is important to note in this context that there are no qualifiers attached to the notion of 'incidental' civilian damage and casualties to be included in the IHL proportionality assessment, in contrast to the military advantage to be taken into consideration, which must be 'concrete' and 'direct'. The extent to which the expected incidental damage is indeed foreseeable and the related issue of the temporal scope will be further elaborated in the next section.

6.5 TEMPORAL SCOPE, DIRECTNESS AND FORESEEABILITY

Linked to the difficult concept of the expectation of a reasonable commander, dealt with in the previous section, are the issues of the temporal scope of the proportionality equation and the question of how direct the effects must be in order to be included. It is already difficult to predict the direct and short-term effects of an attack, but it is even harder to predict indirect and long-term effects, or as they are sometimes labelled: the reverberating effects.[87] These effects are defined by the ICRC as '[t]he effects that are not directly or immediately caused by the attack, but are nonetheless a consequence of it.'[88]

Direct effects are those that are expected to be caused by an attack, such as bullet wounds, but also the effects of an explosion: blast, fragmentation, thermal effects against the human skin and the penetration of those within, which causes damage, often enough to expect the death of the person affected by it. However, the secondary effects of a blast wave caused by an explosion are also included, such as fragments of glass and other material flying through the air as a result of the explosion, the collapse of buildings, dysfunction of objects (such as damaged vehicles), as well as secondary explosions caused by explosive material located at the target of the attack. There are also effects that are not caused by bullets or explosions, such as laser beams, fire, sound blast and electrical shock, which could also be direct effects of an attack. Reverberating effects may, for example, be understood to include the effects of flooding

[87] See, for example, the discussion in Nohle and Robinson: 'the increasing experience of armed forces in urban combat and greater awareness in the public domain about the interconnectedness of essential services arguably makes it objectively foreseeable that damage to or destruction of essential infrastructure will have certain reverberating effects on essential services, such as health care and water distribution'.

[88] ICRC 2015, p. 21. See also Robinson and Nohle, p. 108.

caused by the destruction of a bridge, radiation, the unavailability of medical services, the outbreak of diseases due to the lack of clean water and the like.[89]

With regard to the temporal scope of the expected effects of an attack, there is no explicit guidance in the text of the IHL proportionality rule. However, it is now well settled, according to Schmitt, that '[a]ny consequences, even long-term ones, which are foreseeable and likely in light of the information reasonably available to the attacker, must be factored into the proportionality calculation.'[90] Thus the test does not include any *possible* effect, but only those effects that are foreseeable, whenever they may be expected to materialise. The temporal aspect thus does not impose a restriction on the temporal scope of the effects of a planned attack to be taken into account. Subsequent treaty language confirms this approach.[91]

With regard to the directness of the effects of the planned attack that must be taken into account for the IHL proportionality assessment, a distinction is made between direct effects and indirect effects. It must be noted in this regard that the rule contains a distinction between the civilian side of the proportionality equation and the side of the military advantage. Since, according to the text of the rule, the anticipated military advantage must be 'direct and concrete', it is necessary to distinguish between those effects that are directly militarily advantageous and those that are indirect, because the latter may not be factored into the proportionality assessment. For the civilian side, a distinction between direct and indirect effects is irrelevant, because the standard is that of 'foreseeability', not directness.[92] This is supported, for

89 See generally Robinson and Nohle, pp. 107–145.

90 Schmitt 2006a, p. 296. See also the ILA Study Group Report: '[t]here is, however, no basis in IHL to impose a certain (absolute) time limit on those indirect effects that need to be taken into account.' See International Law Association, p. 25 and the accompanying notes 90 and 91.

91 See, for example, article 3 (10) of the Amended Protocol II to the CCW:

> [a]ll feasible precautions shall be taken to protect civilians from the effects of weapons to which this Article applies. Feasible precautions are those precautions which are practicable or practically possible taking into account all circumstances ruling at the time, including humanitarian and military considerations. These circumstances include, but are not limited to:

(a) the *short- and long-term effect of mines upon the local civilian population for the duration of the minefield*;
(b) possible measures to protect civilians (for example, fencing, signs, warning and monitoring);
(c) the availability and feasibility of using alternatives; and
(d) the *short- and long-term military requirements for a minefield*. (Emphasis added)

92 See, for example, the Program on Humanitarian Policy and Conflict Research, Harvard University 2009b, p. 91: '[t]here is no dispute that indirect effects cannot be taken into account if they are too remote or cannot be reasonably foreseen'; the International Law Association,

example, by the Commentary to the Red Cross Draft Rules of 1956. With regard to the expected collateral damage, it states that '[i]t is reasonable to require an attacker to take into account his assessment of indirect losses and destruction which he could reasonably foresee to occur in the prevailing circumstances.'[93] This means that no assessment is required of the number of steps that may be identified between the attack and the foreseeable effect to determine whether an effect is direct or indirect.[94]

Thus, 'directness', understood in terms of the closeness or remoteness of an effect connected to a planned attack, is only relevant to determine whether an effect of a planned attack contributes directly to the military advantage.[95] For the determination of the incidental effects, however, the directness of the foreseeable effects is irrelevant, as long as the effect is foreseeable. The commentary to the Air and Missile Warfare Manual notes that:

> [t]he members of the Group of Experts could not agree as to what extent (if at all) indirect ('reverberating') effects of attacks have to be factored into the proportionality calculation. In any event, there is no dispute that indirect effects cannot be taken into account if they are too remote or cannot be reasonably foreseen. The Group of Experts could identify no conclusive State practice that settles the issue of indirect effects of attacks.[96]

Similarly, the ICRC Guidance on Direct Participation states that '[t]he relevant threshold determination must be based on "likely" harm, that is to say, harm which may reasonably be expected to result from an act in the prevailing circumstances.'[97] This expectation for the civilian side is thus arguably a 'but-for test': all effects are foreseeable that one would

pp. 23–24: '[t]he prevailing view is that indirect effects of attacks must also be considered alongside direct ones.'

93 ICRC 1956, p. 701, original in French: 'On peut raisonnablement demander à l'attaquant de tenir compte, dans son appréciation, des pertes et destructions indirectes qu'il peut normalement prévoir du fait qu'elles sont attendues et caractéristiques dans les circonstances données' (translation by the author).

94 See also International Law Association, p. 25.

95 Reynolds, p. 90: 'A distinction could be made between direct-effects and indirect effects of an attack. Direct collateral damage may be defined as "any immediate physical effect incidental to any type of attack." Indirect collateral damage may be defined as "any delayed, long-term effect, including physical, economic, social, public health, political or other effect incidental to any type of attack".' See also Henderson, pp. 207–209.

96 Program on Humanitarian Policy and Conflict Research, Harvard University 2009b, p. 91.

97 Melzer 2009, p. 47.

reasonably expect to result from a planned attack and that would not occur but for that attack.[98]

Foreseeability is nonetheless a difficult concept to be applied to, for example, power grids that are used by both the military and civilians. Short-term effects of losing the ability to turn on the light or use computers is clear, but qualify as nuisance rather than damage. However, it may also be foreseen that there are reverberating effects on the civilian population because of the lack of power to water purification plants or hospitals. During the 1990–1991 Gulf War, the number of civilian casualties of the actual attacks on the electrical power grids were outnumbered by the civilian deaths that were the result of the longer-term results of the lack of power at hospital and water purification facilities.[99] It is clear that the water purification facilities and the hospitals themselves were not objects of the attack. In fact, they probably did not suffer any damage from the actual attacks. But that does not seem to imply that the nature of the target (in this case, a dual-use target such as the electricity grid) and the effects that may have can simply be ignored.[100] Even though it may be difficult to quantify the exact effects, they can be foreseen. Provided these effects are reasonably foreseeable, they must be taken into account, especially for dual-use objects. However, it seems that it is an inherently subjective factor in the assessment of whether a certain effect of a planned attack is foreseeable.

6.6 THE CIVILIAN SIDE

The civilian side of the proportionality assessment is composed of a material and a human component. This section deals with the human component and therefore discusses what must be understood by the term 'incidental loss of civilian life [and] injury to civilians'. A crucial part of the proportionality equation is therefore the question of which individuals qualify as 'civilians' in the sense of article 50 (1) API.[101] Here the principle of distinction comes into play. Since armed conflict is waged against the armed forces of the

98 See Gillard, p. 15: '[t]he incidental harm to be considered is that which would not occur but for the attack – with one limitation. Harm that results from the conduct of an actor other than the one carrying out the attack, and does not arise from the physical effects of the attack, is excluded.'

99 Shue and Wippmann, p. 568.

100 Byron, p. 208. According to Byron, '[t]he longer-term threat to civilians from attacks, particularly on electricity stations, *must* be taken into account when making a proportionality assessment' (emphasis in original text).

101 See also Henderson, p. 206.

enemy, the civilian population is immune from attack.[102] Civilians should therefore refrain from participating in hostilities, and combatants should distinguish themselves as such. It must be clear that in principle only injury and loss of life of civilians is counted in the proportionality equation, and not injury or loss of life to the military forces of the opponent, even if this was unintended.

The definition of a civilian under international law is formulated in a negative sense: a civilian is any person who does not fit into the categories of article 4 (A) (1), (2), (3) or (6) of GCIII and article 43 API.[103] Put simply, a civilian is anybody who is not a combatant. A prominent problem for the definition of the notion of civilians in IHL exists in the law applicable to NIACs. The cause of this is the fact that in that context, the notion of combatants is non-existent, at least in the applicable treaty law.[104] The alternative term to be used in an NIAC is that of 'fighter'. A definition is proposed by the ICRC, suggesting that,

> [a]ll persons who are not members of state armed forces or organized armed groups of a party to the conflict are civilians and, therefore, entitled to protection against direct attack unless and for such time as they take a direct part in hostilities. In non-international armed conflict, organized armed groups constitute the armed forces of a non-state party to the conflict and consist only of individuals whose continuous function it is to take a direct part in hostilities ('continuous combat function').[105]

These persons retain civilian status for the purpose of protections once they are captured by their opponents. During hostilities, however, they lose their protection against direct attack continuously, for the duration of the armed conflict or until such time the fighters have disassociated from the NSAG that is a party to the conflict. Civilians participating in a more occasional fashion regain their protection against direct attack as soon as they have stopped participating directly in the hostilities and thus, as of that moment, are included on the civilian side of the proportionality assessment.

[102] See, for example, Rogers 2004, pp. 12–13 and Dinstein 2010, pp. 121–124.

[103] As phrased in the ICRC Interpretative Guidance on DPIH: '[f]or the purposes of the principle of distinction in international armed conflict, all persons who are neither members of the armed forces of a party to the conflict nor participants in a *levée en masse* are civilians and, therefore, entitled to protection against direct attack unless and for such time as they take a direct part in hostilities.' See Melzer 2009, p. 20.

[104] For a discussion of the concepts of civilians in non-international law, see the ICRC Interpretative Guidance on DPIH, Melzer 2009, pp. 27–36.

[105] Melzer 2009, p. 36.

Customary law indicates that the prohibition to attack civilians exists in IHL applicable in both international armed conflicts and non-international armed conflicts.[106] Therefore, for the application of the IHL proportionality rule, it is imperative to distinguish between protected civilians and civilians who participate directly in hostilities. Only the former enjoy the protection awarded to civilians and only the latter may be attacked. The difficulty in making an accurate assessment of which civilians must be included in the proportionality equation, and which must not, is apparent. The ICRC study into the issue of direct participation of hostilities is a clear manifestation of how the issue of direct participation has divided experts in IHL.[107] Although an in-depth study of the issue as such will be omitted for the purpose of this chapter, the next section addresses the specificities of civilian immunity, and the relevance of the notion of direct participation for the application of the proportionality calculation. Subsequently, the focus shifts to a number of difficult issues where there could be doubt on the question of whether an individual should be taken into account in the proportionality calculation. These include whether civilians taking part in a voluntary or involuntary human shield must be taken into account; the allegiance of civilians to one or another party to the conflict; and individuals who work in a military objective. Before these issues are explored, the nature of civilian immunity deserves some further attention.

6.6.1 *Civilian Immunity*

Even though civilians may not be attacked directly, IHL acknowledges the unavoidable reality that they may still be affected by armed violence, without a breach of IHL occurring. It must be noted that not any inconvenience for civilians in armed conflict is included in the phrase 'incidental loss of civilian life [and] injury to civilians'. It is a common understanding that armed conflict causes many unwanted side effects that adversely affect the well-being of the civilian population.

Civilians may be affected by an attack because they are relatively close to a military target, because they are inside a military target, because of a misunderstanding of their status or protection or if a weapons malfunction results in them being hit.[108] Given the definition of an attack, as mentioned earlier,

[106] See ICRC Customary Law Study, Rule 1, see Henckaerts and Doswald-Beck 2005a, p. 3.

[107] Melzer 2009.

[108] Dinstein 1997, p. 6. See also Byron, p. 195, noting an incident in Iraq, where a large number of civilians were killed, and the US and UK forces claimed that this was caused by an anti-aircraft missile that was fired by the defending Iraqi forces.

defensive military operations that may be expected to cause collateral damage must also be proportionate.

Civilians who participate directly in hostilities lose their immunity from attack, which is afforded to them in accordance with their civilian status.[109] Therefore, they may be directly attacked. It has been argued that the provision that has codified this concept in API, was 'a fairly substantial shift in the balance between military necessity and humanity, with a weighting in favour of protecting civilians'.[110] This is particularly due to the fact that civilians are only liable for attack 'for such time as' they participate, and the participation must qualify as 'direct'. For the purpose of the application of the IHL proportionality rule, the question is whether civilians still count in the proportionality equation on the civilian side, or whether they have become part of the military advantage that is expected to result from a planned attack. The issue at stake here is the difference between the 'protection' and 'status' of civilians.[111] It seems safe to conclude on the basis of the text of API that there are indeed only two categories of status that may be attached to persons: either a civilian or a combatant. For the purpose of the conduct of hostilities, it seems self-evident that once the protection against direct attack of a civilian is lifted, due to direct participation in hostilities, the civilian also loses the protection that is awarded by the IHL proportionality rule. That means that although the status remains the same, the civilian does 'change scales' for the purpose of the proportionality calculations. This is a complicating factor for the attacking party to the conflict, because it complicates the proportionality equation in the sense that not all civilians whom the commander expects to be affected by the imminent strike have to be factored in as collateral damage. Also, the commander runs the risk that affected individuals with a civilian status (but not protection) may be exploited as propaganda by the opposing party to the conflict, once the attack is conducted. It is thus submitted that for the purposes of the conduct of hostilities, including the application of the IHL proportionality rule, the focus is more on the protection of the civilian, than on the civilian status.

It has been argued that civilians who have been (but are no longer) participating directly in hostilities, or civilians who have supported the active fighting forces in an indirect manner, must be excluded from the civilian side

109 Article 51 (3) API.

110 Camins, p. 879.

111 See generally, Dörmann 2003b.

of the proportionality assessment.[112] Also, it has been proposed that if civilians are voluntarily participating in a human shield, they can under certain circumstances count for less than other civilians.[113] It is submitted, however, that the former proposal is unacceptable and contrary to IHL. Furthermore, it is submitted that accepting the latter proposal would further complicate the (already difficult) proportionality analysis, and finds no basis in the law. If commanders need to take into account not only the number of civilians, but also add a certain 'value' to these civilians, or multiply the number of civilians with a certain factor, it becomes even more complicated. Therefore, it is submitted here that it is undesirable to step upon this slippery slope. Individuals either enjoy civilian protection and are included on the civilian side of the IHL proportionality assessment, or they are not taken into account because they have lost their protection. As such, civilians must be counted equally in the proportionality equation as long as they refrain from participating directly in the hostilities. It could be argued that this is in accordance with the general principle that '[a]ll human beings are born free and equal in dignity and rights.'[114] While civilians participating in hostilities lose their protection against attack, if they are captured, they benefit from all protection of civilians under IHL on the basis of their civilian status. When civilians are known to be sympathetic to the attacked party, or when it is known that they have participated directly in hostilities in the past, they must not be the subject of a direct attack. Therefore, they must be counted as a civilian on the collateral damage side of the proportionality equation.[115] It is true that if it becomes impossible for a military commander to determine who is a legitimate target and who is a protected civilian, 'his ability to make the necessary proportionality assessments is severely handicapped [and] difficulties will

[112] Blank and Guiora, pp. 66–67. Blank and Guiora suggest that '[p]ersons who participate in hostilities, or assist those who do so, should be counted as legitimate collateral damage, even if they could not be targeted directly at the moment of an attack, and therefore should not factor into the proportionality analysis as civilian casualties.'

[113] See Dinstein 2010, pp. 152–155. This is further explored in the next section.

[114] Article 1, UN Universal Declaration of Human Rights, see www.un.org/en/documents/udhr/index.shtml.

[115] The suggestion of Blank and Guiora seems to amount to a conclusion that in case there is difficulty in determining which civilians still enjoy civilian protection, this protection must therefore be afforded to them in a more limited way. This is, however, contrary to the well-established rule of the assumption of civilian status as codified in both treaty and customary IHL. See, for example, article 52 (3) API. There is no similar rule identified in the ICRC Customary International Humanitarian Law Study, but a brief discussion is included in the rule that regards the protection of civilians who take a direct part in the hostilities. It concludes that 'one cannot automatically attack anyone who might appear dubious'. See also Henckaerts and Doswald-Beck 2005a, pp. 23–24.

correspondingly undermine his ability to carry out his mission within the bounds of the law'.[116] Nonetheless, it is submitted that creating a category that is less protected than 'innocent' civilians finds no basis in the law.

This issue raises the question of whether one's own civilians should also be taken into account in the proportionality equation, and how the value of these civilians must be equated to the opponent's civilians.[117] The following situation may be used to illustrate this. If a valuable military target has malfunctioned, such as a combat helicopter and the enemy is approaching fast, its crew may decide to abandon the helicopter and subsequently call in an airstrike to destroy the helicopter and to prevent it from falling into the hands of the enemy. If, however, the pilot of the aeroplane that is tasked to destroy the helicopter notes that the party's own civilians are in the process of stripping the helicopter of its valuable parts, does he need to take the lives of these 'friendly' civilians into account in his proportionality equation? It is submitted that the allegiance of the civilians should not be decisive in the question of whether the civilians should be factored into the proportionality equation. After all, this would introduce an additional restraint into the definition of a civilian that is not present in the applicable law. It cannot be said that the civilians are participating directly in the hostilities because they are trying to steal scrap metal for reasons of personal gain. Also when the criteria proposed in the ICRC Interpretative Guidance on direct participation of hostilities are applied, it seems safe to assume that the civilians are not participating in the hostilities because a belligerent nexus is lacking. The challenge the pilot is facing is, therefore, a balancing act between the relative value of the lives of the civilians and the military advantage that the enemy will not come into possession of the helicopter.[118]

116 Blank and Guiora, pp. 66–67. Blank clarified their suggestion to this author in email correspondence to mean that '1) on the battlefield there are more people than just combatants or DPH and then totally innocent civilians and 2) that when there is confusion in determining who is who and what is what, commanders will have greater difficulty making proportionality determinations (and other determinations of course)'.

117 See Porat and Bohrer for a view that more value may be attributed to the safety of the party's own troops than to enemy civilians, as well as a plea to attach more weight to the safety of its 'own' civilians than on enemy civilians. Porat and Bohrer, pp. 99–158.

118 Arguably, the helicopter's military value is lost once the civilians have removed so many valuable parts from the helicopter, so that the enemy will no longer be able to fly it, thus diminishing the military advantage to destroy it. The value of depriving the opponent of the ability to require knowledge about the weapons system may be considered important, but that military advantage is probably only indirect.

It is submitted that all civilians should be protected equally by all parties to the conflict.[119] After all, the text of the articles of API governing the protection of the civilian population during the conduct of hostilities give no evidence that there could be any differentiation between the nationality or ethnicity of the civilians.[120] The ICRC Commentary to article 50 API supports this conclusion by stating that '[i]n protecting civilians against the dangers of war, the important aspect is not so much their nationality as the inoffensive character of the persons to be spared and the situation in which they find themselves.'[121] Therefore, it does not seem logical to differentiate between enemy or one's own civilians.

Another issue complicating the assessment of the civilians which should be included in the proportionality equation concerns the fact that in modern military forces, an increasing number of traditional military functions are being performed by civilians. This blurs the status of the military objective. The question also arises whether these individuals should still be included in the proportionality calculation as civilians, or whether they have become part of the military advantage when they are expected to be affected by an attack, even though they are not wearing uniforms.[122]

6.6.2 *Human Shields*

Human shielding is the practice of deliberately collocating civilians or persons *hors de combat* with military objectives with the specific intention of

[119] For a different view, see Dinstein 2016, pp. 159–160.

[120] See articles 48–60 API.

[121] See Sandoz et al., para. 1909, p. 609. It must be noted that there is a clear differentiation between civilians of different nationalities in the provisions protecting the civilian population in Geneva Convention IV (GIV). The ICTY Appeals Chamber, however, seemed to water down this distinction. It held:

> hinging on substantial relations more than on formal bonds, becomes all the more important in present-day international armed conflicts. While previously wars were primarily between well-established States, in modern inter-ethnic armed conflicts such as that in the former Yugoslavia, new States are often created during the conflict and ethnicity rather than nationality may become the grounds for allegiance. Or, put another way, ethnicity may become determinative of national allegiance. Under these conditions, the requirement of nationality is even less adequate to define protected persons. In such conflicts, not only the text and the drafting history of the Convention but also, and more importantly, the Convention's object and purpose suggest that allegiance to a Party to the conflict and, correspondingly, control by this Party over persons in a given territory, may be regarded as the crucial test. (ICTY, Tadic Appeals Chamber Decision, 15 July 1999, para. 166)

[122] See Parks 1997, p. 109.

preventing the enemy from attacking these military objectives or restricting their options.[123] Unfortunately, the use of human shields has been a frequently recurring tactic in a number of armed conflicts.[124] The use of human shields is a specific violation of IHL[125] as well as a violation of the obligation to take precautions against the effects of attack, more specifically the obligation to refrain from placing military objectives in the vicinity of civilians.[126]

Civilians may decide voluntarily to endeavour to shield a military target from attack by their presence, or they may be forced to do so. The question may be asked whether civilians acting as voluntary human shields count differently in the proportionality assessment to those who are forced to do so. The discussion of the protection of civilians participating in a human shield often focusses on the question of whether the participation in a human shield as such constitutes direct participation in hostilities.[127] If the definition of direct participation as it has been formulated in the ICRC Interpretative Guidance on direct participation of hostilities is applied, a human shield does in most cases not qualify as direct participation. This is because there is no direct harm caused to the opponent by the shielding.[128] In those situations, it must be assumed that the civilians do count on the civilian side of the scale. The position of the ICRC thus appears to be that any civilian who is not directly participating in the hostilities and who is voluntarily shielding a military objective must be taken fully into account in the proportionality assessment.[129]

123 Henckaerts and Doswald-Beck 2005a, p. 340.

124 For an overview, see Schmitt 2008, pp. 17–21. See also Geiss and Devaney, pp. 11–12, Henderson, pp. 211–218 and Bouchié de Belle, pp. 883–885.

125 See, for example, articles 23 GCIII, 28 GCIV, 12 (4), 28 (1) and 51 (7) API and Rule 97 of the ICRC Study on Customary International Humanitarian Law.

126 Article 58 API, see also Rules 22–24 of the ICRC Study on Customary International Humanitarian Law.

127 See, for example, Schmitt 2008, p. 45 and Bouchié de Belle, pp. 893–896.

128 See DPIH Interpretative Guidance, Melzer 2009, pp. 56–57:

> [t]he fact that some civilians voluntarily and deliberately abuse their legal entitlement to protection against direct attack in order to shield military objectives does not, without more, entail the loss of their protection and their liability to direct attack independently of the shielded objective. Nevertheless, through their voluntary presence near legitimate military objectives, voluntary human shields are particularly exposed to the dangers of military operations and, therefore, incur an increased risk of suffering incidental death or injury during attacks against those objectives.

See also Sandoz et al., para. 1943, p. 633, and Bouchié de Belle, p. 895, who concludes that the human shield's participation is merely indirect.

129 See Melzer 2009, pp. 56–57. See also Pedrazzi, pp. 98–116.

There is merit in the position that the opposing force must still be reasonably able to wage their war and not be restrained by voluntarily shielding civilians. The 2004 UK Manual on the Law of Armed Conflict states that although the duty of the attacker to take precautionary measures remains in effect, unlawful actions by the opponent 'may be taken into account in considering whether the incidental loss or damage was proportionate to the military advantage expected'.[130] This approach seems to suggest that the status and protection of the civilians remain unchanged due to their placement as a human shield. The presence of a human shield does not alter the character of a military objective itself: it remains liable to attack. However, a heavier burden is borne by the attacking side to take precautionary measures. The approach of the 2004 UK Manual seems to suggest that the ultimate assessment of excessiveness is relaxed for the commander as a result of the unlawful act of the side of the conflict that uses human shields, decreasing the value attributed to the shielding civilians. The updated version of the US DoD Manual has been changed on this point in comparison to the initial version, but still maintains that '[b]ased on the facts and circumstances of a particular case, the commander may determine that persons characterized as voluntary human shields are taking a direct part in hostilities.'[131] These civilians are thus discounted in the proportionality equation and it may be concluded that the US understands civilians voluntarily participating in a human shield as assuming a certain risk and therefore to count differently in the proportionality assessment.[132] Similarly, Dinstein proposes that civilians who are present involuntarily should be 'discounted in value'[133] or that in relation to them at least 'the test of excessive injury to civilians must be relaxed'.[134] This is, however, a minority view. The better view seems to be that civilians involuntarily shielding military objectives retain their full civilian protection and must be fully taken into account in the proportionality assessment as long as their participation does not amount to direct participation in hostilities.[135]

130 See the UK Manual of the Law of Armed Conflict, para. 5.22.1, p. 68. See also Dinstein 2008, p. 15.

131 See the updated US Department of Defense Law of War Manual, para. 5.12.3.3. For a discussion, see also Haque and Dunlap.

132 See on the civilian assumption of risk and the DoD Manual: Khalfaoui, pp. 251–303.

133 Dinstein 2010, p. 131.

134 Dinstein 2008, p. 14.

135 See, for example, Schmitt 2009, p. 301: he proposes *not* 'to relax the incidental injury calculation for involuntary shields [because it] would be to enter upon a normative slippery slope'. See also Henderson, p. 215 and Pedrazzi, pp. 98–116.

Ultimately, it is submitted that the suggestion of attributing different values to civilians who voluntarily shield military objectives than to civilians who do not amounts to accepting that there are different categories of civilians. The law in the Geneva Conventions suggests that this is not appropriate. It may be considered the better view to take all civilians who are part of a human shield into account equally for the purpose of the proportionality assessment, assuming they are not participating in the hostilities.[136] Firstly, for practical reasons, it is very difficult to determine in practice whether a civilian is shielding involuntarily or not. Furthermore, it may be considered prudent to give civilians participating in a human shield the benefit of the doubt, because if there is uncertainty about the status of civilians, they must enjoy the protection of a civilian, which would include the protection of the IHL proportionality rule.[137] That does not mean that shielded military objectives cannot be attacked at all, but rather that it depends on the outcome of the proportionality assessment.[138]

6.6.3 *Physical Injury, Sickness and Mental Harm*

It is debatable whether the phrase 'injury to civilians' in the IHL proportionality rule refers to injury in a broad sense, consisting of physical injury, sickness and mental harm, or whether the two latter categories are excluded. A textual interpretation of the IHL proportionality rule provides no further guidance, but a further interpretation of the rule paints the picture that it is not only the physical injury that is taken into account.

That physical injury may be inflicted incidentally to civilians in the context of hostilities goes without saying. Civilians may be hit by stray bullets, by blast and shrapnel through the detonation of explosives and other foreseeable effects of the use of kinetic force. These effects include pieces of glass that fly around as a result of blast waves that shatter windows, injuries resulting from collapsing buildings and fires that ignite as a result of explosions.

The collateral infliction of sickness may not be expected when a grenade is launched in the direction of military objectives where a limited civilian presence is deemed acceptable incidental harm. However, in other scenarios, the infliction of disease may be highly likely, and therefore foreseeable. The scenarios in which diseases are likely to occur include those carried out with weapons causing severe radiation, such as nuclear weapons; or some chemical

[136] See also Henderson, p. 218.
[137] See article 50 (1) API.
[138] For a thorough analysis of the issue, see Van Schaak.

weapons causing cancers.[139] In addition, when sewage systems may be expected to get hit incidentally, this may lead to catastrophic diseases, especially when the population is already vulnerable as a result of prolonged hostilities. As explained previously, the standard is that of foreseeability.

With regard to the question of whether mental harm is also included in the assessment of expected incidental harm to civilians, the literature on the subject is limited.[140] One could debate whether the ordinary meaning of physical injury must be understood to also include expected mental harm. If that is the case, foreseeable mental harm must be taken into account.[141] Treaty law does contain indications that intentionally inflicted mental harm to the civilian population is taken into account, particularly through the prohibition of terror attacks.[142] To be included in the IHL proportionality assessment, mental harm must amount to more than merely the inconveniences of war, and the fear and anxiety that the conduct of hostilities in the vicinity would instil on the civilian population. But when studies in the realm of psychiatry would show the foreseeability of the expected occurrence of measurable mental harm such as PTSD, there is no reason why this must be excluded from expected incidental injuries to civilians.[143] Furthermore, it has been argued that exposure to blast may cause certain concussive effects, resulting in injuries that are in fact physical in character.[144] This traumatic brain injury is invisible, but must be taken into account nonetheless when the state of science is sufficiently advanced to calculate the impact of the use of certain weapons that are known to cause these effects.[145]

139 Admittedly, chemical weapons are banned and their use would as such already be illegal. Nonetheless, the release of chemicals as a collateral effect may significantly affect the health of civilians through disease.

140 See generally Lieblich, pp. 185–218, Schmitt et al., p.108, Schmitt and Highfill and ILA Report, p. 29.

141 See generally Lieblich, who argues that mental harm can be assessed separately from bodily harm. See Lieblich, p. 188. The ILA report distinguishes between psychological harm and mental harm, suggesting that only the latter must be included because only the latter is 'a biological condition that requires medical treatment'. See ILA Report, p. 29. It is submitted here that this distinction is not useful: foreseeable, but less severe, mental harm would simply be given less weight in the proportionality assessment than more severe types of mental injury.

142 See article 51 (2) API: '[a]cts or threats of violence the primary purpose of which is to spread terror among the civilian population are prohibited.'

143 See also Lieblich, p. 215, arguing that mental harm must be taken into account in the assessment of the IHL proportionality rule. See also Lubell and Cohen, p. 174.

144 Schmitt and Highfill, pp. 76–81.

145 Schmitt and Highfill, p. 98, noting that to take these effects into account in a proportionality assessment is '[g]iven the current state of science . . . arguably premature.'

It is submitted that, in practice, it is not foreseeable for a military commander as to whether the harm that will be caused by a single strike will also include mental harm or disease. Therefore, on a tactical level, except in unusual circumstances, the statistical possibility that the planned attack will also cause mental harm or disease is usually not foreseeable because it is too remote. However, it is suggested that the statistical likelihood of causing mental harm and disease by conducting a large-scale operation must be taken into account at the higher levels of command. As Lieblich notes: '[t]his harm can be accounted for prior to the attack by relying, for instance, on prediction models concerning the risk among injured persons.'[146] Therefore, from the operational level up, statistics and information about the likelihood of an operation causing mental harm and diseases must be taken into account as far as that is reasonably possible. This may, for the time being, be a difficult factor to be applied in practice. Nonetheless, it is a foreseeable factor to be taken into account in the practical application of the IHL proportionality rule in larger, concerted attacks, planned on the operational level. As a result, it may be necessary for States to study the foreseeability of collaterally caused diseases and mental harm on the civilian population and include experts in the respective fields in the planning staff for concerted operations.

6.6.4 *Civilians Inside a Military Objective*

A final controversial issue that must be addressed in this section concerning the protection of the civilian population in the IHL proportionality assessment is that of how civilians who are present inside a military objective must be valued. The often-cited example of such a situation is the civilian worker in an arms or ammunition factory.[147] These civilians are by definition more at risk than other civilians because they are inside what in most circumstances qualifies as a military objective.[148] It is also clear that the status of these civilians is not in doubt.[149] They are civilians, simply because they do not qualify as combatants. The next question therefore is whether they remain protected, or whether they lose their protection because they are participating directly in the hostilities. Although it must be granted that civilian workers in an ammunition or arms factory do indeed contribute to fighting and

[146] Lieblich, p. 213.
[147] See Dinstein 2016, p. 150. See also Khalfaoui, pp. 251–303.
[148] Rogers 2012, p. 12. See also the discussion in Henderson, pp. 218–220.
[149] But see the discussion in Camins, pp. 869–870. The workers inside the ammunition factory were seen as 'quasi-combatants' in the interbellum, for example by Spaight.

war-sustaining capabilities these civilians are not participating directly in hostilities.[150] Therefore, '[a]s civilians who take only an indirect part in the hostilities, these workers continue to enjoy protection.'[151]

The question remains whether these civilians must be treated any differently than other civilians who are not working in the factory, but who only happen to be close to the military objective. It seems that the civilians of the former category are taking a calculated risk to be near that military objective, since it could be attacked. Henderson takes a clear position on this issue: he concludes that '[t]he injury or death to any particular civilian is of no lesser weight than the injury or death to any other civilian.'[152] Given the position discussed earlier with regard to the relative weight that must be attributed to civilians in the case of a human shield, which is shared by Henderson, it is submitted that this is the correct position. This does not mean that the munitions factory may not be attacked. Instead, this places a higher burden on the attacker to take more far-reaching precautions before the attack is launched. However, if the attack is deemed to be proportionate, it may proceed. Rogers agrees that '[s]uch incidental damage is controlled by the rule of proportionality.'[153] He uses as a similar example the civilian truck driver who is driving a military ammunition truck. The driver is a civilian, but the truck is a military objective. When the truck is attacked, the driver will subsequently be viewed as proportionate civilian collateral damage.[154]

As Dill notes, the assertion that the IHL proportionality rule would apply differently to civilians who are within a military objective, and thus choose to be subject to a greater danger than those who stay away, is merely an 'intuition', not a matter of law.[155] An earlier version of the US DoD Manual position on civilians inside an ammunition factory misrepresented this, but this has now been corrected.[156]

[150] This issue led to heated debate during the discussions among the experts. See, for example, Melzer 2005, pp. 21–23. However, according to Schmitt, there is wide agreement that the workers are civilians who are not participating directly in the hostilities. See Schmitt 2008, p. 53. See also Bothe et al., p. 295: '[b]y being within, or in the vicinity of a military objective, these civilians assume the risk of collateral injury from the effects of attack.'

[151] Bouchié de Belle, pp. 896–897.

[152] Henderson, p. 220.

[153] Rogers 2012, p. 12.

[154] Rogers 2012, p. 13.

[155] See Dill 2016 on the Just Security blog: '[i]t is a powerful intuition that what happens to civilians in war should at least to some extent be a result of their own choices. Crucially, this is an intuition about what the law should be, not about what it is. As an intuition about what the law should be, it is deeply misguided.'

[156] See particularly Khalfaoui, pp. 251–303, and Hathaway, Lederman and Schmitt on the Just Security blog.

6.7 WHAT ARE CIVILIAN OBJECTS?

With regard to the scope of the damage included in the IHL proportionality assessment, it may be noted that any 'damage' to civilian objects counts for something, including loss of functionality.[157] As civilian objects are defined as any object that is not a military objective,[158] it is necessary to define what is excluded from the IHL proportionality assessment to determine what is relevant. Only objects that are not military objectives may be included as civilian damage in the proportionality calculation. In short: '[o]nce it is subject to attack, the object itself is not collateral damage.'[159] Therefore, it is instructive to quote the definition of a military objective:

> In so far as objects are concerned, military objectives are limited to those objects which by their nature, location, purpose or use make an effective contribution to military action and whose total or partial destruction, capture or neutralization, in the circumstances ruling at the time, offers a definite military advantage. In case of doubt whether an object which is normally dedicated to civilian purposes, such as a place of worship, a house or other dwelling or a school, is being used to make an effective contribution to military action, it shall be presumed not to be so used.[160]

6.7.1 *Civilian Objects and Military Objectives*

Objects that may be identified as military objectives because of their nature are objects that have an undoubtedly military character, such as military vehicles or platforms (armoured vehicles, fighter jets, attack helicopters). Static examples would include military airfields, military barracks, bunkers or fortresses. As a result of this definition, it may happen that a prima facie civilian object must be included on the military advantage side of the proportionality equation because at the relevant time, its location, purpose or use makes an effective contribution to military action. Objects that may be identified as military objectives because of their location could include strategic points, such as bridges, intersections of important roads or rail tracks, hilltops or mountain passes. These locations could be non-military in character as such but the location of an object in relation to another location could

[157] See International Law Association, pp. 25–26.
[158] Article 52 (1) API.
[159] Henderson, p. 207.
[160] Article 52 (2) and (3) API.

turn a certain object into a military objective nonetheless. Objects that may be identified as military objectives on the basis of their purpose could include objects that could become military objectives because of their intended future use. The intended use of an object is of course difficult to ascertain. Mere potential future use is not sufficient to qualify as a military objective, because there is no concrete military advantage (yet). Only reliable information regarding the future use of an object could be taken into account. A possible example could be the situation where reliable intelligence is available with regard to the intended future military use of a civilian airfield, in a case where the military airfield has been rendered unusable for military aircraft. The intended future use could lead to the conclusion that the civilian airfield becomes a military objective because of its purpose once the military airfield has actually been attacked.[161] Examples of objects that may become military objectives because of their use are civilian objects where combatants or military equipment are located. This could include the use of civilian houses by combatants as shelter, weapons storage, hideouts or shooting positions. Another example could be a school building that is used by military forces as temporary barracks, headquarters or weapons storage.

It is important to stress that there is a fundamental difference between the criteria that render military objectives liable to attack and those that are decisive for persons to be liable for attack, as discussed earlier. For an object to be a military objective it is not only required to have a military nature, location, purpose or use, but in addition, the planned attack must offer a definite military advantage in the circumstances ruling at the time. The test is thus 'two-pronged'. This additional requirement does not exist with regard to individuals: their status as a combatant alone makes them a legitimate military target, to be attacked at all times. The requirement of military advantage is discussed later, because the concept of military advantage is also an important component of the proportionality equation.

It must be noted that the logical result of the two-pronged test for military objectives is that even an object that would be military by nature would count as a civilian object for the purpose of the proportionality assessment in situations where the second prong of the definition of a military objective is not fulfilled. This could potentially lead to the situation in which a military object which is not a military objective, such as a temporarily inoperable tank or empty military barracks, would have to be taken into account as *civilian* collateral damage when a nearby military objective is attacked, unless it is

[161] See Program on Humanitarian Policy and Conflict Research, Harvard University 2009b, pp. 107–108.

known that its purpose fulfils the definition of a military objective. Because that purpose can usually easily be inferred from the circumstances, this situation does not seem to lead to problems in practice. Furthermore, the value that must be attributed to these objects for the protection of the civilian population is arguably zero and therefore they do not count for any real significant counterweight against the military advantage of the destruction of the military objective that is planned to be attacked.

According to the Commentary to the Red Cross Draft Rules of 1956, the terms 'civilian loss' and 'damage' must be interpreted broadly.[162] Therefore, according to this commentary, in case of dual-use objects (such as a train station, cultural object or a school), more weight needs to be attributed in a proportionality calculation to damage to certain important civilian objects, even when the object has become a military objective. This would imply that there are different values to be attributed to civilian objects in the proportionality equation: some types of collateral damage apparently count more than other types. This is supported by the particular rules that apply to some types of civilian objects, such as cultural and religious objects (article 53 API), objects indispensable to the survival of the civilian population (article 54 API) and objects that contain dangerous forces (article 56 API), as well as the example discussed earlier of the inoperable tank and empty military barracks counting marginally as civilian collateral damage.

It is recalled it was rejected that there could be different value categories of civilian individuals. For civilian objects, apparently, some civilian structures are more important than others.[163] This may be illustrated by the example of schools. Schools may be attractive to the military because they could be suitable to be used as barracks.[164] However, the importance of education for children is of high value for the civilian population. This importance in confirmed by recent State practice.[165] Therefore, as compared to shops or a community centre, in some cases more value must be attributed to collateral damage to schools. Similarly, a residential building in which two families are living must be counted for less collateral damage compared to one in which

[162] 'Pertes et destructions infligées à la population civile doivent s'entendre dans un sens très large' (translation by the author). ICRC 1956, p. 701.

[163] See also Henderson, p. 192.

[164] Henderson, p. 207.

[165] See the Safe School Declaration, which declares that '[a]ttacks, and threats of attack, [of schools] can cause severe and long-lasting harm to individuals and societies.' As of 10 November 2020, 106 States have endorsed the Safe School Declaration, see www.regjeringen.no/en/topics/foreign-affairs/development-cooperation/safeschools_declaration/id2460245/. See also the report by Human Rights Watch 2011 on Schools and Armed Conflict.

seven families have their home, assuming similar family sizes. The existence of civilian objects with different values attached to them, does, however, further complicate the proportionality equation, because it is easier to balance equal entities than it is to balance unequal ones, even when they are on the same side of the scale.

With regard to the scope of the notion of incidental civilian damage, the question must be asked whether economic losses and expected displacement of the civilian population also count as collateral damage. In this regard, there is a link with the question of whether reverberating incidental effects must be taken into account. It is submitted that since the applicable standard is that of foreseeability, economic losses and displacement of the civilian population that are foreseeable must indeed be taken into account as civilian damage. It must be emphasised in this respect that it depends on the situation whether these effects are indeed foreseeable for the commander in a specific situation; it is important that the application of the IHL proportionality rule remains realistic. The next section addresses the question of the extent to which damage to the environment must be taken into account in the application of the IHL proportionality rule.

6.7.2 *The Natural Environment as Part of the Proportionality Equation*

A problem in interpreting the component of the natural environment in the proportionality equation is that its interpretation is complicated by the fact that a number of nuclear weapons States are unwilling to accept any rule of IHL that would a priori prohibit the use of these weapons.[166] Outside the scope of nuclear weapons, two major cases on damage to the natural environment as a result of armed conflict pertain to the use of herbicides in the war in Vietnam[167] and the oil spills that occurred during the Gulf Wars in Iraq and Kuwait.[168]

Except in circumstances where a certain part of the natural environment would qualify as a military objective, the natural environment must be

[166] See, for example, Boivin, p. 76, and the discussion in the ICJ Nuclear Weapons Advisory Opinion, p. 226, para. 31.

[167] In fact, Blix argues that the background to the provisions now codified in API 'was the widespread environmental destruction which was brought about during the Indochina war through the use of herbicides, bulldozers and extensive bombardment'. See Blix, p. 149.

[168] Bothe 2007b, p. 237, Schmitt 1997, pp. 9–22 and Dinstein 2001, note 3, p. 524, on the oil spills in the Persian Gulf in 1984 during the war between Iraq and Iran.

deemed to be of a civilian character.[169] In fact, IHL provides for special protection of the natural environment.[170] This includes provisions on the use of certain means and methods of warfare and the rather general statement that '[c]are shall be taken in warfare to protect the natural environment against widespread, long-term and severe damage.'[171] It is worth noting that the provision in article 8 of the Rome Statute that deals with the prohibition of disproportionate attacks in international armed conflicts also mentions 'widespread, long-term and severe damage to the natural environment'.[172]

Although there does not seem to be an agreed definition of the term 'natural environment', it is likely for any substantial attack to have some effect on the natural environment.[173] There seems to be no doubt that the protection of the natural environment should, as a minimum, be taken into account during the planning and executive phases of targeting decisions.[174] According to Koppe, this 'duty of care' (or 'due regard') that is part of article 55 (1) API has developed into customary IHL.[175] The treaty provisions of articles 35 (3) and 55 API were declared part of customary IHL in Rules 43–45 of the ICRC Customary Law Study.[176] However, the customary character of these rules has since been contested.[177] This discussion is reflected in the Commentary on the HPCR Manual on Air and Missile Warfare:

> Some members of the Group of Experts were strongly of the opinion that the protection of the natural environment 'must' be taken into account when planning and conducting air or missile warfare attacks. In their view,

[169] But see Boivin, pp. 74–75, who states that '[t]he principle of proportionality also applies to direct attacks against parts of the environment that have become military objects.' While this is generally correct, the natural environment itself can in that case no longer be part of the civilian side of the equation, since it is liable to direct attack itself.

[170] See articles 35 (3) and 55 of API. See also the ENMOD Convention, that 'prohibits the use of the modified natural environment itself as a weapon (as opposed to damage to the environment, dealt with in API)'. See Program on Humanitarian Policy and Conflict Research, Harvard University 2009b, p. 204.

[171] Article 55 API. The initial proposal of the ban was the clause 'the stability of the ecosystems', but it was deemed insufficiently explicit. See Blix, p. 150.

[172] ICC Statute, article 8(2)(b)(iv). The full provision reads: 'Intentionally launching an attack in the knowledge that such an attack will cause incidental loss of life or injury to civilians or damage to civilian objects or *widespread, long-term and severe damage to the natural environment* which would be clearly excessive in relation to the concrete and direct overall military advantage anticipated' (emphasis added).

[173] See the discussion in Koppe, pp. 165–166.

[174] See for example Dinstein 2001, p. 524, Boivin, p. 74, Koppe, p. 175 and Program on Humanitarian Policy and Conflict Research, Harvard University 2009b, p. 207.

[175] Koppe, pp. 175–177.

[176] Henckaerts and Doswald-Beck 2005a, pp. 143–158.

[177] See, for example, Bothe 2007a, pp. 167–168; Koppe, pp. 170–173.

> expected collateral damage to the environment, if excessive, requires that any missile or missile attack must be aborted. The majority of the Group of Experts reached the conclusion that such a high bar is not mandated by customary international law and that the 'due regard' criterion adequately reflects the state of the law of international armed conflict today.[178]

Yet it seems safe to conclude that the natural environment should be taken into account as part of the collateral side of the proportionality equation, because as such, in principle, the natural environment is a civilian object.[179] However, the value that should be attributed to damage to the natural environment for the purpose of the proportionality calculation does not seem straightforward. It may be argued from the definition of the war crime in the ICC Statute that not any damage to the natural environment should be counted as collateral damage, but only that which is expected to be 'widespread, severe and long-term'. It is notable that for civilians and other civilian objects, there is no such additional requirement. It would imply that damage to the natural environment is not automatically included on the civilian side of the proportionality equation, but only in certain instances, when it is expected that a certain threshold is met, which is that the damage will be sufficiently widespread, severe and long-term. However, given the designation of the natural environment as a civilian object, it is submitted that this interpretation would be incorrect. It is, on the other hand, a reality that the conduct of active hostilities entails consequences for the natural environment. Normally, this damage to the natural environment is not severe enough to add much meaningful weight to the civilian side of the proportionality equation. Yet, if the environmental damage caused by an attack is expected to be disproportionate to the anticipated military advantage, it is still prohibited.[180] When damage to the natural environment is expected, it must be ensured that those means and methods of warfare are chosen that prevent environmental damage as much as possible. Commanders thus particularly need to take expected damage to the natural environment into account when they expect the consequences of a planned attack to be widespread, severe and long-term,

[178] See Program on Humanitarian Policy and Conflict Research, Harvard University 2009b, p. 207.

[179] The natural environment should not be seen as a fully independent entity but rather as a prerequisite for the health and survival of the human population. See also Blix, p. 150. According to Schmitt, 'consensus exists that environmental damage constitutes collateral damage'. See Schmitt 2006a, p. 293. See also Koppe, p. 164; Boivin, p. 74; Henckaerts and Doswald-Beck 2005a, p. 145. See, however, Program on Humanitarian Policy and Conflict Research, Harvard University 2009b, p. 207.

[180] Rogers 2012, p. 234.

because an additional layer of IHL protection needs to be taken into account in that situation. However, as long as the expected damage to the natural environment fails to satisfy the additional requirements, it is taken into account as damage to regular civilian objects. Military commanders must thus assess whether the military objective they plan to attack may be expected to cause grave environmental harm and take that damage into account in the application of the IHL proportionality rule.[181]

6.7.3 *Dual-Use Objects and Proportionality*

'Dual-use object' is as such not a term defined in IHL rules, but it may nonetheless be used to describe objects that are used by both the civilian population and the military.[182] These objects become military objectives as a result of such military use, provided these objects also satisfy the definition of a military objective, including the second prong of that definition. Therefore, these objects lose protection against direct attack as civilian objects. The status of dual-use objects is thus dependent on their concrete use.[183] Examples of dual-use objects include roads, bridges or railroads that are normally used by civilians but are also used during armed conflicts to transport military equipment or personnel. Airports that are simultaneously used by military and civilian aircraft are another example. Some dual-use objects are under certain circumstances essential to both the military and the civilian population, such as oil production facilities, electricity generation facilities and grids.[184] It is important to stress that the mere use of an object simultaneously by civilians and the military is not sufficient to identify it as an object that may be attacked. As becomes clear from the wording of article 52 (2) API, there is an additional requirement. In order to become a legal military objective, it needs to be ascertained that a definite military advantage is to be gained under the circumstances ruling at the time, and subsequently, the proportionality calculation needs to be conducted. Watkin notes that the term dual-use objects is

181 As the ICTY OTP Kosovo report notes: '[i]n order to satisfy the requirement of proportionality, attacks against military targets which are known or can reasonably be assumed to cause grave environmental harm may need to confer a very substantial military advantage in order to be considered legitimate. At a minimum, actions resulting in massive environmental destruction, especially where they do not serve a clear and important military purpose, would be questionable.' See International Tribunal for the former Yugoslavia, Office of the Prosecutor, para. 22.

182 Sassòli and Cameron, p. 57.

183 Kolb and Hyde, p. 132, see also Benvenuti, p. 516 and Sassòli and Cameron, pp. 57–58.

184 See Watkin 2007, p. 16; Dörmann 2008, p. 87.

problematic because the term masks the fact that an object is either a valid military target, or a civilian object that is not liable for attack.[185] It seems that the special characteristic of a dual-use object is that if it is attacked, it 'inevitably affects the civilian population'[186] and the collateral civilian damage is thus inherent.[187] Dual-use objects may thus 'change sides' in the proportionality equation as soon as the military starts using them or weigh in partly on both sides of the proportionality equation. This last point does not seem straightforward because it means that even though a certain object has been identified as a military objective, it nonetheless also counts partly on the civilian side of the proportionality equation.

It is clear that the simultaneous use by civilians and the military of a dual-use object will put a larger burden on the attacker. The military advantage that may be gained must be sufficiently significant in order to prevent the attack from being disproportionate. Especially when there are many civilians present in the vicinity of the object, additional precautionary measures may be necessary. As long as the object is still also used by civilians, the remaining civilian characteristics should not be discounted altogether on the civilian side of the equation.[188] The object itself has lost its protection from direct attack, but 'the loss of the civilian function also performed by that object cannot be allowed to disappear from all calculations as if it had never been performed'.[189] The following example may illustrate how this may be dealt with in practice.

Suppose during an armed conflict a section of a large bridge crossing a big river is used as cover for a military objective, such as a surface-to-surface multiple launch rocket system (MLRS) and its crew. The bridge is therefore now used for a clear military purpose, and makes an effective contribution to the military action because it is expected to be used in the ongoing struggle between the parties to the conflict. The bridge is normally used for civilian purposes and therefore it would be a civilian object if the MLRS was not hidden underneath. It is clear that possible harm to civilians as they happened to be driving their car over the bridge at the time of the attack on the MLRS may be foreseen and must thus be taken into account as incidental damage.

185 Watkin 2007, p. 16.

186 Dörmann 2008, p. 87.

187 Sandoz 2002, p. 273: '[t]he attack on a dual-use object can be considered as the attack on a military objective with collateral damages.'

188 Dörmann 2008, p. 87: '[t]he civilian part of the object affected by the attack, including foreseeable reverberating effects, must be counted among the incidental civilian damage in addition to the possible civilian damage to civilian property in the vicinity.'

189 Shue and Wippmann, p. 565.

The question now is whether the damage to the bridge itself and the indirect effects this may have on the civilian population must also be taken into account as incidental civilian damage. It seems to this author that because of the use of the bridge as cover for the MLRS, that particular section of the bridge has lost its protection as a civilian object. That is not to say that the entire bridge has now become a military objective, but the section that serves to hide the MLRS has and therefore it has lost its protection as a civilian object. As a result, the direct damage done to the bridge when planning the attack on the MLRS should not be taken into account as incidental civilian damage. However, foreseeable indirect effects the attack on the bridge may have for the civilian population, depending on the circumstances ruling at the time, must be taken into account.

It may be noted that the solution as proposed in this section is also of use for cultural objects that have become military objectives, because it would enable, if not require, the attacking side to take the cultural value of a military objective into account.[190]

6.8 COMBATANTS *HORS DE COMBAT* AND OTHER PROTECTED PERSONS AND OBJECTS

The two previous sections address the civilian side of the proportionality equation. The text of the IHL proportionality rule is clear. Civilians, including those who are wounded, sick or detained, as well as civilian objects are incorporated into the proportionality equation on the basis of their civilian status. Excluded are civilians who participate directly in hostilities, because they have lost their protection against direct attack for such time as they directly participate. Nonetheless, one may wonder whether other categories of persons and objects specifically protected by the rules of IHL must also be taken into account in the application of the IHL proportionality rule, on the basis of that protection and because these are as such also exempted from direct attack.

The first example of such persons is the category of combatants or fighters *hors de combat*, such as wounded, sick, shipwrecked and captured soldiers. Just like civilians, they may (no longer) be attacked. The question may be raised whether these persons must therefore also be included in the civilian side of the IHL proportionality equation despite their status as members of the military. Secondly, the same question may be asked for military medical

[190] See the discussion in the Chatham House Report on proportionality, Gillard, p. 35.

personnel and military chaplains, because they are not combatants, although they are clearly not civilians either.[191] Similar questions may arise with regard to specifically protected objects, such as military medical installations and holding facilities for prisoners of war or detained opponents. It must be noted that there are absolute protections in the Geneva Conventions prohibiting the direct attack of these objects. Nonetheless, it is unclear to what extent they must be included in the IHL proportionality assessment if they are expected to be affected by a planned attack on a military objective.

The text of the IHL proportionality rule is clear and refers only to civilians and civilian objects. Thus, applying the most common method of interpretation of treaty provisions, that of the ordinary meaning of the terms, would imply that only civilians and civilian objects are included.[192] Furthermore, looking at the object and purpose of the text, the articles containing the IHL proportionality rule are placed in part IV of API, which has as its topic the 'Civilian population'. The protection of medical personnel is covered in part II of API ('Wounded, sick and shipwrecked'), and the rules regarding combatants in part III of API ('Methods and means of warfare – Combatant and prisoner-of-war status'). A logical inference thus seems to be that the decisive criterion according to the proportionality equation is the question of whether the person or object is of a civilian character.[193] As noted earlier, civilians are defined as any person who does not fit into the categories of article 4 (A) (1), (2), (3) or (6) of GCIII and article 43 API.[194] Damage to military medical objects, and injury and loss of life to medical military personnel, military chaplains and military personnel *hors de combat* thus seem prima facie excluded from the proportionality equation, because they are not of a civilian character and not included in the categories referred to in the previous sentence. However, the purpose of the protective articles in API is clearly to also provide strong protection to the other categories of protected persons and

[191] See generally also Gisel, pp. 215–230.

[192] See article 31 (1) of the 1969 Vienna Convention on the Law of Treaties: '[a] treaty shall be interpreted in good faith in accordance with the ordinary meaning to be given to the terms of the treaty in their context and in the light of its object and purpose.'

[193] Henderson, p. 206. However, during an expert meeting on the principle of proportionality on 27 October 2018 in Chatham House, London, one expert noted that not too much weight should be attached to the placement of the IHL proportionality rule in this part of API, because this was not viewed as decisive during the drafting of the rules.

[194] As phrased in the ICRC Interpretative Guidance on DPIH: '[f]or the purposes of the principle of distinction in international armed conflict, all persons who are neither members of the armed forces of a party to the conflict nor participants in a *levée en masse* are civilians and, therefore, entitled to protection against direct attack unless and for such time as they take a direct part in hostilities.' See Melzer 2009, p. 20.

objects. The 2016 update of the US Department of Defense Manual explicitly excludes non-civilians from the proportionality rule and instead refers to the obligation to take precautionary measures for the protection of non-civilian protected persons and objects.[195] In academic doctrine, Henderson and Merriam, among others, make the point that only civilians are part of the IHL proportionality equation.[196]

However, other modes of interpretation of treaty obligations are available, such as the assessment of subsequent practice in the application of the treaty, which establishes the agreement of the parties regarding its interpretation and the existence of other relevant rules of international law applicable in the relations between the parties.[197] With regard to the latter, it is noted that these categories of persons and objects enjoy strong protection under IHL, not only in the specific rules,[198] but also in the obligations concerning precautions in attack.[199] According to Fleck, this protection 'goes beyond' the protection of civilians under the IHL proportionality rule.[200]

Including other protected persons and objects in the civilian side of the equation would presumably increase their protection, a result that would be in accordance with many well-established rules and principles of IHL. A situation may, for example, be envisaged where a legitimate military objective, such as military equipment of high importance,[201] is located adjacent to a medical unit where many wounded soldiers and their carers are present. Of course, medical installations and equipment enjoy a high degree of protection,[202] and the presence of a military objective adjacent to it may under the circumstances be a violation of IHL. Is the military commander who is planning an attack on the military equipment required to include the persons

195 See DOD Manual, para. 7.3.3.1 on pp. 441 and 442: '[t]he respect and protection due to the wounded, sick, and shipwrecked do not prohibit incidental damage or casualties due to their proximity to military objectives or to a justifiable mistake. Combatants who are wounded, sick, or shipwrecked on the battlefield are deemed to have accepted the risk of death or further injury due to their proximity to military operations.'

196 Henderson, p. 206, and generally Merriam on the Just Security blog.

197 Article 31 (3) (b) and (c) of the 1969 Vienna Convention on the Law of Treaties.

198 International Law Association, p. 27. See, for example, for wounded and combatants, article 12 (1) GCI: '[m]embers of the armed forces ... shall be respected and protected in all circumstances.'

199 Article 57 (2) (a) (ii) API.

200 Gasser and Dörmann, p. 246. However, it must be noted that this rule is subject to a 'feasibility' qualifier.

201 For example, an anti-aircraft installation.

202 See articles 21 and 22 of GCI. Particularly, their protection against direct attack is absolute and not to be lifted unless they are used to commit acts harmful to the enemy and a warning to stop those acts is ignored.

present near the military objective into his proportionality assessment? Is there an additional, separate, proportionality obligation for non-civilian protected persons and objects military commanders must apply? Or are these categories of persons simply ignored in the application of the IHL proportionality rule when attacking the military objective? This last conclusion seems to contradict the protection provided to these categories of protected persons and objects.[203]

There is some State practice that indicates that protected persons or objects other than civilian ones are included in the proportionality equation. For example, the Military Manual of New Zealand refers to the 'possible harmful effects upon protected persons and objects'.[204] Similarly, the ICRC argues in the updated Commentary to GCI in favour of the inclusion of wounded members of the armed forces into the IHL proportionality equation.[205] In doctrine, the position to include protected persons other than civilians into the proportionality analysis is posited by a number of authors.[206]

Civilians who are directly participating in the hostilities do not count as incidental casualties during their direct participation, but once they have

[203] As Clarke notes, this result would be ridiculous'. See Clarke, p. 107.

[204] See ICRC Customary Law Study, Practice (Volume II, Part I), Henckaerts and Doswald-Beck 2005b, p. 302. See also International Law Association, note 97 on p. 28.

[205] 2016 updated ICRC Commentary to GCI, para. 1357:

> [i]n view of the specific protections accorded to the wounded and sick, namely the obligation to respect (and to protect) them in all circumstances, a fortiori they should also benefit from the protection accorded to civilians. In other words, if civilians are to be included in the proportionality assessment all the more so should the wounded and sick. Indeed, if the wounded and sick were not to be considered for purposes of the proportionality principle, their presence in the vicinity of legitimate military objectives would be legally irrelevant. However, this would contradict the explicit obligation to respect them in all circumstances and the basic rationale of according special protection to them. It would be unreasonable to consider that direct or indiscriminate attacks against the wounded and sick would be strictly prohibited and would amount to a grave breach, while incidental harm and even excessive incidental casualties would not be prohibited. Accordingly, the presence of wounded and sick members of the armed forces in the vicinity of a military objective is to be taken into consideration when carrying out a proportionality assessment prior to an attack. In addition, and on the basis of the same rationale, an attacker must take precautions in accordance with Article 57 of Additional Protocol I in relation not only to civilians but also to wounded and sick members of the armed forces, to protect them from direct attack and collateral damage.

[206] See International Law Association, pp. 27–28; Bartels 2013, p. 304; Corn and Culliver; Gisel; and Kleffner 2017. Note, however, that except for Bartels and Culliver, the other authors, including the present author, were part of the ILA Study Group responsible for drafting the ILA Report. See also the San Remo Manual on International Law Applicable to Armed Conflicts at Sea, para. 13.9.

become wounded, they are always included in the proportionality assessment for the purpose of a planned attack on another military objective in their proximity. The first reason for this is the fact that they never lose their status as a civilian for the purpose of their treatment after they are captured, but that only the accompanying protection against direct attack is suspended until their participation has ended. Secondly, it may be assumed that the direct participation in the hostilities of the civilians has indeed ended as soon as they are *hors de combat*. As a result, civilians who were directly participating but are now *hors de combat* are included in the proportionality calculation. To exclude those permanently participating in the hostilities thus seems to imply that their protection is lower after they are rendered *hors de combat*, even though there are no reasons of military necessity to justify this.

Medical personnel generally enjoy a higher level of protection than 'ordinary' civilians.[207] For medical personnel, there are no convincing reasons that explain why civilian medical personal would factor into the proportionality equation, and military medical personnel would not. In practice, their tasks are mostly identical. The only relevant differences between the two categories of persons are that the institution that pays their wages differs and that military medical personnel may be armed with small arms for self-defence purposes. Moreover, it seems impossible in practice to take the differences in protection into account when a medical installation that is expected to be affected by an attack on a nearby located military objective contains both wounded civilians and wounded combatants, and both military and civilian medical personnel. As for prisoners of war, there are a number of categories that are also protected as civilians, such as civilian persons who accompany the armed forces without actually being members thereof and crews of civilian aircraft.[208] Depriving these of their protection as civilians under the IHL proportionality rule is in clear contradiction to the purpose of their protection as prisoners of war. Excluding these civilian POWs from their protection as civilians under the IHL proportionality rule would therefore be both illogical and inconsistent.

It is submitted that the protection under IHL of persons *hors de combat*, medical personnel and protected objects is simply too strong to ignore this category of persons and objects altogether in the application of the IHL

[207] Dinstein 2016, p. 160: '[a] dozen civilians dining in a restaurant do not weigh as much a dozen patients and doctors in an infirmary. Otherwise, what is the real meaning of the special protection accorded to the latter?'

[208] Article 4A (4) and (5) GCIII.

proportionality rule. A number of legal bases for this conclusion have been suggested in doctrine, including the specific articles that provide specific protection to the different categories of persons and objects, assimilation into the categories of 'civilians and civilian objects' as included in the IHL proportionality rule and the invocation of the Martens Clause and general principles of IHL.[209]

There are also approaches excluding the categories of protected persons and objects from the IHL proportionality assessment. Corn and Culliver note, for example, that in practice members of the armed forces cannot be required to constantly take into account whether earlier attacks resulted in wounded opponents. It is submitted that this approach is unconvincing, because it confuses the principle of the proportionality calculation during such a situation with the actual outcome of the equation. In the example used to illustrate the issue, Corn and Culliver state that it is incompatible with the attack on entrenched Iraqi forces that are about to be enforced by other forces to take the wounded into account.[210] It is submitted that the wounded must nonetheless be taken into account and balanced against the military aim of decisively destroying the military objective. This does not necessarily 'require the US commander to postpone a subsequent attack decision in order to first conduct a proportionality assessment to protect the wounded Iraqi soldiers and military personnel in the target area'. In this example, the proportionality assessment can be done on the spot and does not need to take hours, given the direct and concrete military advantage that is at stake. Furthermore, (additional) wounding or killing enemies *hors de combat* and military medical personnel does not offer any military advantage. If anything, in the long run, affecting them will turn into a disadvantage for all parties to the conflict. After all, it is detrimental to the protection of their own military personnel *hors de combat* and medical personnel if massive numbers of protected persons are killed during an attack on an otherwise legitimate military objective. As far as medical personnel are concerned, it may be added that both attackers and defenders would benefit from their work and therefore causing injury or death to them during an attack on a legitimate military objective is disadvantageous from an operational point of view.

With regard to objects, Gisel makes the point that the category of civilian objects consists of all objects that do not meet the definition of a military objective. Since this definition for objects is two-pronged, in contrast to the

[209] See specifically: Gisel, pp. 221–226, Corn and Culliver, pp. 464–466 and Kleffner 2017.

[210] Corn and Culliver, pp. 456–457.

definition of combatants and members of an NSAG with a continuous combat function, the *military* medical installations and arguably also *military* detention facilities for detained opponent fighters must be designated as civilian objects. For this reason, they are covered by the protection of the IHL proportionality rule.[211] This seems confusing, given the fact that these objects are certainly 'military' in the ordinary meaning of the term. Nonetheless, it is submitted that these objects must be included in the proportionality assessment nonetheless, treating them in the same way as civilian objects (using the word civilian in its ordinary meaning).

In the end, it is not the status of a person or object that invokes their protection by the IHL proportionality rule, but the protection it enjoys at the moment an attack is planned or executed. Any person or object enjoying protection against direct attack, as can be reasonably foreseeable for the attacker, must be included on the civilian, or protective, side of the proportionality assessment. It is submitted that as a minimum, this is also what any reasonable military commander would do on the basis of common sense.[212] The legal basis for this conclusion is the respective specific protectionary rules of IHL, reinforced by the IHL principle of precautions and a broader IHL proportionality principle (as opposed to the IHL proportionality rule).[213] This protection may be attained in three ways. First, one could argue that a separate proportionality obligation applies for non-civilian protected persons and objects. Second, one could interpret the terms in the treaty rules of 'loss of civilian life, injury to civilians, damage to civilian objects or a combination thereof' in a broader way, including other protected persons and objects. Thirdly, one may argue that these categories are included in the customary IHL proportionality rule, which is then understood as broader than the treaty rules containing the IHL proportionality rule.[214] It is submitted that this third option is to be preferred.

[211] Gisel, pp. 219–220.

[212] According to Merriam, the US CDE methodology does take specifically protected persons and objects into account: '[a]t least in the US, our collateral damage estimation process requires us to consider not only civilians, but also other specially protected persons or objects. But that collateral damage methodology is a process, which is not the same thing as a position on the law.' See Merriam. See also Scott Adams, discussing policy restrictions beyond the requirements of IHL: https://harvardnsj.org/2017/08/lancelot-in-the-sky-protecting-wounded-combatants-from-incidental-harm/

[213] Here, the positions of Corn and Culliver, based on the Martens Clause, and Kleffner 2017, based on the general principles of IHL, seem to be in agreement with each other and congruent with the position taken in this book.

[214] See also Sari and Tinkler.

6.9 HOW TO EVALUATE A 'COMBINATION' OF INCIDENTAL LOSS OF CIVILIAN LIFE, INJURY TO CIVILIANS AND DAMAGE TO CIVILIAN OBJECTS

Having analysed which civilian individuals and objects must be taken into account in the proportionality calculation, the next question is how the 'combination' of incidental loss of civilian life, injury to civilians and damage to civilian objects should be calculated. Even though the IHL proportionality rule is not a mathematical formula, it seems safe to conclude that at least to determine the absolute total amount of direct collateral damage, a simple sum of the totals of expected casualties and total damage to civilian objects could be calculated. It may be more difficult to compare the relative totals of collateral damage when different means and methods of attack may be used in an attack. This would necessitate the assessment of the relative value of the components of the expected collateral damage. It may be more difficult to put foreseeable indirect effects into concrete numbers.

It has been suggested that the value of the damage to civilian objects should be discounted.[215] The rationale of this approach seems to be that in both the statements of States and the media, the emphasis is always on human casualties, not on destroyed civilian property. Although it seems correct that this emphasis is prevalent, it is submitted that this does not imply that there is no legal obligation to include civilian objects in the proportionality calculation. It rather indicates that civilian casualties should be counted more than damage to civilian objects. It is submitted that this is indeed the way the two components of civilian harm must be interpreted, but this is not unlimited. In particular, when some objects are indispensable for the survival of the civilian population in a particular area, or when it may be expected to contain dangerous forces leading to more foreseeable civilian death and injury, arguably, more weight must be attached to the object than to civilians who are expected to be affected by the attack directly.

Obviously, injury is normally less severe than death, since one still has a chance of recovery, which may be assessed on the basis of recognised medical

[215] Watkin 2007, p. 13. See also Parks 1997, pp. 97–98: '[t]he record of concern for collateral damage to enemy civilian property is virtually nonexistent, suggesting that the pairing up of protection for lives and property in Additional Protocol I may not even see application in future conflicts.'

criteria. Yet, the IHL principle prohibiting serious injury or unnecessary suffering (the SIRUS principle) paradoxically points in a different direction. The SIRUS principle dictates that some types of weapon and methods of warfare are prohibited under IHL because the injury they cause is deemed to be superfluous and the suffering this causes unnecessary. This principle leads to the effect that sometimes a certain non-lethal weapon may not be employed against the adversary, because it is outlawed through the application of the SIRUS principle, such as permanently blinding laser weapons. Thus, instead, a kinetic means or methods of warfare must be employed, leading to more civilian collateral damage. However, paradoxical as this may seem, it is the legal reality military commanders have to deal with in the conduct of operations. Military commanders are generally used to being guided in their actions by the law and additional restraints such as rules of engagement.

With regard to civilian objects, it may be argued that it is too simple to qualify damage to civilian objects only in the monetary value of rebuilding the object. After all, the destruction of some civilian objects is less severe than that of others. The destruction of civilian objects that are indispensable for the survival of the civilian population is placed in a more important category by the Geneva Conventions.[216] In addition, the collateral destruction of a modern shopping mall, it could be argued, is not such a great loss as the destruction of unique and irreplaceable cultural property would be. As an example, one could compare the loss of a modern shopping mall to the destruction of the ancient Buddhas of Bamiyan by the Taliban government of Afghanistan in 2001.

Another question is how injury to civilians and loss of civilian life may be valued as compared to damage to civilian objects in the longer term. It would seem, as noted earlier, that loss of civilian life is always more severe than damage to an object. This may, however, change if the expected damage to the civilian object will inevitably lead to significant loss of civilian lives in the long term. There is unfortunately no universally accepted method of measurement available to solve this issue and the situation is very different for every single attack. It will be a separate evaluation for every attack that is planned or executed. It is therefore impossible to provide more clarity for this component of the equation other than flagging the issue and add that the sum of all expected civilian damage, injury and casualties must be taken into account. It must be left to the discretion of the military commander to evaluate how the combination calculation must be executed for a future planned attack.

[216] See article 54 API.

6.10 THE MILITARY ADVANTAGE SIDE

The concept of 'military advantage' is both part of the proportionality equation as an important component in itself and as part of the definition of a military objective, which also dictates whether an object is a civilian object. The meaning of the phrase 'military advantage' for the determination of an object to be a military objective is, however, not necessarily identical to the definition of the military advantage that needs to be factored into the proportionality analysis.[217] For example, in the latter case, the security of the attacking force may be taken into account, as is discussed subsequently in this chapter. This is not the case for the determination of whether the destruction of a military objective leads to a definite military advantage. Obviously, for the identification of an object as a military objective, there is no assessment required of the civilian damage that may occur in the destruction of that object, because this is part of the proportionality equation that will need to be conducted in the next phase of the targeting cycle. The threshold for the concept of military advantage for the purpose of identifying a military objective, it is submitted, is thus rather low. This type of military advantage may be defined as 'any consequence of an attack which directly enhances friendly military operations or hinders those of the enemy' under the circumstances ruling at the time.[218] It must be borne in mind, however, that the question of whether this military objective may actually be attacked is subject to additional requirements, such as the precautionary measures and proportionality assessment. Therefore, the appreciation of the military advantage that will arise from a certain attack says nothing in itself, because it depends on the counterweight of the expected collateral damage whether it is sufficient to execute the attack

It is also important to note that the notion of 'military advantage' does not equate to 'military necessity'.[219] The mere fact that an attack may result in some type of military advantage does not in itself mean that an attack is militarily necessary. The mere fact that something *could* be attacked does not mean that it *must* be attacked.

6.10.1 *Concrete and Direct Military Advantage*

The IHL proportionality rule puts the additional qualifiers of 'concrete', 'direct' and 'military' to the assessment of the advantage of an attack. These

217 Contra: Watkin 2007, p. 18.
218 Program on Humanitarian Policy and Conflict Research, Harvard University 2009b, p. 45.
219 See generally Redse Johansen, pp. 271–308.

qualifiers clearly place extra limitations on the extent to which effects of a planned attack may be factored into the IHL proportionality assessment. These factors imply that there must be a measurable effect[220] with a 'close connection between the action and the attainment of the military purpose'.[221] Clear examples of militarily advantageous results that may be expected from an attack are the ground that is conquered by the attack or the effect on the opposing forces, both in terms of casualties and damage to the objects and installations of the enemy.[222] However, military advantage may be deemed to be somewhat broader.[223]

A definition of military advantage that may be included in the proportionality equation is formulated in Rule 1 (w) of the HCPR Air and Missile Warfare Manual: '"Military advantage" means those benefits of a military nature that result from an attack. They relate to the attack considered as a whole and not merely to isolated or particular parts of the attack.' This military advantage must be sufficiently tangible: '[t]he advantage concerned should be substantial and relatively close.'[224] It cannot be 'based merely on hope or speculation'.[225] Military advantage cannot include advantage that is only political, psychological, economic, financial, social or moral in nature.[226] There is no debate on the fact that the notion of military advantage is comprised of a wide range of tactical gains and military considerations. Furthermore, the components of that military advantage 'need not necessarily derive from the destruction of the specific object under attack [but] may be considered cumulatively'.[227] Military advantageous effects may be valued in terms of importance (strategic, operational or tactical advantage) and in terms of urgency (urgent advantage, moderate advantage, distant advantage). Whether the terms 'concrete and direct' call for a single 'causal step' approach or rather must be defined in terms of a temporal link is debatable and depends highly on the type of military objective subject to attack. There is no single formula outlining how the concrete and direct military advantage must be evaluated in relation to the underlying plan, or commander's intent. However, an authoritative interpretation is found in the elements of crimes explaining the meaning of the 'overall' military advantage as included in

220 Watkin 2007, p. 22.
221 Hampson 1992, p. 47.
222 Sandoz et al., para. 2218, p. 685.
223 Watkin 2007, p. 19; Geiss 2012, p. 77.
224 Sandoz et al., para. 2209, p. 684.
225 Program on Humanitarian Policy and Conflict Research, Harvard University 2009b, p. 92.
226 Program on Humanitarian Policy and Conflict Research, Harvard University 2009b, p. 45.
227 Geiss 2012, p. 77.

article 8 (2) (b) (iv) of the Rome Statute of the International Criminal Court. It refers to '[a] military advantage that is foreseeable by the perpetrator at the relevant time. Such advantage may or may not be temporally or geographically related to the object of the attack.'[228] Finally, it needs to be emphasised that the probability of success of a planned attack plays a role in the proportionality equation: the probability of a high military advantage may not result in a reckless attack.

The ultimate limit to military advantage is that military advantage cannot be attributed to damage to civilian objects and civilian casualties. This is why the morale of the civilian population cannot be deemed to amount to a military advantage.[229] Military advantage may, however, be derived from the blockade of a transportation route or a communication line. These types of object may often be 'dual-use' objects. Therefore, the military advantage that is achieved by attacking these objects also determines whether the objects qualify as military objects in the first place. Similarly, the military advantage that results from attacking objects that support the economic sustainability of the enemy may only become part of the military advantage if the armed conflict has developed into a situation where it is expected to become a conflict that will stretch over a longer period of time. If not, economic targets must be deemed to be insufficiently 'military' to be part of the military advantage of a planned attack and the military advantage that is thus attained is too indirect to be included in the proportionality calculus.

For some types of military operation, such as counter-insurgency operations, the military advantage also consists in part of protecting the civilian population against the dangers of attacks. In this type of operation, attacking an enemy may be dependent not only on its status as a targetable individual, but also on 'how much harm the targeted insurgent could do if allowed to escape.'[230] It could thus also be the conduct, not just the status of the individual, that must be taken into account in this specific type of operation.

6.10.2 *The 'Overall' Military Advantage*

It is controversial to what extent the military advantage from an attack should be limited to the tactical level of one isolated attack, or if it must be regarded

[228] Dörmann 2003a, p. 161.

[229] On this subject, see for example Sassòli and Cameron's discussion of Dunlap's and Meyers' proposal to include civilian objects in the list of legitimate military objectives, Sassòli and Cameron, pp. 59–62. See also Parks 1997, pp. 77–84.

[230] Wright, p. 845.

as part of a larger attack. As a result of the negotiations for the formulation of the definition of war crime of article 8 (2) (b) (iv) of the ICC Statute, the adjective 'overall' was added to the concrete and direct military advantage, because it was deemed that this was now customary law.[231] The ICRC has, however, argued that adding the word 'overall' to the definition of the crime 'could not be interpreted as changing existing law'.[232] The ICRC explained that if 'overall' indicates that with regard to a certain military objective, the importance of the military advantage extends a lengthy period of time and affects military action in areas other than in the direct vicinity of the objective, then 'this meaning is included in the existing wording of Additional Protocol I and the inclusion of the word "overall" is redundant'.[233]

The conclusion of Section 6.2 of this chapter may be recalled, which is that the proportionality assessment, including the assessment of the military advantage, must be done at all levels of authority (strategic, operational and tactical), with the exception that a proportionality assessment on a tactical level does not need to be repeated if it has been done previously on the operational level in a situation in which three conditions are fulfilled: when the tactical operations are (1) part of a pre-existing plan on the operational level; and (2) the tactical commander is aware of the fact that he will encounter a certain degree of prima facie excessive collateral damage; and (3) the situation as it becomes apparent to the tactical commander in the course of the execution of the operation is as expected in the planning phase.

6.10.3 *Military Advantage and Force Preservation*

The proportionality equation is meant as a protective rule for the sake of the civilian population, in particular that of the adversary.[234] Thus it may be assumed that it has not developed because there is a need to protect one's own forces. For this reason, it seems cynical at first glance to include the responsibility for a commander to protect the life of his own soldiers in the IHL proportionality equation when attacking a military objective. It seems to

[231] Dörmann 2003a, p. 169.

[232] Henckaerts and Doswald-Beck 2005a, p. 50, referring to the ICRC Paper submitted to the Working Group on Elements of Crimes of the Preparatory Commission for the International Criminal Court.

[233] Roscini, p. 422.

[234] See, for example, Krüger-Sprengel, p. 181: 'La règle de proportionnalité n'a pas pour objet de faciliter les operations de guerre, mais d'en limiter les effets nuisibles': 'The purpose of the rule of proportionality is not to facilitate military operations during armed conflict, but to limit its damaging effects' (translation by the author).

deny the very basis of the IHL proportionality rule, which aims to protect civilians. In general terms, one would therefore assume that the definition of military advantage in the proportionality equation regards the damage that is done to the fighting capacity of the adversary, not the capacity of one's own forces. This does not mean that military commanders must disregard the lives of their own soldiers, or that they have no rights at all. The omnipresent balance between military necessity and humanity in IHL argues against that. One could, however, argue that the IHL proportionality rule is a clash between the right to life of the civilians of the adversary, and that of the soldier. Put in those simple terms, it would seem based on the rationale of IHL that the right to life of the civilians of the adversary should be more unconditional than the competing right of the soldiers of one's own military. Indeed, the belligerent privilege to participate in hostilities comes with the inescapable fact that soldiers may also be wounded or killed in combat. The protection of soldiers is framed in different rules, such as those based on the SIRUS principle prohibiting superfluous injury and unnecessary suffering. When commanders conclude that a planned attack could be executed in accordance with the IHL proportionality rule, but a large number of their own soldiers may be expected to become casualties in the course of the operation, commanders may simply decide to cancel or postpone the planned attack to preserve the lives of their own soldiers. International humanitarian law does not oblige them to do so, but nor does IHL prohibit it. International humanitarian law does, on the other hand, prohibit proceeding with an operation when the expected civilian collateral damage would be disproportionate.

Yet, both doctrine and State practice show that the proportionality equation is in fact influenced by the responsibility that is put upon a commander to protect the lives of his own soldiers. In the words of a US Army general: 'commanders are morally responsible not to waste lives of their soldiers because they are charged to protect soldiers' right to life'.[235] This is a factor that may be regarded as part of the military advantage that is to be gained. After all, it is militarily advantageous to military commanders not to lose soldiers in combat, because it will negatively influence the morale of their soldiers, and they will have fewer men to fight the next battle. This applies equally to military equipment that may be lost in an attack. Thus, when identifying a military objective, the commander will take the question into account whether the military advantage is sufficiently significant to justify the danger

[235] Major General James M. Dubik in 1982, quoted by McPherson, p. 89.

that his troops and equipment will be subjected to when the attack would be executed.

Canada, New Zealand and Australia declared upon ratification of API that they view the protection of the attacking forces as part of the military advantage that could be gained from an attack.[236] In Operation Allied Force in Kosovo, the concept of 'zero casualty warfare' was defended, that is in that operation the aim was that no casualties were to be suffered on the side of the NATO armed forces.[237] The Prosecutor of the ICTY deemed it to be one of the most difficult and yet unresolved questions surrounding the application of the IHL proportionality rule. As noted in the Final Report on Operation Allied Force:

> there is nothing inherently unlawful about flying above the height which can be reached by enemy air defences. However, NATO air commanders have a duty to take practicable measures to distinguish military objectives from civilians or civilian objectives. The 15,000 feet minimum altitude adopted for part of the campaign may have meant the target could not be verified with the naked eye. However, it appears that with the use of modern technology, the obligation to distinguish was effectively carried out in the vast majority of cases during the bombing campaign.[238]

Also, there are notable authors suggesting the inclusion of the protection of one's own forces in the assessment of military advantage for the purpose of the application of the IHL proportionality rule.[239] Others note that '[t]he security of the attacking forces is a factor that must be weighed in the balance when assessing military advantage'[240] and 'in an effort to improve security of the attacking force, increased collateral damage is permissible'.[241] Schmitt acknowledges that '[s]urvival is a valid factor in the assessment', adding that the protection of one's own forces is particularly a question of precautions.[242] Survival of one's own troops would then be a valid factor in the assessment of

236 See, for example, Canada's Declaration, at https://ihl-databases.icrc.org/applic/ihl/ihl.nsf/Notification.xsp?action=openDocument&documentId=172FFEC04ADC80F2C1256402003FB314.

237 For a general discussion of the concept of 'zero-casualty warfare', see Rogers 2000.

238 International Tribunal for the former Yugoslavia, Office of the Prosecutor, para. 56.

239 See, for example, Dinstein 2010, p. 141 and Henderson, p. 205. See also Henderson and Cavanagh, pp. 73–94 and The Commander's Handbook on the Law of Naval Operations, para. 8.3.1: 'Naval commanders must take all reasonable precautions, taking into account military and humanitarian considerations, to keep civilian casualties and damage to the minimum consistent with mission accomplishment and the security of the force.'

240 United Nations General Assembly 2009, p. 39.

241 Henderson, p. 205.

242 Schmitt 2006a, pp. 297–298.

the proportionality equation but only when 'collateral damage and incidental injury are excessive . . . one must further factor in the military advantage that is inherent in combatant and weapon survival'.[243] An example is the circumstances under which it may not be possible to give an 'effective advance warning' because of the safety of the attacking force. In the situation of the US 'Linebacker II' air raids on Vietnam in 1972, '[g]iven the extremely heavy air defenses surrounding Hanoi during the campaign, circumstances obviously did not permit warning the Vietnamese civilians before each raid.'[244]

On the other hand, a number of writers discount own casualties in the proportionality equation.[245] As an example, Fenrick notes that one's casualties among one's own forces conducting the attack may not be calculated in the analysis of the military advantage that will be gained.[246] Geiss concludes that the safety of the attacking force must be seen as part of the military advantage, but that the real issue is whether that military advantage is sufficiently concrete and direct.[247] He states that 'the overall aim of protecting one's own forces would indeed be too abstract to be considered'; however, if the planned attack 'will prevent the imminent annihilation' of the attacking forces, the military advantage of their protection seems to be sufficiently concrete and direct.[248] The requirement that there must indeed be 'imminent annihilation' at stake seems to be overly strict. It is submitted that in the event that significant losses are expected, this also may be factored into the expected military advantage. There is a limit to this: '[t]he focus must be on the forces that are in fact being protected, and the maximum value that may be considered when conducting a proportionality assessment is the relative military value of these forces.'[249] However, when there is a choice between different modes of attack, and the mode of attack that saves most lives of the attacking forces is chosen, this in itself does not allow for factoring in the possible losses that would have accrued from the mode of attack that was not chosen. Since that attack never happened, the military advantage of the safety of the attacking troops was in that case never sufficiently concrete and direct to be included in the proportionality equation.[250]

In conclusion, even though it seems counterintuitive and the protection of the attacking forces was never the basis of the IHL proportionality rule, in reality, the safety of the attacking forces is included in the calculation of the

[243] Schmitt 2006a, p. 298.
[244] Carnahan, p. 866.
[245] See the discussion in Geiss 2012, pp. 73 and 74, referring to Fenrick, Solis and Oeter.
[246] Fenrick 2000, p. 78.
[247] Geiss 2012, p. 79.
[248] Geiss 2012, pp. 81–82.
[249] Geiss 2012, p. 86.
[250] Geiss 2012, pp. 87–88.

military advantage that may be achieved by an attack. However, the view of Geiss must be accepted that the advantage must be particularly concrete and direct. It may be seen as the far edge of the military advantage that may be included in the proportionality calculation. And even then, caution remains necessary, since 'whenever "force protection" is at issue, self-preservation is at stake'[251] which has the potential to be overstated by the person who feels that his life is on the line, at the expense of the civilian population. In the end, '[t]he idea that the armed forces' own soldiers could be ascribed a greater value in the balancing exercise than civilians is incompatible with the [IHL rule of] proportionality, and would in fact undermine [it].'[252] Self-preservation of the military must not be tantamount to a personalised military necessity exception to the IHL proportionality rule.

6.11 CONCLUSION

It has been suggested that the uncertainty of the proportionality assessment that is present in the fact that every attack must be assessed on its own merits, renders its protective value presently null and void.[253] The analysis of the components of the proportionality equation in this chapter reveals that diverging opinions indeed exist on almost all components of the proportionality equation,[254] and thus the unsurprising conclusion of this chapter is that 'there is no mathematical proportionality formula'.[255]

But must the fact that there is no a mathematical formula be understood to mean that the proportionality equation is nothing more than 'a thankless game of guesswork'?[256] It is submitted that the IHL proportionality rule requires military commanders to conduct a thorough analysis of its components as far as circumstances permit. The fog of war may make it impossible to acquire more information concerning possible civilian casualties, or the expectations of military commanders with regard to the military advantage of their planned attack may be misperceived. Nonetheless, military commanders need a sufficient understanding of the components to enable them to conduct an assessment of these factors.

[251] Geiss 2012, p. 88.
[252] International Law Association, p. 34.
[253] See, for example, Shamash, pp. 103–105.
[254] As early as 1979, Krüger-Sprengel had proposed in Ankara initiating efforts on the international level to reach a uniform interpretation of the principle of proportionality. See Krüger-Sprengel, p. 195.
[255] Garraway 2005, para. 21.
[256] Anderson 2003.

7

Proportionality in Practice

7.1 INTRODUCTION

Having established the place of the proportionality assessment in the targeting process, as well as its place in the legal framework applicable to that process, the attention in the previous chapter turned to the analysis of the components of which the IHL proportionality rule consists. This chapter turns to an analysis of its application in practice. A number of examples of factual situations are therefore examined, the purpose of which is to assess which difficulties arise in the practical application of the proportionality analysis in different situations.

Some preliminary remarks with regard to this chapter are required. Although a thorough methodology has been proposed to assess practical incidents, the selection of the situations in this chapter is relatively random and its description not based on extensive field research.[1] This touches upon an important obstacle to analysing the practical application of the IHL proportionality rule. Commanders, or the authorities of their States, are generally reluctant to share how they conduct a proportionality assessment.[2] There are some valid reasons for this. The most important of these is the fact that States regard the actual assessments and the considerations on which these are based as classified. States thus wish to prevent their opponent from being able to predict how operations will be conducted. In addition, States prefer to keep the proportionality assessments classified in order to prevent claims adjudicated before civilian courts in which victims of the hostilities claim compensation for any collateral damage.[3] Although there have been

[1] Fellmeth 2012, pp. 136–141. For more case studies on the principle of proportionality, see for example Sassòli et al.

[2] See Krupiy, p. 5, and Fellmeth 2012, p. 131.

[3] Fellmeth 2012, pp. 131–133.

calls on States to declassify the records of proportionality assessments after a certain period of time, this has thus far not happened often.[4]

This book is not intended to focus particularly on air or land operations, nor is there any particular preference for one or another side in the armed conflicts from which the proportionality assessments in this chapter are taken. Rather, any selection of factual situations with the purpose of providing further clarity to the application of the principle of proportionality in practice depends, in particular, on the availability of material from which the actual operation of the proportionality principle may be derived. Therefore, no effort is made to present a representative set of case studies to cover all aspects and types of armed conflict, operation or political objective. The situations presented are furthermore not intended to be understood as representing State practice. Attacks conducted before the IHL proportionality rule came into existence in API have been omitted, since the commanders deciding on these attacks may be assumed not to have based decisions on the IHL proportionality rule as it exists today.[5]

As was mentioned earlier, the proportionality rule needs to be applied in advance of as well as during an attack. Therefore, the actual outcome of an attack is only relevant for an analysis of an attack, if exactly that has happened, that was expected in advance. It seems safe to assume that in practice, this does not always happen. Finding proof, or even State practice, of how the proportionality principle has been applied in factual situations is therefore a difficult endeavour. Also, in assessing an attack after the fact, it is difficult not to be biased by its actual outcome. Judicial decisions on the matter are not always clear either.[6] Furthermore, since the aim of this chapter is to assess the application of the proportionality rule in practice, the analysis will not include issues of classification of the conflict. It will be assumed that IHL is applicable as a matter of law.

The general division of the tiers of command in a military organisation consists of a distinction between the strategic, operational and tactical levels. Proportionality assessments need to be made not only at the tactical level, but also at the operational and strategic levels, as was mentioned in the previous chapter.[7] The analysis of the application of the proportionality rule in the next

4 Sassòli 2005, pp. 204–205.

5 See for example Gaughan, pp. 229–285. Gaughan studied the Allied air campaign preceding D-Day in 1944 on the basis of the proportionality rule, concluding that the proportionality rule 'leaves all but the most extreme and incontestable cases of excessive collateral damage beyond the reach of international law'. See Gaughan, p. 284.

6 See for example Bartels 2013 and Ponti.

7 To recall: The strategic command is the higher command, overseeing the big picture, whereas the tactical level relates to the lower level of command. In simple terms: at the tactical level, a

section includes proportionality assessments on the strategic or the operational levels, and Section 7.3 assesses a number of incidents on the tactical level. The incidents are presented in chronological order.

7.2 THE STRATEGIC AND OPERATIONAL LEVELS

The assessment of the actual collateral damage of an entire armed conflict, compared to the actual tonnage of bombs dropped, cannot count as a practical assessment of the proportionality of an attack on the strategic or operational level.[8] This may be different for a proportionality assessment for the purpose of the *ius ad bellum*. However, the assessment for the IHL proportionality rule must be done in advance of and during an operation. The actual effects would only have some relevance in the unlikely event all tactical attacks went exactly according to plan and produced exactly both the military advantage and the collateral damage anticipated. It is thus much more difficult to assess the proportionality of a planned attack on the strategic or operational level. In particular, it has proven difficult to obtain sufficient information for the purpose of analysing an actual attack on the strategic and operational level. However, in this section, three examples are analysed: the NATO bombing campaign in Serbia-Montenegro during the war in Kosovo in 1999; the 2003 UK intervention in Iraq; and an artillery exchange of fire between North and South Korea in 2010.

7.2.1 *Kosovo 1999: The NATO Bombing Campaign*

The NATO bombings during the Kosovo crisis in 1999 have been the subject of extensive scholarly analysis.[9] The NATO-led air campaign against military

commander needs to take decisions incident-by-incident, at the operational level, the commander plans and decides on an attack-by-attack basis, while at the strategic level the decisions regard the overall military campaign. In addition, a 'grand strategic' or political level could be defined to which may be referred in *ius ad bellum* and that is thus outside the scope of IHL. NATO defines the levels as follows: The strategic level: The level at which a nation or group of nations determines national or multinational security objectives and deploys national, including military, resources to achieve them. The operational level: The level at which campaigns and major operations are planned, conducted and sustained to accomplish strategic objectives within theatres or areas of operations. The tactical level: The level at which activities, battles and engagements are planned and executed to accomplish military objectives assigned to tactical formations and units. See NATO Glossary of Terms and NATO, 3.9, p. 31 v. See also Olasolo, pp. 158–159, but compare: Henderson, pp. 238–241.

8 See Fenrick 2001, p. 493.

9 See for example: Rowe, Rogers 2000, Shamash, Laursen, Benvenuti, Bring, Byron, Fenrick 2001, Medenica and the proceedings of the ASIL Conference of 2002 and the proceedings of a

targets of the Milošević regime started on 24 March 1999 and lasted for roughly two and a half months.

The ICTY Office of the Prosecutor (ICTY OTP) established a committee to assess allegations of violations of IHL, including the IHL proportionality rule, to advise the Prosecutor on the question of whether a criminal investigation was opportune into some of the incidents that occurred during the bombing campaign. The work of the committee resulted in the ICTY OTP Kosovo Report.[10] The Kosovo Report contains a general analysis of the law applicable during the Kosovo air campaign, as well as an analysis of five specific incidents and a number of recommendations to the ICTY OTP. The ICTY OTP Kosovo Report concludes that

> [e]ither the law is not sufficiently clear or investigations are unlikely to result in the acquisition of sufficient evidence to substantiate charges against high level accused or against lower accused for particularly heinous offences ... [and] [o]n the basis of information available, the committee recommends that no investigation be commenced by the OTP in relation to the NATO bombing campaign or incidents occurring during the campaign.[11]

The committee draws a general conclusion from the statistics of the entire bombing campaign. It states that

> [d]uring the bombing campaign, NATO aircraft flew 38,400 sorties, including 10,484 strike sorties. During these sorties, 23,614 air munitions were released (figures from NATO) ... [and] it appears that approximately 500 civilians were killed during the campaign. These figures do not indicate that NATO may have conducted a campaign *aimed at causing substantial civilian casualties either directly or incidentally*.[12]

It may be noted that the committee found it appropriate to conduct the proportionality equation on such a high (campaign/strategic) level, although there is no further explanation of the yardstick the committee used to reach this conclusion. That the committee based its conclusion with regard to the proportionality analysis on a strategic level is confirmed by the statement that '[i]t has not been possible for the committee to look at the NATO bombing campaign on a bomb by bomb basis and that was not its task.'[13] Furthermore,

Conference of 8–10 August 2001on the subject of the Kosovo Crisis as published in the Naval War College ILS 78 (2002), edited by A. E. Wall.

[10] ICTY OTP Kosovo Report, available online: www.icty.org/x/file/Press/nato061300.pdf

[11] ICTY OTP Kosovo Report, p. 31.

[12] ICTY OTP Kosovo Report, para. 54 on p. 21 (emphasis added).

[13] ICTY OTP Kosovo Report, p. 5.

support for the position that a proportionality analysis must also be conducted on the tactical level of the separate attacks of the operation can be found in the statement of the committee that it 'reviewed public information concerning several incidents ... [and] endeavoured to examine, and has posed questions to NATO, concerning all other incidents in which it appears three or more civilians were killed'.[14] These incidents refer to the tactical level and are therefore addressed in Section 7.3.

7.2.2 *The 2003 UK Intervention in Iraq*

Section 17 of the Iraq Inquiry Report, or Chilcot Report, published on 6 July 2016 (hereinafter: the Report) contains an analysis of expected civilian casualties, and assessments of actual civilian casualties resulting from the 2003 intervention in Iraq that the United Kingdom carried out as part of the US-led Coalition.[15] The Report addresses in section 17 assessments of the human cost of not intervening in Iraq; expected civilian casualties resulting from attacking Iraq; and the reports on actual civilian casualties and the UK Government's response to these latter reports. Apart from an analysis of one particular attack on General 'Chemical' Ali Hasan Al-Majid, which is analysed in Section 7.3.5, the Report contains an analysis on a strategic level before the invasion of Iraq started on 20 March 2003.

Of course, an assessment of the legality of the invasion of Iraq by the US-led Coalition in 2003 is outside the scope of this chapter, because it would concern an analysis of the proportionality of the attack on the basis of the *ius ad bellum*. It is striking to note, however, that the Report seems to suggest that the question whether the attack on Iraq was legal under the *ius ad bellum* is dependent also on the degree to which civilians were suffering as a result of repression by the government of Saddam Hussein. Furthermore, the Report seems to take into account the expectation of the UK Government of a number of strategies the Iraqi forces might use that would possibly cause significant Iraqi civilian casualties, including the use of chemical and biological weapons against Coalition forces that would also affect the civilian population and also human shields, suicide attacks and the use of 'scorched earth' policies.[16]

The Report proves that the UK Government did take expected civilian casualties into account before the invasion of Iraq started. Two months before

[14] ICTY OTP Kosovo Report, p. 5.
[15] Chilcot Report.
[16] Chilcot Report, paras. 21–26, pp. 176–177.

the start of the invasion, the UK Ministry of Defence produced an assessment of the expected civilian casualties from planned UK air attacks following a future invasion.[17] The UK Ministry of Defence noted in this regard that expected civilian casualties would have to be assessed in more detail on a case-by-case basis, and '[t]he target set was not yet sufficiently well-defined to allow an estimate to be produced for the air campaign as a whole.'[18] However, an analysis of earlier operations over Iraq in 1998 and 1999 'suggested that the civilian casualties for an air campaign would be around 150 killed and 500 injured'.[19] Aside from air operations, ground operations were expected to cause additional collateral civilian casualties. Based upon experiences from World War II, the United Kingdom expected that if British troops became engaged in urban warfare in Basra, this was likely to cause another 200–2,000 civilian casualties, depending on the 'circumstances, duration and the degree to which civilian casualties are minimised'.[20] Admiral Sir Michael Boyce, who was the British Chief of Defence Staff, expected civilian casualties to be in the 'low hundreds'.[21]

Although it is questionable whether World War II experiences were still relevant for any assessment of expected civilian casualties in 2003, given developments in weaponry and tactics in the meantime, it seems positive that lessons learned from earlier armed conflicts were used to assess proportionality on a strategic level. The other issue at hand here is that there is no assessment in section 17 of the Report of the other end of the proportionality equation of civilian casualties. Proportionality is of course more than just an assessment of the expected killed and injured civilians, without taking destruction of and damage to civilian objects into account. Furthermore, that assessment would be worthless for the purpose of the IHL proportionality assessment if it is not subsequently put in relation to the military gain sought from the planned operation. The interesting point of the analysis of the Chilcot Report, however, is that it seems that factors were taken into account in assessing the civilian damage of the entire invasion, other than those that would be taken into account in the proportionality analysis of a single attack (i.e. on a tactical level). An example of a factor that was mentioned with regard to the entire operation is the human cost that could be expected if the abusive government in power stayed in place. It would, however, seem to be difficult to determine

17 Chilcot Report, note 27, p. 177, referring to Minute Fry to COSSEC, 3 February 2003, Casualty Estimates – Op TELIC' attaching Paper MOD.

18 Chilcot Report, paras. 29–30, p. 177.

19 Chilcot Report, para. 30, p. 177.

20 Chilcot Report, para. 31, p. 178.

21 Chilcot Report, para. 40, p. 179.

the extent to which the prevention of possible future victims of the regime may be meaningfully included as 'concrete and direct military advantage'. Furthermore, the Report mentions the potential adverse effects on the safety of the civilian population in post-conflict Iraq as a relevant factor.[22] It may be assumed that the Report thus regards this to be part of the expected incidental loss of civilian life and injury to civilians.

It seems the Report suggests that the UK Prime Minister himself made the decision on the issue of the proportionality of the planned invasion of Iraq on the strategic level: 'Mr Blair concluded that "we must set our strategy: to destroy the regime but minimise civilian casualties".'[23]

In sum, the analysis in the Report is probably meant as a proportionality analysis on the basis of the *ius ad bellum* standard rather than an analysis of the IHL proportionality of the UK intervention in Iraq. Nonetheless, the material presented in the Report is valuable to assess prima facie how proportionality on the strategic level can be conducted.

7.2.3 *The 2010 Artillery Attack on South Korea*

In June 2014, the Prosecutor of the ICC issued a Report with regard to possible war crimes under the jurisdiction of the ICC.[24] The Report is the result of a preliminary investigation opened by the ICC Prosecutor on 6 December 2010 to evaluate the shelling of South Korea's Yeonpyeong Island by the North Korean Armed Forces (DPRK) on 23 November 2010 and assess whether the attack could amount to war crimes under the ICC jurisdiction.[25] The ICC Prosecutor inquired in its preliminary investigation whether there was intentional targeting of civilians (articles 8 (2) (b) (i) or (ii)) or a disproportionate attack (article 8 (2) (b) (iv)).[26] For the purpose of its preliminary investigation, the Prosecutor asked both States for additional information with regard to the incidents under review. North Korea did not respond to this request.

The facts of the attack, according to the ICC Prosecutor, were as follows:

> The shelling of Yeonpyeong Island occurred after military exercises with prior notification by the [South Korean] ROK Marine Corps stationed on the island, including an artillery firing exercise. Such exercises have been conducted annually since 1974. The shelling by the DPRK on 23 November

[22] Chilcot Report, paras. 35–38, p. 178.
[23] Chilcot Report, para. 41 on p. 179.
[24] See International Criminal Court, Office of the Prosecutor (ICC Korea Report).
[25] ICC Korea Report, p. 3
[26] ICC Korea Report, p. 12.

> 2010 came in two waves, the first between 14h33 and 14h46, and the second between 15h11 and 15h29. It resulted in the killing of four people (two civilians and two military), the injuring of sixty-six people (fifty civilians and sixteen military) and the destruction of military and civilian facilities on a large scale, estimated to cost $4.3 million. In addition to the military base in the southwestern part of the island and other marine positions, several civilian installations were hit, including the History Museum, locations close to Yeonpyeong Police Station and the Maritime Police Guard Post, the township office, a hotel, a health center and other civilian structures in the town of Saemaeul. As to the total number of artillery shells and rockets fired by the DPRK, the report of the U.N. Command states that a total of 170 rounds were fired, of which 90 landed in the water surrounding Yeonpyeong Island. The ROK Government indicated that 230 rounds were fired, of which 50 landed in the surrounding waters. The DPRK publicly acknowledged responsibility for the shelling.[27]

According to the International Crisis Group (ICG), the 23 November 2010 artillery attacks on Yeonpyeong Island killed two civilians and two South Korean Marines, and injured two civilians and fifteen South Korean Marines.[28] In addition, the ICG Report mentions that the North Korean attack 'was preceded by several warnings, and was executed after meticulous planning'.[29] The ICG held that:

> The ROK had six K9 155-mm self-propelled howitzers deployed on Yŏnp'yŏng Island and they began a live fire exercise at about 10:00am on 23 November. At 2:34pm, after the exercise had finished, the [North Korean] KPA began to fire at Yŏnp'yŏng Island from two bases, Kaemŏri, on the DPRK coast, and Mu Island, which are only about 12-13km from Yŏnp'yŏng Island.... About 80 of some 170 rounds fired from the North hit the island and around 90 fell into the surrounding waters. The shells hit military and civilian targets killing two civilians and wounding three others. Two ROK Marines were killed and fifteen were wounded. Several homes were damaged and the shells were described as special incendiary rounds designed to penetrate structures and cause extensive damage. The cost of the damage initially was estimated to be about $4.3 million. The KPA shelling came in two volleys. Between 2:34 and 2:46 the KPA fired 150 rounds from Kaemŏri and Mu Island; 60 shells hit Yŏnp'yŏng Island and 90 fell into the surrounding waters during the first wave. The ROK howitzers on the island had their barrels pointing south for their firing exercise; three were unable to pivot and

[27] ICC Korea Report, p. 4.
[28] International Crisis Group (ICG Report), p. 48.
[29] ICG Report, p. 27.

> point their fire north. The radar on Yŏnp'yŏng Island also malfunctioned and it took thirteen minutes to return fire. The KPA had deployed MLRS vehicles to Kaemŏri shortly before the attack, and during the first wave of artillery fire, the ROK unit only returned fire to Mu Island while shells were also being launched from Kaemŏri. The slow response enabled the KPA to fire another twenty shells from 3:12 to 3:29; all twenty hit Yŏnp'yŏng Island. The ROK returned fire according to the rules of engagement, which restricted counter-fire to similar weapons systems attacking from the North. ROK fighter planes were scrambled but were restricted from attacking the KPA artillery bases at Kaemŏri and Mu Island.[30]

The analysis of the proportionality of the North Korean artillery attack on the island is complicated by the fact that there is no detailed information available with regard to the DPRK planning process that preceded the attacks. With regard to the South Korean Army that fired back at the North Korean forces, information is also lacking about any expected civilian damage from these attacks in response.[31]

The ICC Report indicates that the analysis of the Prosecutor of the attacks by the DPRK has been after the fact and did not look at the planning stage of the attacks. It states that:

> [a]lthough the attack resulted in injury to civilians and damage to civilian objects, it is not clear that they were the objects of the attack. There are other possible explanations for the striking of civilian objects other than intentional targeting. The fact that military objectives, including the military base on the southwestern part of Yeonpyeong Island, were attacked eliminates any reasonable basis to believe that civilians or civilian objects were the sole object of the attack.[32]

Furthermore, the ICC Prosecutor notes that '[o]ut of 180 rounds, approximately 150 landed in and around 8 different military areas in various locations on the island and 30 on the civilian area immediately surrounding ... [and] there are alternative explanations for the civilian impact (targeting accuracy of artillery weapons).'[33] The Prosecutor held that since a number of military

[30] ICG Report, pp. 27–28 (footnotes omitted).

[31] According to a news agency, the South Korean armed forces' response consisted of firing eighty artillery rounds, and a South Korean military spokesman is reported to have stated that military barracks were hit, resulting in 'many casualties and considerable property damage'. See YonHap News Agency.

[32] ICC Korea Report, pp. 24–25.

[33] ICC Korea Report, p. 25.

objectives were hit, the attacks did not violate the prohibition of directly attacking the civilian population.

Since the exchange of artillery fire is not limited to a single strike, it can be qualified as an attack on an operational level. With regard to a possible violation of the IHL proportionality rule, in line with the analysis of the application of the IHL proportionality rule in the previous chapters, it is necessary to identify the expected military advantage from the attack as well as the anticipated collateral damage.

The first question is whether the attack was directed at military objectives. According to the ICC Report, most of the attacks were aimed at military objectives and the incidental damage was inherent to the type of weapons that were used.[34] The ICC Report notes, on the basis of information provided by South Korea, that '230 rounds were fired, of which 180 struck the island and 50 landed in the surrounding waters. Out of 180 rounds, approximately 150 landed in and around 8 different military areas in various locations on the island and 30 on the civilian area immediately surrounding'.[35] The ICC Report obviously does not specify which exact military objective the attacks were aimed at. Since the North Korean military had warned South Korea not to conduct the artillery training exercise, it may be assumed that the artillery pieces that were used during the exercise were the targets of the attack, but lacking information from the North Korean authorities, this remains pure speculation.

The next question is whether precautionary measures had been taken to avoid or minimise damage to civilian objects or civilian casualties. This also includes a preliminary proportionality assessment. A first factor is whether the North Korean military commanders could have reasonably expected any civilian damage to occur. On this point, the ICC Prosecutor notes that:

> In assessing the anticipated civilian damage or injury, a number of factors are relevant. The DPRK had access to maps of Yeonpyeong Island and thus would have been aware of the proximity of the civilian areas to the military objects. The DPRK allegedly conducted a firing drill near the Northern Limit Line in January 2010 using the same 'time on target' method used in the Yeonpyeong attack. If the DPRK equipment did have low targeting accuracy, leading to the incidental civilian impact, one can presume that the DPRK was aware of this and of the likelihood of the subsequent civilian impact after the January drill.... [T]he island is a total 7.3km2 and at the time of the attack had a civilian population of 1,361. Thus, while the DPRK could

[34] ICC Korea Report, p. 21.

[35] ICC Korea Report, p. 20.

> have anticipated a likely civilian impact from its attack, it does not appear that a reasonably well-informed person in the circumstances of the actual perpetrator would have expected such civilian impact to be very high. The civilian population on the island (1,361) was concentrated in one area near the island's main port; this population does not appear to have been the intended object of the attack. . .. The size of the island and its civilian areas meant that many of the shells that missed their targets would fall in uninhabited areas of the island or in the surrounding waters (rather than on civilian areas).[36]

It may be added that the North Korean authorities issued an advance warning of an attack in the event that the South Korean military proceeded with its exercise, even though at the time it was issued it may have been understood as a threat to the South Korean military rather than a warning directed at the civilian population.

The next phase is to identify the military advantage expected from the attack, after which the actual proportionality assessment can be made. The ICC Prosecutor Report suggests that internal political reasons were behind the attack by North Korea;[37] however, this advantage would present itself on a political level, and is thus not of a military character and irrelevant for the IHL proportionality equation, because the IHL proportionality rule requires the advantage to be of a military nature. The ICC Report concludes that '[g]iven the context of the attack, principally the DPRK fashioning it as a response to South Korean military activity, one may surmise that the perceived military advantage of the attack was a reassertion of DPRK territorial control of particular waters and a demonstration of its military power in the area.'[38] This could be perceived as a military advantage on an operational level, but it is difficult to understand why this would be *directly* militarily advantageous at this particular moment in time, because the same training exercises had been conducted on a yearly basis since 1974. On a tactical level, the ICC Prosecutor notes that

> [t]he attack resulted in damage to military objectives and appears to have been directed towards those objectives, including the military base on the southwestern part of the island, three marine helipads, and K-9 howitzers that had been deployed outside of their hardened positions for a firing drill earlier on the same day. Those military objects were damaged or destroyed during the attack, and the attack may have been timed, in part, to catch the K-9s outside of their hardened positions. It would thus appear that the neutralization of South Korean military assets was also part of the concrete and direct overall military

[36] ICC Korea Report, p. 22 (footnote omitted).

[37] ICG Report, p. 1.

[38] ICC Korea Report, p. 23 (footnote omitted).

> advantage anticipated by DPRK, in addition to the military advantage related to the demonstration of DPRK's military power in the area.[39]

It is unfortunate that the ICC Prosecutor could only base their findings with regard to the expected military advantage arising from the attack on assumption and actual results, instead of on an operational plan of the North Korean armed forces. However, the assumed expected military advantage seems to be sufficiently significant to be assessed in relation to the expected civilian casualties and damage, because the latter could be expected to be rather limited.

The ICC Prosecutor acknowledges in the paragraph comparing the military advantage and the civilian damage that '[t]he difficulties of calculating anticipated civilian losses and anticipated military advantage and the lack of a common unit of measurement with which to compare the two make this assessment difficult to apply, both in military decision-making and in any ex post facto assessment of the legality of that action.'[40] Nonetheless, the Prosecutor starts the proportionality equation with a mathematical and quantitative proportionality assessment based on the outcomes of the attacks. With regard to civilian casualties, the ICC Report notes that, '[t]he attack resulted in two military personnel killed and 16 injured, as compared to two civilians killed and 52 injured.' With regard to material damage, the ICC Prosecutor notes on the basis of information provided by the South Korean authorities that the attacks resulted in damage worth 'US$4.3 million, but this figure does not distinguish between damage to civilian or military objects'.[41] In the final paragraph, the ICC Prosecutor concludes with regard to the feasibility of a criminal prosecution in relation to the artillery attacks on the South Korean island that

> [w]hile a reasonably well-informed person in the circumstances of the actual perpetrator, would have expected some degree of civilian casualties and damage to result from the attack given the relative proximity of military and civilian objects, the information available is insufficient to provide a reasonable basis to believe that the anticipated civilian impact would have been clearly excessive in relation to the anticipated military advantage of the attack, considering the size and population of the island, and the fact that military targets appeared to be the primary object of the attack.[42]

A few conclusions may be drawn from the ICC Korea Report, it is submitted. One is that although the ICC Prosecutor admits that it has no information on

39 ICC Korea Report, p. 23 (footnote omitted).

40 Ibid.

41 ICC Korea Report, p. 24.

42 Ibid.

the planning of the attacks by the North Korean armed forces, it nonetheless uses the result of the attacks for drawing conclusions with regard to the expected military advantage and anticipated civilian casualties and damage. Although it may seem safe to conclude from the outcomes of the attacks that there is insufficient proof to start a criminal investigation, the information as presented in the Report provides insufficient information to draw any conclusions as to whether the IHL proportionality rule was applied or violated. After all, the yardstick in international criminal law that the anticipated civilian damage was not *clearly* excessive is not the applicable yardstick for IHL, which uses the test of excessiveness, not clear excessiveness. Furthermore, it is worth noting that the Prosecutor looked at the 170–230 projectiles that were launched in two waves as one concerted attack. This seems in line with the opinion of a number of States that the proportionality rule must take into account the *overall* military advantage expected from the attack. The conclusion of the ICC Prosecutor that 'the information available is insufficient' to prosecute the North Korean military commander for a violation of the ICL proportionality rule applies therefore similarly to the question of whether North Korea violated the IHL proportionality rule.

Finally, given the acknowledgement in the ICC Report that the South Korean authorities complied with the request by the ICC to provide information about the attacks, it is peculiar to note that the Report provides no in-depth analysis of the counter-attacks on North Korea by the South Korean armed forces. After all, it is not the actual outcome of those artillery attacks, of which there is little information available, but the expectation in advance that dictates whether these attacks were proportionate. That information presumably could have been made available to the ICC Prosecutor by the South Korean authorities. Since the forces are located rather close to each other, it could be expected that the South Korean armed forces would continuously monitor civilian presence near closely located North Korean artillery and make peacetime assessments of expected civilian damage and casualties, including a ratio of the collateral damage it would be ready to accept in the event of future use of the artillery assets on Yeonpyeong Island against North Korea.

7.3 THE TACTICAL LEVEL

There is general agreement on the position that a proportionality assessment must be conducted on the tactical level of an operation.[43] This section

[43] Note, however, that according to some States, this must be understood to mean that an on-scene commander must make proportionality calculations, but the individual soldier does not.

presents a number of attacks of which information is available in the open domain with regard to the proportionality analysis that was conducted in the course of the planning of that attack. It must be noted that even if information is available in the public domain, it appears that it is still difficult to distinguish where an issue of proportionality arises, or whether there were questions of distinction and precautions at issue.[44]

This position, it is submitted, is incorrect. This became clear during an expert meeting on the principle of proportionality in Quebec in 2016, which this author attended. The position of one expert working for a State was explained as follows: if individual soldiers engaged in combat are ordered to execute a certain attack with their unit, they are not in a position to conduct a separate proportionality assessment for every bullet they fire. It is submitted, however, that the individuals may have to conduct a separate proportionality analysis, albeit in a split second. An example is the situation in which an individual soldier is ordered to clear a house of hostile fighters in an urban situation where civilians are also known to be present. The individual soldier who wants to attack an opposing fighter who is in a room where civilians are also present has to calculate himself whether killing the civilians by tossing a grenade inside the room is excessive. In that case the soldier himself must apply the IHL proportionality rule.

44 See for example R. J. Barber, p. 499: Barber looks at two particular incidents in Afghanistan and comes to the conclusion that in both cases there was a violation of the principle of proportionality. However, in neither case does she actually perform a proportionality calculation. Her conclusion should have been that it was unknown how many civilian casualties could be expected. Therefore, the problem here is not one of proportionality, but of precautions. Another example is the ICTY case of the *Prosecutor* v. *Galic*, in which the ICTY Trial Chamber considered proportionality with regard to the shelling of a football game where military personnel were present in the stadium. According to Bartels:

> The incident concerned a recreational football match in Sarajevo, held on a parking lot surrounded by tall buildings. The match, in which some members of the Bosnian Muslim forces took part, was watched by a crowd of approximately 200, consisting of both civilians and soldiers. Evidently, neither the soldiers nor the civilians were at the time directly participating in hostilities. Naturally, the soldiers themselves remained legitimate targets but, owing to the circumstances, it was not possible to see who was and who was not targetable. The Trial Chamber noted that none of the evidence suggested that the Serbian forces knew that soldiers were amongst the players and spectators at the football match, but went on to consider that had the SRK troops been informed of this gathering and of the presence of ABiH soldiers there, and had [they] intended to target these soldiers, this attack would nevertheless be unlawful. Although the number of soldiers present at the game was significant, an attack on a crowd of approximately 200 people, including numerous children, would clearly be expected to cause incidental loss of life and injuries to civilians excessive in relation to the direct and concrete military advantage anticipated. It would not have been necessary to make this observation. The Bosnian-Serb forces were not able to make a distinction between civilians and the soldiers, first, because they could not see the location that was being targeted and, second, because of the means used. Therefore, the group consisting of spectators and football players was targeted as a whole. The attack in itself was thus indiscriminate on that basis, irrespective of the anticipated incidental damage.

See Bartels 2013, pp. 285–286 (footnotes omitted).

7.3.1 The Destruction of Mostar's Old Bridge

The attack on the Old Bridge (Stari Most) in Mostar, Bosnia-Herzegovina was dealt with during the *Prlić Case* at the ICTY. In its judgment, the Trial Chamber ruled that the destruction of the bridge was disproportionate. At the time of its destruction, the historic Old Bridge, built about 427 years earlier,[45] was one of two bridges still intact between the territories held by the Bosniak armed forces on the east bank of the river Neretva, that cuts the town of Mostar in two, and a small enclave on the west bank of the Neretva.[46] The Old Bridge was used by the civilian population to obtain supplies, but also by the Bosniak troops at the frontline on the west bank for supplies and communications with the forces located at the east bank. Furthermore, there was another makeshift bridge (the Kamenica Bridge) and a small and dangerous path over the mountains to Jablanica that still connected the Bosniak troops on the west bank to their headquarters.[47] The Old Bridge was destroyed by a tank of the Bosnian Croat forces (HVO) that fired at it 'all day long'[48] on 8 November 1993. The next day, '[a] few tank shells, which landed at the base of the eastern side of the arch on the south side of the Bridge, brought it down.'[49] The Kamenica Bridge was destroyed just days after the Old Bridge, leaving the Bosniak troops as well as the Bosniak residents on the western bank of the Neretva mostly isolated.

The Trial Chamber conducted an assessment of the attack on the Old Bridge, concluding that

> [a]lthough the destruction of the Old Bridge by the HVO may have been justified by military necessity, the damage to the civilian population was indisputable and substantial. It therefore holds by a majority, with Judge Antonetti dissenting, that the impact on the Muslim civilian population of Mostar was disproportionate to the concrete and direct military advantage expected by the destruction of the Old Bridge.[50]

45 Petrovic, p. 265.
46 See also Bartels 2013 on the EJILTALK blog.
47 ICTY Trial Chamber, *Prlić et al.*, Judgment, Part III, para. 1583.
48 ICTY Trial Chamber, *Prlić et al.*, Judgment, Part III, para. 1581.
49 Petrovic, p. 75.
50 ICTY Trial Chamber, *Prlić et al.*, Judgment, Part III, para. 1584. In his dissent, Judge Antonetti states on this topic on p. 325: 'I fail to see how the principle of proportionality could be applicable in this case. If the Old Bridge was a military objective, it quite simply had to be destroyed. In any event, there is no such thing as proportionate destruction.' This is clearly an incorrect statement: the proportionality rule instead applies only in cases where the target is a military objective.

With regard to the military advantage of destroying the Old Bridge, the Trial Chamber held that the bridge was 'essential to the [Bosniak troops] for combat activities of its units on the front line, for evacuations, for the sending of troops, food and material, and that it was indeed utilised to this end … [and furthermore the Bosniak troops were] holding positions in the immediate vicinity of the Old Bridge'.[51] Therefore, 'its destruction cut off practically all possibilities for the [Bosniak Army] to continue its supply operations'.[52] The question of whether the Old Bridge qualified as a military objective, by use, location or both, may thus be answered in the affirmative. Referring to the second prong of the definition of a military objective of article 52 (2) API, Petrovic argues that, '[a]s for the use of the Bridge itself for military purposes, there is no evidence that there was fighting between the two opposing forces at the time. Even if the Bridge was used for military purposes there is no evidence that such a use was posing any significant threat to the HVO forces at the time.'[53] It is submitted, however, that in general terms, there does not necessarily need to be proof of a direct plan of the HVO soldiers to attack the Bosniak enclave on the west bank of the Neretva, or that the use of the bridge posed a threat to the HVO soldiers, in order for it to be targetable at that time. That seems to be too restrictive an understanding of the second prong of the definition of a military objective. Therefore, it is assumed that the Old Bridge was a military objective at the time it was destroyed,[54] although it must be accepted that there was also a continued civilian use of the Old Bridge and that it was important for transporting food and other goods to the remaining civilians in the enclave.

The military gain the HVO sought by destroying the Old Bridge may be assumed to have been the defeat of the remaining Bosniak soldiers on the west bank of the Neretva, as well as repressing the positions of the Bosniak troops near the bridge. However, the objective of making it impossible to use the Old Bridge for bringing reinforcements to the opposite side of the river seems to have been achieved already on the evening of 8 November.[55] In fact, the

[51] ICTY Trial Chamber, *Prlić et al.*, Judgment, Part III, para. 1582.

[52] Ibid.

[53] Petrovic, p. 266.

[54] But see Petrovic, p. 127, arguing that there was no significant military use of the Old Bridge. Also, since article 23 (g) of the 1907 Hague Regulations states that it is forbidden '[t]o destroy or seize the enemy's property, unless such destruction … be imperatively demanded by the necessities of war', it would have been interesting to see how the Trial Chamber would weigh this factor.

[55] ICTY Trial Chamber, *Prlić et al.*, Judgment, Part III, para. 1581 and Judgment, Part II, para. 1318.

civilian population on the west bank only got fully isolated after the Kamenica Bridge was destroyed. Furthermore, there was a system of pulleys installed that allowed food and other supplies to be transported over the River Neretva in baskets.[56]

On the other end of the proportionality equation, the destruction of the Old Bridge also resulted in 'the Muslim enclave on the right bank of the Neretva, in virtually total isolation, making it impossible for them to get food and medical supplies resulting in a serious deterioration of the humanitarian situation for the population living there'.[57] Thus, although there is no mention in the Trial Chamber Judgment of the presence of civilians on the bridge during the attacks, the collateral damage seems to consist of the more indirect results of the destruction of the bridge. The Trial Chamber also attached value to the 'significant psychological impact on the Muslim population of Mostar',[58] although unfortunately there is no explanation of the weight the Trial Chamber attached in the proportionality assessment to the loss of the Old Bridge, which was found to be of 'great symbolic importance primarily for the Muslims'.[59] Instead, the Trial Chamber concluded that 'the destruction of the Old Bridge, in view of its immense cultural, historical and symbolic value for the Muslims in particular was extensive'.[60]

It is unfortunate that the ICTY Trial Chamber did not include an appreciation of the fact that the Old Bridge may be seen as protected cultural property, and how that would have impacted the proportionality assessment. The Old Bridge obviously enjoyed general protection under article 27 of the 1907 Hague Regulations and customary IHL, and although it was never added to the lists of cultural property protected by the UNESCO Convention, it was certainly eligible for the protection provided by the UNESCO Convention.[61] Furthermore, there is no assessment in the ICTY Trial Chamber Judgment of whether the destruction of the Old Bridge would be in violation of the restrictions on attacking objects indispensable for the survival of the civilian population.[62]

56 ICTY Trial Chamber, *Prlić et al.*, Judgment, Part II, para. 1291.
57 ICTY Trial Chamber, *Prlić et al.*, Judgment, Part III, para. 1583.
58 Ibid.
59 ICTY Trial Chamber, *Prlić et al.*, Judgment, Part II, para. 1364.
60 ICTY Trial Chamber, *Prlić et al.*, Judgment, Part III, para. 1585.
61 Petrovic, pp. 121–148 and 268. Petrovic notes that the Old Bridge was also not entitled to the special protection as provided for in article 8 of the 1994 UNESCO Convention. See Petrovic, p. 134.
62 Article 54 API and its customary law corollary.

In conclusion, although it seems that the Trial Chamber left room[63] for the Appeals Chamber to further clarify the application of the IHL proportionality rule to the attack on the Old Bridge, this has not happened.[64]

7.3.2 *The Attack on Milan Martić*

The trial of General Ante Gotovina at the ICTY has given rise to a number of critiques to both the judgments of the Trial Chamber and of the Appeals Chamber.[65] The case focussed on a number of issues that related to the conduct of hostilities taking place during Operation Storm in August 1995, among which was the shelling of the town of Knin. In particular, the artillery shelling that targeted the leader of the Serbian Kraijna region, Milan Martić, raises issues regarding the proportionality rule. The Trial Chamber found that the Croatian forces (HV) 'reported firing a total of twelve shells of 130 millimetres at Milan Martić's apartment on two occasions between 7:30 and 8 a.m. on 4 August 1995. Further, on the evening of 4 August 1995, the HV fired an unknown number of 130-millimetre shells at a location marked R on [map] P2337 where they believed Martić to be present'.[66]

The first issue in a proportionality assessment is the question of whether it was aimed at a military objective. Martić himself was commander in chief of the Serb forces and president of the Republic of Serbian Krajina, and as such, he may be labelled as a valid military objective. However, the Trial Chamber did not make it clear whether Martić himself was the target of the attacks on Knin.[67] Rather, the Trial Chamber referred to the military advantage of the attack on his apartment. The Trial Chamber noted that

> [f]iring at Martić's apartment could disrupt his ability to move, communicate, and command and so offered a definite military advantage. [The testimony of witness] Rajčić recognized that the chance of hitting or injuring Martić by firing artillery at his building was very slight. Rajčić testified that the HV sought to harass and put pressure on Martić and that the HV took the rules of distinction and of proportionality into account when deciding whether to target the apartment block.[68]

[63] See also Lederman on the Just Security blog.

[64] As Milanovic noted in his summary of the judgment on the EJILTALK blog, it 'does not directly engage with the "pure" IHL proportionality question, as the majority and dissent did at trial'.

[65] See for example Blank, Bartels 2013, and Ariav.

[66] ICTY Trial Chamber, *Gotovina et al.*, para. 1910, pp. 966–967.

[67] Ariav, p. 343.

[68] ICTY Trial Chamber, *Gotovina et al.*, para. 1910, p. 967.

It may be recalled that when an attack is aimed at a combatant during an international armed conflict, there is no need to emphasise how the attack renders any military advantage, because combatants may be attacked at any time. The fact that Martić was the commander in chief of the Serb Krajina forces (although it is debatable whether this armed conflict was international in character) obviously makes killing him more militarily advantageous than killing a regular soldier. However, if it was the residence of Martić that was the subject of the attack, it needs to be examined whether it qualified as a military objective.[69] The first prong of the definition of a military objective dictates that it must be determined whether the object made an effective contribution to military action. For a residential building, arguably, that may only be true when Martić was present himself, or when there was knowledge that the structure was used by Martić for military purposes, or contained military objectives, such as military planning documents, communication systems or weapons. Since it appears that the Trial Chamber could not conclude that the attacking Croatian forces knew the location of Martić, even though it seems that two locations were attacked where it was assumed that he was present, it is difficult to imagine the Trial Chamber meant to conclude that Martić himself was the target of the attacks. With regard to the second prong of the definition, however, disrupting Martić's ability to effectively command his forces seems to have the potential to render a substantial military advantage to the attacking Croatian forces.[70]

[69] Article 52 (2) API: 'Attacks shall be limited strictly to military objectives. In so far as objects are concerned, military objectives are limited to those objects which by their nature, location, purpose or use make an effective contribution to military action and whose total or partial destruction, capture or neutralization, in the circumstances ruling at the time, offers a definite military advantage.'

[70] Blank, p. 9: A group of experts discussing the *Gotovina Case* found that:

> [i]t is essential then to examine the value of the target in the context of the entire operation (and not merely as an individual object of attack) – in this case, Martić was the supreme military commander of the SVK during a deliberate attack against improved enemy defensive positions protecting their most vital strategic asset: their capital city. The experts agreed that almost any military commander would consider disrupting the ability of such a commander to influence the command, control, and communication of his forces during the decisive phase of an attack to be one of the highest priority targets. In the context of Operation Storm, Martić was perhaps the most valuable target in the city of Knin.... Disrupting Martić's ability to influence the battle, whether by targeting him directly, severing his command and control capabilities, or fixing him in place and isolated from his operational command post, for example, therefore offered a tremendously significant military advantage, particularly from the perspective of the commander at the time of the attack. Intelligence showing that Martić was in the building at the designated time would be relevant as well to the determination of the value of the building as a military objective.

For the purpose of the discussion of the proportionality assessment with regard to the attack on Martić's residence, it is necessary to assume that the attacks were aimed at a military objective. The next questions are whether any collateral damage was anticipated and whether sufficient precautionary measures were taken to minimise it. With regard to the issue of expected collateral damage, the Trial Chamber considered that,

> Martić's apartment was located in an otherwise civilian apartment building and ... both the apartment and the area marked R on P2337 were in otherwise predominantly civilian residential areas. The Trial Chamber has considered the use of artillery in light of the evidence on the accuracy of artillery weapons ... and the testimony of expert Konings on the blast and fragmentation effects of artillery shells. At the times of firing, namely between 7:30 and 8 a.m. and in the evening on 4 August 1995, civilians could have reasonably been expected to be present on the streets of Knin near Martić's apartment and in the area marked R on P2337. Firing twelve shells of 130 millimetres at Martić's apartment and an unknown number of shells of the same calibre at the area marked R on P2337, from a distance of approximately 25 kilometres, created a significant risk of a high number of civilian casualties and injuries, as well as of damage to civilian objects.[71]

However, any reference to precautionary measures taken by the attackers is missing in the analysis of the ICTY.[72]

With regard to the assessment of the excessiveness of the expected damage to civilian objects and civilian casualties, the Trial Chamber considers 'that this risk was excessive in relation to the anticipated military advantage of firing at the two locations where the HV believed Martić to have been present'.[73] The Appeals Chamber, however, stated with regard to the proportionality assessment of the Trial Chamber that it 'was not based on a concrete assessment of comparative military advantage, and did not make any findings on resulting damages or casualties'.[74] It is noted that this is a particularly incorrect statement, since it is not the actual resulting damages and casualties that must be taken into account in accordance with the IHL proportionality rule, but the *expected* incidental damage.

It may be noted that the proportionality analysis as conducted by the ICTY Trial Chamber concerns only the attack on Martić's apartment and the other area where he was believed to be present. No proportionality analysis was

71 ICTY Trial Chamber, *Gotovina et al.*, para. 1910, p. 967.
72 See also Blank, pp. 11–12.
73 ICTY Trial Chamber, *Gotovina et al.*, para. 1910, p. 967.
74 ICTY Appeals Chamber, *Gotovina et al.*, para. 82, p. 28.

conducted by the Trial Chamber with regard to the totality of the artillery attacks on the four towns during the first phase of Operation Storm.[75] Therefore, it seems that the analysis of the Trial Chamber was limited to the tactical level, whereas an (additional) analysis on the operational level could also have resulted in valuable insight into the way the proportionality analysis must be conducted. The Appeals Chamber in a footnote 'also notes that the Trial Chamber declined to determine the proportionality of the overall attack on Knin'.[76] In addition, both the Trial and the Appeals Chamber failed to properly identify which military advantage could arise from attacking the regional military commander, although the Trial Chamber did state that there was significant risk of causing incidental civilian damage.[77]

In conclusion, despite the potential in the facts of the case, as well as the extensive evidence that was available in the case, the *Gotovina Case* has provided little useful guidance on the practical application of the IHL proportionality rule.[78]

7.3.3 *Kosovo 1999: The NATO Bombing Campaign*

With regard to the five separate incidents the committee reviewed, the first incident (the attack on the bridge over the Grdelica Gorge on 12 April 1999) concerned a military objective which, only just before it was hit, a civilian train had crossed. As a result, it is reported that ten civilians died. The pilot expected no civilians to be present on or near the bridge when the bomb was released. Once the pilot saw the train, it was already too late to divert the missile. Therefore, the proportionality rule did not play a role in this incident. However, since the pilot noted that the bridge was not destroyed, it was attacked again by the same aircraft in a subsequent run. This time, again, the pilot became aware only at the very last moment before the bomb hit the bridge that the train was still present on the bridge. Consequently, it was once again impossible to divert the bomb, and the train was hit for the second time. It is debatable whether the pilot should have refrained from attacking the

75 Ariav, p. 347.
76 ICTY Appeals Chamber Judgment, note 252 on p. 28.
77 Bartels 2013, p. 291.
78 There was significant debate concerning the decision of the Trial Chamber to assess only those attacks that resulted within a 200-metre radius of a military objective in Knin. It is submitted that the 200-metre radius is merely a factual finding with no connection to a correct application of the IHL proportionality rule. See also Kolb 2017, p. 484. The Judgment of the Appeals Chamber in particular has been heavily criticised. See for example Kolb 2017, p. 487, claiming that the Appeals Chamber 'rendered a disgraceful service to the Tribunal'.

bridge for a second time until he was certain that the train was no longer on the bridge, given the fact that the pilot knew the train had been hit. One might debate whether this precautionary measure would have been appropriate in this case; however, the pilot gave priority to fulfilling the mission assigned to him, which was to destroy the bridge.[79]

The second incident (the attack on the Djakovica convoy on 14 April 1999) regarded objects that were mistakenly identified as military objectives. According to the Report, the attacks were suspended 'as soon as the presence of civilians in the convoy was suspected'.[80] It thus follows that no proportionality assessment has been conducted, since the attackers did not expect a civilian presence at the location of the attack.

The third incident concerns the attack of 23 April 1999 on the Serbian Radio and TV Station (RTS) in Belgrade and the only incident of the Kosovo Report in which the application of the IHL proportionality rule is discussed. The Kosovo Report estimates that between ten and seventeen individuals lost their lives during this attack, all of them civilians.[81] The discussion with regard to this attack focussed mostly on the question of whether the station could be identified as a legitimate military objective in the circumstances prevailing at the time of the attack. Unfortunately, the Committee does not share the reasoning behind its conclusion that '[a]ssuming the station was a legitimate objective, the civilian casualties were unfortunately high but do not appear to be clearly disproportionate.'[82] However, some effort is put by the committee into explaining the military advantage that the deciding military commander was aiming to obtain:

> At a press conference on 27 April 1999, another NATO spokesperson similarly described the dual-use Yugoslav command and control network as 'incapable of being dealt with in a single knock-out blow….' The proportionality or otherwise of an attack should not necessarily focus exclusively on a specific incident. (… referring to the need for an overall assessment of the totality of civilian victims as against the goals of the military campaign). With regard to these goals, the strategic target of these attacks was the Yugoslav command and control network. The attack on the RTS building must therefore be seen as forming part of an integrated attack against numerous objects, including transmission towers and control buildings of the Yugoslav radio relay network which were 'essential to Milosevic's ability to direct and control the repressive

79 See also Shamash, p. 138.

80 ICTY OTP Kosovo Report, p. 24.

81 ICTY OTP Kosovo Report, p. 25. Amnesty International claims that sixteen civilians lost their lives. See Amnesty International Report, 'Collateral Damage or Unlawful Killings?', p. 26.

82 ICTY OTP Kosovo Report, p. 26.

> activities of his army and special police forces in Kosovo' (NATO press release, 1 May 1999) and which comprised 'a key element in the Yugoslav air-defence network' (ibid, 1 May 1999).... Not only were these targets central to the Federal Republic of Yugoslavia's governing apparatus, but formed, from a military point of view, an integral part of the strategic communications network which enabled both the military and national command authorities to direct the repression and atrocities taking place in Kosovo (ibid, 21 April 1999).[83]

One additional point with regard to this attack is that there had been a warning of the impending attack on the building, but it is debated whether this was an effective advance warning as required by IHL.[84]

From the text of the Kosovo Report, it becomes clear that the committee regarded the separate attack of the RTS building as part of a much larger operation to disrupt the operations the Yugoslav forces were conducting in Kosovo. This aim could be interpreted as contributing to the military advantage at the strategic level. The committee apparently felt that given the contribution of eliminating the RTS building to the military advantage sought on a strategic level, justified the expected collateral damage of the attack on the building. It is to be regretted that no further underlying analysis of the proportionality assessment of the attack on the RTS building is provided by the committee.[85] If this would have been done, it may have become clear whether the committee, in analysing the attack on the RTS building as part of the larger operation, took possible collateral damage of other components of the operation into account as well.[86]

The fourth incident that the committee analysed is the 7 May 1999 attack on the Chinese embassy in Belgrade, which was clearly a civilian object that was hit by mistake. Therefore, the committee did not discuss proportionality in its analysis of this incident. The fifth incident regarded a military objective where no civilians were present as far as the NATO troops were aware. Therefore, the proportionality rule played no role here, although one could perhaps debate whether the attackers could have taken more extensive precautionary measures to attain more certainty with regard to the presence of civilians.

83 ICTY OTP Kosovo Report, pp. 27–28.

84 ICTY OTP Kosovo Report, pp. 26–27.

85 See also Shamash, p. 141, and Laursen, p. 791, calling the treatment of the proportionality assessment by the committee 'confusing'.

86 See also Shamash, pp. 118–120.

In sum, only the attack on the RTS building that was analysed in the Kosovo Report concerns an example of the IHL proportionality rule application on the tactical level. However, there is very little substance in this analysis. Rather, the statements of the committee seem to be focussed on a more overall approach in the attack in the RTS building, but offered little clarification for its conclusion that the expected collateral damage of that attack was not clearly disproportionate.

7.3.4 *The Killing of Salah Shehadeh*

A situation that has attracted quite some attention is the Israeli attack that killed Salah Shehadeh in Darge Street in Gaza City on 22 July 2002.[87] Salah Shehadeh was 'one of [Hamas'] senior leaders and Head of its Operational Branch'.[88] The Israel High Court of Justice ruled on a petition asking the Israeli authorities to instigate criminal proceedings against a number of persons involved in the decision-making with regard to the attack. The High Court decided that 'the petitioners were not able to carry the burden allotted to them, to point out a flaw in the judgment of the JAG and the Attorney General'.[89] It was therefore decided not to open a criminal investigation. The attack has, however, been the subject of an investigation by a Special Investigatory Commission (SIC). The SIC Report reveals a number of interesting approaches with regard to the practical application of the IHL proportionality rule in this case.[90]

As far as the facts are concerned, the SIC concluded that

> [d]uring the operation, a one-ton bomb was dropped on the house in which Shehadeh was staying, killing him, Hamas activist Zahar Natzer, Shehadeh's wife Layla and his 15-year-old daughter Iman, who were with him in the house ... [and in addition] 13 civilians including women and children, who were not directly involved in terrorist activities, ... and dozens of civilians in the vicinity were injured.[91]

87 *The Guardian*.

88 Israel Ministry of Foreign Affairs 2011 (SIC Report), para. 6.

89 See The Supreme Court in Jerusalem Sitting as the High Court of Justice, Petition 8794/03 submitted by Yoav Hass, Ruling on 23 December 2008, para. 11, available at www.geneva-academy.ch/RULAC/pdf_state/HCJ-decision-8794-03-1-.pdf.

90 SIC Report, see also Friedman, and Barak, www.haaretz.com/israel-news/israel-s-2002-hit-of-hamas-leader-was-justified-despite-civilian-casualties-1.346067. See also Weill, pp. 624–627.

91 SIC Report, para. 1.

The house in which Shehadeh was staying was located in a densely populated civilian neighbourhood, and as a result of the bomb, the houses close by were either destroyed or severely damaged.[92] The task of the SIC was to 'examine the justification for the strike on Salah Shehadeh, the circumstances in which he and the other casualties of this operation were hit and the question of whether there was an effective alternative means to the strike on Shehadeh'.[93]

Remarkably, the SIC concluded that

> the difficult collateral consequences of the strike against Shehadeh, in which uninvolved civilians, mostly women and children, were killed and many others injured, became clear in hindsight, as disproportionate in the circumstances of the incident in question. Such was the view of the Commission and this was also the assessment in hindsight of the great majority of the senior officials involved in the planning and implementation of the operation, who stated that if they had foreseen in real-time the scope and gravity of the collateral damage which actually resulted, the operation would not have been carried out. The said consequence was unintended, undesired and unforeseen. It did not stem from disregard or indifference to human lives.[94]

Furthermore, the SIC stated that

> . . . a gap arose between what was expected and what actually occurred. The central reason for this gap was incomplete, unfocused and inconsistent intelligence information with regard to the presence of civilians in the structures adjacent to the Shehadeh house (the garage and huts), where most of the civilians died.. . . This gap stemmed from incorrect assessments and mistaken judgment based on an intelligence failure in the collection and transfer of information to the various echelons involved in the points of contact between the different agencies involved, and from a lack of sufficient understanding regarding the uncertainty that was created as a result of this unfocused, inconsistent and incomplete intelligence information which was before the decision-makers.[95]

The conclusion of the SIC is that '[t]he decision-makers foresaw proportionate harm to uninvolved civilians.'[96] They, however, misjudged the magnitude of the expected civilian harm. The SIC concludes that there is no reason to assume that criminal responsibility may arise from the attack because there

92 See Weill, p. 617.
93 SIC Report, para. 3.
94 SIC Report, para. 10.
95 SIC Report, paras. 11–12.
96 SIC Report, para. 14.

were some failures that led the decision makers to expect that the attack to be proportionate.

The SIC Report reveals that the SIC was willing to deliver an appraisal of the application of the IHL proportionality rule, in this case based on its outcomes and conveys its opinion that the attack would have been disproportionate if the decision makers had anticipated the collateral damage that actually occurred. Approval for the conclusion of the SIC comes from a notable author, the late professor and Judge Antonio Cassese. He states, in a witness statement relating to the *Shehadeh Case*, that '[t]here can be no doubt that the damages caused were awfully out of proportion to the advantages gained: nobody would deny the manifest disproportion between the death of 15 innocent civilians, the injury of 150 persons and the destruction of 9 buildings, on the one hand, and the objective to kill one single individual, however dangerous he might have been, on the other.'[97]

Although it is commendable that Cassese shares his view with regard to the excessiveness of the collateral damage in this situation, his statement seems quite categorical. It seems possible that the military advantage of killing certain crucial figures during armed conflict could in some situations justify the collateral damage as it presented itself in this attack.

With regard to these conclusions, however, Niv notes that the SIC

> neither specifies its line of thinking nor lays down the legal analysis which underpins its determined decision. It appears that the Commission relies primarily on the fact that most of the security officials who testified before it, stated that had they known the consequences of the attack in advance they would not have executed it, as, in their opinion, the said result is not proportional.[98]

Also, Niv notes that it is 'hard to understand how the Commission decided that the deaths of 13 civilians and the wounding of dozens was not proportional when the target was a master terrorist who was responsible, in one year alone, for the deaths of hundreds of civilians and soldiers and the wounding of thousands – which seems to illustrate the military advantage in his elimination'.[99] Therefore, the military advantage of disrupting these operations by taking out the person deciding upon these attacks, as well as protecting civilians that were a substantial part of the victims of the attacks by Hamas, seem to result in considerable military advantage. Whether the commanders

97 Cassese 2006.
98 Niv.
99 See Niv.

deciding upon the attack could reasonably have expected the magnitude of collateral civilian damage that actually resulted in attacking Selah Shehadeh is unknown. Niv notes that '[t]he limited legal practice publicized in this matter [i.e. the *Kunduz Fuel Trucks Case* and the ICTY OTP Kosovo Report on the airstrike on the RTS in Belgrade] does not support the conclusions of the Commission.'[100]

In sum, the *Selah Shehadeh Case* firstly proves that any proportionality calculation is only as good as the information on which it is based. In situations where military commanders are expecting a substantive military advantage, but are unable to attain more or better information on the expected outcomes of an attack, the main question seems to be whether the commanders would have a duty to wait for the next opportunity to launch the attack. That is an issue of precautions, however, rather than proportionality. The option to postpone an attack seems more viable in a targeted killing operation during armed conflict where the threat of the person targeted is not imminent than in an attack during a large-scale conventional armed conflict where own troops and civilians are under a direct threat. It may be said that the situation in Gaza at the time of the attack on Selah Shehadeh, as not being a 'hot battlefield' at the time, may have played a role in the SIC's conclusion that the attack would be proportionate if the decision makers had more information. Furthermore, unfortunately, in both the SIC Report on the attack on Selah Shehadeh and in Cassese's statement, as has been the case in most reports dealing with the practical application of the IHL proportionality rule, a thorough factual and legal analysis supporting the conclusion is lacking.

7.3.5 *The Attack on General 'Chemical' Ali Hasan Al-Majid*

The Chilcot Report contains an analysis of one particular attack on the tactical level that was carried out at 05:30 local time on 5 April 2003 against General Ali Hasan Al-Majid. General Al-Majid was known as 'Chemical Ali' as a result of his earlier involvement in the attack on Kurdish regions using chemical weapons.[101] In April 2003, however, General Al-Majid was 'described as responsible for co-ordinating resistance to the Coalition within Southern Iraq and therefore as a combatant'.[102]

[100] See Niv.

[101] Chilcot Report, paras. 54–80, pp. 182–185.

[102] Chilcot Report, para. 56, p. 182; see also Human Rights Watch 2003, p. 28:

> U.S. aircraft bombed a building in al-Tuwaisi, a residential area in downtown Basra at approximately 5:20 a.m. on April 5, 2003, in an attempt to kill Lieutenant General Ali

With regard to the military advantage of attacking General Al-Majid, therefore, it was assessed that this consisted not only of the killing of one member of the Iraqi armed forces, but the removal from command of a 'key Iraqi military figure [which] was expected to deliver considerable military advantage thus ultimately minimising casualties on both sides'.[103] It is clear that in the international armed conflict between the Coalition and the Iraqi regime in 2003, General Al-Majid was a legitimate military objective, because he was not just a regular combatant, but a leading general in the Iraqi military that the Coalition had fought in the early days of the invasion, and who was now a leading figure in the resistance against the occupying Coalition troops. The military advantage of killing General Al-Majid may thus be described as considerable.

With regard to expected civilian damage and casualties, the Report states that the UK military had undertaken an assessment on 4 April 2003 using a procedure called the 'Rapid Collateral Damage Assessment'[104] based on the expectation that General Al-Majid would visit a small group of houses in Basra. It assessed that in addition to the house where the general was expected to reside, seven other civilian houses might be affected by the strike on General Al-Majid. The assessment predicted that thirty-nine casualties might be expected if the strike were launched during the day, and fifty-one if the strike were launched during the night.[105] Even though General Al-Majid was identified as a time-sensitive target, the authority for approving the strike was referred up to the political level. The advice of the UK Contingency Commander in that process was that the attack would not violate the proportionality rule, although a description of a thought process on which that advice was based is not cited in the Report.[106] There is furthermore no mention in the Report whether this assessment is based on the attack being launched during the day or during the night, which would enable a more exact analysis of the proportionality assessment. Ultimately, the attack was approved by the UK Defence Secretary, but it was subsequently cancelled since it was reported that General Al-Majid had already left the location.

Hassan al-Majid. Al-Majid, known as 'Chemical Ali' because of his role in gassing the Kurds in the 1988 Anfal Campaign, was in charge of southern Iraq during the recent war. Initial British reports indicated that al-Majid was killed in the attack. CENTCOM later reversed this claim and changed al-Majid's status back to 'at large.' Coalition forces ultimately captured al-Majid on August 21, 2003 (footnotes omitted).

[103] Chilcot Report, para. 78, p. 185.

[104] Chilcot Report, para. 56, p. 182.

[105] Chilcot Report, para. 57, p. 182.

[106] Chilcot Report, para. 59, p. 182.

One day later, however, at 05:20 in the morning, the location was attacked by US forces, using a 500 lb precision guided bomb. General Al-Majid was not hit by the attack. The bomb destroyed at least two adjacent civilian houses, killing a considerable number of civilians.[107] Human Rights Watch reports that '[t]he collateral damage estimate done on the target appears to have allowed for a high level of civilian damage. This attack may have been approved due to the perceived military value of al-Majid. Had smaller weapons been used, however, many civilian lives may have been spared.'[108]

Combining the available facts presented in this case, it could mean that in cases where considerable military advantage is expected because an important military leader is expected to be hit, a number of more than fifty expected civilian casualties is not deemed excessive. This is based on the assessment of the British armed forces that fifty civilians would be killed in an attack at night and the timing of the actual attack. Whether such a quantitative approach was indeed followed in planning this attack remains uncertain, however, due to insufficient information. In the particular case of General Al-Majid, the intelligence on which the planners of the attack relied proved to be inaccurate. This leads to the conclusion that the civilians who died in this particular attack died as a result of a proportionality analysis that was based on inaccurate information with regard to the expected military advantage. One may wonder whether the probability of attaining the desired military gain in this attack was sufficiently likely to occur. There is, however, insufficient information available to evaluate whether this constitutes a violation of the precautionary measure to ascertain that the attack is aimed at a military objective, or how the presumably low probability of success in this attack was taken into account.

7.3.6 *The Attack on the Kunduz Fuel Trucks*

On 3 September 2009 at about 20:00 local time, two fuel tankers filled with gasoline and diesel fuel were stolen from a private company at a location about 15 kilometres from the Afghan city of Kunduz. The commander of the nearby German unit, Colonel Klein, was made aware of the theft, and when the two tankers were located some hours later, the fuel trucks were stuck in a sand bank in the Kunduz River. Eventually, in the early morning of 4 September, the two fuel trucks were destroyed by bombs dropped by two

[107] Human Rights Watch reports that seventeen civilians died as a result of the attack. Human Rights Watch 2003, p. 30.

[108] Human Rights Watch 2003, p. 32.

US aircraft, on the orders of Colonel Klein. A substantial number of persons were killed in the attack, including a number of civilians.[109]

The attack on the Kunduz fuel trucks was investigated by the United Nations Assistance Mission in Afghanistan (UNAMA), the German Parliament[110] and the NATO-led International Security Assistance Force (ISAF).[111] In addition, the case was the subject of proceedings resulting in the decision of 16 April 2010 of the Federal Prosecutor General, dismissing criminal proceedings against Colonel Klein and another member of the German armed forces. According to one commentator, '[i]t remains unclear what exactly happened before the bombing, what the commander's motivations for the airstrike were and how many of the victims were civilians.'[112] Another commentator held that the case proved the 'lack of definite criteria by which to evaluate the proportionality of an attack'.[113]

The military advantage expected from the attack on the fuel trucks must be evaluated in the light of the fact that fuel tankers had been used as driving bombs during recent attacks elsewhere in Afghanistan. In addition, the German forces had been warned in the months preceding this incident that their camp would be attacked by vehicle bombs in the near future. The commander estimated during the night of 3 September 2009 that there was no alternative to destroying the stolen fuel tankers, because a recovery operation was too dangerous, given the estimate he had obtained from a human source that there were about seventy opposing fighters located at or near the location of the tankers, including one or more regional commanders.

However, Heintschel von Heinegg and Dreist conclude from the available facts that '[a]t no point in time did the colonel have reason to believe that civilians were present at the location [and] he only wanted to know as much about the situation as possible and to receive all available information about any changes whatsoever which might have occurred on the sand bank.'[114] Thus, it is submitted, there could be no violation of the proportionality rule by Colonel Klein, because he expected no civilian casualties and he had no further options to verify whether civilians were present at the sand bank. Nonetheless, the German Federal Court of Justice conducted a

109 Exact numbers are unknown, however the estimates range between 40 and 140 individuals, including 'many' civilians. See von der Groeben, p. 473.

110 Deutscher Bundestag (PIC Report).

111 Henn, p. 623.

112 Henn, p. 623. See for one summary of the facts of the case: Heintschel von Heinegg and Dreist, pp. 834–851. For cockpit footage of the attack: see for example YouTube.

113 Andresen, p. 25.

114 Heintschel von Heinegg and Dreist, p. 838, deriving this from the PIC Report.

proportionality assessment on the basis of the assumption that the presence of civilians on the location of the fuel tankers was expected.[115]

The German Federal Court of Justice found that:

> [e]ven if the killing of several dozen civilians would have had to be anticipated (which is assumed here for the sake of the argument), from a tactical-military perspective this would not have been out of proportion to the anticipated military advantages. The literature consistently points out that general criteria are not available for the assessment of specific proportionality because unlike legal goods, values and interests are juxtaposed which cannot be 'balanced.' Therefore, considering the particular pressure at the moment when the decision had to be taken, an infringement is only to be assumed in cases of obvious excess where the commander ignored any considerations of proportionality and refrained from acting 'honestly,' 'reasonably,' and 'competently.' This would apply to the destruction of an entire village with hundreds of civilian inhabitants in order to hit a single enemy fighter, but not if the objective was to destroy artillery positions in the village. There is no such obvious disproportionality in the present case. Both the destruction of the fuel tankers and the destruction of high-level Taliban had a military importance which is not to be underestimated, not least because of the thereby considerably reduced risk of attacks by the Taliban against own troops and civilians. There is thus no excess.[116]

Furthermore, the German Federal Court of Justice found that

> [t]he standard of prohibiting excess first requires a military advantage of a tactical nature…, such as the destruction or weakening of hostile troops or their means of combat, or territorial gain.… Collateral damage such as the death of civilians is not out of proportion merely because the military advantage is only a short-term advantage which does not decide the conflict. Thus, the bombarding of a broadcasting centre by NATO in Belgrade with the foreseeable result of numerous civilian deaths was not considered to be out of proportion, even though the anticipated tactical advantage only lay in the interruption of the adversary's telecommunication for a few hours.… In the present case the bombing pursued to military goals, namely the destruction of the fuel tankers robbed by the Taliban and of the fuel as well as the killing of the Taliban, including not least the high-level regional commander of the insurgents. The anticipated military advantage, namely on the one hand the final prevention of using the fuel and the fuel tankers as 'driving bombs' or to fuel the insurgents' militarily used vehicles and on the other

115 A similar approach is taken by von der Groeben. See von der Groeben, pp. 478–483.

116 Germany, Federal Court of Justice, Federal Prosecutor General, *Fuel Tankers Case*, Decision, 16 April 2010, para. 2 on p. 63.

> hand the at least temporary disruption of the Taliban's regional command structure fall within the usual, recognized tactical military advantages.... The fact that the goal mentioned in second place was not fully achieved is irrelevant for the legal assessment because the expectations at the time of the military action based on the facts are decisive.[117]

Von der Groeben's analysis of the attack on the fuel trucks, which also assumes that the commander had knowledge of the presence of civilians at the sand bank of the Kunduz River (which he reportedly did not), differentiates between a defensive and an offensive military aim. He argues that a mathematical approach is possible if it is assumed that the attack was aimed at enhancing the safety of the German soldiers at the nearby German camp, because in the case of a non-imminent threat, the number of soldiers and the number of civilians that are expected to be harmed by, respectively, the expected attack on the German camp and the civilians expected to be affected by an instant attack on the fuel tankers stuck in the river, could be compared. Therefore, according to von der Groeben, the three decisive factors are the 'aim to protect soldiers, the non-imminence of the threat, and the comparison between civilians' and soldiers' lives'.[118] He then argues that the attack is disproportionate if the absolute number of affected civilians is expected to be higher than the absolute number of affected German soldiers, based on three arguments:[119]

(1) The soldiers, given their belligerent privilege, have to accept some degree of risk in order to save civilians. This argument is even more important during missions in which the strategic goal is the protection of civilians.
(2) Given the fact that there is no imminent threat, other options must be considered, especially since the harm caused to soldiers by a non-imminent attack is less certain than the harm that will be caused to the civilian population by striking the fuel tankers immediately.
(3) Comparing the risk to the lives of the soldiers and those of the civilians 'at least allows us to put numbers on both sides of the equation',[120] whereas in most cases of attacks it is much more problematic to compare the desired

[117] Germany, Federal Court of Justice, Federal Prosecutor General, *Fuel Tankers Case*, Decision, 16 April 2010, para. 4 on p. 66.
[118] Von der Groeben, p. 481.
[119] Von der Groeben, pp. 481–482. Von der Groeben admits that '[t]he suggested formula is of course a very tentative attempt to clarify the notion of proportionality, and it is only applicable where an attack is intended to protect soldiers' lives. But it shows that the proportionality test can go beyond just describing the evident cases.'
[120] Von der Groeben, p. 482.

military gain to expected civilian damage in terms of death and injury of civilians as well as damage to objects.

Von der Groeben notes that the tables turn when the desired military gain consists not only of a defensive component, but also of an offensive one, particularly the objective to attack the opposing forces, including some important local commanders. The military advantage would then be of a higher value, adding to the defensive military advantage that would arise from enhancing the safety of the German troops by depriving the opposing forces of vehicles that would probably be turned into 'driving bombs' and the fuel that could be used for the vehicles of the opposing forces.

It is submitted that the approach taken by von der Groeben differentiating between an offensive and a defensive military advantage, makes sense as a model to further analyse the components of which the IHL proportionality rule is comprised. The effort to 'put numbers on both sides of the equation', however, seems to oversimplify the assessment of the anticipated military advantage in this case. It is therefore submitted that the approach is useful in terms of enabling a thorough analysis of the values that must be attached to the two sides of the equation, but the probability of the expected result is the main complicating factor that von der Groeben's analysis fails to take sufficiently into account. It is submitted that the high degree of uncertainty whether the expected results will materialise makes it impossible to use an exclusively quantitative analysis.

To sum up, based on the publicly available information about the attack on the Kunduz fuel trucks, the IHL proportionality rule was never an issue, because the commander did not expect civilians to be present. Whether additional precautionary measures should have been taken to confirm this is unclear on the basis of the available information. Nonetheless, the incident demonstrates (when it is assumed that the commander did have reason to believe that civilians were present) that the military advantage expected from an attack may also include defensive considerations. It is submitted that although in some cases a mathematical comparison between expected collateral damage and anticipated military advantage may be possible, the Kunduz fuel trucks incident is not an example in point.

7.3.7 *Firefight along the Baghlan River*

Written as a diary of operations (in German), Mike Zimmermann, commander of a company deployed to Afghanistan in 2010, describes a firefight in which he and his unit were engaged in for sixteen hours, during a patrol in an area along the Baghlan River.[121] During this period, the company lost a 'Dingo' military vehicle, but Zimmermann's troops suffered no casualties. Nonetheless, the diary provides exemplary insight into the considerations of an on-scene commander who is balancing the purpose of his operation, the safety of his own troops and the legal boundaries that apply to the operation, including a proportionality assessment. The description proves particularly that the proportionality rule finds application not only in offensive operations, but also in attacks in response to an attack. Although the diary contains no description of the legal framework applicable to the operation and the rules of engagement guiding the commander in this specific operation, it is assumed that the rules of customary IHL apply to the situation, including the IHL proportionality rule.

The facts of the case, as described by Zimmermann, regard the assignment to his unit of conducting a patrol aimed at the reconnaissance of an area called Wazgari. The aim of the operation was to meet with local leaders and to explore the area to enable a future operation to be conducted there. During the operation, one of the military vehicles gets stuck in the Baghlan River, and quickly thereafter it becomes clear that opposing forces are present in the region. Soon, the company finds itself ambushed and it starts to receive small-arms fire from different sides. The firefight gets intense, leaving the company pinned down to its position near the river, and their enemy attacks them using small-calibre firearms, RPGs and BM-1 rockets. After a while, the company identifies the location of the main firebase of their opponents, overseeing the entire area, some 900–1,200 metres to the east of their location. The company commander decides to attack the main firebase of the opponent using their 120 mm calibre 'Mörser' mortar, in order to be able to retreat from the firefight. However, the mortar observer, who is responsible for directing the mortar grenades to the correct location, reports to Zimmermann that he has observed a number of women and children near the opposing fighters. Zimmermann describes how he inquires whether the mortar observer is able to confirm the direct participation of the women and children in the hostilities towards his company, or whether the presumed civilians are used as a human shield. Zimmermann notes that both circumstances were common practice during earlier incidents, and that the opponents were well aware of the restrictions this would place on his response. Since the observer was unable to confirm either situation 'with a hundred percent certainty',[122] the

121 Zimmermann, pp. 31–38.

122 Zimmermann, p. 35: '. . . er kann es nicht mit hundertprozentiger Sicherheit sagen'.

commander decides to refrain from firing the mortar for the time being, because he considers 'the risk to hit uninvolved women and children'[123] to be too big.

The company commander proceeds to describe the underlying difficult dilemma he faced, which is the question of why he decided to prefer the lives of the civilians over his own soldiers.[124] He asks himself the question of whether he should protect the women and children and sacrifice his soldiers, or whether he should protect his soldiers and sacrifice the women and children.[125] The commander then justifies his decision by explaining that although he tries his best to protect the lives of his soldiers, others too have the right to life. The commander solves his dilemma by trying a different option, which is to drop two air-delivered bombs closing in on the enemy's position, which gives the commander the opportunity to regroup and give the order to retreat during the lull in the shooting following the impact of the air-delivered munitions.

It is submitted that the description of the firefight along the Baghlan River proves that military commanders do not necessarily put the safety of themselves and their men above the possibility of causing collateral civilian damage. Even though the dilemma is vexing, the commander in the situation described above seemed to conduct a proportionality calculation for the planned operation to attacking the enemy's main firebase by a mortar. He assessed the expected military advantage, consisting of retreating from the firefight without sustaining casualties as well as killing hostile troops. Furthermore, he assessed the expected collateral damage based on the information available to him, consisting of killing or wounding civilians (an unknown number of women and children) present at the location from which the opponent fired. He concluded that the proportionality equation would result in excessive collateral damage and postponed the mortar attack. He then proceeded to figure out an alternative course of action that also resulted in the military gain he was aiming to achieve.

In conclusion, it is important to note that the commander did not fall into the trap of the understandable reaction of thinking that in this situation the notion of self-defence or self-deprivation would bypass a meaningful proportionality analysis. Also, it may be noted that the commander seems to have required a 100 per cent certainty in the assessment of whether the women and

[123] Zimmermann, p. 35: 'Das Risiko, unbeteiligte Frauen und Kinder zu treffen, ist mir zu gross'.
[124] Zimmermann, p. 36: 'Warum nicht, Herr Hauptmann? Sollen lieber wir sterben?'
[125] Zimmermann, p. 36: 'Soll ich also Frauen und Kinder schützen und meine Männer opfern oder soll ich Frauen und Kinder opfern um meine Männer zu schutzen?'

children may have lost their protection due to directly participating in the hostilities or by functioning as a voluntary human shield. This would seem to comply with the presumption of civilian protection of article 50 (1) API.

It is submitted that the firefight illustrates that military commanders do not necessarily take the safety of their own troops as an absolute factor in their proportionality analysis. He takes it into account as a relevant factor for determining the military advantage of the planned attack, but accepts that the possibility of collateral damage serves as a contra weight against the responsibility he feels to bring his soldiers home safely.

7.4 CONCLUSION

The situations analysed in this chapter could easily be augmented by an unlimited number of further analyses of attacks at all appropriate levels. As an example, no studies have been included in the realm of cyber-operations. Furthermore, human rights organisations have produced a massive number of reports concerning incidents that involved a very wide variety of contexts.

The proportionality analysis on the strategic or operational level reveals that in none of these situations is a detailed yardstick used to come to a conclusion. The committee in the Kosovo Bombing held that it found no evidence to conclude that the entire bombing campaign was aimed at causing substantial incidental civilian casualties, looking at the totality of civilian victims. It is submitted that this methodology seems insufficient for assessing the potential excessiveness of the incidental civilian damage and casualties of that bombing campaign. This is true, first of all, because the anticipated military advantage of the campaign does not seem to be made explicit. As a result, there is no factor of military advantage against which the expected civilian damage can be balanced. Second, looking primarily at situations in which three civilians died has no causal relationship to the factor of incidental damage that should be assessed by the committee for the purpose of a proportionality analysis on a campaign level because (a) the three civilian deaths are looked at in hindsight, whereas the proportionality analysis should be made on a prospective basis, and (b) the number of three civilian deaths seems to be chosen randomly. After all, an attack can be prohibited because it is disproportionate even in situations in which no civilian deaths actually occurred, although excessive civilian deaths were expected. Furthermore, it is incorrect to exclude damage to civilian objects from the analysis. The conclusion is therefore that the report contains only helpful statements on the overall proportionality of the entire bombing campaign in the sense that the IHL proportionality rule must be applied at the various levels of command.

The Chilcot Report may be used to assess prima facie some factors to be taken into account in the IHL proportionality analysis on the strategic level. The Report shows that States can, and in this situation apparently do, take expected civilian damage and casualties into account before a campaign is launched. The Chilcot Report thus seems to indicate that the British Government took its responsibilities under API seriously in the sense that an analysis was made of the expected civilian damage before the invasion of Iraq was started. It is commendable that the British armed forces looked into the expected collateral effects of both their planned air and ground operations and based this assessment on the lessons learned during earlier operations. The methodology for that assessment seems to be a primarily quantitative analysis and, with regard to the scope of the expected incidental civilian damage and casualties, the phase after the removal of the Saddam Hussein government is also taken into account. The military advantage side of the proportionality assessment seems to take into account the civilian suffering that would be avoided by removing Saddam Hussein from power. Nonetheless, the Chilcot Report is indeterminate about whether the analysis is meant to be based on the *ius ad bellum* or must be understood as a description of the IHL proportionality analysis by a State on a strategic level.

In the situation of the Korean artillery attacks, the ICC Prosecutor acknowledges that the conclusions were not based on the prospective plans of the North Korean armed forces, but instead on the results. This alone makes inevitable the conclusion that no prosecution is recommended for violation of the ICL proportionality rule. The Report is nonetheless interesting because it indicates that the ICC Prosecutor believes that a quantitative analysis is appropriate. It is, however, unclear why the ICC Prosecutor bypasses the issue of the application of the IHL proportionality rule to the South Korean counter-attack, given the fact that the South Korean authorities reportedly showed a willingness to provide information to the ICC Prosecutor with regard to the incident.

The situations on a tactical level reveal that sometimes the assessment of the military advantage of an attack is complicated by the different levels on which that advantage is expected to materialise. The military advantage of the attack on the RTS building alone was small, but must be assessed in relation to the bigger picture of the objective to disable the communications and command and control system of the entire Yugoslav armed forces. Similarly, the military advantage of the attack on Martić was disrupting his ability to exercise his command, not necessarily attacking the two buildings in which he was believed to be present. The military advantage of killing Salah Shehadeh and General Al-Majid could also be deemed to be more significant than killing one commander: it may be argued that it was also intended to end the string of attacks that they had reportedly ordered, and safeguard both their own troops and the civilians that could be affected by future attacks ordered by these commanders. The question, however, arises as to what extent these uncertain future advantages may be taken into account, because they would potentially allow a higher ratio of permissive collateral damage but perhaps not qualify as 'direct and concrete'. Nonetheless, in terms of quantitative assessment, the attacks on Salah Shehadeh and General Al-Majid show that, presumably, expected casualties of between twenty and fifty civilian lives may be considered acceptable by States when a high-level commander is attacked.

The two situations involving German armed forces indicate that the safety of one's own forces is taken into account when the military advantage of an attack is assessed. This is the opinion of the German Federal Court of Justice in the Kunduz Fuel Tankers situation and of the on-scene commander in the situation of the firefight along the Baghlan River. The latter situation, however, indicates that there is a limit to that: the safety of their own forces does not justify a full disregard for civilian casualties on that basis, but it also proves that the IHL proportionality rule finds application not only in offensive operations, but also in attacks in response to an attack.

In sum, it is submitted that the situations in this chapter demonstrate that commanders do conduct proportionality analysis on different levels, and may adjust their operations, or even in some cases refrain from launching an attack they were planning or even ordered to execute. Still, it remains difficult to deduct actual guidance for how the assessment of proportionality must be done according to military practice, primarily due to the absence of accounts of military commanders that describe their thought process. It is, however, submitted that the practice presented in this chapter enables a further elaboration on the application of the IHL proportionality rule in practice in the next chapter.

8

Assessing Proportionality

If the proportionality principle does fail to protect civilians, one suspect is the highly subjective and discretionary phrasing of the principle.[1]

8.1 INTRODUCTION

Having established the place of the proportionality assessment in the targeting process, as well as its place in the legal framework applicable to that process, the attention turned to the analysis of the components of the IHL proportionality rule. In the previous chapter, a number of factual situations were analysed in order to illustrate how the IHL proportionality rule was, or was not, applied in practice.

This chapter aims to formulate guidance for conducting a proportionality assessment of a planned attack. This chapter therefore turns to a further analysis of how the IHL rule on proportionality must be applied. To this end, Section 8.2 discusses whether the factors of which the assessment consists can be meaningfully balanced or must be seen as inherently incomparable. Section 8.3 discusses the question of whether an objective application of the proportionality rule is possible and the measures parties to a conflict may take to improve the objective application of the IHL proportionality rule. Section 8.4 assesses whether the term ‘reasonable military commander’ must be understood to constitute the correct yardstick for applying the IHL proportionality rule. Section 8.5 builds on this by seeking to provide guidance for military commanders that may assist them in assessing proportionality by providing a preliminary analysis of the question of how the term ‘excessive’ must be understood.

[1] Fellmeth 2010, p. 8.

8.2 ARE THE COMPONENTS OF THE IHL PROPORTIONALITY RULE COMPARABLE?

Military operators and commanders have to consider a large number of factors and determine the relative value of each factor as precisely as is feasible, using all the information that is reasonably available to them, before they can decide whether the planned attack is in accordance with the IHL proportionality rule. Some commentators have made the remark that the expected 'concrete and direct military advantage' and the 'incidental loss of civilian life, injury to civilians, damage to civilian objects, or a combination thereof' are incomparable as unequal factors. Olasolo mentioned that the two factors of the proportionality calculation have 'hardly anything in common'.[2] Fenrick notes, '[i]t is much easier to formulate the principle of proportionality in general terms than to apply it to a particular set of circumstances because the comparison is often between unlike quantities and values. One cannot easily assess the value of innocent human lives as opposed to a particular military objective.'[3] The IHL proportionality rule nonetheless requires the commander to perform an analysis of the underlying factors, to make an assessment of the two sides of the equation and, finally, to decide whether the expected collateral damage is excessive compared to the anticipated military gain. Furthermore, there is a legal obligation in the principle of proportionality, based on the obligation to protect civilians as much as possible, to assess the correct value of those components that can be objectively determined.[4] Therefore, pointing to the fact that the factors are dissimilar is at times correct but never very helpful.

It is clear that the proportionality assessment is not only comprised of quantitative factors, but qualitative factors also play a role. For example, the military advantage of killing three ordinary foot soldiers must be deemed to be much lower than an attack, the expected military advantage of which is that the three most important commanders of a NSAG will be killed. Similarly for collateral damage, the destruction of one civilian building may be minor collateral damage if it is an abandoned shepherd's shed in a rural area, compared to a school or an important museum. Therefore, incommensurate factors may perhaps only in exceptional cases be compared in a quantitative sense, but they certainly can in a qualitative sense. A mathematical assessment may be possible only in exceptional cases, for example, when a planned attack will destroy a military objective where 100 enemy combatants are present and

2 Olasolo, p. 158.
3 Fenrick 2000, p. 58.
4 This obligation is based on articles 51 (1) and 57 (1) and (2) (ii) API.

the attack is expected to cause the death of only two civilians. But usually, the expected military advantage and collateral damage remain dissimilar in nature, for example, when the expected destruction of vital civilian infrastructure needs to be compared to the destruction of a number of enemy tanks that block the advancement of the attacking forces. Comparing dissimilar factors is, however, not unique to IHL proportionality. As has been noted in Chapter 2, different manifestations of the proportionality principle are found in many branches of international law, as well as in national law. In each different field, it is used to strike a certain balance. Mostly, the law requires a balancing between rather different things. In fact, almost every proportionality equation that is found in international law is a matter of comparing unequal entities. It is therefore submitted that different factors can certainly be compared, it just depends on the question one is asking.

Coming back to the IHL proportionality rule, it may be relevant to assess whether the quantitative and qualitative factors in the IHL equation result in an objective test of excessiveness. The next section analyses this issue.

8.3 THE SEARCH FOR AN OBJECTIVE IHL PROPORTIONALITY RULE

This section clarifies whether balancing the quantitative and qualitative factors in the IHL proportionality equation result in an objective test of excessiveness, and if not, whether there would be a need to restrict the subjectivity of the application of the proportionality rule. Furthermore, this section addresses which measures may be taken to improve the objectivity of the proportionality rule. In essence, these measures do not relate to the rule itself, but to its application, and these measures may be expected to assist in putting the IHL proportionality rule into practice.

Many authors have commented on the subjectivity of the IHL proportionality rule.[5] For example, Blix stated that the line between permissible and excessive collateral civilian damage 'necessarily contains a large subjective element'.[6] Similarly, Oeter noted that '[o]bjective standards for the appraisal and balancing of expected collateral damage and intended military advantage are virtually non-existent.'[7] The experts who drafted the HPCR Manual on Air

5 Sloane labelled the standard of proportionality as a 'singularly subjective and indeterminate legal standard'. See Sloane, pp. 301–302. See also Guisández Gómez 1998, p. 358: '[b]ecause of the degree of subjectivity involved, this principle is considered as the Achilles' heel of the law of war.' Sassòli 2005, p. 204.

6 Blix, p. 148.

7 Oeter 2013, p. 197.

and Missile Warfare, however, view the IHL proportionality rule as 'objective in that the expectations must be reasonable'.[8]

One could ask why one would want to search for an objective rule of proportionality and what it means for a rule to be 'objective'. According to one dictionary, 'objective' means 'not influenced by personal feelings or opinions; unbiased or fair'.[9] The term 'objective' is used here to mean that the outcome of an analysis is not only dependent on the personal ideas of the individual who conducts the proportionality assessment, but that the law speaks for itself, and anybody applying the rule would come to the same outcome in the same situation. One may argue that only if that is the case, the rule is clear enough to function as a legal rule, and sufficiently precise to be applied by the professionals who are trusted with the responsibility of deciding on life or death of civilians who happen to be in the vicinity of military objectives. As such, an objective rule would exist if the balance consists only of quantitative factors that may be measured against a set metric yardstick. An example of such a rule would be if it read that an attack is always disproportionate if it is expected to kill five civilians more than it is expected to kill enemy soldiers. Thus, if the planned attack is expected to affect no civilian objects, but it is expected to kill ten civilians and only three enemy soldiers, and there is no other direct and concrete military advantage attached to killing the three soldiers, the planned attack is illegal in this example. Unfortunately, the IHL proportionality rule does not operate as objectively as the rule that was just introduced, primarily because there is no mathematically quantifiable yardstick applicable as in the fictive interpretation of the rule in the example. Depending on who the three enemy soldiers are, the value of killing these three soldiers could be non-excessive when compared to the expected collateral damage of killing ten civilians. Therefore, even if the IHL proportionality rule included a mathematically quantifiable yardstick (which it does not), the rule would still not be fully objective because the personal ideas of the individual who conducts the proportionality assessment play a role in assessing the value of the factors that need to be balanced.

Nonetheless, it would be of great assistance to military commanders when as many factors as possible are assessed as objectively as possible before the IHL proportionality assessment is conducted. The next section assesses why this is the case.

8 Program on Humanitarian Policy and Conflict Research, Harvard University, Commentary, p. 97. See also Gardam 1993, p. 407.

9 Cowie, p. 849.

8.3.1 *The Passive and Active Protection Rationales for an Objective Proportionality Rule*

A first and obvious ground why the rule on proportionality should be objective may be called the 'passive protection rationale'. This entails that the rule aims to protect the civilian population by prohibiting excessive casualties among civilians who refrain from taking a direct part in the hostilities. This protection of those who do not, or no longer, participate in the hostilities is one of the major underlying rationales of IHL in general, and the IHL proportionality rule in particular. It is submitted that, in order to obtain that purpose, the protection of these civilians should not be dependent on the subjective perspective of the military commander, but on objective parameters.

A second reason why an objective rule must be preferred over a subjective rule is that of the 'active protection rationale'. This means that with the responsibilities of the members of the armed forces to lawfully attack military objectives, they also cause civilian casualties and destroy civilian objects, so these professionals run the risk of prosecution for a violation of IHL. The advantage of a more objective IHL proportionality rule is that it would provide military commanders with more clarity and guidance on how to implement the rule. Objective parameters would allow them to make decisions that are more predictable and decrease their chances of ending up being prosecuted for violating the proportionality rule. The active protection rationale thus requires the rule to be sufficiently objective for the members of armed forces to be protected from prosecution, since the parameters of the rule are clear enough to be applied in a more or less predictable manner.[10] In addition to the active protection rationale for individuals, this applies similarly to States. Wright notes in this context that '[b]ecause an attack with excessive collateral damage engages both [S]tate and individual responsibility, there must be an objective quality to the assessment.'[11]

As such, the proportionality rule enhances the protection of civilians in armed conflict and similarly assists the commanders in remaining within the limits to warfare set by IHL. There is, however, another side to this coin.

10 See for example Olasolo, p. 162:

> [l]ogically, the more intense the pressure of the media and public opinion concerning the adequate application of the proportionality rule (and the more numerous the national and international investigations and prosecutions of serious breaches of the proportionality rule), the greater the motivation for military commanders to take the expected incidental civilian damage into consideration in the targeting process and during the preparation and execution of attacks.

11 Wright, p. 840.

One may argue that if the States that codified the proportionality rule in Additional Protocol I had wanted a more precise or objective rule, they would have come up with one. Professor Frits Kalshoven was one of the persons present during the drafting of the part of API in which the proportionality rule is laid down. He wrote: 'weighing the expected collateral damage against the anticipated military advantage will never be a job for one's pocket calculator'.[12] In doctrine, it is widely acknowledged that the proportionality principle is a very subjective rule.[13] This would decrease the relevance of the active protection rationale and raises the question of whether this rule is of any use to military commanders at all. However, it may be argued – and has been – that a subjective or imprecise rule provides the members of the military with more leeway and flexibility in targeting than a very precise rule would. Given this latitude for military commanders, it seems difficult to successfully prosecute military commanders for violating the proportionality rule.[14] There are indeed very few cases in which a violation of the IHL proportionality rule has been established. To shield their military commanders from prosecution for causing collateral damage except in the clearest cases may have been a desired outcome for the States that negotiated the IHL proportionality rule as it stands today.

It is submitted that in the circumstances where the IHL rule on proportionality must be applied, no rule can be formulated that covers every possible scenario in which an attack is planned. The question thus remains how objective the proportionality rule can be formulated in the first place. It is furthermore submitted that an objective rule does not necessarily mean that the outcome of the rule must be measurable in mathematical terms. Objectivity can also follow from relative factors. For example, the IHL proportionality rule can assist in finding when an expected outcome of an attack must be deemed to be more proportionate than another outcome. Thus, a commander who assesses these two different outcomes is able to decide which outcome is less and which is more excessive in terms of the balance between expected collateral damage and military advantage. Therefore it follows that even if the components of the proportionality equation perhaps cannot be determined in a measurable way, they can still be compared and the rule is thus useful.

12 Kalshoven 1992, p. 44.

13 See for example Dinstein 2008, p. 5: '[t]he difficulty is that military advantage and civilian casualties are like the metaphorical apples and oranges: a comparison between them is an art, not science.'

14 Bartels 2013, pp. 271–315.

In order to be able to decide whether the collateral damage of an attack is inside the limits set by the IHL proportionality rule, it is necessary to assess the subjective or objective character of the different factors that need to be taken into account in the application of this rule, because it impacts on the subsequent question of whether the IHL proportionality rule as a whole can be seen as either an objective or a subjective rule.

8.3.2 *Are the Factors in the IHL Proportionality Rule Objective or Subjective?*

The IHL proportionality rule is comprised of many different factors, as was analysed in depth in Chapter 6. As follows from the debates among academics, a number of the aspects of the proportionality analysis could profit from further clarification in order to improve the protection the civilian population may enjoy from this important rule as well as assist commanders in applying the rule. Unfortunately, the conclusion is that the exact legal meaning of many of these factors remains unsettled and subject to heated scholarly debate. Furthermore, the value attached to these factors in a proportionality assessment is dependent on the actual circumstances and context of the planned attack.

Firstly, there is the fact that only military objectives may be attacked. Although IHL provides for a definition of a military objective, that definition itself consists of a number of subjective factors.[15] Secondly, once a military objective has been identified, the next question in the context of the IHL proportionality rule is what the 'concrete and direct military advantage' is that would follow from attacking that military objective. In order to justify the loss of life and limb of civilians and damage to their belongings, the military advantage that justifies that loss must be sufficiently (1) concrete, (2) direct and (3) military, which is a more elaborate test than that which is necessary to identify a military objective. The question whether the military advantage may be expected to be 'concrete and direct' depends on many factors, such as the information available to the attacking commander and the importance of the target in the overall campaign. Thus, even if the military advantage may be determined easily in a quantitative sense (such as the number of enemies expected to be killed or injured or the expected number of enemy tanks destroyed), the military advantage that these effects have on the operation still

15 For example, whether an object is a legitimate military objective based on its location, such as a bridge or a certain hill, depends primarily on the question of whether, given the circumstances ruling at the time, that object plays a role in the hostilities. Only when that role would render a military advantage may the object in question be targeted.

depends on other factors, such as the proximity to the zone of hostilities and the danger they pose to own troops. The concrete and direct anticipated military advantage that will result from a planned attack will therefore be too dependent on its context to characterise it as completely objective. A qualitative analysis is always required to compare different outcomes that are expected from different possible modes of attack and as a result the military advantage expected from an attack will always remain a subjective factor.

The factors that play a role on the other side of the balance include the expected injury or death to civilians and damage to civilian objects. The protection of civilians depends on the question of whether the civilians refrain from participating directly in the hostilities. This too is a difficult question, depending on a number of subjective parameters. But for the purpose of assessing the proportionality of a planned attack, it is crucial to establish the civilian status and protection of persons who are expected to be affected by the planned attack. After all, that is decisive for the side of the proportionality equation where these individuals must be counted. For civilian objects, the difficulty is that any civilian object can be, and often is, used also for military purposes. That means that it can be unclear whether the destruction of an object must count as collateral damage or as part of the military advantage that follows from an attack. Nonetheless, for technologically advanced militaries, it will be possible to actually place a quantitative number to the civilians that are expected to be affected by a planned attack, using sophisticated collateral damage estimation (CDE) methodology. In addition, it will in some cases be possible to put a monetary value on the expected damage to civilian objects. Therefore, it is submitted that it is possible, at least in theory, to find an objective value for the expected civilian damage.

Nonetheless, when the foreseeability of reverberating effects on the collateral damage for civilians must be assessed, the analysis turns into a qualitative analysis, which will consequently be assessed differently by different military commanders.[16] Therefore, the expected collateral damage for larger operations may be expected to have a subjective character. This is the result of the fact that the temporal aspect of both the anticipated military advantageous outcome of the attack and the civilian damage that it is expected to cause are undefined. Although it is a given that the anticipated military advantage must be 'direct', it is questionable whether effects from the attack that will become militarily advantageous in a later stage of the operation may also be given

[16] See ICRC Commentary on API, Sandoz et al., para. 2208: 'this system [referring to article 57(2)(a)(iii)] is based to some extent on a subjective evaluation'; Bothe et al., para. 2.6.2 on article 51: 'the judgment must be subjective'; Wright, p. 839; Oeter 2013, p. 197.

weight in the equation. The test of whether the effects are foreseeable is only satisfactory up to a certain point in this respect. Direct effects of wounds may certainly be counted as collateral damage, but the question may be asked whether effects on the health (including mental harm) of the civilian population that may only be expected to materialise a number of years later must also be taken into account as being foreseeable. In this respect, one may also think of an attack using weapons that could cause serious diseases after a certain period, or attacking water facilities that will perhaps not directly lead to serious consequences for the civilian population, but may after a longer period lead to a decline in sanitary conditions, depending on how the conflict develops.

Henderson[17] and Wright claim that the IHL proportionality test of excessiveness is 'hybrid', because it is an objective ('reasonable') assessment of the subjective factors of military advantage and civilian damage.[18] The subjective element of the proportionality assessment, according to Henderson and Wright, is thus the evaluation in good faith of the factors such as military advantage and civilian damage. The objective part follows, from the 'resulting balancing [to be] objectively reasonable in ensuring that the civilian deaths, injury, or property destruction are not excessive'.[19] In most scenarios, the value of both the expected military advantage and the expected collateral damage is not clear-cut and must be characterised at least as partly subjective.

It is thus submitted that the IHL proportionality assessment remains a partly subjective standard, although in some instances, parts of the components of the IHL proportionality assessment may be valued objectively. Taken in its totality, the IHL proportionality is thus both subjective and objective, and thus a hybrid assessment. However, the objectivity may be determined to a certain extent by labelling the standard as 'objective but qualified'.[20] Then it seems that the question of whether an objective proportionality assessment can be accomplished is moot, in spite of the preference for an objective test for reasons of the passive and active protection rationale. Instead, it is submitted that every attempt to phrase the IHL proportionality assessment in purely objective terms at some point ends up in the assertion that it must be made

[17] There are both subjective and objective elements in the proportionality calculation, but 'the assessment is not capable of precise analysis or determination by a mathematical equation'. See Henderson, p. 222.

[18] Wright, p. 846 and Henderson, p. 223.

[19] Wright, p. 847.

[20] See Henderson and Reece, p. 6: '[a]s the proportionality decision requires an assessment, it is imperative to understand whether the assessment is subjective (e.g. "where a person believes"), objective but unqualified (e.g. "where a person reasonably believes"), or objective but qualified (e.g. where a doctor reasonably believes)'.

reasonably. Nonetheless, the qualification of those that need to conduct the proportionality assessment as a reasonable military commander must be made as objective as possible. Therefore, the next section assesses in what ways the objectivity of the IHL proportionality assessment could be enhanced.

8.3.3 *Measures to Limit the Subjective Application of the IHL Proportionality Rule*

It is submitted that even if it were impossible to achieve a fully objective proportionality rule in IHL, there is nonetheless a number of measures that may be taken to increase the objectivity of the IHL proportionality rule. These measures are to a certain extent procedural in nature.

The first procedural measure that can be taken to enhance the trust that can be given to the military commander is through maximising the efforts in providing them with proper training in IHL in general. A thorough knowledge of the interpretation of the factors that need to be taken into account in the proportionality analysis, as discussed in Chapter 6, will increase the objectivity of the proportionality assessment of an actual attack during armed conflict. It must, however, be acknowledged that setting high standards for the training of military commanders is not the whole story, because some targeting decisions are often made at a much lower level. Therefore, group commanders and even foot soldiers must also, as a minimum, be trained in the principles and basic rules of IHL.

Connected to the measure of improving the knowledge on how the factors of the proportionality assessment must be understood is conducting training in peacetime through different exercise scenarios during which proportionality assessments must be made. The experience that results from these proportionality assessments made in a training environment is likely to increase the 'reasonableness' of a proportionality analysis that needs to be conducted during actual armed conflict. This is the result of an enhanced familiarity with the process of balancing the different components and of discussions with other military commanders and staff officers that is possible in the context of military exercises. Thus, the outcomes of proportionality assessments will become more predictable – and thus more objective.

Furthermore, armed forces may achieve a higher degree of objectivity in the application of the proportionality principle by institutionalising their targeting procedures, such as those that have been analysed in Chapter 5. The purpose of these procedures is to ensure that the targeting process takes all relevant factors into account and includes a genuine effort to minimise collateral damage by taking precautionary measures and to ensure that the proportionality of the attack is assessed before the decision is taken to launch, postpone or cancel a planned attack.

Fourth, the objectivity of the process may be enhanced by ensuring that the military commander has access to well-trained (military) legal advisers.[21] It is crucial that these legal advisers are aware of the effects of the means and methods that the military commander has at his disposal to execute the attack. It is the job of the legal adviser to provide the military commander with advice on the options the commander has to launch a planned attack or attain a sought military gain within the limits set by the rules of IHL. Wright has argued that in this role, military lawyers are often 'the first-line defenders of human rights in combat environments'.[22]

Fifth, a more objective IHL proportionality rule can be strived for by using procedures, software and equipment that maximise the correct assessment in advance of the likely effects of weapons and modes of attack under consideration. In Chapter 5, a description of systems such as CDE Methodology was provided. It has been argued that following a checklist may be of assistance here. Types of checklists do exist, and mostly follow the IHL rules as explained in Chapter 5. Many of the procedures the military uses for targeting purposes are classified, but some are available in the open domain. An example is the collateral damage sheet or form for US Air Force support in urban operations.[23]

Sixth, although the IHL proportionality rule is to be applied before an attack, evaluating an attack after it has happened can also be useful for enhancing the objectivity of future attacks. These evaluations could include a permanent procedure of conducting a thorough battle damage assessment (BDA) after an attack.[24] It must be noted that BDAs would first and foremost serve to analyse whether the sought military advantage has been attained, or whether an additional attack is necessary. Arguably, however, the knowledge

[21] As required by article 82 API.

[22] Wright, p. 821. See also generally Newton, and more specifically the 'Populated Area Targeting Record' on p. 894.

[23] According to US military doctrine, Battle Damage Assessment (BDA) is part of the Combat Assessment procedure. It aims to 'to compare post-execution results with the projected results generated during target development'. See United States, Joint Chiefs of Staff 2007.

[24] There have been a number of writers who have suggested that it should be imperative to permanently assign units the task of conducting ex post investigations of all attacks that resulted in collateral damage. See for example Reynolds, pp. 104–106, who suggests that 'collateral damage response teams' should be deployed. Also, Cohen suggests that the proportionality rule should be supplemented by the duty to conduct an ex post review if civilian deaths have resulted. See Cohen 2009, p. 38. This resembles the international human rights law duty to investigate, see generally Margalit.

that an attack will be investigated in cases where collateral damage has occurred will be an incentive for military commanders to ensure that they plan attacks in such a manner that the outcome will be proportionate. Moreover, the military commander may as a result adopt the practice to better document the considerations that were at the basis of the decision to launch the attack. Obviously, investigating an attack after it has occurred entails that the ex post investigators have the difficult task of seeking to acquire the value of the factors relevant for the proportionality assessment as they were perceived by the military commander ex ante. Furthermore, presumably, the parties to an armed conflict may not be too enthusiastic about accepting a duty upon their forces to conduct these types of investigation. This applies particularly to less-sophisticated armed forces, and in cases where conducting an ex post investigation is not feasible.

Another measure is that parties to an armed conflict must conduct in-depth studies into the effects certain weapons have under certain circumstances, through intensive testing of these weapons. This obligation already exists to a certain extent, since States that are parties to API are bound by its article 36, that prescribes that States review the legality of new weapons systems. When it is clear what damage will be done by a certain mode of attack using a certain weapon, it is also possible to conduct a more precise CDE, as discussed in Chapter 5. Presumably, this will enhance both the knowledge of the commander about the anticipated military advantage of the attack and the magnitude of the expected civilian collateral damage. When these factors can be determined to a very detailed level, a more precise – and arguably more objective – proportionality analysis can subsequently be conducted.

Other measures that could be taken to strive for a maximum degree of objectivity of the proportionality assessment include efforts to maximise the quality of the sources of intelligence for commanders, and measures that aim at ensuring the mental and physical fitness of commanders at the time they need to decide on the proportionality of a planned attack. In practice, however, these decisions often need to be made under time pressure in the stressful and chaotic circumstances of hostilities.

Some procedures that are in place in more sophisticated militaries restrain the execution of attacks much more than the proportionality rule could ever do in practice. These procedures are the result of policy, rather than law, and may be put down in certain rules of engagement. A specific example is the requirement that in cases where a higher number of collateral casualties is expected, the decision must be taken up the chain of command. Corn describes these measures as 'civilian casualty benchmarks'. He notes, 'higher levels of command establish limits on the maximum number of anticipated civilian casualties a subordinate commander may permissibly risk through a targeting judgment'.[25] In these cases where the collateral damage is expected to surpass a certain threshold of magnitude, the decision to launch the attack needs to be taken by a commander in a more senior position. The potential restraining factor contained in this is that the commander referring the decision up to higher levels of command will consider the planned attack with more precision, and the targeteer will draft the target folder with more care. The reason for this is that the subordinate military officers may be expected to refrain from wasting the valuable time of their superiors with targeting requests of poor quality. Also, in these cases, the decision is made by a more experienced commander who is less emotionally involved with the planned attack, feels less sense of urgency and has a broader view of how the tactical operation fits into the bigger picture. Furthermore, higher commanders may be assumed to have a larger number of more experienced staff officers and specialists at their disposal, who are able to further refine the analysis of the components of the proportionality assessment of the planned attack. Thus, a more objective outcome of the proportionality assessment may be expected.[26] Furthermore, there is another 'highly significant benefit of reserving proportionality judgments to higher levels of command, because as the judgment is progressively elevated, the commander entrusted with the judgment will be able to consider a broader range of alternative targeting options'.[27]

The following section addresses the concept of the 'reasonable military commander'. After a discussion of the question of whether the 'reasonable military commander' constitutes an objective element of the proportionality assessment, the issue is addressed whether the 'reasonable military commander' must be seen as the applicable legal standard providing the yardstick for assessing the components of the IHL proportionality rule.

8.4 THE 'REASONABLE MILITARY COMMANDER'

It was concluded earlier that the military commander, no matter their level of decision-making, is responsible for the IHL proportionality assessment.[28] The question of whether military commanders may be trusted with such a

[25] Corn 2014, p. 461.

[26] Corn calls these types of procedures as 'a procedural tool to enhance the ultimate substantive proportionality judgment'. See Corn 2014, p. 462.

[27] Corn 2014, pp. 463–464.

[28] It must be noted that the individual conducting the IHL proportionality assessment is not necessarily a commander in the usual sense of the word, of being responsible for subordinates

daunting task is therefore not relevant, because it is a truism that anybody who plans, decides upon or executes an attack *is* responsible for conducting this assessment. But that does not mean that there are no limits to how the responsible military commander must apply the IHL proportionality rule. One of the most important of these limits is reasonableness.

It needs to be reminded in assessing the concept of the reasonable military commander that this concept has been introduced by the jurisprudence of international criminal tribunals. In that context, the tribunals need to apply, ex post, a different yardstick of proportionality than the military decision maker needs to in planning and deciding on future attacks. At first sight, it thus seems to be a valid question whether this concept of the reasonable military commander could potentially add substance to the legal obligations of commanders that are to apply the IHL proportionality rule in practice. However, to reverse the issue: if it is not the reasonable military commander, then how can the person responsible for conducting the IHL proportionality assessment be referred to? Furthermore, as Henderson and Reece note, there are good reasons to use the term reasonable military commander, because 'this standard has the advantage of having gained acceptance among practicing lawyers, academics, NGOs and militaries'.[29]

This section assesses first to what extent the concept of the 'reasonable military commander' provides an objective yardstick for assessing excessiveness. Subsequently, remaining subjective factors are identified. Finally, the question is addressed of whether the concept of the 'reasonable military commander' constitutes a meaningful yardstick for assessing excessiveness in applying the IHL proportionality rule.

8.4.1 *The Objectivity of the Concept of the 'Reasonable Military Commander'*

The concept of the 'reasonable military commander' was suggested by the office of the Prosecutor in the Kosovo Report of 2000. It held that '[a]lthough there will be room for argument in close cases, there will be many cases where *reasonable military commanders* will agree that injury to non-combatants or the damage to civilian objects was clearly disproportionate to the military advantage gained.'[30] The ICTY Trial Chamber echoed the relevance of the

in the military chain of command. Nonetheless, the term 'military commander' is used to refer to the person who is responsible for conducting the IHL proportionality assessment.

29 Henderson and Reece, p. 21. See also Israel Ministry of Foreign Affairs 2015, para. 317, p. 181.

30 ICTY OTP Kosovo Report, p. 19 (emphasis added).

reasonable commander in addressing the IHL proportionality rule in the *Galić Case*. The Trial Chamber held that '[i]n determining whether an attack was proportionate it is necessary to examine whether a reasonably well-informed person in the circumstances of the actual perpetrator, making reasonable use of the information available to him or her, could have expected excessive civilian casualties to result from the attack.'[31] The Trial Chamber thus does not require the person *as such* to be reasonable in the assessment of excessiveness, but whether the military commander is *reasonably well-informed* and whether the available information is *reasonably used*. It may be suggested that these two issues are embedded in the standard concerning causality and foreseeability of the effects of the planned attack and the precautionary obligations rather than in the assessment of whether the persons conducting the assessment of the two sides of the proportionality analysis are reasonable themselves.

According to one dictionary, the term 'reasonable' means in this context 'in accordance with reason, not absurd'. The term 'reason' in this context must be understood as 'what is right or practical or possible; common sense or judgement'.[32] A preparatory background document for an ICRC Expert meeting held in Quebec in June 2016 notes a number of further descriptions found in military manuals describing the terms 'reasonable' in connection with a military commander carrying out IHL proportionality assessments. These descriptions basically boil down to the conclusion that the 'reasonable' military commander is expected to act in 'good faith', 'rationally', 'honestly' and even 'objectively'.[33] These different words used to describe how military commanders must make proportionality assessments, it is submitted, do not amount to a materially different yardstick. Rather it may be assumed that military commanders conduct their proportionality assessments reasonably. This is because the training and experience of military professionals is aimed at respecting the principles and basic rules of IHL, among which is the IHL proportionality rule. The respect for this is 'a matter of sound military judgement [and the IHL proportionality rule serves] not so much to limit military effectiveness as to provide legal reinforcement for professional military values'.[34] Thus, it is submitted, the adjective 'reasonable' in the term reasonable military commander may be understood to be satisfied when the

[31] ICTY, *Prosecutor* v. *Stanislav Galić*, Trial Chamber, Judgment, 5 December 2003, para. 58.

[32] Cowie, p. 1046.

[33] ICRC, Background Document 2016, pp. 21–22, on file with the author. See also ICRC 2018, pp. 57–62.

[34] Carnahan, p. 868.

subjective features of military commanders have been sufficiently limited. It has been submitted in Section 8.3.3 that the subjective features of military commanders can be limited to a certain extent by ensuring that a number of procedural measures have been taken.

The objectivity of the reasonable military commander may be argued to increase when all the measures that enhance their objectivity have been taken into account. In more concrete terms, this means that the reasonableness is enhanced as long as, for example, it can be proven that the commanders have been well-trained, particularly in IHL. In addition, it can be determined whether the subordinate staff officers, targeteers, group commanders and foot soldiers have also been trained in the principles and basic rules of IHL. This could relatively easily be ascertained by requiring a minimum number of training hours, or by requiring the members of the military to pass an exam on their respective level of required knowledge. It is furthermore the duty of the leadership of armed forces to ensure that a sufficient level of knowledge and training exists within the different components of the armed forces, including forces consisting of conscripts or reserves. In addition, it can be objectively established whether the military commander has access to well-trained legal (military) advisers. This, too, would constitute an objective element in the total calculation. Furthermore, a minimum number of years of military experience in targeting decisions can be required from military commanders. With regard to specific attacks, it can be assured by using checklists whether military commanders have had sufficient access to the information that assists them in determining whether the expected civilian casualties may be excessive.[35] If available, this applies equally to whether auxiliary means such as CDE methodology have been used to assess the damage the planned attacks may cause and predict the expected collateral damage. These systems are often able to provide reliable expectations on the damage the use of certain munitions or fuses may cause, thus enabling commanders to assess the expected collateral damage as accurately as possible. These types of decision-support tools, including computer programs that provide calculations for different options for decision makers, are obviously not available in all circumstances and to every level of decision-making.

[35] Checklists may assist in following the right sequence of assessment that lead to the commander being able to make an informed decision and in making sure that no factors are accidently left out of the assessment because the military commander forgot to take it into account. Obviously, no matrix or checklist could be all-compassing, because there are indefinite factors, with different levels of certainty and expectations.

8.4.2 *Remaining Subjective Factors for 'Reasonable Military Commanders'*

Even when all procedural measures have been taken, subjective factors remain that influence the outcome of the proportionality analysis. Some of these remaining subjective factors seem inherent to the judgement of human beings. For example, when the decision makers and their staff have already put considerable effort into determining the factors of a planned attack, it may perhaps be understandable that they develop the preference to go ahead with the attack. This psychological effect may arguably entail that slightly more emphasis is put on the importance of the military advantage sought by the attack than is put on preventing harm from occurring to the civilian population.

Another subjective element that remains is the assessment military commanders will make of the value of human life. The ICTY OTP Kosovo Report notes that with regard to the excessiveness of a planned attack the answer different military commanders will give 'will differ depending on the background and values of the decision-maker'.[36] Some commentators have expressed their general scepticism towards military commanders, because they expect that 'the military will naturally tend to overstate the importance of the military advantage part of the equation'.[37] This statement is not new. The commentary to the 1956 Red Cross Draft Rules includes a statement warning that the importance of the expected military advantage should not be overstated. Instead, it must be assessed in the light of experience, which often shows how much the obtained result is inferior to the one that was anticipated.[38] During the deliberations that led to the adoption of the 1977 Additional Protocols, a Swedish representative is reported to have stated that

> [a] man responsible for an attack against a military object, will sometimes say himself that the suffering that may be caused – as far as he can judge – to the civilian population is not disproportionate to the military advantage he gains by destroying the object, but the people who will suffer by the attack will find the suffering too grave and the military advantage less important. Who is right?[39]

[36] ICTY OTP Kosovo Report, para. 50.

[37] Sassòli and Cameron, p. 64.

[38] ICRC 1956, p. 702: 'L'avantage militaire ne doit pas se voir attribuer une valeur excessive; il doit, au contraire, être apprécié à la lumière de l'expérience, qui montre souvent combien le résultat obtenu est inférieur à celui qui avait été escompté.'

[39] ICRC 1957.

According to one author, this tendency particularly exists when one of the parties is militarily superior.[40] During Operation Allied Force it was reported with regret by one author that '[t]he extensive process of target review combined with a preoccupation to avoid collateral damage resulted in cancelled targets, delayed engagements, failure to produce enough targets to adequately mass, and limited strikes producing inconsequential effects.'[41] The missing factor here seems to be the human factor. Instead of the apparent disappointment of the author that there may have been missed opportunities, there must also have been civilian lives saved. Nonetheless, it may be that political pressure to engage a larger number of targets, or operational considerations to apply 'overwhelming' force during an overall attack may lead to commanders dedicating less attention to their obligation to minimise civilian casualties and damage, leading to an approach in which the civilian side of the proportionality assessment is undervalued.

A further complication for finding an objective standard of reasonableness may be that commanders from different cultures may attach different values to the components of the IHL proportionality rule.[42] It seems furthermore to be a common feature of mankind to be, or become, more or less indifferent to the suffering of the adversary. Yet, the IHL proportionality rule serves to protect all civilians equally. For that reason, a number of writers have suggested that this perception may be prevented by including in the proportionality equation, a 'reversed assumption' whether the commander would consider the attack lawful if the expected collateral damage consisted of civilians of his own side. Gomez writes that the subjective character of the IHL proportionality rule is 'the Achilles heel' of the law of war. The rule could perhaps be seen in more practical terms if it stated that an aerial attack expected to cause civilian casualties would be acceptable should it have the same degree of approval as a similar action taking place over a part of the country's own territory under enemy occupation, in which case the civilian casualties would be

[40] McPherson, p. 94: '[o]ur tendency when we are in a position of considerable advantage will be to identify with the possible benefits to ourselves and others for whom we have special concern and to dissociate from the costs to persons likely to bear the burdens of use of force.'

[41] Reynolds, p. 87.

[42] Reynolds, p. 71:

> [t]he value of life ranges among individuals and cultures, making a value determination of civilian casualties compared to a military objective highly variable.... A military commander from a depressed, under-developed state with little access to the resources necessary to make the most prudent command decisions cannot be held to the same standard of reasonableness as commanders from highly advanced military states with extensive resources, information, technology, and high situational awareness of the battle space.

compatriots'.[43] In this rather simple way, the danger may be avoided that the lives of civilians of the adversary are seen as less valuable than the lives of 'own' civilians would be.[44] This, it is submitted, may be a tool for military commanders to apply in order to enhance the quality of their decisions.

In the end, it must be stressed that making decisions with regard to the IHL proportionality assessment must be done by military commanders, but the outcome of such assessments must not only be acceptable in *military* terms. After all, the military is part of the civil society as a whole and must not only take military considerations into account when assessing the excessiveness of expected collateral damage. As Bothe put it: '[i]n democratic systems, the values pursued by the military and those society at large cannot be far apart. The value system on the basis of which the military is operating has to conform to that of the civil society, not *vice versa*.'[45]

8.4.3 *Sub-conclusion*

Military commanders are responsible for the application of the IHL proportionality rule in practice, but their margin of appreciation is not unlimited. It is suggested that the IHL proportionality calculation is a subjective standard, although some of its components can and must be as objective as possible in the process of the proportionality calculation. Nonetheless, '[e]ven when the comparison is between the number of military casualties and civilian casualties, the comparison is still not between human lives and human lives',[46] because the military advantage of killing different people varies. There is no option other than to 'rely on judgement, although it must be judgement influenced by a reasonable understanding of what will be generally acceptable and understood in humanitarian terms'.[47] Military commanders must act in good faith, but 'persons acting in good faith may make mistakes'.[48] Kalshoven and Zegveld note that it is decisive 'whether a normally alert attacker who is reasonably well-informed and who, moreover, makes reasonable use of the available information, could have expected the excessive damage among the civilian population'.[49] However, different military commanders may come to

43 Guisández Gómez 1998, p. 358.
44 See also Krüger-Sprengel, pp. 192–193 and Henderson, p. 229.
45 Bothe 2001, p. 535.
46 Henderson, p. 223.
47 Haines, p. 9.
48 Fenrick 2000, p. 77.
49 Kalshoven and Zegveld, p. 115.

different conclusions when faced with identical circumstances.[50] This alone suggests that there is no objective yardstick in the phrase 'reasonable military commander' other than that the rule is violated in cases where the relationship between the two is such that it was unreasonable for military commanders to have proceeded with the attack.

The references to reasonableness that were made earlier are not included in the text of the IHL proportionality rule. Nonetheless, there seems to be agreement that reasonableness is a key factor in the application of the IHL proportionality rule. This should not come as a surprise, as 'in all . . . fields of international law, it is necessary that the law be applied reasonably'.[51] Furthermore, it was concluded that reasonableness is used for a clash between unequal interests, which requires a more qualitative assessment. It is submitted that the IHL proportionality rule fits that description and therefore the 'reasonable military commander' is not a separate component of the IHL proportionality rule, but instead the manifestation of the general principle of the international law of reasonableness. The term 'reasonable military commander', it is submitted, does not provide guidance for implementing the IHL proportionality rule additional to that of the general principles of international law. Moreover, the phrase 'reasonable military commander' does not in itself enhance the objectivity of the IHL proportionality rule. However, it is submitted that the measures mentioned earlier will be of assistance in establishing an a priori expectation that military commanders have not acted unreasonably in their assessment of the excessiveness of a planned attack. Procedural measures alone are, however, insufficient to determine a priori the reasonableness of commanders in their targeting decisions, because there is also a material component. In the field of IHL, as a branch of international law, it is the general principle of reasonableness that provides this obligation for States to ensure that their agent (the reasonable military commander) conducts the IHL proportionality assessment reasonably. In sum, the concept of the 'reasonable military commander' is the standard for evaluating the decision on the basis of the proportionality assessment by a commander. That commander is 'a person with all the experience, training and understanding of military operations'.[52] It can therefore be understood to mean that in the context of the application of the IHL proportionality rule, military commanders need to make a thorough assessment in good faith of all the different components of the rule as well as the circumstances at the time, and take a reasonable

[50] See also Henderson, pp. 221–224.

[51] *Barcelona Traction Case*, ICJ Reports 1970, para. 93.

[52] Henderson and Reece, p. 11.

decision to launch, postpone or cancel an attack because of their obligations under the IHL proportionality rule.

8.5 WHAT IS 'EXCESSIVE'?

Even though it has been established earlier that the definition of the components of the proportionality equation is subject to extensive debate, to determinate the ratio between the two major components is 'the most difficult of all'.[53] As an example, referring to the same attack, Amnesty International and the ICTY OTP reach a very different conclusion on the question of whether the NATO attack on a Serbian television station was proportionate.[54]

If it is accepted that the 'reasonable military commander' does not provide definitive guidance for establishing the excessiveness of a planned attack, further analysis of the term 'excessive' is required. The interpretation of this term determines the difference between a lawful attack and an unlawful attack in the IHL proportionality rule. The draft that was drawn up by the ICRC contained the word 'proportionate', but after the draft article was discussed in the drafting committee, Frits Kalshoven claims to have proposed using the word 'excessive', which was subsequently accepted.[55]

It is useful to stress that when an attack is planned where it is expected that a large number of civilian casualties and massive damage to civilian objects will occur, this extensive civilian damage does not necessarily lead to a violation of the IHL proportionality rule. Yet, it is worth exploring the fine line between extensive and excessive collateral damage. This is the subject of Section 8.5.1. Subsequently, the attention turns to the question of whether the standard of excessiveness is drawn in terms of 'excessiveness' or 'clear excessiveness' (Section 8.5.2).

8.5.1 *Extensive or Excessive?*

It seems fair to say on the basis of the various arguments made earlier that even an attack that is expected to cause 'extensive', or 'massive' collateral damage

53 Kalshoven and Zegveld, p. 109.

54 See Amnesty International 2000, p. 49: '... NATO deliberately attacked a civilian object, killing 16 civilians, for the purpose of disrupting Serbian television broadcasts in the middle of the night for approximately three hours. It is hard to see how this can be consistent with the rule of proportionality' and the ICTY OTP Kosovo Report, para. 71. See also Henderson, p. 221. And see previous chapter, Section 7.3.3.

55 As indicated by Frits Kalshoven during a presentation of this author on 'Controversial issues surrounding the principle of proportionality in international humanitarian law' at a research meeting of the Kalshoven-Gieskes Forum on International Humanitarian Law at Leiden Law School on 27 November 2012.

may be lawful, provided that an even more significant military advantage is expected to be the result of that attack. Rogers concludes that 'extensive' collateral damage is irrelevant, since 'the more important the military objective, the greater the incidental losses before it could be said that the rule of proportionality had been violated'.[56] Geiss agrees that IHL 'does not prescribe any absolute limit in relation to collateral damage'.[57] Thus, a very considerable military advantage could potentially justify significant civilian damages and even casualties, that is extensive as opposed to excessive collateral damage. Also, the scope of an attack needs to be taken into account to assess the extensiveness of collateral damage: 'proportionality is not assessed by looking at the total amount of collateral damage at the end of an armed conflict and then determining whether that collateral damage is excessive when compared against the goals of the armed conflict'.[58]

Yet, obviously, attacks that cause a large quantity of collateral damage are among the first suspects of attacks where the IHL proportionality rule may have been disregarded. Also, the question may be raised of whether the sheer magnitude (extensiveness) of expected collateral damage could be the absolute boundary of the test of excessiveness, even when the expected military advantage is expected to be immense. In other words: may the expected vast *extensiveness* of an attack render an attack that is not excessive nonetheless illegal?[59]

The ICRC Commentary to API states on this topic that

> [t]he idea has also been put forward that even if they are very high, civilian losses and damages may be justified if the military advantage at stake is of great importance. This idea is contrary to the fundamental rules of the Protocol – in particular it conflicts with Article 48 '(Basic rule)' and with paragraphs 1 and 2 of the present Article 51. The Protocol does not provide any justification for attacks which cause extensive civilian losses and damages. Incidental losses and damages should never be extensive.

This statement has, however, been criticised.[60]

According to Kalshoven,

> [t]he principle of proportionality was introduced as a last line of defense [to protect the civilian population]. Must we now recognize yet another,

[56] Rogers 2012, pp. 25–26.

[57] Geiss 2010, p. 127.

[58] Henderson, p. 201, referring also to Laursen, pp. 795–796 and Dinstein 2004, p. 123. Henderson also mentions Sassòli as another supporter of this view.

[59] Kalshoven 1992, p. 44.

[60] See for example Henderson, p. 224, Watkin 2007, p. 29.

> ultimate upper limit beyond which collateral damage that is not excessive in view of the absolutely imperative military necessity of the attack, will by its terrible scale become unacceptable nonetheless?[61]

Kalshoven answers his own question negatively, however, it may be worth exploring the argument slightly further.

The question may be asked whether lawful extensive damage to the civilian population is in line with the historical idea of IHL, which is to provide a humanitarian baseline for the accepted fact that the warring parties must be able to conduct their operations. It seems unlikely that the rules of IHL were crafted to allow for extensive civilian damage for reasons of military advantage in the planning phase of an operation, because IHL seeks to prevent massive civilian casualties through a large number of protective rules. It may be argued that all those protective rules, such as the principle of distinction and the prohibition to conduct indiscriminate attacks, are rendered irrelevant when operations are planned with such a high military advantage that extensive civilian damage may be lawful. This is of particular relevance for the use of certain types of weapon. It must be realised that the principle of proportionality only became an accepted part of the codified rules of IHL in 1977. At that time, the nuclear era was thirty years old and the magnitude of the civilian damage and casualties to be expected from the use of nuclear weapons and the devastating effects of the bombings on cities during World War II were clear. The rule of proportionality may therefore have been one of the underlying reasons why the International Court of Justice concluded in their Advisory Opinion that the use of nuclear weapons could be lawful in some cases. This is the claim that any operation is legal, no matter how reckless and potentially devastating for the civilian population, provided it is militarily sufficiently advantageous. Clearly extensive collateral damage and the use of illegal means or methods of warfare could thus potentially be justified, because the stakes are so high. This is exactly the argument that the International Court of Justice has used in its appraisal of the legality of Nuclear Weapons, and the suggestion put forward by Michael Walzer that it is justified to violate the rules of IHL in cases of 'Supreme Emergency'.[62]

It is true that the IHL rule of proportionality does not allow the incidental damage that is expected from an attack to be viewed in isolation.[63] However, it is submitted, there is a difference between the civilian side and the military advantage side, when both are stretched to their extremes. The outer limit of

[61] Kalshoven 1992, p. 44.

[62] Walzer, pp. 251–268.

[63] Henderson, pp. 224–225.

the humanitarian part of the proportionality equation is the prohibition on the attack of civilians and launch of indiscriminate attacks. These are absolute legal obligations. The outer limit of the military advantage, at least for a large-scale planned attack, ultimately still leaves a choice to the attacker. There is no absolute legal obligation to launch an attack, no matter how advantageous it may be. The ultimate incentive to conduct an attack that would cause extensive civilian casualties, which could be acceptable because of the massive military advantage that is expected from it, is found in *ius ad bellum*, not in IHL. It may therefore be argued that the limit for the humanitarian side of the IHL proportionality equation is contained within the law, whereas the limit for military advantage is not. This could, in extreme cases, be taken as the legal rationale why attacks that may cause extensive collateral damage could be illegal, even though there is a massive military advantage to be gained. Judge Higgins seems to acknowledge this situation where she writes that

> [i]t must be that, in order to meet the legal requirement that a military target may not be attacked if collateral civilian casualties would be excessive in relation to the military advantage, the 'military advantage' must indeed be one related to the very survival of a State or the avoidance of infliction (whether by nuclear or other weapons of mass destruction) of vast and severe suffering on its own population; *and that no other method of eliminating this military target be available.*[64]

It is thus submitted that planned attacks expected to cause extensive civilian damage may comply with the IHL proportionality rule only in cases where there is no other choice at all to attain a certain enormous military advantage. In all other cases, where extensive collateral damage occurs, the planned attack should be cancelled. The legal basis for this rule would be article 57 (1) of API, which contains the obligation to take constant care of the civilian population. Of course, the next question is when the expected civilian damage may be labelled as 'extensive'. However, for this, it may be possible for States to address this question in consultations, leading to expectations of operations that will cause more than a certain number of civilian casualties as 'extensive', and thus contrary to the rules of IHL at first sight.

To be clear, practical examples of the situation that has just been described may be found only on strategic levels and in the situations to which the ICJ referred in its Nuclear Weapons Advisory Opinion: when the survival of the State is at stake. In the vast majority of situations, there is no situation where

[64] *Legality of the Threat or Use of Nuclear Weapons*, Advisory Opinion, Dissenting Opinion of Judge Higgins, ICJ Reports 1996, para. 21, p. 588 (emphasis added).

such a huge military advantage could be attained that the extensiveness of civilian casualties would stand in the way of a planned attack. However, the possibility that the extensiveness of an attack stands in the way of its lawfulness under the IHL proportionality rule, it is submitted, should not be dismissed categorically. Nonetheless, the applicable standard of the IHL proportionality rule is 'excessive'.

8.5.2 *Excessive or* Clearly *Excessive?*

The next issue to be determined is the question of what the exact standard is, because the standard of 'excessive' as included in the treaty text of Additional Protocol I differs slightly from the standard of '*clearly* excessive' that is included in article 8 (2) (b) (iv) of the Rome Statute, adopted in 1998. The 'clearly excessive' standard was copied in the Report of the ICTY Prosecutor on Kosovo of 2000, referring to the attacks of 23 April 1999 on the Serbian Radio and TV Station in Belgrade.[65] It is striking to note, however, that in one of the first cases before a criminal tribunal, that of *Galić*, the ICTY Trial Chamber did not refer to the clearly excessive standard in its explanation of the rule;[66] however, it does note with regard to a specific attack on a football match that 'although the number of soldiers present at the game was significant, an attack on a crowd of approximately 200 people, including numerous children, was *clearly* excessive in relation to the direct and concrete military advantage anticipated'.[67] This of course does not prove anything, because when the collateral damage is 'clearly excessive', it is by definition also 'excessive'.

Rogers is of the opinion that the formulation in the Rome Statute that includes the adjective 'clearly' is '[p]erhaps the closest one can get to an acceptable formulation of the customary law principle of proportionality'.[68] It must be noted that he seems to primarily have phrased this conclusion when it concerns questions of individual criminal responsibility, and it is for a tribunal to consider that the collateral damage 'must be "clearly" excessive before criminal liability can be established'.[69] Dinstein has suggested that the meaning of the word 'clearly' was already implicitly included in the proportionality test, and that it was merely made explicit by the formulation used in

65 ICTY OTP Kosovo Report, p. 26.
66 ICTY Trial Chamber, *Galić*, para. 58.
67 ICTY Trial Chamber, *Galić*, para. 387 (emphasis added).
68 Rogers 2008, p. 208.
69 Rogers 2008, p. 210.

the Rome Statute[70] and that the benefit of the insertion of the adjective is 'unclear'.[71] Boothby, however, notes that the text of API does 'not necessarily imply this "clearly disproportionate" element, although its practical application probably does'.[72]

The difference in wording, it is submitted, should not be interpreted to be of importance for military commanders planning an attack.[73] It is their obligation to cancel or postpone an attack if they believe it will cause excessive civilian damage. Military commanders will normally be well aware that whenever an attack is expected to be 'clearly' excessive, they need to consider an alternative. These are the easy cases for military commanders, where the intended operative mode for IHL becomes apparent: it plays its role as a preventive framework guiding military commanders. The fact that the adjective 'clearly' is now included in the Rome Statute 'must be understood as not to change the existing law'.[74] For international criminal law, on the other hand, the inclusion in the Rome Statute means that for international criminal responsibility to arise, the word 'clearly' must be seen as an additional requirement for a disproportionate attack to constitute a war crime under the Rome Statute.[75] The fact that the formulation in the Rome Statute contains the word 'clearly' in the definition is not surprising, given the fact that the adjective is added for criminal law purposes. It means that an attack that is not 'clearly' disproportionate (but nonetheless disproportionate) is not a war crime under the Rome Statute. This means that when a commander has conducted a fair proportionality calculation, after which he concluded that the planned attack would be disproportionate, he needs to cancel or postpone it. If he proceeds with it nonetheless because he believes it is not 'clearly' disproportionate, he has violated the rules of IHL, but he is off the hook where it regards his individual criminal liability under international criminal law. This is understandable because it is difficult, if not impossible, for a judge to assess ex post

70 Dinstein 2004, p. 120, but in the 2016 version of his handbook on the conduct of hostilities under the law of international armed conflict, he calls the 'value added of the adverb "clearly" *obscure*' (emphasis added). See Dinstein 2016, note 869 on p. 153. See also Watkin 2007, p. 8.

71 Dinstein 2012, p. 269.

72 Boothby, p. 97.

73 See, however, Boothby, p. 97:

> [w]hile accepting that the Rome Statute fulfills its own purpose in international criminal law and that its interpretation is not determinative of the meaning to be given to the API provision, the former text should, nevertheless be borne in mind when we consider the proportionality principle, not least because it represents the most recent internationally adopted text on the subject.

74 Dörmann 2003a, p. 169.

75 McCormack and Mtharu, p. 196.

the exact circumstances as they appeared to military commanders at the time they had to make proportionality decisions. In fact, that is already hard enough for military commanders themselves, and the IHL proportionality rule thus seems to leave room for situations in which there may be a disproportionate attack that may be blamed on the commander, and on his State of origin, but that does not give rise to individual criminal liability.

Thus, the application of the IHL proportionality rule requires that even when a planned attack is not expected to be 'clearly' excessive, but excessive nonetheless, it needs to be cancelled or postponed.

8.6 CONCLUSION

It is submitted in this chapter that there are a number of objective factors in the proportionality equation, but that it is ultimately a subjective assessment. A number of measures should be taken in order to further objectify the IHL proportionality assessment by military commanders. The remaining subjective components of the calculation must be assessed in good faith and the assessment with regard to the excessiveness of incidental civilian death, injury or damage must be conducted in a reasonable manner, on all levels of command. That does not mean that the 'reasonable military commander' provides an objective yardstick. The possibility of a reasonable proportionality calculation conducted in good faith does exist, it is submitted, although much work needs to be done before consensus exists on the interpretation of the different components and thus a more clear-cut application of the IHL rule of proportionality becomes possible. In addition, the yardstick of excessive must not be confused with the term 'extensive', or with the yardstick of 'clearly' excessive.

The aim of this chapter, which is to formulate guidance for conducting a proportionality assessment of a planned attack, is perhaps only attained to a limited extent. It is concluded that ultimately, the IHL proportionality rule must be accepted as it is: an inherently imprecise and flexible yardstick that nonetheless does play its role as the last line of protection for the civilian population, and an obligation for reasonable military commanders to take that protection seriously into account by refraining from attacks that may cause excessive collateral damage. The ultimate question therefore is how the term excessive must be interpreted in light of all factors impacting on the IHL proportionality rule. This is the subject of the next chapter.

9

Determining Excessiveness and a Plea for Tilting the Balance towards Humanity

9.1 INTRODUCTION

This chapter proceeds to further explore the term 'excessive' and dissects a number of factors that affect the assessment of military commanders as to whether expected collateral damage may be excessive in Section 9.2. One of these factors is the probability of success of an attack, which is proposed as a third component of the IHL proportionality rule in Section 9.3. A number of rationales for attaching more weight to the prevention of causing collateral civilian damage and casualties than is done traditionally is proposed in Section 9.4, which may result in a refocussed application of the IHL proportionality rule, tilting the balance more towards humanity. In Section 9.5, some policy and operational factors are discussed that may affect the assessment of excessiveness of collateral damage. Section 9.6 revisits the discussion about the level of authority making a proportionality assessment in the context of how this level affects the factors to be taken into account. The last two sections of this chapter address the question of whether there is a need to clarify or change the IHL proportionality rule and suggest one way ahead to acquire more practical guidance for commanders to apply the IHL proportionality rule.

9.2 DETERMINING EXCESSIVENESS

A preliminary remark for the discussion in this chapter is that since the assessment of excessiveness in applying the IHL proportionality rule is a case-by-case analysis, it is particularly difficult to draw general conclusions about how excessiveness must be determined. Sivakumaran warns that '[t]he concept of excessive is such that any explanation, even that designed to elucidate the test, may have the effect of distorting rather than clarifying the meaning.'[1] Wright similarly concludes that '[t]here is no overarching definition of "excessive" because the variables in the proportionality standard are relative to each other.'[2] Nonetheless, the proportionality calculation must be conducted, notwithstanding the fact that shedding more light on the interpretation of the term excessive is a difficult task.

When an imprecise word contained in a legal text, such as the term 'excessive', must be interpreted, the first and most obvious way is to look at the normal use of the word.[3] According to one dictionary, 'excessive' means 'greater than what is normal or necessary' or 'extreme'.[4] In other words, the term excessive is used to assess the relation between two or more factors. If that relation is in balance, it may be said that the situation is normal, and thus not excessive. It is tempting to use the example of a scale in this respect. As long as the scale is in balance, none of the factors is excessive in relation to the other. In terms of collateral damage and military advantage, this means that as long as the balance tilts in the direction of where the collateral damage is expected to be less significant than the anticipated military advantage, the planned attack is not excessive. It may even be argued that even when the collateral damage is slightly more than the military advantage, it is not excessive because the imbalance is not 'extreme', nor is the collateral damage 'clearly' excessive compared to the anticipated military advantage. This ordinary use of the word 'excessive' in balancing military advantage and civilian casualties and damage then seems to tilt the scale in favour of military advantage, because it seems to suggest that even when the two factors are in balance, the collateral damage cannot be said to be excessive. The standard of 'excessiveness' rules out a standard of 'clearly excessive'. As was explained in the previous chapter, this is the standard that applies for prosecutions under international criminal law; thus military commanders must apply a yardstick in IHL that is more protective of civilians and civilian objects than the standard that would constitute a violation under international criminal law. As a result, claims that attacks are only disproportionate in situations where the ratio between the expected collateral damage and the anticipated military advantage is 'clearly' out of balance is incorrect. However, there are a number of reasons suggesting that the interpretation of the term 'excessive' may not be as clear-cut as the ordinary use of the term would suggest.

1 Sivakumaran 2012, p. 351.

2 Wright, p. 853.

3 Article 31(1) of the Vienna Treaty on the Law of Treaties: 'A treaty shall be interpreted in good faith in accordance with the ordinary meaning to be given to the terms of the treaty in their context and in the light of its object and purpose.'

4 Cowie, p. 416.

If an attack is likely to cause any collateral damage after precautionary measures are taken, the question comes up of whether the military advantage sought by the attack is significant enough to justify the expected collateral damage. The resulting balancing act that is required must not be understood as a precise measurement between military advantage and civilian injury and loss. In doctrine, a number of writers have attempted to clarify the term 'excessive'. Dinstein, for example, notes that 'excessive' means 'that disproportionality is not in doubt'.[5] This, however, resembles the test of 'clearly' excessive, and may therefore seem to permit military commanders too much leeway. According to Kalshoven and Zegveld, military commanders are not expected to conduct 'an all too subtle weighing process...: the attacker is obliged to refrain from the attack only if the disproportion between the two sides in the equation "becomes apparent"'.[6] This merely substitutes the term 'excessive' for that of 'disproportion'.

One useful approach to assist military commanders in determining excessiveness may be to introduce a scaled approach. For example, the HPCR Manual on Air and Missile Warfare Commentary proposes the use of the qualifiers, 'marginal', 'substantial' and 'high'.[7] Wright proposes using the scales of 'marginal', 'moderate' and 'substantial'.[8] It is, however, submitted that a scaled model of only three qualifiers lacks sufficient granularity and is therefore unable to do justice to the plurality of situations that military commanders face in actual combat circumstances. Therefore, a more refined approach seems preferable for providing useful guidance for military commanders in order to determine excessiveness in applying the IHL proportionality rule. The qualifiers that may be proposed are then (ranging from small to large): marginal, minor, medium, major, massive.

It will still prove to be difficult to categorise these two components of the IHL proportionality rule in one of the five qualifiers. What needs to be taken into account, however, is the fact that the factors could be calculated to a certain extent in objective terms before they are balanced in the assessment of excessiveness. Here, States may be able to develop objective guidelines for the assessment of the respective factors, taking into account those factors that count on each level of decision-making. As Wright notes with regard to incidental civilian damage: 'national militaries may find it useful to establish

5 Dinstein 2016, p. 155.

6 Kalshoven and Zegveld, p. 115.

7 Program on Humanitarian Policy and Conflict Research, Harvard University, Commentary, p. 92.

8 Wright, p. 852.

objective guidelines concerning what amount of civilian death, injury, or destruction would generally be marginal, moderate, and substantial (e.g., anticipated civilian casualties is marginal, 2–4 is moderate, and 5+ is substantial)'.[9] In fact, it seems that sophisticated militaries could connect the categorisation into the five qualifiers introduced earlier to the assessment they already make for determining when the authorisation for the execution of an attack needs to be referred up the chain of command because of the number of civilians that is expected to be affected by the planned attack.

As far as the anticipated military advantage of a planned attack is concerned, again, many factors are relevant, such as the scale of the attack and whether there is a threat to own forces. Some authors note the need to differentiate between the proportionality assessments for attacks with a defensive objective on the one hand, and those with an offensive military aim on the other.[10] Here, context matters so much that it is more difficult to establish a baseline that may be put into more objective guidelines in order to categorise the military advantage in terms of the five qualifiers mentioned earlier. To the extent States have developed such guidelines to qualify military advantage, such information is mostly classified. In the public domain, Guisández Gómez has suggested an approach to provide different types of military advantageous aspects of a planned attack with points, with different factors to subtract or add points.[11] The aspects taken into account include the importance of the target to the opposing forces; the importance of the target to the attacking side and the distance to the target. It is submitted that depending on the level of command under which the attack is taking place and the context of the planned attack, it may be possible to devise a methodology to attach value to the anticipated military advantage and subsequently classify it in terms of one of the five qualifiers identified earlier. This is, however, an effort that only more sophisticated militaries would be able to conduct in the planning phase of attacks, and which militaries would presumably not be willing to share in public sources. Not too much may be expected from a resulting guidance document, however, because the method may be completely useless in situations that do not allow any time for elaborate planning and calculations. Also, because of the overriding importance of the unique circumstances of each planned attack, the resulting parameters can only be understood as guiding, not as authorising. A common-sense reality

[9] Wright, note 192 on p. 848.

[10] See von der Groeben, discussing the *Kunduz Fuel Tankers Case*, pp. 479–482.

[11] Guisández Gómez 2007, pp. 197–243 (in Spanish).

check must always accompany the guidance that military commanders can derive from the proposed five-step scaled analysis.

When framed in a matrix, a picture may become clear. There is a line somewhere in the middle where the anticipated military advantage and the expected collateral damage are in balance. As long as the expected collateral damage remains above the diagonal line, these decisions may be deemed to be taken in accordance with the IHL proportionality rule. The subjective and qualitative characters of the IHL proportionality rule will normally not allow for determinations of the excessiveness of an attack that are exactly on that line. Rather, a zone or area is more likely to exist in which reasonable military commanders may differ in their opinions of whether the civilian damage expected from a planned attack is excessive.

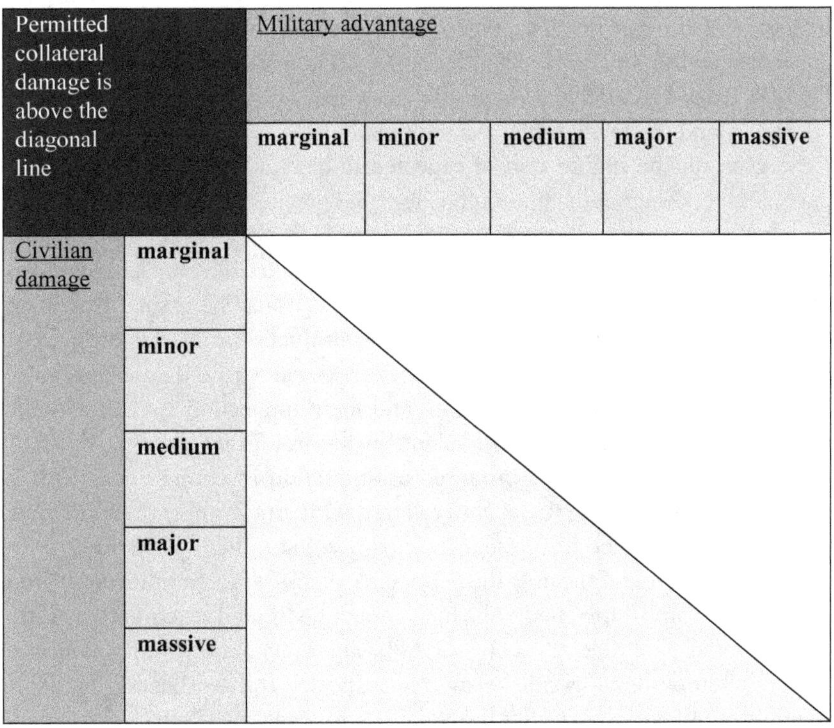

It also needs to be pointed out that the ratio between military advantage and collateral damage is not a straight line. There are some indicators already embodied in IHL that show how the term excessiveness must be interpreted.

These factors prove that there is no complete linear relation between the two factors to be balanced, because the law already provides for guidance in some situations.

First, on the lower end of expected military advantage and collateral damage, the qualifier 'concrete and direct' in the definition of the military advantage anticipated means that where a planned attack is expected to result in marginal military advantage and also marginal collateral civilian damage, it is likely that the planned attack must be labelled as causing excessive collateral damage. This is because when the military advantage is likely to be marginal, it may also be expected to be insufficiently 'concrete and direct' compared to the marginal collateral damage, and the law does not contain an additional qualifier to the expected collateral damage. Thus, in cases of marginal expected military advantage that is not 'concrete and direct', where some limited collateral damage is expected to occur, the balance will usually tilt in favour of the collateral damage. In other words, not all types of military advantage counts, but *any* civilian harm does. This means that the attack must in most cases be cancelled or postponed where both the expected military advantage and the civilian harm is only marginal.

Second, on the higher end of expected military advantage and collateral damage, the law contains some indicators that dictate that certain ratios must be labelled as disproportionate attacks. These indicators can be found in the attacks defined as indiscriminate attacks, in particular, the attacks prohibited by article 51 (4) (c) and article 51 (5) (a) of API. It may be argued that these prohibitions are related to the principle of distinction, not proportionality. However, in the author's view, the IHL proportionality rule is an extension of the IHL rules concerning distinction, and their application is not so fundamentally different that this would stand in the way of considering the IHL proportionality rule and the principle of distinction in conjunction. This is particularly true because the attacks referred to in article 51 (4) (c) and article 51 (5) (a) of API are both in essence aimed (also) at military objectives.

The first of these indicators thus concerns attacks which employ a method or means of combat the effects of which cannot be limited as required by IHL, as prohibited by article 51 (4) (c) of API. These attacks are prohibited also under the proportionality rule because the expected collateral damage is likely to increase uncontrollably after the military advantage of the attack is reached. This may be understood to mean that where it is expected that initially (right after the attack), the collateral damage is not (yet) excessive, but when it is foreseeable that the effects produced by the means or method of attack cannot be contained or limited as required by the proportionality rule, the collateral damage may be expected to eventually reach the point when the collateral damage becomes excessive in relation to the military advantage sought by the attack.

The second types of attack (those by bombardment by any methods or means which treats as a single military objective a number of clearly separated and distinct military objectives located in a city, town, village or other area containing a similar concentration of civilians or civilian objects) are prohibited under the IHL proportionality rule because the practice of World War II had shown that in these types of attack the expected ratio of military advantage and collateral damage was in such imbalance that these attacks would produce excessive collateral damage to the civilian population.[12] Thus, these types of attack are both specifically prohibited as indiscriminate attacks in API, as well as by the prohibition to launch disproportionate attacks under the IHL proportionality rule.

Furthermore, it has been submitted earlier that, for the purpose of the proportionality calculation, while there is no difference in value to be attached to one civilian or another, this is not true for civilian objects. The law determines, for example, that cultural objects and objects that are indispensable for the survival of the civilian population enjoy special protection. With regard to civilians, although the law does not state this explicitly nor implicitly, one could argue that if the amount of media attention is taken as an indicator of who enjoys broader protection, children and (pregnant) women and the elderly generally would enjoy special protection against attacks. It may be argued that as such, they should attribute extra weight to the civilian scale of the balance as compared to other civilians. By analogy to the law applicable to civilian objects, the same may be argued, depending on the factual situation, for other categories of civilian persons that are 'indispensable for the survival of the civilian population', namely firefighters or police officers, or those persons who provide the main source of a family's income. This is not reflected in the law, but may arguably be elaborated upon in policy considerations to which States commit themselves in their practice.

[12] See ICRC Commentary to API: Sandoz et al., p. 624, para. 1968:

> [t]he first type includes area bombardment, sometimes known as carpet bombing or saturation bombing. It is characteristic of such bombing that it destroys all life in a specific area and razes to the ground all buildings situated there. There were many examples of such bombing during the Second World War, and also during some more recent conflicts. Such types of attack have given rise to strong public criticism in many countries, and it is understandable that the drafters of the Protocol wished to mention it specifically, even though such attacks already fall under the general prohibition contained in paragraph 4.

When reduced to a step-by-step model, the IHL proportionality test requires military commanders to (1) assess the two components of the proportionality assessment; (2) assign a value to both components; (3) compare these two values; and (4) decide on the basis of that assessment whether the planned attack would produce excessive collateral damage in the prevailing circumstances, and to therefore launch, postpone or cancel the planned attack. The dominance of the prevailing circumstances at the moment the attack is planned make it impossible to formulate a one-size-fits-all formula commanders may use. Nonetheless, using a checklist to make sure all factors that need to be taken into account are part of the ultimate assessment may benefit military commanders who are in the midst of active hostilities. It would assist them in ensuring that all factors that are part of the IHL proportionality rule are taken into account.

It is submitted, however, that the IHL proportionality rule is not as simple as the scaled model, described in the previous paragraph, would suggest and that the ordinary meaning of the word excessive seems to indicate. Indeed, it seems that there is another factor that impacts the determination of excessiveness, and that is the *probability* that the anticipated collateral damage, and military advantage will indeed materialise as expected. Furthermore, it is submitted that the perceived understanding of the word excessive, attaching more weight to the expected military advantage than to civilian damage, must be adjusted in the other direction. These two proposals of adjustments of the ordinary literal interpretation of the word 'excessive' will be further expounded in the following two sections.

9.3 PROBABILITY OF SUCCESS AS A FACTOR DETERMINING EXCESSIVENESS

It is submitted that the IHL proportionality rule requires military decision makers not only to balance the value of military advantage and civilian damage, but also, as a third factor, the probability of success. This factor concerns the estimation of how likely it is that the operation will in fact go as planned, that is that the expected military advantage will in fact materialise and the probability that the collateral damage will not exceed what is expected in advance.[13] This factor deals with a different aspect than foreseeability,

[13] This factor is referred to as 'likelihood' in a background paper prepared by Chatham House for an expert round table held at Chatham House on 9 March 2018, as part of the Chatham House project on 'Proportionality in the conduct of hostilities: the incidental harm side of the assessment'. This author is part of that project and the background paper is on file with the

which concerns the effects of a planned attack that are expected, and the question of causality, which concerns the expectation that a certain effect will result from the planned attack.

Taking this factor into account may prevent operations from which a high value of military gain is expected, and a similarly high (but not excessive) expected value of collateral damage is anticipated, but with only a small probability that the operation will materialise as planned. The operations that come to mind in this respect are those attacks by the United States in 2003 that sought to kill Saddam Hussein, but that ended up only killing large scores of civilians.[14] Although it may be accepted that at the time, it was very militarily advantageous to kill Saddam Hussein, the probability of the attacks actually hitting Saddam Hussein was very low, if not merely speculative, because the attackers were aware that they were relying on very unreliable information. A similar example is the attack on General 'Chemical' Ali Hasan Al-Majid as well as the attack on Milan Martić as discussed in Chapter 7.

It is submitted that adding the factor of probability of success leads to a more refined IHL proportionality assessment, because it may assist in tipping the balance between excessive and non-excessive in close cases. It is, however, difficult to find a yardstick that defines the probability of success of a planned attack. As noted in the previous chapter, expectations of the success of the planned attack are subjective by definition, yet an expectation may become more objective when there is sufficient information available on the nature of the military objective and the number of civilian objects and civilians surrounding it. This is furthermore a matter of conducting thorough precautionary measures in the planning phase. The availability of surveillance assets and other information sources are therefore important in order to be able to obtain a clear picture of the target and the presence of civilians and civilian objects. Of course, military planners and commanders will prefer reliable equipment and information, because if 'there are difficulties in anticipating the consequences, that is not of any use to military planners'.[15] The Commentary to the HPCR manual suggests that '"[e]xpected" collateral damage and "anticipated"

author. See also the final report: Gillard, pp. 17–18 and 20. This book draws a different conclusion than the Chatham House Report: the Chatham House Report concludes that likelihood must be addressed when assigning weight to the two factors in the IHL proportionality rule.

14 As was claimed by Mr Garlasco (former chief of US high-value targeting) during an interview on 60 Minutes, a 'couple of hundred' civilians were killed during fifty airstrikes aimed at killing Saddam Hussein and other high-value targets, whereas none of the targets was actually hit. See Wikipedia.

15 Garraway 2005, p. 3.

military advantage, for these purposes, mean that that outcome is probable, i.e. more likely than not.'[16] It seems that such an 'at least fifty-fifty' approach is unsatisfactory, because it significantly erodes both the protection of the civilian population and the effectiveness of the military effort. Lacking a better term in which probability of success can be measured, as well as taking into account that the IHL proportionality assessment by its nature is a matter of prediction rather than an exact science, it is submitted that military commanders and planners must be 'pretty sure' or 'very confident' that the planned operation will have the effects it is expected to have in terms of both components of the IHL proportionality assessment. This may be expressed as a percentage, but it seems more practicable to assess this in terms of the degree of confidence a reasonable military commander may have in expecting a certain effect. Therefore, when a military commander is not sufficiently confident and sure that an attack will have the planned effects, the planned attack is simply very risky. In these situations, it is submitted that commanders must accept levels of collateral damage that are far beneath what would be non-excessive in an operation that has a very high probability of success. Of course, it remains a forward-looking assessment, but that does not justify gambling with certain high civilian casualties and damage against a very small probability of attaining a military advantage. To attack a military objective with a very low probability of success is furthermore contrary to the required level of expected military advantage that must be assessed in the IHL proportionality assessment, which is required to be 'concrete and direct'.

It is thus submitted that the probability of success must be taken into account not when determining the respective values of military advantage and collateral damage, but at a later stage, when the assessment is made whether the equation of comparing the two factors may be expected to result in excessive collateral damage. An example may assist in illustrating why it is important at what point during the application of the IHL proportionality rule the factor of the probability of success of an attack is brought into the assessment. Suppose an attack is planned on a high-ranking military commander of the opposing forces. The attack, if it succeeds, will clearly provide a major military advantage. The expected collateral damage is calculated to be medium. Normally, the proportionality rule could be argued not to stand in the way of this attack, because the medium expected civilian damage is not excessive in relation to the major military advantage anticipated from the attack. If the probability of success of the operation is only very small, however,

[16] Program on Humanitarian Policy and Conflict Research, Harvard University, Commentary, pp. 91–92.

this, it is submitted, puts the civilian population in harm's way to such an extent that the IHL proportionality assessment must be deemed to be excessive. The result is a three-dimensional assessment of excessiveness, taking into account (1) the military advantage anticipated from the planned attack; (2) the expected collateral damage; and (3) the probability that the results of (1) and (2) will materialise as expected.

9.4 TILTING THE BALANCE OF EXCESSIVENESS TOWARDS HUMANITY?

According to some authors, the application of the principle of proportionality is not a question of 'balancing' but rather a 'test of excessiveness'.[17] Schmitt explains that in his view, it is not a matter of determining whether the concrete and direct military advantage would 'outweigh' resulting collateral damage and incidental injury, as in a scale 'with the slightest difference tipping the balance'.[18] The test of excessiveness would in his view only ban attacks

> in which there is no proportionality at all between the ends sought and the expected harm to civilians and civilian objects.... Focusing on excessiveness avoids the legal fiction that collateral damage, incidental injury, and military advantage can be precisely measured. Ultimately, the issue is reasonableness in light of the circumstances prevailing at the time.[19]

As may be derived from the earlier discussion, this study concludes that the analogy of balancing two different values is the most useful model to use. However, that model does not explain what happens when the scale is more or less in balance. Wright argues that in those cases '[w]hile the proportionality standard provides constructive ambiguity, the scale should always be tilted in favour of furthering the protection of the civilian population.'[20] Thus this study comes to a similar conclusion. Taking all considerations into account, it is submitted that the consideration of protecting the civilian population must take precedence over considerations of military advantage in close cases, or when there is a balance between the two components of the IHL proportionality assessment.[21]

17 Schmitt 2006a, p. 293 and Boothby, p. 97.
18 Schmitt 2006a, p. 293.
19 Ibid.
20 Wright, p. 853.
21 For a similar view: see Sandoz et al., para. 1979: '[i]n some situations there will be no room for doubt, while in other situations there may be reason for hesitation. In such situations the interests of the civilian population should prevail.' See also ICTY, *Prosecutor* v. *Galić*,

In the hypothetical situation that a military commander concluded that the ratio is in balance, two different interpretations of the rule on proportionality are possible: one is to conclude that since there is a balance, the planned attack apparently does not produce 'excessive' damage. As noted earlier, the interpretation of the word 'excessive' in its ordinary meaning, attaches more weight to the expected military advantage than to civilian damage. This interpretation would mean that an attack is proportionate as long as the expected collateral damage does not exceed the expected military advantage too much. There are however a number of indications arguing against this interpretation of the term 'excessive'. This may be of assistance for military commanders in these close cases, or in other words, in those situations where the expected civilian damage and casualties are beneath the standard of 'clearly excessive' when compared to the expected military advantage. It is submitted that the preferred interpretation is that when in balance, there is not more military advantage than there is expected collateral damage, and therefore the planned attack must be postponed or cancelled.

The rationales for the latter interpretation, it is submitted, are (1) the context and purpose of the proportionality rule; (2) the fact that the component of military advantage is qualified in the IHL proportionality rule with the additional qualifiers 'concrete and direct'; (3) the API and customary rule of precautions to take 'constant care' to spare the civilian population; (4) the application of IHL principles through the application of the Martens Clause; and (5) the allocation of risk on the civilian population for the militaries' mistakes, faulty intelligence, malfunction of weapons systems or misreading and misunderstanding of information and other factors that cannot be controlled, such as the influence of weather.[22]

9.4.1 *Context and Purpose*

The first rationale is connected to the context and purpose of the IHL proportionality rule. In accordance with article 31 (1) of the Vienna Treaty on the Law of Treaties, the ordinary meaning of the term 'excessive' as found in API must be interpreted in its context and in the light of its object and purpose. It is submitted that the place of the rule is of relevance and indicates the context for the interpretation of the IHL proportionality rule. The IHL

IT-98-29-T, Trial Judgment, 5 December 2003, para. 58: '[t]he basic obligation to spare civilians must guide the attacking party when considering the proportionality of an attack.'

22 See Dinstein 2004, p. 135 for a list of all the 'things that can go wrong as far as civilians are concerned'.

proportionality rule is codified in article 51 (Protection of the Civilian Population) of Part IV (Civilian Population), in Section I (General Protection Against Effects of Hostilities), Chapter II (Civilians and Civilian Population) of API, as well as in article 57, placed in Chapter IV (Precautionary Measures) of the same section, providing an indication that the rule is aimed at protecting civilians. There is not only a duty to take the precautionary measures, but an additional duty on the part of the attacker emanating from the objective of the section where the IHL proportionality rule is formulated as a protective rule for the civilian population. It may then be concluded that the object and purpose of the IHL proportionality rule is that it is a protective rule for the civilian population. Therefore, when no clarity exists as to which side of the scale must take precedence in close cases, the context of the IHL proportionality rule in API, as well as its purpose concerning the protection of the civilian population, points to the conclusion that the interpretation of the ordinary meaning of the term excessiveness needs refocussing in light of the protection of the civilian population.

9.4.2 *Qualifiers in the IHL Proportionality Rule*

The second rationale, it is submitted, is the fact that the component of military advantage is qualified in the IHL proportionality rule with the additional qualifiers 'concrete and direct', whereas the component of the civilian damage does not have these additional qualifiers. This points to a conclusion that the drafters of the IHL proportionality rule meant to define the military advantage component as more restrictive in the IHL proportionality assessment than the factor of the collateral damage. It obliges military commanders to take *any* collateral damage into account, whereas for military advantage, only those militarily advantageous outcomes of a planned attack can be taken into account that are 'concrete and direct'.

9.4.3 *The Constant Care Obligation*

The third rationale that points in the direction of tilting the proportionality scale in favour of the protection of civilians in close cases is the rule of customary IHL embodied in article 57 (1) of API that 'constant care shall be taken to spare the civilian population, civilians and civilian objects'. Since this provision applies to not only attacks but to all types of military operation, the rule may be understood to apply to factual situations where an imprecise rule of IHL must be interpreted. Thus, as the interpretation of 'excessive' in close cases is one of these rules, it is submitted that the obligation to take constant care of the civilian population points to an interpretation of the IHL proportionality rule that in close cases, the protection of the civilian population must take precedence rather than the military advantage that may be expected from a planned attack.

9.4.4 *The General Principle of Proportionality*

A fourth rationale, although its scope is subject to debate, is the application of the Martens Clause, which points to the possibility of using a general proportionality principle (as opposed to the IHL proportionality *rule*) that may be used to interpret the IHL proportionality rule to the benefit of those not participating in the hostilities, and thus for the protection of civilians.[23] This general proportionality principle may be derived from the different manifestations of proportionality mitigating the use of armed force in international law, applicable during armed conflict. The different standards of moderation in IHL aim to prevent excessive effects from the use of armed force during armed conflict.[24] The multitude of other proportionality standards applicable during armed conflict in the *ius ad bellum* and IHRL supports this. This general proportionality principle could be understood as a substantive legal principle that may fill gaps and interpret specific rules of IHL, without being able to set other rules or principles of international law aside. The objective of this principle is to mitigate suffering of both civilians and opposing forces and is more specific than the foundations of IHL, humanity and military necessity.[25]

When proportionality is interpreted as a broad concept that is present in many different branches of international law, it can be regarded as a general principle of the entirety of international law. When applied to the law pertaining to situations of armed conflict, it could be interpreted as '*une*

[23] See also Section 2.2.2.

[24] See Chapter 3.

[25] The ICRC Interpretative Guidance (primarily written by Melzer) states that '[i]n conjunction, the principles of military necessity and of humanity reduce the sum total of permissible military action from that which IHL does not expressly prohibit to that which is actually necessary for the accomplishment of a legitimate military purpose in the prevailing circumstances.' See Melzer 2009, p. 79. Another ICRC legal adviser, Cordula Droege, wrote that

> [t]here is a growing position that even under humanitarian law the ability to use lethal force is limited not only by a principle of proportionality protecting incidental loss of civilian life or damage to civilian objects, but also by other limitations inherent to humanitarian law, in particular the principle of military necessity and the principle of humanity.

See Droege 2008, p. 526.

doctrine générale limitative de la violence dans les conflicts armés'.[26] The existence of such a general proportionality principle in IHL is recognised by some authors, courts and States. For example, Philippe argues that proportionality is a 'central' principle of IHL.[27] The Israeli *Beit Sourik Case* of 2004 states that '[p]roportionality is recognized today as a general principle of international law'.[28]

Some of the practice that has been collected by the ICRC in the customary law database with regard to the IHL rule on collateral damage also relates to a more general statement of moderation in the use of force during armed conflict.[29] The 2015 US Manual on Law of Armed Conflict (LOAC), updated in 2016, also refers to a general principle of proportionality. It states on the

[26] Philippe, p. 1183. For a similar view, David 2001, pp. 237–239.

[27] Philippe, p. 1187: 'Le principe de proportionnalité occupe donc un place enviable en droit international humanitaire et sous-tend l'ensemble du droit des conflits armés.' Philippe proposes to integrate an explicit proportionality criterion in any decision-making process during armed conflict to prevent the principle to be only an ideal, but a reality instead. See Philippe, p. 1192. See also Gardam 1993, p. 11, writing that the 'theory of proportionality' is a 'central element of the modern law of armed conflict'. Also, Melzer states with regard to an obligation to 'capture rather than kill', that the argument that this applies could be based, except on the military necessity principle in IHL and on IHRL proportionality, also on 'a wider proportionality requirement, which would constitute a general principle of international law'. See Melzer 2010b, p. 299 and Melzer 2006, pp. 87–113.

[28] *Beit Sourik Case* (HCJ 2056/04, *Beit Sourik Village Council et al.* v. *Government of Israel et al.* 58(5) PD, or the English translation in 43 ILM 1099 (2004)) With regard to this case, Pertile states that

> the view that the principle of proportionality, although never finding explicit recognition, operates in the application of [IHL] can be safely shared. The principle is the normative tool that reconciles the opposing values of humanity and military necessity. However, contrary to what the reasoning of the Court seems to imply, it is submitted that the reasons of military necessity are not recognised by every norm applicable to the case at hand and that the balancing operated through the principle of proportionality is possible only when reference to military necessity is explicitly admitted in a derogatory clause.

See Pertile, pp. 679–680.

[29] See for example the Military Manual of the Philippines: '[t]he use of force to accomplish authorized missions should be reasonable in intensity, duration and magnitude.' See also Kenya's LOAC Manual, which states that '[o]ne of the main principles which places constraints on the conduct of hostilities is "the principle of proportionality which calls for the avoidance of unnecessary suffering and damage and therefore prohibits all forms of violence not indispensable for the overpowering of the enemy"'. See Military Manual of the Philippines. In addition, the United Kingdom is on the record stating that '[a]ll our military planning is conducted in full accordance with our obligations under international law to employ *the minimum necessary use of force* to achieve military effect and to avoid injury to non-combatants or civilian infrastructure.' See Mr Adam Ingram, Minister of State for the Armed Forces, see House of Commons, Official Report, 2 April 2003, column 738W (emphasis added), as quoted in the Chilcot Report, available on www.iraqinquiry.org.uk, para. 51 on

subject that IHL 'requires that even when actions may be justified by military necessity, such actions not be unreasonable or excessive'.[30] This definition of proportionality is clearly a different, more general, notion than the proportionality rule on collateral civilian damage, since it refers to proportionality as a means to balance the more general principle of military necessity on the one hand and unreasonableness and excessiveness on the other hand.[31] It thus seems that the US Manual on LOAC adequately acknowledges that manifestations of proportionality apply in different rules of IHL. However, it seems that in the reference to the principle of proportionality requiring that even actions justified by military necessity must not be disproportionate, proportionality works as a general principle that serves to connect the separate rules of IHL into a coherent system.[32]

It must be noted that this general principle is not undisputed. Some notable authors maintain that no normative guidance may be derived from the principles of IHL.[33] However, there may also be potential to see

p. 180. This seems to indicate that the United Kingdom views its proportionality obligations under IHL to be broader than the IHL proportionality rule.

30 US Department of Defense Law of War Manual (US DoD Manual) p. 51.

31 Military necessity is defined as the 'principle' that 'justifies certain actions necessary to defeat the enemy as quickly and efficiently as possible'. See US DoD Manual, p. 51. It is not entirely clear whether the United States understands this proportionality principle as a more general notion that entails legal obligations for US soldiers. In the further elaboration of proportionality, the principle is explained by referring to the military concept of the economy of force, the IHL 'standard applicable to persons conducting attacks' (i.e. the collateral damage rule, JvdB), the rule on precautions against the effects of attacks and with reference to the prohibition on the use of weapons that are calculated to cause superfluous injury and unnecessary suffering. US DoD Manual, pp. 60–62.

32 The accompanying footnote, however, refers to Vattel and Grotius; and also to the *Caroline Case*, where proportionality is explained to mean that even actions taken in self-defence should not be 'unreasonable or excessive' since such actions 'justified by the necessity of self-defense, must be limited by that necessity and kept clearly within it'. If this phrase is meant to introduce a military necessity justification to use armed force based on the *ius ad bellum*, even when that would not be in accordance with the rules of IHL, it must be rejected. If this notion of proportionality is, however, meant to refer to a legally binding principle of IHL that is legally restricting the use of armed force during armed conflict, the references in the footnotes make no sense. US DoD manual, note 67 on p. 60.

33 See for example Kleffner and Dinstein. A general proportionality principle would in Kleffner's view not have an independent normative value that would apply directly to the battlefield. He states:

> [t]o approach the law on the conduct of hostilities from the opposite permissive starting point – that parties to an armed conflict are allowed to use those methods and means which are not expressly prohibited – is more in tune with the nature of the law of armed conflict as a law that governs a state of exception rather than normality. Hence, there are good reasons for maintaining that, in the area of the law governing the conduct of hostilities, any restriction on what parties to an armed conflict may do when using force

proportionality as one of the principles that applies as an independent source of international law, or it may be accepted as a principle or as a rule of international customary law.[34]

This general principle of proportionality applies as a touchstone for rules of IHL which have indeterminate components. The discussion in the previous chapters shows that the IHL proportionality rule is certainly a rule comprised of subjective factors that require further interpretation. These factors need to be assessed in light of the circumstances ruling at the time, with the general proportionality principle in mind to moderate the effects of armed conflict on the civilian population. This calls for an interpretation of the IHL proportionality rule that favours the protection of the civilian population in the close cases.

9.4.5 *Mistakes by Soldiers Are Not Violations*

The fifth rationale for attaching more weight to the prevention of causing civilian damage in cases where only a small difference of value exists between the two components of the proportionality assessment is that IHL allocates the risks of accidents causing civilian damage exclusively to the civilian population. The IHL proportionality rule does not take into account the inescapable fact that the military may make honest mistakes when they are planning attacks. Furthermore, the military may rely in good faith on intelligence that proves to be wrong and use weapons systems that may malfunction from time to time, without running the risk of being blamed for that in terms of a violation of the IHL proportionality rule.[35] In addition, a violation of the IHL proportionality rule does not occur in situations where the military has

against military objectives in their quest to overcome the adversary must derive from an express restriction stipulated in a rule or principle of positive international law.

See Kleffner 2012, p. 40. Compare, however, Kleffner 2018, p. 43. Dinstein similarly states that '[i]t is sometimes maintained (for instance, by the Supreme Court of Israel, in the *Beit Sourik Case* of 2004) that "[p]roportionality is recognized today as a general principle of international law". This is a completely untenable proposition. Indeed, proportionality is not even a general principle of IHL: it is patently excluded insofar as combat operations are concerned.' See Dinstein 2013, p. 74.

34 Cottier et al., p. 671: '[a]s a "fundamental rule of international law", the principle of proportionality is "able to apply in its own right". . . . The normative difference between customary international law and a legal principle of law is important as the latter does not operate on its own but informs and supports the process of application and interpretation of specific rules.'

35 However, when there is a certain failure rate attached to the use of a certain weapons system which has proven to cause certain collateral damage, this must be taken into account on the civilian side of the proportionality assessment.

misread the information on a military advantage to be attained by accident, or plotted the wrong coordinate in a system that serves to deliver a piece of ammunition to a pinpoint location. Furthermore, attacks that cause unforeseen damage to civilian objects or civilian casualties as a result of other factors that cannot be controlled, such as the influence of weather conditions, are not in violation of the IHL proportionality assessment either. It is submitted that in return for the immunity the military enjoys from accidents such as these, it is only fair that in close cases, the IHL proportionality rule must provide some additional protection to the civilian population when compared to the attainment of a certain military advantage.[36]

9.5 POLICY OR OPERATIONAL FACTORS AFFECTING THE EXCESSIVENESS OF COLLATERAL DAMAGE

It has been suggested that in particular in operations such as the NATO operation Allied Force in Kosovo, the threshold of proportionality should be higher, because it was an operation to save the civilian population, sometimes referred to as a 'humanitarian intervention' or an operation arising from the concept of the 'Responsibility to Protect'.[37] Similarly, it was argued that 'the tolerance of collateral damage would be very different for an invaded nation in the desperate state of survival compared to a state participating in war for economic gain'.[38] This distinction must be rejected as a matter of law since it is based on *ius ad bellum* concepts, not IHL. Nonetheless, further restrictions for acceptable collateral damage may be placed on the proportionality assessment on the basis of policy considerations. As far as policy is concerned, it seems that the tolerance for collateral damage in accordance with the IHL proportionality rule is lower among the general public than it is according to the law. This may impact on the legitimacy of military operations in the long term, as an experienced general from a sophisticated armed force notes.[39] For example, the IHL proportionality rule provides no basis for placing more weight on the collateral damage side for young children than for adults.

[36] To be fair, it must be noted that in targeting processes conducted by sophisticated armed forces, the worst-case scenario for the civilian population is taken into account when a CDE is assessed. Therefore, in these cases where such an elaborate procedure is in place, this does not allocate most of the risk to the civilian population.

[37] Bothe 2001, p. 535.

[38] Reynolds, p. 88.

[39] See Efroni, p. 82: '[e]xperience has shown that, in the realm of legitimacy, the tolerance level for collateral damage – and particularly the extent and nature of such damage – is infinitely lower than the tolerance level for collateral damage set by international law.'

However, military commanders are more likely to accept a higher burden of attempting to minimise civilian casualties in cases where the collateral damage consists predominantly of children. The reasons for this are unrelated to the IHL proportionality rule as it stands today. One of these may be a desire of military commanders to live without the knowledge that they knowingly placed children in harm's way, and thus as a preventive measure for their own mental well-being. Second, because they are aware of the fact that children dying as part of collateral damage from a legitimate attack are more likely to shock the general public and cause complications on the political level, for example as a result of reports in the press and through advocacy by human rights organisations.

There may also be operational reasons to apply a different understanding of excessiveness, that is a more protective one for the civilian population. A frequently quoted example is any operation that may be characterised as a counter-insurgency operation (COIN). During COIN operations, such as the ISAF operation in Afghanistan that started in 2002, the acceptable foreseeable collateral damage would preferably amount to zero.[40] Although an attack that is expected to cause minor civilian casualties would thus be illegal under the restrictions of that particular operation, depending on the military advantage sought, it would not per se be in violation of the IHL proportionality rule. These restrictions would typically be imposed through rules of engagement. Another example of an operational consideration that may possibly influence the proportionality assessment to the benefit of the protection of the civilian population is the practice of economy of force. This practice may be defined as 'the judicious employment and distribution of forces so as to expend the minimum essential combat power on secondary efforts in order to allocate the maximum possible combat power on primary efforts'.[41] It may thus be that even though an attack may be legal under IHL in using an expensive and scarce military asset, military commanders may choose not to launch it for economic reasons.

It is likely that policy and operational factors provide a higher level of protection to the civilian population than any strict application of the IHL proportionality rule. But as these factors exceed the scope of the legal rule which is the subject of this study, the description in this section suffices for the purpose of this study.

40 Because, as Wright notes: '"collateral damage", quite simply, has the capacity to fuel further violence'. See Wright, p. 854. See also the so-called McCrystal Tactical Directive: NATO/ISAF HQ Kabul.

41 Pratzner, p. 91, referring to JCS, JP 1-02, 2013, p. 81.

9.6 DIFFERENT FACTORS FOR DIFFERENT LEVELS OF DECISION-MAKING

The application of the IHL proportionality rule is particular in one sense: it applies to States, but also to the single member of the fighting party in the midst of an armed conflict, as well as to those planning and ordering attacks on much higher levels of command. It was established earlier that proportionality assessments, including those in the phase in which precautionary measures are taken, need to be conducted at all operational levels.[42]

Thus, when an operation is conducted on a limited scale, it is only that level on which the IHL proportionality analysis must be conducted. An example is taking out one particular offensive asset of the adversary that is a threat to own troops, or may become so in the near future. This is a limited attack that has no bearing on a larger operation that may be planned and decided at a higher level, such as the operational level. It could be a planned attack, through a precision airstrike, on an enemy battle tank situated in a village, where there is no plan (yet) to attack that village in order to bring it under the control of the attacking forces. Under these circumstances, that tank is highly likely to become a threat to own forces in the course of the near future, and therefore qualifies as a military objective. Attacking this tank has no bearing on any level other than the tactical level, and therefore the only incidental damage to civilian objects and civilian casualties that needs to be taken into account is the collateral damage from this single attack. This is consistent with the interpretation that the military advantage of a planned attack must be assessed for the operation 'as a whole', because the scope of the operation in this example is limited to this single airstrike.

It must be noted, however, that sometimes, the character of the targets may be labelled as 'strategic' targets, even when it concerns one isolated attack. For example, in order to achieve air superiority, anti-aircraft systems may be labelled as such. It is of crucial importance on the strategic level that these types of target are neutralised as soon as possible when a larger military operation starts, because it enables future operations on the operational and tactical level. In these cases, even though it may concern only a limited operation, it may still be a show-stopper for other operations to commence. This type of attack may take into account more than only the military advantage to be expected on the tactical level. In other words: not only the military advantage of this single strike

[42] See also Corn: '[a] requirement to take "constant care" to mitigate the risk to civilians and civilian property must animate all strategic, operational, and tactical decision-making.' See Corn 2015.

is relevant, but also the important strategic implications of the ability to launch the following strikes that are dependent on this tactical operation. However, if it does so, it also needs to broaden the scope of the foreseeable collateral damage. It would be incorrect to argue that the military advantage that may be gained on a strategic level by a limited attack should only consist of the civilian casualties expected from the limited tactical attack.

Similarly, if a number of attacks form part of a more comprehensive military operation, the military advantage of the operation may be assessed in relation to the operation as a whole, consistent with the declarations of a number of States upon accession to API,[43] and not only from one particular part of the attack.[44] It is also clear that where the level of operations that are planned or decided upon at an even higher level, that of the strategic level, it must be assured that the operation does not turn into a proportionality assessment on the level of the *ius ad bellum*.

Depending on the level of the proportionality assessment, different factors need to be taken into account. For example, expected weapons malfunctions may normally not be factored in for a single attack, but cannot be ignored for larger operations. This is because the attacking force normally has figures on the failure rate of its weapons systems, based on previous experience, testing or on assessments provided by the producer of the weapons system. Therefore, these foreseeable factors need to be taken into account in assessing the proportionality of an attack 'as a whole', thus often on an operational level. This also includes other factors that are mostly irrelevant for a proportionality assessment on the tactical level, but do play a role in the proportionality assessment on an operational level. First, this must include the factor that not all intelligence that is the basis of some attacks is reliable. This also makes sense from an operational perspective: commanders will seek to achieve a certain objective or effect, and they need to allocate sufficient use of force in order to achieve that goal. In cases where the information whether that goal may indeed be attained is based on speculation rather than reliable information, the operational objectives are similarly uncertain to be attained. Therefore, the magnitude of the military advantage expected from the operation is also uncertain, and this factor must be balanced against the risk to harming the civilian population by that operation.

A second factor is the extent to which foreseeable reverberating effects must be taken into account. These effects may be more foreseeable on an operational level than they are on a tactical level. Here too, planning staff on the

[43] See for example the Declarations on Article 51 and 57 API by Italy (27 February 1986), Germany (14 February 1991), the United Kingdom (2 July 1992) and France (11 April 2001).

[44] Oeter 2008, p. 186.

operational level are expected to analyse the foreseeable reverberating effects on the civilian population, and take these into consideration in the proportionality assessment. These reverberating effects may, for example, also include environmental harm and mental harm to the civilian population, when these are foreseeable based on reliable reports, past experience and feasible research. This is not applicable of course on the tactical level of a single attack, but these factors enter the IHL proportionality assessment when conducted at higher levels of command.

Conversely, there are also factors that are less relevant in the proportionality assessment on the operational level, but more relevant on the tactical level. One of these is the factor of self-preservation of the individual soldier or unit. In offensive operations on a large scale, the expected own troops that may be killed by a planned attack is a very relevant operational factor for a commander. Here, the level of decision-making and the urgency of the attack also play a role and may result in a less stringent interpretation of 'excessive' in cases where it concerns emerging targets, as opposed to deliberate and preplanned targeting.[45] It is not a factor, however, that can be balanced against the expected civilian casualties and damage to civilian structures. On a tactical level, however, a group commander who finds himself and his unit surrounded by enemies and pinned down on a certain location, may certainly take this factor into account when he is planning his next course of action. This right to save your own life is not unlimited, because of the nature of the profession of the soldier. IHL attaches a different degree of protection to the status of combatants to that of civilians, which implies that some risk must be assumed by the former in order to safeguard the latter.

It is submitted that the awareness among military commanders to include the correct factors into the IHL proportionality assessment at the appropriate level must be thoroughly integrated into procedures and training. This ensures a realistic application of the IHL proportionality rule that safeguards both the requirements of military necessity as envisioned in the rule as well as the protection of the civilian population.

9.7 IS THERE A NEED TO CLARIFY OR CHANGE THE IHL PROPORTIONALITY RULE?

In recent years, a number of subjects and issues within the realm of IHL that needed clarification have been addressed. These issues include, for example,

45 Clarke, pp. 79–80.

the notion of direct participation in hostilities,[46] detention,[47] the rules that apply to private military companies,[48] the rules that achieved the status of customary IHL,[49] and the rules for air and missile warfare.[50] It is noteworthy that there have not been successful efforts to conclude new, additional treaties on these subjects, but that instead there have been a number of expert processes that have sought to clarify the challenges that were faced in practice. New treaties have been negotiated in the last decades only on specific types of weapon, more particularly on cluster munitions (2008) and nuclear weapons (2017).

With regard to all the uncertainties and controversial issues that accompany the application of the IHL proportionality rule in practice, one may ask the question whether there is a need for new rules on the IHL proportionality rule, or whether interpretative guidance would be useful for the IHL proportionality rule. A proposal to conduct some kind of international process with a view to clarifying the application of the IHL proportionality rule in practice is not a new idea. Krüger-Sprengel underscored the need for the clarification of the IHL proportionality rule in October 1979, just two years after its codification in API, acknowledging that an international process was necessary aimed at reaching a uniform interpretation of the IHL proportionality rule.[51]

Fenrick noted in 2000 that the rules with regard to targeting and proportionality must become more transparent: 'outsiders, including military experts and legal advisers not directly involved in particular conflicts, should learn from the military planning process. A vigorous informed discussion of targeting and proportionality issues based on case studies, both historical and hypothetical, can contribute substantially to clarification of how the law can and should be applied.'[52] Bothe noted in 2001 that '[w]hat is necessary in this respect is the dialogue between civil society and the military, which then has to be reflected

46 Melzer 2009.

47 The Copenhagen Process on the handling of detainees in international military operation: principles and guidelines, 2014.

48 Swiss Federal Department of Foreign Affairs and the ICRC (2008): The Montreux Document on pertinent international legal obligations and good practices for States related to the operations of private military and security companies during armed conflict.

49 Henckaerts and Doswald-Beck 2005.

50 Program on Humanitarian Policy and Conflict Research at Harvard University.

51 Krüger-Sprengel, p. 195: 'A l'avenir, il s'agira de trouver, tant à l'échelon national qu'à l'échelon international, une solution aux problèmes suivants posés par l'application de la règle de proportionnalité ... les efforts entrepris à l'échelon international en vue d'une interprétation uniforme de la règle de proportionnalité.'

52 Fenrick 2000, p. 80.

in military decision making.'[53] It is, however, unclear how this dialogue with civil society must be held.

Dill noted in 2010 that proportionality is 'largely ineffective' and 'features a number of design flaws and remains extremely vague'.[54] Therefore, she proposed that a similar expert process would be started as the one that was conducted under the auspices of the T.M.C. Asser Institute in The Hague and the ICRC that resulted in the 2009 ICRC Guidance on direct participation in hostilities.[55] Furthermore, Clarke launched a proposal in 2012 to draft a guidance document on the application of the IHL proportionality rule, outlining a number of issues that should be addressed in such a document.[56] Clarke also noted that 'ideally, the ICRC would coordinate expert meetings on proportionality and also the drafting of the text'.[57]

In more recent years, three separate groups have indeed attempted to clarify parts of the IHL proportionality rule.[58] First, a Study Group of the International Law Association on current challenges of IHL devoted considerable effort to offering a further interpretation of the IHL proportionality rule. The Final Report of the ILA Study Group was published in 2017.[59] The ICRC has also repeatedly called for further clarification of the IHL proportionality rule.[60] The ICRC organised an expert meeting devoted to the clarification of the IHL proportionality rule in June 2016 in conjunction with Laval University in Quebec, Canada. A report of the meeting was published in 2018. Thirdly, Chatham House organised an expert group process that published its report on 10 December 2018 on the 'civilian side' of the proportionality principle.[61]

What may be drawn from all proposals to clarify how the IHL proportionality rule must be applied in practice is firstly that it is difficult to attain a common understanding of all the components of the IHL proportionality rule. Secondly, it seems that the assessment of the excessiveness of collateral damage for a specific planned attack by military commanders is an inherently subjective factor. Shamash wonders whether the difficulties in clarifying the IHL proportionality rule result from the reluctance of the international legal

53 Bothe 2001, p. 535.
54 Dill 2010, p. 1.
55 Dill 2010, p. 8.
56 Clarke, p. 121.
57 Clarke, p. 122.
58 The current author was part of these three processes, and a number of points in the current study have also been proposed in the context of those processes.
59 For documents related to the Study Group, see www.ila-hq.org/en/study-groups/index.cfm/cid/1040. For the Final Report of the Study Group see International Law Association.
60 For an overview of the statements of the ICRC on this issue: see Clarke, pp. 96–97.
61 See Gillard 2018.

community to 'come out and say that twenty civilians are worth a bridge'.[62] Given the inherent subjective character of the assessment of expected military advantage, this seems highly unlikely. It is therefore submitted that Dinstein's observation may be accepted, that although the 'subjective evaluation of proportionality is viewed with a jaundiced eye by certain scholars, ... there is no serious alternative'.[63] Therefore, not even a survey among a large number of experienced and well-trained military commanders would provide, for example, an answer to the question posed by Shamash of how many civilian casualties would be acceptable for the destruction of one bridge. Nonetheless, the points noted earlier in this and previous chapters may provide at least some additional guidance for military commanders.

Another option would obviously be to dismiss the current IHL proportionality rule because of its inherently subjective character, and draft a new, preferably more objective rule protecting the civilian population. It must be stressed at the outset that this author would not necessarily support changing the existing IHL rule on proportionality, because the outcome of such a process is uncertain and may even result in a rule that is even less useful for the military, and less protective for the civilian population. Nonetheless, for the purpose of having a starting point for a discussion on the subject, it is worth exploring how a different formulation of the IHL proportionality rule could read.

One option in this regard that may be feasible is to introduce a rebuttable prohibition of causing collateral civilian damage and civilian casualties. However, to be clear, such a rule is outside the law as it currently stands in both treaty and international customary IHL. It would presumably also be found unacceptable to States and to military commanders who need to apply that rule in practice, because it would arguably tilt the balance within the IHL proportionality rule too much to civilian protection, ignoring reasons of military necessity. Thus, in a possible new draft of the rule aiming to minimise excessive expected incidental damage and casualties, some kind of exception based on military necessity is necessary. Therefore, a rule prohibiting incidental civilian damage and casualties needs to refer to a certain proportionate ratio between the military advantage and civilian loss expected to result from the attack. An advantage for adopting a new rule would be that certain small alterations could already be implemented into the rule, such as attaching more weight to human lives than to damage to civilian objects, except specifically protected objects. Also, combatants *hors de combat*, medical

62 Shamash, p. 127.
63 Dinstein 2004, p. 122.

personnel and other protected persons and objects could be brought into the equation explicitly. Furthermore, the element of probability of success could be made explicit. Lastly, arguably, the rule could be brought closer in line with an interpretation of the level of excessiveness that is more protective to the civilian population than the rule may be understood from the ordinary meaning of the term 'excessive' in the IHL proportionality rule.

This rule could read as follows:

a. Taking into account the probability that the effects of the attack will be as expected, it is prohibited to plan or launch an attack on a military objective which may be expected to cause incidental loss of civilian life or injury to civilians and specifically protected objects, or a combination thereof, except in cases where military necessity imperatively requires the military objective to be attacked and the expected concrete and direct military advantage of that or the overall attack would clearly justify the expected incidental loss.
b. Taking into account the probability that the effects of the attack will be as expected, it is also prohibited to plan or launch an attack on a military objective which may be expected to cause incidental damage to civilian objects, or incidental loss of life or injury to combatants *hors de combat* and medical personnel, or a combination thereof, except in cases where considerations of military necessity requires the military objective to be attacked and the expected concrete and direct military advantage of that or the overall attack would justify the expected incidental loss.

An advantage of a rule that would be formulated as such is that there is a stronger prohibition on causing collateral damage. Military commanders would be forced to take an additional mental step in asking themselves whether there would be reasons of imperative military necessity to override the prohibition to cause incidental civilian casualties. This is a moderate version of Shamash's idea to place the burden of proof that an attack is proportionate on the attacker, since that person is best placed to assess the legality of the attack in terms of proportionality,[64] without placing military commanders in a position where it is presumed that they violate the IHL proportionality rule in any event that collateral damage occurs. However, the inherent subjective components remain part of the rule and as such, the prohibition still would need further clarification with regard to the question of when one or the other component of the rule would take precedence. It is

[64] Shamash, p. 146.

assumed that military commanders would not necessarily be in favour of an alternative and more elaborate proportionality rule as formulated above, although the rule may be of use in situations where operational or policy considerations would require a more restrictive regime with regard to causing collateral damage.

9.8 EMPIRICAL ANALYSIS AS A POSSIBLE WAY AHEAD

Another possible avenue to strive for a more objective IHL proportionality rule and to clarify the interpretation of the rule could be empirical analysis. The US Law of War Manual notes that '[t]he weighing or comparison between the expected incidental harm and the expected military advantage does not necessarily lend itself to empirical analysis',[65] but fails to provide a further explanation as to why this would be the case. Obviously, however, the exact meaning of excessiveness has been established as a subjective factor, but this does not mean per se that empirical research would a priori be useless. Shamash suggests that much of the uncertainty in the proportionality equation may be eliminated by changing the figures and debating the excessiveness of cases between the two extreme cases of clear disproportionate attacks and clear proportionate attacks.[66] It may thus be valuable to take an empirical approach in order to attempt to reach some general conclusions on excessiveness.

It may be possible to conduct a large-scale survey, in order to find out an average norm where operators and civilians draw the line between excessive and acceptable collateral damage in a number of scenarios.[67] It must be noted, however, that such a survey would presumably require States' willingness to subject their military and civil personnel to the survey. The data that follows from that survey could provide a wealth of State practice from which more refined assessments with regard to planned attacks may be made. If nothing else, a survey such as the one suggested may provide training opportunities for assessing excessiveness to military commanders and planners.

Furthermore, the results of this survey could be fed into software containing artificial intelligence and machine learning that is subsequently tasked with

[65] US Department of Defense Law of War Manual 2015, update May 2016, para. 5.12.4, p. 244.

[66] Shamash, p. 130.

[67] For an example in this direction: see also Janine Dill's online survey and the critique on this survey by Jensen, Corn and Blank on the Just Security blog: www.justsecurity.org/21474/surveying-proportionality-reasonable-commander/ as well as her response: www.justsecurity.org/21529/meaning-proportionate-collateral-damage-care-civilians/. See for another suggestion to conduct an empirical study, Whittemore, pp. 632–634.

running an infinite number of slight alterations to the circumstances of the initial survey. Indeed, it is expected by some people that in the future, autonomous weapons systems will be capable of conducting a proportionality analysis without a human decision maker in the loop, using artificial intelligence.[68] Possibly, using artificial intelligence may provide an opportunity to narrow down the grey area between excessiveness and non-excessiveness of collateral civilian damage on the basis of empirical research. Such algorithms could perhaps subsequently be made available to planners and military commanders, for the purpose of assisting them in their responsibility to make decisions. Perhaps these autonomous weapons systems would thus provide an opportunity in the future for creating a more refined and objective understanding of the IHL proportionality rule. Whether this would lead to a situation in which the proportionality analysis reaches the level of an objective rule remains unlikely. In addition, it seems questionable whether we should trust an autonomous weapons system, which is really only a very sophisticated 'pocket-calculator', to autonomously decide whether collateral damage to civilians is excessive.[69]

Empirical research could potentially provide an insight into the question of whether military decision makers would make different decisions when they base themselves on the current IHL proportionality rule, or on the one as formulated above. This insight could potentially provide an incentive to persuade States to agree to altering the current text of the IHL proportionality rule to a more elaborate or precise rule.

9.9 FINAL REMARKS

This chapter shows that there are a number of factors that would support the assumption that the term 'excessive' could be interpreted as more protective for the civilian population than it would seem at first sight. A scaled approach may be used by commanders in order to assist them in taking a more structured approach in applying the IHL proportionality rule in practice. The probability of success of the operation to materialise as planned must also be taken into account as an inherent part of the proportionality assessment, given its prospective character. The result is a three-dimensional model of proportionality, consisting of an assessment of the military advantage anticipated, the expected civilian damage and the probability that these two components will materialise as planned.

[68] Backstrom and Henderson, pp. 493–494. See also Schmitt and Thurnher, pp. 253–257.
[69] Van den Boogaard 2015, p. 283, quoting Kalshoven 1992.

The aim of this study is to formulate guidance for conducting a proportionality assessment of a planned attack. In its practical application, the IHL proportionality rule must be accepted as it is: an inherently imprecise and flexible yardstick that nonetheless does play its role as the last line of protection for the civilian population, and an obligation for military commanders to take that protection seriously into account. Nonetheless, this study suggests that the balance of the proportionality assessment should in close cases be refocussed and tilt more towards protecting the civilian population than the ordinary meaning of the term 'excessive' in the rule may suggest. Changing the rule has some advantages. It could, for example, provide the opportunity to include combatants *hors de combat*, medical personnel and other protected persons and objects in the proportionality assessment. Applying a general IHL principle of proportionality may for the time being be accepted as one of the factors arguing in favour of such a suggestion. There is no certainty, however, that States would be willing to alter the IHL proportionality rule at this point in a way that would improve the protection of the civilian population. Empirical research may in the future possibly be used as an avenue to further define the fine line between acceptable and excessive collateral civilian damage and casualties.

Bibliography

MONOGRAPHS, ARTICLES, CHAPTERS AND CONTRIBUTIONS

Akehurst, M., 'Custom as a source of international law' (1977) vol. 47, *British Yearbook of International Law*, pp. 1–53.

Aldrich, G. H., 'Some reflections on the origins of the 1977 Geneva Protocols' in C. Swinarski (ed.) *Studies and essays on international humanitarian law and Red Cross principles in honour of Jean Pictet*, Nijhoff, 1984, pp. 129–137.

'The work of the Eritrea-Ethiopia Claims Commission' (2003) vol. 6, *Yearbook of International Humanitarian Law*, pp. 435–442.

Alexy, R., *A theory of constitutional rights*, Oxford University Press, 2002.

Amerasinghe, C. F., 'History and sources of the law of war' (2004) vol. 16, *Sri Lanka Journal*, pp. 263–287.

Andresen, J., 'Challenging the perplexity over *jus in bello* proportionality' (2014) vol. 7, no. 2, *European Journal of Legal Studies*, pp. 19–35.

Arai-Takahashi, Y., 'Excessive collateral civilian casualties and military necessity: awkward crossroads in international humanitarian law between state responsibility and individual criminal liability' in C. Chinkin and F. Baetens (eds.) *Sovereignty, statehood and state responsibility: essays in honour of James Crawford*, Cambridge University Press, 2015, pp. 325–339.

Arancibia, J., 'The intensity of judicial review in the commercial context: defence and proportionality' in C. Forsyth (ed.) *Effective judicial review: a cornerstone of good governance*, Oxford University Press, 2010, pp. 287–299.

Ariav, R., 'Hardly the "Tadić" of targeting: missed opportunities in the ICTY's "Gotovina" judgements' (2015) vol. 48, no. 3, *Israel Law Review*, pp. 329–355.

Backstrom, A. and I. Henderson, 'New capabilities in warfare: an overview of contemporary technological developments and the associated legal and engineering issues in Article 36 weapons reviews' (2012) vol. 94, no. 886, *International Review of the Red Cross*, pp. 483–514.

Baker, R. B., 'Customary international law in the 21st century: old challenges and new debates' (2010) vol. 21, no. 1, *European Journal of International Law*, pp. 173–204.

Barber, P., 'Scuds, shelters and retreating soldiers: the laws of aerial bombardment in the Gulf War' (1993) vol. 31, no. 4, *Alberta Law Review*, pp. 662–691.

Barber, R. J., 'The proportionality equation: balancing military objectives with civilian lives in the armed conflict in Afghanistan' (2010) vol. 15, no. 3, *Journal of Conflict & Security Law*, pp. 467–500.

Barnidge, R. P. Jr, 'The principle of proportionality under international humanitarian law and Operation Cast Lead' in W. C. Banks (ed.) *New battlefields, old laws: critical debates on asymmetric warfare*, Columbia University Press, 2011, pp. 171–189.

Bartels, R. J., 'Timelines, borderlines and conflicts: the historical evolution of the legal divide between international and non-international armed conflicts' (2009a) vol. 91, no. 873, *International Review of the Red Cross*, pp. 35–67.

'Humanitarian intervention after 9/11: the link between *ius ad bellum* and *ius in bello*' in W. J. M. van Genugten et al. (eds.) *Criminal jurisdiction 100 years after The 1907 Hague Peace Conference: proceedings of The Eighth Hague Joint Conference held in The Hague, The Netherlands, 28–30 June 2007*, Asser Press (2009b), pp. 219–226.

'Dealing with the principle of proportionality in armed conflict in retrospect: the application of the principle in international criminal trials' (2013) vol. 46, no. 2, *Israel Law Review*, pp. 271–315.

Bassiouni, M. C., 'A functional approach to "general principles of international law"' (1990) vol. 11, no. 3, *Michigan Journal of International Law*, pp. 768–818.

Bellinger, J. B. and W. J. Haynes, 'A US Government response to the International Committee of the Red Cross Study *Customary International Humanitarian Law*' (2007) vol. 89, no. 866, *International Review of the Red Cross*, pp. 443–471.

Benvenuti, P., 'The ICTY Prosecutor and the review of the NATO Bombing Campaign against the Federal Republic of Yugoslavia' (2001) vol. 12, no. 3, *European Journal of International Law*, pp. 503–526.

Besson, S., 'Theorizing the sources of international law' in S. Besson and J. Tasioulas (eds.) *The philosophy of international law*, Oxford University Press, 2010, pp. 163–185.

Best, G. F. A., *War and law since 1945*, Clarendon Press, 1994.

Bethlehem, D., 'The methodological framework of the Study' in E. Wilmshurst and S. Breau (eds.) *Perspectives on the ICRC study on customary international humanitarian law*, Cambridge University Press, 2007, pp. 3–14.

Beyerlin, U., 'Different types of norms in international law: policies, principles, and rules' in D. Bodansky, J. Brunée and E. Hey (eds.) *The Oxford handbook of international environmental law*, Oxford University Press, 2007, pp. 425–448.

Bílková, V., 'Belligerent reprisals in non-international armed conflicts' (2014) vol. 63, no. 1, *International and Comparative Law Quarterly*, pp. 31–65.

Bill, B. J., 'The Rendulic "Rule": military necessity, commander's knowledge, and methods of warfare' (2009) vol. 12, *Yearbook of International Humanitarian Law*, pp. 119–155.

Blank, L. R., 'Operational law experts roundtable on the Gotovina judgment: military operations, battlefield reality and the judgment's impact on effective implementation and enforcement of international humanitarian law' (2012) Emory Public Law Research Paper No. 12-186, https://papers.ssrn.com/sol3/papers.cfm?abstract_id=1994414.

Blank, L. R. and A. Guiora, 'Teaching an old dog new tricks: operationalizing the law of armed conflict in New Warfare' (2010) vol. 1, *Harvard National Security Journal*, pp. 45–85.

Blix, H., 'Means and methods of combat' in Henri Dunant Institute and UNESCO (eds.) *International dimensions of humanitarian law*, Henri Dunant Institute/UNESCO/Martinus Nijhoff, 1988, pp. 135–151.

Bohlander, M. and D. L. Rothe, 'Assassination of regime elites versus collateral civilian damage' in D. L. Rothe and C. W. Mullins (eds.) *State crime: current perspectives*, Rutgers University Press, 2011, pp. 245–261.

Bohrer, Z. and M. Osiel, 'Proportionality in military force at war's multiple levels: averting civilian casualties vs. safeguarding soldiers' (2013) vol. 46, no. 3, *Vanderbilt Journal of Transnational Law*, pp. 747–822.

Boivin, A., 'The legal regime applicable to targeting military objectives in the context of contemporary warfare', Research Paper 2006/2, University Centre for International Humanitarian Law, www.adh-geneve.ch/recherche/pdf/travaux/2/CTR_objectif_militaire.pdf.

Boothby, W. H., *The law of targeting*, Oxford University Press, 2012.

Bothe, M., 'The protection of the civilian population and the NATO bombing on Yugoslavia: comments on a report to the Prosecutor of the ICTY' (2001) vol. 12, *European Journal of International Law*, pp. 531–535.

'Customary international humanitarian law: some reflections on the ICRC study' (2007a) vol. 8, *Yearbook of International Humanitarian Law*, pp. 143–178.

'Military activities and the protection of the environment' (2007b) vol. 37, no. 2/3, *Environmental Policy and Law*, pp. 232–238.

Bothe, M. et al. (eds.), *New rules for victims of armed conflict: commentary to the Two 1977 Protocols Additional to the Geneva Conventions of 1949*, Martinus Nijhoff, 1982.

Bouchié de Belle, S., 'Chained to cannons or wearing targets on their T-shirts: human shields in international humanitarian law' (2008) vol. 90, no. 872, *International Review of the Red Cross*, pp. 883–906.

Bring, O., 'International humanitarian law after Kosovo: is lex lata sufficient?' in A. Wall (ed.) *Legal and ethical lessons of Nato's Kosovo campaign*, International Law Studies, vol. 78, U.S. Naval War College, 2002, pp. 257–272.

Brown, B. L., 'The proportionality principle in the humanitarian law of warfare: recent efforts at codification' (1976) vol. 10, no. 1, *Cornell International Law Journal*, pp. 134–155.

Brownlie, I., *International law and the use of force by states*, Clarendon Press, 1963.

Buchan, R., 'The Palmer Report and the legality of Israel's naval blockade of Gaza' (2012) vol. 61, no. 1, *International and Comparative Law Quarterly*, pp. 264–273.

Byron, C., 'International humanitarian law and bombing campaigns: legitimate military objectives and excessive collateral damage (2010) vol. 13, *Yearbook of International Humanitarian Law*, pp. 175–211.

Camins, E., 'The past as prologue: the development of the "direct participation" exception to civilian immunity' (2008) vol. 90, no. 872, *International Review of the Red Cross*, pp. 853–881.

Cannizzaro, E., *Il principio della proporzionalità nell'ordinamento internazionale*, Giuffrè, 2000.

Carcano, A., *The transformation of occupied territory in international law*, Brill Nijhoff, 2015.

Carnahan, B. M., 'Linebacker II and Protocol I: the convergence of law and professionalism' (1982) vol. 31, *American University Law Review*, pp. 861–870.

Cassese, A., *International Law*, second edition, Oxford University Press, 2005.

'Declaration of Professor Antonio Cassese [on the subject of targeted killing and Gaza]', 21 April 2006, Center for Constitutional Rights, http://ccrjustice.org/sites/default/files/assets/files/Professor%20Cassese%20declaration.pdf.

Charlton, L. E. O., *War from the air*, Thomas Nelson and Sons, 1935.

Cheng, B., *General principles of law as applied by international courts and tribunals*, Stevens and Sons, 1953.

Chetail, V., 'The contribution of the International Court of Justice to international humanitarian law' (2003) vol. 85, no. 850, *International Review of the Red Cross*, pp. 235–269.

Clapham, A., 'Human rights obligations of non-state actors in conflict situations' (2006) vol. 88, no. 863, *International Review of the Red Cross*, pp. 491–523.

Clark, W. K., *Waging modern war: Bosnia, Kosovo and the future of combat*, PublicAffairs, 2002.

Clarke, B., 'Proportionality in armed conflicts: a principle in need of clarification?' (2012) vol. 3, no. 1, *Journal of International Humanitarian Legal Studies*, pp. 73–123.

Cohen, A., 'The principle of proportionality in the context of Operation Cast Lead: institutional perspectives' (2009) vol. 35, *Rutgers Law Record*, pp. 23–38.

'Proportionality in modern asymmetrical wars' (2010) Jerusalem Center for Public Affairs, www.jcpa.org/text/proportionality.pdf.

Conot, R. E. *Justice at Nuremberg*, Harper & Row, 1983.

Corn, G. S., 'Expert Report', see Defendant Ante Gotovina's Submission of Expert Report of Professor Geoffrey Corn pursuant to Rule 94 bis, ICTY Prosecutor v. Gotovina et al., IT-06-90-T, 30 June 2009, Appendix A, p. 12.

'War, law, and the oft overlooked value of process as a precautionary measure' (2014) vol. 42, *Pepperdine Law Review*, pp. 419–466, https://digitalcommons.pepperdine.edu/plr/vol42/iss3/2

Corn, G. S. and G. P. Corn, 'The law of operational targeting: viewing the LOAC through an operational lens' (2012) vol. 47, no. 2, *Texas International Law Journal*, pp. 337–380.

Corn, G. S. and A. Culliver, 'Wounded combatants, military medical personnel, and the dilemma of collateral risk' (2017) vol. 45, no. 3, *Georgia Journal of International and Comparative Law*, pp. 445–473.

Corn, G. S. et al. (eds.) *The law of armed conflict: an operational approach*, Wolters Kluwer, 2012.

Cottier, T. et al., 'The principle of proportionality in international law: foundations and variations' (2017) vol. 18, no. 4, *The Journal of World Investment and Trade*, pp. 628–672.

D'Amato, A. A., *The concept of custom in international law*, Cornell University Press, 1971.

Darcy, S., 'Law of belligerent reprisals' (2003) vol. 175, *Military Law Review*, pp. 184–251.

David, E., 'The opinion of the International Court of Justice on the legality of the use of nuclear weapons' (1997) vol. 37, no. 316, *International Review of the Red Cross*, pp. 21–34.

Droit des conflicts armés, Bruylant, 2001.

Degan, V. D., 'General principles of law (A source of general international law)' (1992) vol. 3, *Finnish Yearbook of International Law*, pp. 1–102.

Dill, J., 'Applying the principle of proportionality in combat operations', Policy paper, December 2010, Oxford Institute for Ethics, Law and Armed Conflict, www.elac.ox.ac.uk/downloads/Proportionality_policybrief_%20Dec_2010.pdf.

Dinstein, Y., 'Air, missile and nuclear warfare' (1997) vol. 27, *Israel Yearbook on Human Rights*, pp. 1–16.

'Protection of the environment in international armed conflict' (2001) vol. 5, *Max Planck Yearbook of United Nations Law*, pp. 523–549.

The conduct of hostilities under the law of international armed conflict, Cambridge University Press, 2004.

War, aggression and self-defence, 4th edition, Cambridge University Press, 2005.

'The ICRC customary international humanitarian law study' (2006) vol. 36, *Israel Yearbook on Human Rights*, pp. 1–15.

'Distinction and loss of civilian protection in international armed conflicts' (2008) vol. 38, *Israel Yearbook on Human Rights*, pp. 1–16.

The international law of belligerent occupation, Cambridge University Press, 2009.

The conduct of hostilities under the law of international armed conflict, 2nd edition, Cambridge University Press, 2010.

War, aggression and self-defence, 5th edition, Cambridge University Press, 2012.

'The principle of proportionality' in K. Mujezinovic Larsen and C. Guldahl Cooper (eds.) *Searching for a 'principle of humanity' in International Humanitarian Law*, Cambridge University Press, 2013, pp. 72–85.

The conduct of hostilities under the law of international armed conflict, 3rd edition, Cambridge University Press, 2016.

War, aggression and self-defence, 6th edition, Cambridge University Press, 2017.

Dörmann, K., *Elements of war crimes under the Rome Statute of the International Criminal Court: sources and commentary*, Cambridge University Press (2003a).

'The legal situation of "unlawful/unprivileged combatants"' (2003b) vol. 85, no. 849, *International Review of the Red Cross*, pp. 45–74.

'The definition of military objectives' in G. L. Beruto and G. Ravasi (eds.) *The conduct of hostilities, revisiting the law of armed conflict*, Proceedings of the 30th Round Table, San Remo, 6–8 September 2007, International Institute of Humanitarian Law, 2008, pp. 85–90.

Doswald-Beck, L., 'New protocol on blinding laser weapons' (1996) vol. 36, no. 312, *International Review of the Red Cross*, pp. 272–299.

'International humanitarian law and the Advisory Opinion of the International Court of Justice on the legality of the threat or use of nuclear weapons' (1997), vol. 37, no. 321, pp. 35–55.

'The right to life in armed conflict: does international humanitarian law provide all the answers?' (2006) vol. 88, no. 864, *International Review of the Red Cross*, pp. 881–904.

Draper, G. I. A. D., 'Military necessity and humanitarian imperatives' (1973) vol. 12, *Revue de droit pénal militaire et de droit de la guerre*, pp. 129–151.

Droege, C., 'The interplay between international humanitarian law and international human rights law in situations of armed conflict' (2007) vol. 40, no. 2, *Israel Law Review*, pp. 310–355.

'Elective affinities? Human rights and humanitarian law' (2008) vol. 90, no. 871, *International Review of the Red Cross*, pp. 501–548.

Ducheine, P. A. L., 'Non-kinetic capabilities: complementing the kinetic prevalence to targeting' in P. A. L. Ducheine et al. (eds.) *Targeting: the challenges of modern warfare*, Asser Press, 2016, pp. 201–230.

Ducheine, P. A. L. et al., 'Introduction' in P. A. L. Ducheine et al. (eds.) *Targeting: the challenges of modern warfare*, Asser Press, 2016, pp. 1–5.

Dupuy, P.-M., 'Between the individual and the State: international law at crossroads?' in L. Boisson de Chazournes and P. Sands (eds.) *International Law, the International Court of Justice and nuclear weapons*, Cambridge University Press, 1999, pp. 449–461.

Dworkin, R., *Taking rights seriously*, Duckworth, 1977.

Efroni, D., 'Challenges posed by international law in the context of urban warfare: insights from Operation Pillar of Defense' (2014) Special Issue, *Military and Strategic Affairs*, pp. 81–87.

Else, R. C., 'Proportionality in the law of armed conflict: the proper unit of analysis for military operations' (2010) vol. 5, no. 1, *University of St. Thomas Journal of Law & Public Policy*, pp. 195–213.

Fellmeth, A. X., 'Interpreting proportionality doctrine through the lens of international custom', Paper presented at the Conference 'Proportionality in Armed Conflicts' at the Minerva Center for Human Rights, Jerusalem, Israel, 22 November 2010, http://law.huji.ac.il/upload/7_AaronFellmeth_p.pdf.

'The proportionality principle in operation: methodological limitations of empirical research and the need for transparency' (2012) vol. 45, no. 1 *Israel Law Review*, pp. 125–150.

Fellmeth, A. X. and D. J. Sylvester, 'Targeting decisions and consequences for civilians in the Colombian civil strife' (2017) vol. 26, no. 2, *Minnesota Journal of International Law*, pp. 501–560.

Fenrick, W. J., 'The rule of proportionality and Protocol I in conventional warfare' (1982) vol. 98, *Military Law Review*, pp. 91–127.

'The law applicable to targeting and proportionality after Operation Allied Force: a view from the outside' (2000) vol. 3, *Yearbook of International Humanitarian Law*, pp. 53–80.

'Targeting and proportionality during the NATO bombing campaign in Yugoslavia' (2001) vol. 12, no. 3, *European Journal of International Law*, pp. 489–502.

Fitzmaurice, G., 'The general principles of international law considered from the standpoint of the rule of law' (1958) vol. 92, *Recueil des cours*, pp. 1–227.

Fortin, K., *The accountability of armed groups under human rights law*, Oxford University Press, 2017.

Friedmann, W., 'The uses of "general principles" in the development of international law' (1963) vol. 57, *American Journal of International Law*, pp. 278–299.

Gardam, J. G., *Non-combatant immunity as a norm of international humanitarian law*, Martinus Nijhoff, 1993.

Necessity, proportionality and the use of force by States, Cambridge University Press, 2004.

Garner, J. W., *International law and the world war*, Longmans, 1920.

Garraway, C., 'How does existing law address the issue of explosive remnants of war?' CCW/GGE/XII/WG.1/WP.15 (15 December 2005), available through the online official UN Documents System https://documents.un.org/prod/ods.nsf/home.xsp.

'International humanitarian law in self-defence operations' in T. D. Gill and D. Fleck (eds.) *The handbook of the international law of military operations*, Oxford University Press, 2010, pp. 213–215.

Gasser, H.-P. and K. Dörmann, 'Protection of the Civilian Population' in D. Fleck (ed.) *The Handbook of International Humanitarian Law*, Oxford University Press, 2013, pp. 231–320.

Gaughan, A. J., 'Collateral damage and the laws of war: D-Day as a case study' (2015) vol. 55, no. 3, *American Journal of Legal History*, pp. 229–285.

Geiss, R., 'The conduct of hostilities in asymmetric conflicts: reciprocity, distinction, proportionality, precautions' (2010) vol. 23, no. 3, *Humanitäres Völkerrecht*, pp. 122–132.

'The principle of proportionality: force protection as a military advantage' (2012) vol. 45, no. 1, *Israel Law Review*, pp. 71–89.

Geiss, R. and J. G. Devaney, 'Zealots, victims and captives: maintaining adequate protection of human shields in contemporary international humanitarian law' (2017) vol. 47, *Israel Yearbook on Human Rights*, pp. 11–33.

Gill, T. D., 'The Nuclear Weapons Advisory Opinion of the International Court of Justice and the fundamental distinction between the *jus ad bellum* and the *jus in bello*' (1999) vol. 12, *Leiden Journal of International Law*, pp. 613–624.

Gill, T. G., 'The temporal dimension of self-defense: anticipation, pre-emption, prevention and immediacy' in M. N. Schmitt and J. Pejic (eds.) *International law and armed conflict: exploring the faultlines: essays in honour of Yoram Dinstein*, Nijhoff, 2007, pp. 113–155.

'Chivalry: a principle of the law of armed conflict?' in M. Matthee et al. (eds.) *Armed conflict and international law: in search of the human face: liber amicorum in memory of Avril McDonald*, Asser Press, 2013, pp. 33–51.

Gill, T. D., 'Some thoughts on the relationship between international humanitarian law and international human rights law: a plea for mutual respect and a common sense approach' in Y. Haeck et al. (eds.) *The realisation of human rights: when theory meets practice: studies in honour of Leo Zwaak*, Intersentia, 2014, pp. 335–350.

'Some considerations concerning the role of the *ius ad bellum* in targeting' in P. A. L. Ducheine et al. (eds.) *Targeting: the challenges of modern warfare*, Asser Press, 2016, pp. 101–119.

Gillard, M. C., 'Proportionality in the conduct of hostilities: the incidental harm side of the assessment', Chatham House Report, Chatham House, 10 December 2018, www.chathamhouse.org/publication/proportionality-conduct-hostilities-incidental-harm-side-assessment.

Gillich, I., 'The normativity of principles within the positivist theory of international law' (2015) vol. 41, *North Carolina Journal of International Law and Commercial Regulation*, pp. 1–30.

Gisel, L., 'Can the incidental killing of military doctors never be excessive?' (2013) vol. 95, no. 889, *International Review of the Red Cross*, pp. 215–230.

Green, L. C., *The contemporary law of armed conflict*, 3rd edition, Manchester University Press, 2008.

Greenwood, C. J., 'Self defense and the conduct of international armed conflict' in Y. Dinstein (ed.) *International law at a time of perplexity*, Nijhoff, 1989a, pp. 273–288.

'The twilight of the law of belligerent reprisals' (1989b) vol. 20, *Netherlands Yearbook of International Law*, pp. 35–69.

'Customary law status of the 1977 additional protocols' in A. J. M. Delissen and G. J. Tanja (eds.) *Humanitarian law of armed conflict: challenges ahead*, Martinus Nijhoff, 1991, pp. 93–114.

'The advisory opinion on nuclear weapons and the contribution of the International Court to international humanitarian law' (1997) vol. 37, no. 316, *International Review of the Red Cross*, pp. 65–75.

Greenwood, C., 'Historical development and legal basis' in D. Fleck (ed.) *The handbook of international law*, 2nd edition, Oxford University Press, 2008, pp. 15–27.

Gross, A. M., 'The construction of a wall between The Hague and Jerusalem: the enforcement and limits of humanitarian law and the structure of occupation' (2006) vol. 19, no. 2, *Leiden Journal of International Law*, pp. 393–440.

Gross, O., 'The new way of war: is there a duty to use drones?' (2015) vol. 67, *Florida Law Review*, pp. 1–71.

Grossgeneralstab of the Kingdom of Prussia, *Kriegsbrauch im Landkriege* (1902) translated as War Book of the German General Staff by J. H. Morgan, originally published in 1915, reprinted by Stackpole Books, 2005.

Grotius, H., *The rights of war and peace (de jure ac bella paci), Book I*, first published by in 1625, edited by R. Tuck, republished by Liberty Fund, 2005.

Guisández Gómez, F. J., 'The law of air warfare' (1998) vol. 38, no. 323, *International Review of the Red Cross*, pp. 347–363.

Guisández Gómez, J., 'El principio de la proporcionalidad y los daños colaterales, en enfoque pragmático' in R. A. Prieto Sanjuán (ed.) *Conducción de hostiliades y derecho internacional humanitario: a propósito del Centenario de las Convenciones de La Haya de* 1907, Biblioteca Jurídica Diké, 2007, pp. 197–243.

Haines, S., 'The developing law of weapons: humanity, distinction and the need for proportionality' in A. Clapham and P. Gaeta (eds.) *The Oxford handbook of international law in armed conflict*, Oxford University Press, 2014, pp. 273–295.

Hall, J. A., *The law of naval warfare*, 2nd edition, Chapman and Hall, 1921.

Hampson, F. J., 'Belligerent reprisals and the 1977 Protocols to the Geneva Conventions of 1949' (1988) vol. 37, *International and Comparative Law Quarterly*, pp. 818–843.

'Implementing limitations on the use of force: the doctrine of proportionality and necessity: proportionality and necessity in the Gulf Conflict' (1992) vol. 86, *American Society of International Law Proceedings*, pp. 45–54.

'Other areas of customary law in relation to the study' in E. Wilmshurst and S. Breau (eds.) *Perspectives on the ICRC study on customary international humanitarian law*, Cambridge University Press, 2007, pp. 50–73.

'The relationship between international humanitarian law and international human rights law' in S. Sheeran and N. Rodley (eds.) *Routledge handbook of international human rights law*, Routledge, 2013, pp. 185–213.

Hayashi, N., 'Requirements of military necessity in international humanitarian law and international criminal law' (2010) vol. 28, no. 1, *Boston University International Law Journal*, pp. 39–140.

Heintschel von Heinegg, W., 'Naval blockade' in M. N. Schmitt (ed.) *International law across the spectrum of conflict: essays in honour of Professor L.C. Green on the occasion of his eightieth birthday*, Naval War College, 2000, pp. 203–230.

'The law of naval warfare' in D. Fleck (ed.) *The handbook of international humanitarian law*, 3rd edition, Oxford University Press, 2013, pp. 463–547.

Heintschel von Heinegg, W. and P. Dreist, 'The 2009 Kunduz air attack: the Decision of the Federal Prosecutor-General on the dismissal of criminal proceedings against members of the German armed forces' (2010) vol. 53, *German Yearbook of International Law*, pp. 835–866.

Henckaerts, J.-M., 'Study on customary international humanitarian law: a contribution to the understanding and respect for the rule of law in armed conflict' (2005) vol. 87, no. 857, *International Review of the Red Cross*, pp. 175–212.

'Customary international humanitarian law: a response to US comments' (2007) vol. 89, no. 866, *International Review of the Red Cross*, pp. 473–488.

Henckaerts, J.-M. and L. Doswald-Beck, *Customary IHL, Volume 1, Rules*, Cambridge University Press (2005a).

Henckaerts, J.-M. and L. Doswald-Beck, *Customary IHL, Volume 2, Practice*, Cambridge University Press (2005b).

Henderson, I., *The contemporary law of targeting*, Martinus Nijhoff, 2009.

Henderson, I. and B. Cavanagh, 'Military members claiming self-defence during armed conflict: often misguided and unhelpful' in J. Petrovic (ed.) *Accountability for violations of international humanitarian law: essays in honour of Tim McCormack*, Routledge, 2016, pp. 73–94.

Henderson, I. and K. Reece, 'Proportionality under IHL: the "reasonable military commander" standard and reverberating effects' (2018) vol. 51, no. 3, *Vanderbilt Journal of Transnational Law*, pp. 1–22.

Henn, E. V., 'The development of German jurisprudence on individual compensation for victims of armed conflicts: the "Kunduz" Case' (2014) vol. 12, no. 3, *Journal of International Criminal Justice*, pp. 615–637.

Jachec-Neale, A., *The concept of military objectives in international law and practice*, Routledge, 2015.

Jensen, E. T., 'Precautions against the effects of attacks in urban areas' (2016) vol. 98, no. 1, *International Review of the Red Cross*, pp. 147–175.

Kalshoven, F., *Belligerent reprisals*, Martinus Nijhoff, 1971, reprinted in 2005.

'Implementing limitations on the use of force: the doctrine of proportionality and necessity, Remarks by Frits Kalshoven' (1992) vol. 86, *American Society of International Law Proceedings*, pp. 40–45.

'The respective roles of custom and principle in the international armed conflict' (2006) *Acta Societatis Martensis*, on file with author (previously available online at http://acta.martens.ee/article/view/288/49), pp. 48–68.

'Bombardment: from Brussels 1874 to Sarajevo 2003' in J. Doria, H.-P. Gasser and M. C. Bassiouni (eds.) *The legal regime of the International Criminal Court: essays in honour of Professor Igor Blishchenko: in memoriam Professor Igor Pavlovich Blishchenko (1930–2000)*, 2009, pp. 103–139. Reprinted in F. Kalshoven, Reflections on the law of war, Collected essays, Martinus Nijhoff, 2007, pp. 431–463.

Kalshoven, F. and L. Zegveld, *Constraints on the waging of war: an introduction to international humanitarian law*, Cambridge University Press and International Committee of the Red Cross, 2011.

Kammerhofer, J., 'International legal positivism' in J. Kammerhofer and J. D'Aspremont (eds.) *International legal positivism in a post-modern world*, Cambridge University Press, 2014, pp. 81–113.

Kelsen, H., *Principles of international law*, Rinehart & Company, 1952.

The pure theory of law, 2nd edition, 1967, translated by M. Knight, original German text Reine Rechtslehre, 1960.

Khalfaoui, A., 'The curious case of civilians working in munitions factories: civilian assumption of risk in armed conflict and the United States DoD Law of War Manual' (2017–2018) vol. 56, no. 2, *The Military Law and the Law of War Review*, pp. 251–303.

Kleffner, J. K., 'Section IX of the ICRC Interpretive Guidance on direct participation in hostilities: the end of *jus in bello* proportionality as we know it' (2012) vol. 45, no. 1, *Israel Law Review*, pp. 35–52.

'Sources of the law of armed conflict' in R. Liivoja and T. McCormack (eds.) *Routledge handbook on the law of armed conflict*, Routledge, 2016, pp. 71–88.

'Military collaterals and *ius in bello* proportionality' (2018) vol. 48, *Israel Yearbook on Human Rights*, pp. 43–62.

Kolb, R., 'Origin of the twin terms *jus ad bellum/jus in bello*' (1997) vol. 37, *International Review of the Red Cross*, pp. 553–562.

'Principles as sources of international law (with special reference to good faith)' (2006) vol. 53, no. 1, *Netherlands International Law Review*, pp. 1–36.

'Gotovina and the ICTY' (2017) vol. 27, no. 4, *Swiss Review of International and European Law*, pp. 483–487.

Kolb, R. and R. Hyde, *An introduction to the international law of armed conflicts*, Hart, 2008.

Koppe, E. V., 'The use of depleted uranium and the direct protection of the natural environment under *jus in bello*' in A. McDonald, J. K. Kleffner and B. Toebes (eds.) *Depleted uranium weapons and international law: a precautionary approach*, Asser Press, 2008, pp. 161–185.

Koskenniemi, M., *From apology to utopia*, Cambridge University Press, 2005.

Kravetz, D., 'The protection of civilians in war: the ICTY's Galić Case' (2004) vol. 17, no. 3, *Leiden Journal of International Law*, pp. 521–536.

Krieger, H., 'A conflict of norms: the relationship between humanitarian law and human rights law in the ICRC Customary Law Study' in R. Cryer and

C. Henderson (eds.) *Law and the use of force and armed conflict*, vol. 3, Edward Elgar, 2017.

Krüger-Sprengel, F., 'Le concept de proportionnalité dans le droit de guerre', *Military Law and Law of War Review*, 1980, pp. 179–197.

Krupiy, T., *A toolbox for the application of the rules of targeting*, Cambridge Scholars Publishing, 2016.

Kunz, J. L., 'The laws of war' (1956) vol. 50, *American Journal of International Law*, pp. 313–337.

Lachenmann, F., 'Legal positivism', in *Max Planck Encyclopedia of Public International Law*, Oxford University Press, 2011.

Lammers, J. G., 'General principles of law recognised by civilised nations' in F. Kalshoven, P. J. Kuyper and J. G. Lammers (eds.) *Essays on the development of the international legal order: in memory of Haro F. van Panhuys*, Sijthoff & Noordhoff, 1980, pp. 53–75.

Laursen, A., 'NATO, the war over Kosovo, and the ICTY investigation' (2002) vol. 17, no. 4, *American University International Law Review*, pp. 765–782.

Lauterpacht, H., 'War' in L. Oppenheim (ed.) *International law: a treatise; Vol. 2: Disputes, war and neutrality*, 5th edition, Longmans, 1935.

'War' in L. Oppenheim (ed.) *International law: a treatise; Vol. 2: Disputes, war and neutrality*, 6th edition, Longmans, 1944.

Lieblich, E., 'Beyond life and limb: exploring incidental mental harm under international humanitarian law' in D. Jinks et al. (eds.) *Applying international humanitarian law in judicial and quasi-judicial bodies: international and domestic aspects*, Asser Press, 2014, pp. 185–218.

Lubell, N., 'Parallel application of international humanitarian law and international human rights law: an examination of the debate' (2007) vol. 40, no. 2, *Israel Law Review*, pp. 648–660.

Lubell, N. and A. Cohen, 'Strategic proportionality' (2020) *International Legal Studies*, https://digital-commons.usnwc.edu/ils/vol96/iss1/6/.

Margalit, A., 'The duty to investigate civilian casualties during armed conflict and its implementation in practice' (2012) vol. 15, *Yearbook of International Humanitarian Law*, pp. 155–186.

Matheson, M., 'Additional Protocol I as an expression of customary international law' (1987) vol. 2, *American University Journal of International Law and Policy*, pp. 419–436.

Maxwell, M. D. and R. V. Meyer, 'The principle of distinction: probing the limits of its customaries' (2007) March, *The Army Lawyer*, pp. 1–11, www.loc.gov/rr/frd/Military_Law/pdf/03-2007.pdf.

McCormack, T. L. H. and P. B. Mtharu, 'Cluster munitions, proportionality and the foreseeability of civilian damage' in W. Engdal and P. Wrange (eds.) *Law at war, the law as it was and the law as it should be, liber amicorum Ove Bring*, Koninklijke Brill BV, 2008, pp. 191–206.

McCormack, T. L. H. et al., 'Report on States Parties' responses to the IHL questionnaire on international humanitarian law and explosive remnants of war' (2006) *Asia Pacific Centre for Military Law*, p. 17.

McDougal, M. S. and F. P. Feliciano, *Law and minimum world order: the legal regulation of international coercion*, Yale University Press, 1961.

McNair, A., 'War' in L. Oppenheim (ed.) *International law: a treatise; Vol. 2: Disputes, war and neutrality*, 4th edition, Longmans, 1926.

McNeal, G. S., 'The U.S. practice of collateral damage estimation and mitigation' (2011) on file with the author.

McPherson, L. K., 'Excessive force in war: a golden rule test' (2006) vol. 7, no. 1, *Theoretical Inquiries in Law*, pp. 81–95.

Medenica, O., 'Protocol I and Operation Allied Force: did NATO abide by principles of proportionality?' (2001) vol. 23, no. 3, *Loyola of Los Angeles International & Comparative Law Review*, pp. 329–426.

Melzer, N., 'Summary expert meeting on the notion of direct participation in hostilities', Summary report, ICRC 2005, www.icrc.org/eng/assets/files/other/2005-09-report-dph-2005-icrc.pdf

'Targeted killing or less harmful means? Israel's High Court Judgment on targeted killing and the restrictive function of military necessity' (2006) vol. 9, *Yearbook of International Humanitarian Law*, pp. 87–113.

Targeted killing in international law, Oxford University Press, 2008.

'Interpretive guidance on the notion of direct participation in hostilities under international humanitarian law', International Committee of the Red Cross, 2009.

'Conceptual distinction and overlaps between law enforcement and the conduct of hostilities' in T. D. Gill and D. Fleck (eds.) *Handbook of the international law of military operations*, Oxford University Press, 2010a, pp. 33–49.

'Targeted killings in operational law perspective' in T. D. Gill and D. Fleck (eds.) *Handbook of the international law of military operations*, Oxford University Press, 2010b, pp. 277–301.

Meron, T., *Human rights and humanitarian norms as customary law*, Clarendon Press, 1989.

'Revival of customary humanitarian law' (2005) vol. 99, no. 4, *American Journal of International Law*, pp. 817–834.

Mitchell, A. D., 'Law of reprisals: does one illegality merit another?' (2001) vol. 170, *Military Law Review*, pp. 158–161.

Moneta, F., 'Direct attacks on civilians and indiscriminate attacks as war crimes' in F. Pocar et al. (eds.) *War crimes and the conduct of hostilities: challenges to adjudication and investigation*, Edward Elgar, 2013, pp. 59–77.

Mosler, H., 'General principles of law' in R. Bernhardt (ed.) *Encyclopedia of public international law*, Elsevier, 1995, vol. II, pp. 511–527.

Mumford, P. S., *Humanity, air power and war*, Jarrolds, 1936.

Murphy, J. F., 'Some legal (and a few ethical) dimensions of the collateral damage resulting from Nato's Kosovo campaign' (2002) vol. 31, *Israel Yearbook on Human Rights*, pp. 51–77.

Nasser, S. H., *Sources and norms of international law: a study on soft law*, Galda + Wilch, 2008.

Neuman, N., 'Applying the rule of proportionality: force protection and cumulative assessment in international law and morality' (2004) vol. 7, *Yearbook of International Humanitarian Law*, pp. 79–112.

Newton, M. A., 'Modern military necessity: the role & relevance of military lawyers' (2007) vol. 12, no. 3, *Roger Williams University Law Review*, pp. 877–903.

Nirmal, B. C., 'International humanitarian law in Ancient India' in V. S. Mani (ed.) *Handbook of international humanitarian law in South Asia*, Oxford University Press, 2007, pp. 25–38.

Oeter, S., 'Methods and means of combat' in D. Fleck (ed.) *The handbook of international humanitarian law*, 2nd edition, Oxford University Press, 2008, pp. 119–235.

'Collateral damages: military necessity and the right to life' in C. Tomuschat et al. (eds.) *The right to life*, Nijhoff, 2010, pp. 167–193.

'Methods and means of combat' in D. Fleck (ed.) *The handbook of international humanitarian law*, 3rd edition, Oxford University Press, 2013, pp. 115–230.

Olasolo, H., *Unlawful attacks in combat situations: from the ICTY's case law to the Rome Statute*, Martinus Nijhoff, 2008.

Oppenheim, L., *International law, a treatise, Vol. II, Disputes, war and neutrality*, 7th edition, Longmans, Green and Co, 1952.

Orford, A., *The Oxford handbook of the theory of international law*, Oxford University Press, 2016.

Osinga, F. P. B. and M. P. Roorda 'From Douhet to drones, air warfare, and the evolution of targeting' in P. A. L. Ducheine et al. (eds.) *Targeting, the challenges of modern warfare*, Springer/Asser Press, 2016, pp. 27–76.

Parks, W. H., 'Rolling thunder and the law of war' (1982) vol. 22, *Air University Review*, www.airpower.maxwell.af.mil/airchronicles/aureview/1982/jan-feb/parks.html.

'Linebacker and the law of war' (1983) vol. 15, *Air University Review*, www.airpower .maxwell.af.mil/airchronicles/aureview/1983/jan-feb/parks.html.

'Air war and the law of war' (1990) vol. 32, *Air Force Law Review*, pp. 1–226.

'The protection of civilians from air warfare' (1997) vol. 27, *Israel Yearbook on Human Rights*, pp. 65–112.

Pedrazzi, M., 'Using human shields as a war crime' in F. Pocar et al. (eds.) *War crimes and the conduct of hostilities: challenges to adjudication and investigation*, Edward Elgar, 2013, pp. 98–116.

Penna, L. R., 'Customary international law and Protocol I: an analysis of some provisions' in C. Swinarski (ed.) *Studies and essays on international humanitarian law and Red Cross principles in honour of Jean Pictet*, Nijhoff, 1984, pp. 201–225.

Pertile, M., 'Beit Sourik Village Council v. The Government of Israel: a matter of principle (and neglected rules)' (2005) vol. 65, *Heidelberg Journal of International Law*, pp. 677–734.

Petersen, N., 'Customary law without custom? Rules, principles, and the role of State practice in international norm creation' (2008) vol. 23, no. 2, *American University International Law Review*, pp. 275–310.

Petrovic, J., *The Old Bridge of Mostar and increasing respect for cultural property in armed conflict*, Nijhoff, 2013.

Philippe, X., 'Brèves réflexions sur le principe de proportionnalité en droit humanitaire' in F. Delperée et al. (eds.) *En Hommage à Francis Delpérée: itinéraires d'un constitutionnaliste*, Bruylant, 2007, pp. 1183–1196.

Pictet, J. S., *The principles of international humanitarian law*, ICRC, 1966.

Development and principles of international humanitarian law: course given in July 1982 at the University of Strasbourg as part of the courses organized by the International Institute of Human Rights, Nijhoff, 1985.

PoKempner, D. et al., 'Off Target on the Iraq Campaign: a response to Professor Schmitt' (2006) vol. 6, *Yearbook of International Humanitarian Law*, pp. 111–125.

Ponti, C., 'The crime of indiscriminate attack and unlawful conventional weapons: the legacy of the ICTY Jurisprudence' (2015) vol. 6, no. 1, *Journal of International Humanitarian Legal Studies*, pp. 118–146.

Porat, I. and Z. Bohrer, 'Preferring one's own civilians: may soldiers endanger enemy civilians more than they would endanger their state's civilians' (2015) vol. 47, no. 1, *The George Washington International Law Review*, pp. 99–158.

Pouw, E. H., 'International human rights law and the law of armed conflict in the context of counterinsurgency', dissertation, NLDA, 2013.

Pratzner, P. R., 'The current targeting process' in P. A. L. Ducheine et al. (eds.) *Targeting: the challenges of modern warfare*, Springer/Asser Press, 2016, pp. 77–97.

Prud'homme, N., 'Lex specialis: oversimplifying a more complex and multifaceted relationship?' (2007) vol. 40, no. 2, *Israel Law Review*, pp. 356–395.

Quéguiner, J.-F., 'Precautions under the law governing the conduct of hostilities' (2006) vol. 88, no. 864, *International Review of the Red Cross*, pp. 793–821.

Ratner, S. R., 'Sources of international humanitarian law and international criminal law: war/crimes and the limits of the doctrine of sources' in J. D'Aspremont and S. Besson (eds.) *Oxford handbook of the sources of international law*, Oxford University Press, 2017, pp. 912–935.

Redse Johansen, S., 'On military necessity and the commander's assessment of military necessity under the international law of armed conflict during conduct of hostilities', PhD dissertation, University of Oslo, 2017.

Reed, W., 'Laws of war: the developing law of armed conflict: some current problems' (1977) vol. 9, no. 1, *Case Western Reserve Journal of International Law*, pp. 17–38.

Reynolds, J. D., 'Collateral damage on the 21st century battlefield: enemy exploitation of the law of armed conflict and the struggle for a moral high ground' (2005) vol. 56, *Air Force Law Review*, pp. 1–108.

Roberts, A. and R. Guelff, *Documents on the laws of war*, 3rd edition, Oxford University Press, 2000.

Robinson, I. and E. Nohle, 'Proportionality and precautions in attack: the reverberating effects of using explosive weapons in populated areas' (2016) vol. 98, no. 1, *International Review of the Red Cross*, pp. 107–145.

Rogers, A. P. V., 'Zero-casualty warfare' (2000) vol. 82, no. 837, *International Review of the Red Cross*, pp. 165–181.

Law on the battlefield, 2nd edition, Manchester University Press, 2004.

'The principle of proportionality' in H. M. Hensel (ed.) *The legitimate use of military force: the Just War tradition and the customary law of armed conflict*, Ashgate, 2008, pp. 189–218.

Law on the battlefield, 3rd edition, Manchester University Press, 2012.

Ronen, Y., 'International humanitarian law' in J. Kammerhofer and J. D'Aspremont (eds.) *International legal positivism in a post-modern world*, Cambridge University Press, 2014, pp. 475–497.

Ronzitti, N., 'The codification of law of air warfare' in N. Ronzitti and G. Venturini (eds.) *The law of air warfare: contemporary issues*, Eleven International Publishing, 2006, pp. 3–15.

Roscini, M., 'Targeting and contemporary aerial bombardment' (2005) vol. 54, no. 2, *The International and Comparative Law Quarterly*, pp. 411–444.

Rowe, P., 'Kosovo 1999: the air campaign: have the provisions of Additional Protocol I withstood the test?' (2000) vol. 82, no. 837, *International Review of the Red Cross*, pp. 147–164.

Royse, M. W., *Aerial bombardment and the international regulation of warfare*, Harold Vinal Publishers, 1928.

Salmon, J., *Dictionaire de droit international public*, Bruylant/AUF, 2001.

Sandoz, Y., 'Advisory opinion of the International Court of Justice on the legality of the threat or use of nuclear weapons: preliminary remarks' (1997) vol. 37, no. 316, *International Review of the Red Cross*, pp. 6–8.

'Commentary' in A. E. Wall (ed.) *Legal and ethical lessons of NATO's Kosovo Campaign*, US Naval War College's International Law Studies, vol. 78, Newport, 2002, pp. 273–279.

Sandoz, Y., C. Swinarski and B. Zimmermann, *ICRC commentary on the Additional Protocols of 8 June 1977 to the Geneva Conventions of 12 August 1949*, Martinus Nijhoff, 1987.

Sanger, A., 'The contemporary law of blockade and the Gaza Freedom Flotilla' (2010) vol. 13, *Yearbook of International Humanitarian Law*, pp. 397–446.

Sari, A. and K. Tinkler, 'Collateral damage and the enemy' (2019) *British Yearbook of International Law*, pp. 1–107, doi:10.1093/bybil/brz004.

Sassòli, M., 'Targeting: the scope and utility of the concept of "military objectives" for the protection of civilians in contemporary armed conflicts' in D. Wippman and M. Evangelista (eds.) *New wars, new laws?: applying the laws of war in 21st century conflicts*, Transnational, 2005, pp. 181–210.

'*Ius ad bellum* and *ius in bello*: the separation between the legality of the use of force and humanitarian rules to be respected in warfare: crucial or outdated?' in M. Schmitt and J. Pejic (eds.) *International law and armed conflict: exploring the faultlines: essays in honour of Yoram Dinstein*, Nijhoff, 2007, pp. 241–264.

Sassòli, M. and L. Cameron, 'The protection of civilian objects: current state of the law and issues de lege ferenda' in N. Ronzitti and G. Venturini (eds.) *Current issues in the international humanitarian law of air warfare*, Eleven International Publishing, 2006, pp. 63–64.

Sassòli, M. and L. M. Olson, 'The relationship between international humanitarian and human rights law where it matters: admissible killing and internment of fighters in non-international armed conflicts' (2008) vol. 90, no. 871, *International Review of the Red Cross*, pp. 599–627.

Sassòli, M. and A. Quintin, 'Active and passive precautions in air and missile warfare' (2014) vol. 44, *Israel Yearbook on Human Rights*, pp. 69–123.

Sassòli, M. et al., How does law protect in war? Proportionality, https://casebook.icrc.org/casebook/doc/glossary/proportionality-glossary.htm.

Schindler, D. and J. Toman, *The laws of armed conflict: a collection of conventions, resolutions and other documents*, 4th revised and completed edition, Martinus Nijhoff, 2004.

Schmitt, M. N., 'Green war: an assessment of the environmental law of international armed conflict' (1997) vol. 22, *Yale Journal of International Law*, pp. 1–109.

'Fault lines in the law of attack' in Breau, S. C. and A. Jachec-Neale (eds.) *Testing the boundaries of international humanitarian law*, The British Institute of International and Comparative Law (2006a), pp. 277–307.

'The conduct of hostilities during Operation Iraqi Freedom: an international humanitarian law assessment' (2006b) vol. 6, *Yearbook of International Humanitarian Law*, pp. 73–109.

'The law of targeting' in E. Wilmshurst and S. C. Breau (eds.) *Perspectives on the ICRC study on customary international humanitarian law*, Cambridge University Press, 2007, pp. 131–168.

'Human shields in international humanitarian law' (2008) vol. 38, *Israel Yearbook on Human Rights*, pp. 17–59.

'Human shields in international humanitarian law' (2009) vol. 47, no. 2, *Columbia Journal of Transnational Law*, pp. 292–338.

'Foreword' in W. H. Boothby, *The law of targeting*, Oxford University Press, 2012, pp. vii–ix.

'Targeting in operational law' in T. D. Gill and D. Fleck (eds.) *The handbook of the international law of military operations*, 2nd edition, Oxford University Press, 2016, pp. 269–306.

Schmitt, M. N. and C. E. Highfill, 'Invisible injuries: concussive effects and international humanitarian law' (2018) vol. 9, *Harvard National Security Journal*, pp. 72–99.

Schmitt, M. N. and J. S. Thurnher, 'Out of the loop: autonomous weapon systems and the law of armed conflict' (2013) vol. 4, no. 2, *Harvard National Security Journal*, pp. 231–281.

Scobbie, I., 'The approach to customary international law in the study' in E. Wilmshurst and S. Breau (eds.) *Perspectives on the ICRC study on customary international humanitarian law*, Cambridge University Press, 2007, pp. 15–49.

Scott, J. B., *The reports to the Hague Conferences of 1899 and 1907*, Clarendon Press, 1917.

Scott Adams, R., 'Lancelot in the sky: protecting wounded combatants from incidental harm' (8 August 2017) https://harvardnsj.org/2017/08/08/lancelot-in-the-sky-protecting-wounded-combatants-from-incidental-harm/.

Shamash, M. E., 'How much is too much? An examination of the principle of *ius in bello* proportionality' (2005–2006) vol. 2, *IDF Law Review*, pp. 104–148.

Shaw, M. N., *International law*, 7th edition, Cambridge University Press, 2014.

Shue, H. and D. Wippmann, 'Limiting attacks on dual-use facilities performing indispensable civilian functions' (2002) vol. 35, no. 3, *Cornell International Law Journal*, pp. 559–579.

Simma, B. and P. Alston, 'The sources of human rights law: custom, *jus cogens* and general principles' (1992) vol. 12, *Australian Yearbook of International Law*, pp. 82–108.

Sivakumaran, S., 'International humanitarian law' in D. Moeckli et al. (eds.) *International human rights law*, Oxford University Press, 2010, pp. 521–539.

The law of non-international armed conflict, Oxford University Press, 2012.

Slaughter, A.-M. and S. R. Ratner, 'Appraising the methods of international law: a prospectus for readers' (1999) vol. 93, no. 2, *American Journal of International Law*, pp. 291–302.

Sloane, R. D., 'Puzzles of proportion and the reasonable military commander: reflections on the law, ethics, and geopolitics of proportionality' (2015) vol. 6, no. 2, *Harvard National Security Journal*, pp. 299–343.

Solis, G. D., *The law of armed conflict: international humanitarian law in war*, 2nd edition, Cambridge University Press, 2016.

Spaight, J. M., *Air power and war rights*, Longmans, Green and Co, 1924.

Air power and the cities, Longmans, Green and Co, 1930.

Air power and war rights, 2nd edition, Longmans, Green and Co, 1933.

Bombing vindicated, Geoffrey Bles, 1944.

Stahn, C., 'The International Committee of the Red Cross' influence on related areas of international law' in R. Geiss et al. (eds.) *Humanizing the laws of war: the Red Cross and the development of international humanitarian law*, Cambridge University Press, 2017, pp. 139–212.

Stone, R. W., 'Protecting civilians during operation allied force: the enduring importance of the proportional response and NATO's use of armed force in Kosovo' (2001) vol. 50, *Catholic University Law Review*, pp. 501–537.

Stürchler, N., *The threat of force in international law*, Cambridge University Press, 2007.

Turns, D., 'At the "vanishing point" of international humanitarian law: methods and means of warfare in non-international armed conflicts' (2002) vol. 45, *German Yearbook of International Law*, pp. 115–148.

van den Boogaard, J. C., 'Fighting by the principles: principles as a source of international humanitarian law' in M. Matthee et al. (eds.) *Armed conflict and international law: in search of the human face: Liber Amicorum in memory of Avril McDonald*, Asser Press, 2013, pp. 3–31.

'Proportionality and autonomous weapons systems' (2015) vol. 6, *Journal of International Humanitarian Legal Studies*, pp. 247–283.

'Knock on the roof: legitimate warning or method of warfare?' (2018a) vol. 19, *Yearbook of International Humanitarian Law*, pp. 183–209.

'Laser weapons' in D. Djukić and N. Pons (eds.) *The companion to international humanitarian law*, Brill Nijhoff, 2018b, pp. 462–464.

van den Boogaard, J. C. and A. Vermeer, 'Precautions in attack and urban and siege warfare' (2019) vol. 20, *Yearbook of International Humanitarian Law*, pp. 163–198.

van Dijk, B., 'Human rights in war: on the entangled foundations of the 1949 Geneva Conventions' (2018) vol. 112, no. 4, *American Journal of International Law*, pp. 553–582.

van Engeland, A., 'When two visions of a just world clash: international humanitarian law and Islamic humanitarian law' (2006) vol. 100, *Proceedings of the Annual Meeting* (American Society of International Law), pp. 155–156.

van Hoof, G. J. H., 'Rethinking the Sources of International Law', dissertation, 1983.

van Houtte, H., 'The Eritrea-Ethiopia Claims Commission and international humanitarian Law' in G. Venturini and S. Bariatti (eds.) *Individual Rights and International Justice, Liber Fausto Pocar*, Giuffrè, 2009, pp. 383–398.

van Schaak, B., 'The Law and Policy of Human Shielding' in C. M. Ford and W. S. Williams (eds) *Complex battlespaces: the law of armed conflict and the dynamics of modern warfare*, Oxford University Press, 2018, pp. 463–514.

van Steenberghe, R., 'Sources of international humanitarian law and international criminal law: specific features' in J. D'Aspremont and S. Besson (eds.) *Oxford handbook of the sources of international law*, Oxford University Press, 2017, pp. 891–911.

Vité, S., 'Typology of armed conflicts in international humanitarian law: legal concepts and actual situations' (2009) vol. 91, no. 873, *International Review of the Red Cross*, pp. 69–94.

von der Groeben, C., 'Criminal responsibility of German soldiers in Afghanistan: the case of Colonel Klein' (2010) vol. 11, no. 5, *German Law Journal*, pp. 469–492.

Voon, T., 'Pointing the finger: civilian casualties of NATO bombing in the Kosovo Conflict' (2001) vol. 16, no. 4, *American University International Law Review*, pp. 1083–1113.

Wall, A. E. (ed.) *Legal and ethical lessons of NATO's Kosovo Campaign*, International Law Studies, vol. 78, U.S. Naval War College, 2002.

Walzer, M. L., *Just and unjust wars: a moral argument with historical illustrations*, Basic Books, 1977 (4th edition, 2006).

Watkin, K., 'Controlling the use of force: a role for human rights norms in contemporary armed conflict' (2004) vol. 98, no. 1, *American Journal of International Law*, pp. 1–34.

'Assessing proportionality: moral complexity and legal rules' (2007) vol. 8, *Yearbook of International Humanitarian Law*, pp. 3–53.

Watson, G. R., 'Humanitarian law: law of belligerent occupation: proportionality of security measures taken in occupied territory: self-defense against terrorism: effect of ICJ decisions in domestic courts' (2006) vol. 100, no. 4, *American Journal of International Law*, pp. 895–901.

Weill, S., 'The targeted killing of Salah Shehadeh: from Gaza to Madrid' (2009) vol. 7, *Journal of International Criminal Justice*, pp. 617–631.

Wells-Greco, M., 'Operation "Cast Lead": jus in belli proportionality' (2010) vol. 57, no. 3, *Netherlands International Law Review*, pp. 397–422.

Werres, B., 'Der Targeting-Prozess in der NATO: die Methode Collateral-Damage-Estimation (CDE)' in M. Gillner and V. Stümke (eds.) *Kollateralopfer: die Tötung von Unschuldigen als rechtliches und moralisches Problem*, Nomos, 2014, pp. 47–50.

Whittemore, L. A., 'Proportionality decision making in targeting: heuristics, cognitive biases, and the law' (2016) vol. 7, *Harvard National Security Journal*, pp. 577–636.

Wilmshurst, E., 'Conclusions' in E. Wilmshurst and S. Breau (eds.) *Perspectives on the ICRC study on customary international humanitarian law*, Cambridge University Press, 2007, pp. 401–413.

Winter, E., 'Pillars not principles: the status of humanity and military necessity in the law of armed conflict' (2020) vol. 25, no. 1, *Journal of Conflict & Security Law*, pp. 1–31.

Wood, M., 'The evolution and identification of the customary international law of armed conflict', vol. 51, *Vanderbilt Journal of Transnational Law*, pp. 727–736.

Wright, J. D., '"Excessive" ambiguity: analysing and refining the proportionality standard' (2012) vol. 94, no. 886, *International Review of the Red Cross*, pp. 819–854.

Zimmermann, M., 'Hinterhalt am Baghlan River in Afghanistan: eine Tagebuchaufzeichnung' in M. Gillner and V. Stümke (eds.) *Kollateralopfer: die Tötung von Unschuldigen als rechtliches und moralisches Problem*, Nomos, 2014, pp. 31–38.

Zöckler, M. C., 'Commentary on Protocol IV on blinding laser weapons' (1998) vol. 1, *Yearbook of International Humanitarian Law*, pp. 333–340.

ONLINE RESOURCES

Anderson, K., 'Who owns the rules of war?', *The New York Times Magazine*, 13 April 2003, pp. 38–43, www.nytimes.com/2003/04/13/magazine/who-owns-the-rules-of-war.html or www.faculty.umb.edu/gary_zabel/Courses/Morals%20and%20Law/M+L/news-iraq6.html.

BBC News, 'Saddam's Iraq: key events', 2003, http://news.bbc.co.uk/2/shared/spl/hi/middle_east/02/iraq_events/html/ground_war.stm.

Friedman, R., 'Deaths in 2002 Shehadeh killing came from faulty intel', *The Jerusalem Post*, 28 February 2011, www.jpost.com/National-News/Deaths-in-2002-Shehadeh-killing-came-from-faulty-intel.

Human Rights Watch, 'Sudan: Southern Kordofan civilians tell of air strike horror', 30 August 2011, www.hrw.org/news/2011/08/30/sudan-southern-kordofan-civilians-tell-air-strike-horror.

Hyland, T., 'Lost in the fog of war', *The Sydney Morning Herald*, 12 February 2012, www.smh.com.au/national/lost-in-the-fog-of-war-20120211-1sybr.html.

Information Directorate, Wright-Patterson Air Force Base, 'Joint targeting toolbox successfully integrated at JEFX 2006', 5 December 2006, https://www.wpafb.af.mil/News/Article-Display/Article/401562/joint-targeting-toolbox-successfully-integrated-at-jefx-2006/.

Niv, A., 'The disproportion in the Shehadeh Commission's proportionality test', Association for the Promotion of International Humanitarian Law, 29 November 2012, https://sites.google.com/site/almaihl2010en/opeds/the-disproportion-in-the-shehadeh-commission-s-proportionality-test.

Northrop Grumman, 'Rainstorm: advanced precision targeting', 2014, www.northropgrumman.com/Capabilities/RainStorm/Documents/RainStorm.pdf.

Roth, K., 'Barrel bombs, not ISIS, are the greatest threat to Syrians', *Human Rights Watch*, 5 August 2015, www.hrw.org/news/2015/08/05/barrel-bombs-not-isis-are-greatest-threat-syrians.

Schmitt, R. J., 'U.S. Army buried Iraqi soldiers alive in Gulf War', *New York Times*, 15 September 1991, www.nytimes.com/1991/09/15/world/us-army-buried-iraqi-soldiers-alive-in-gulf-war.html.

Sloyan, P. J., 'What I saw was a bunch of filled-in trenches with people's arms and legs sticking out of them. For all I know, we could have killed thousands', *The Guardian*, 14 February 2003, www.theguardian.com/world/2003/feb/14/iraq.features11

The Guardian, 'Israeli jets attack Hamas', 23 July 2002, www.theguardian.com/world/2002/jul/23/israel.

Wikipedia, 'Marc Garlasco', https://en.wikipedia.org/wiki/Marc_Garlasco.

Yonah, J. B., 'Meet the godfather of Israeli experts on international law and war crimes', *The Jerusalem Post*, 24 April 2016, www.jpost.com/Israel-News/Meet-the-godfather-of-Israeli-experts-on-international-law-and-war-crimes-452131.

YonHap News Agency, '(2nd LD) Military suggests counterfire caused "many casualties" in N. Korea', 2 December 2010, http://english.yonhapnews.co.kr/national/2010/12/02/83/0301000000AEN20101202009100315F.HTML?2181af00.

YouTube, 'New details on September Kunduz bombing', Kunduz Attack Cockpit footage, Al Jazeera English, 4 February 2010, www.youtube.com/watch?v=nexiUdImS68.

BLOGS

Bartels, R. J., 'Prlić et al.: The destruction of the Old Bridge of Mostar and proportionality', EJILTALK, 31 July 2013, www.ejiltalk.org/prlic-et-al-the-destruction-of-the-old-bridge-of-mostar-and-proportionality/.

Blank, L. et al., 'Surveying proportionality: whither the reasonable commander?' Just Security, 25 March 2015, www.justsecurity.org/21474/surveying-proportionality-reasonable-commander/.

Corn, G. S., 'Precautions to minimize civilian harm are a fundamental principle of the law of war', Just Security, 8 July 2015, www.justsecurity.org/24493/obligation-precautions-fundamental-principle-law-war/.

Dill, J., '"Proportionate" collateral damage and why we should care about what civilians think', Just Security, 27 March 2015, www.justsecurity.org/21529/meaning-proportionate-collateral-damage-care-civilians/.

'The DoD Law of War Manual and the false appeal of differentiating types of civilians', Just Security, 1 December 2016, www.justsecurity.org/35068/dod-law-war-manual-false-appeal-differentiating-types-civilians.

Dunlap, C. J., 'Human shields and the DOD Law of War Manual: can't we improve the debate?' Just Security, 25 June 2015, www.justsecurity.org/24199/human-shields-dod-law-war-manual-cant-improve-debate/#more-24199.

Haque, A. A., 'Human shields in the DOD Manual: a new mistake or an old one?' Just Security, 29 October 2015, www.justsecurity.org/27173/human-shields-dod-manual-mistake-one/.

Hathaway, O. et al., 'Two lingering concerns about the forthcoming Law of War Manual amendments', Just Security, 30 November 2016, www.justsecurity.org/35025/lingering-concerns-forthcoming-law-war-manual-amendments.

Kleffner, J. K., 'Transatlantic workshop on international law and armed conflict: wounded and sick and the proportionality assessment', ICRC, Intercross, 12 October 2017, http://intercrossblog.icrc.org/blog/transatlantic-workshop-on-international-law-and-armed-conflict-wounded-and-sick-and-the-proportionality-assessment.

Lederman, M., 'Is it legal to target ISIL's oil facilities and cash stockpiles?' Just Security, 27 May 2016, www.justsecurity.org/31281/legality-striking-isils-oil-facilities-cash-stockpiles/.

Merriam, J., 'Must military medical and religious personnel be accounted for in a proportionality analysis?' Just Security, 8 July 2016, www.justsecurity.org/31905.

Milanovic, M., 'An eventful day in The Hague: channelling Socrates and Goering', EJILTALK, 30 November 2017, www.ejiltalk.org/an-eventful-day-in-the-hague-channeling-socrates-and-goering/.

Nohle, E. and I. Robinson, 'War in cities: the "reverberating effects" of explosive weapons', Humanitarian Law and Policy, ICRC blog, 2 March 2017, http://blogs.icrc.org/law-and-policy/2017/03/02/war-in-cities-the-reverberating-effects-of-explosive-weapons/.

van den Boogaard, J. C., 'Reimagining IHL principles, Part I: the wrong principles', Articles of War, 8 December 2020, https://lieber.westpoint.edu/reimagining-ihl-principles-part-i-wrong-principles/.

van den Boogaard, J. C., 'Reimagining IHL principles, Part II: a new framework', Articles of War, 11 December 2020, https://lieber.westpoint.edu/reimagining-ihl-principles-part-ii-new-framework/.

MILITARY MANUALS AND DOCTRINE

Canada

Law of Armed Conflict at the Operational and Tactical Levels, Joint Doctrine Manual, National Defence Canada, Office of the Judge Advocate, 2001, B-GJ-005-104/FP-021, pp. 2-1–2-3, www.fichl.org/fileadmin/_migrated/content_uploads/Canadian_LOAC_Manual_2001_English.pdf.

Germany

Humanitarian Law in Armed Conflicts – Manual, The Federal Ministry of Defence of the Federal Republic of Germany, VR II, 3 August 1992, www.humanitaeres-voelkerrecht.de/ManualZDv15.2.pdf.

Law of Armed Conflict – Manual, Bundesministerium der Verteidigung, Joint Service Regulation (ZDv) 15/2, May 2013, DSK AV230100262, p. 25.

Israel

2006 Israel Military Manual, Rules of Warfare on the Battlefield, Military Advocate-General's Corps Command, 2nd edition, IDF School of Military Law, 2006.

NATO

NATO, 2008, Allied Joint Publication, AJP 3.9, Allied Joint Doctrine for Joint targeting.

NATO Glossary of Terms, www.nato.int/docu/stanag/aap006/aap-6-2010.pdf.

Norway

The Military Manual of Norway, Draft-English translation of the Norwegian military manual, on file with the author, pp. 19–20.

Philippines

Military Manual of the Philippines, www.icrc.org/customary-ihl/eng/docs/v2_rul_rule14.

Switzerland

Basic Military Manual (1987), http://www.icrc.org/customary-ihl/eng/docs/v2_rul_rule15.

The Netherlands

The Handbook on International Humanitarian Law, VS 27-412/1, Handleiding Humanitair Oorlogsrecht, published by the Royal Netherlands Army, 2005.

United Kingdom

The United Kingdom Manual of the Law of Armed Conflict, Oxford University Press, 2004

United States

Instructions for the Government of Armies of the United States in the Field, promulgated as General Orders No. 100 by President Lincoln on 24 April 1863, Adjutant General's Office, prepared by Francis Lieber, LL.D., reprinted in Schindler and Toman, pp. 3–20.

1956 US Army Field Manual, Department of the Army Field Manual, The Law of Land Warfare (FM 27-10), July 1956.

Annotated Supplement to the Commander's Handbook on the Law of Naval Operations, NWP 9 (REV. A)/FMFM 1-10 (1989)

Air Force Pamphlet 14-210 Intelligence, http://citeseerx.ist.psu.edu/viewdoc/download?doi=10.1.1.131.8965&rep=rep1&type=pdf.

United States Joint Targeting Doctrine, Joint Publication 3-60, published 17 January 2002, page A2 of Appendix A, www.bits.de/NRANEU/others/jp-doctrine/jp3_60(02).pdf.

US Interservice Field Manual FM 3-06 Aviation Urban Operations, July 2005, pp. I–6, www.scribd.com/doc/12777654/fm306.

The Commander's Handbook on the Law of Naval Operations, NWP I-14 M, July 2007 edition.

United States, Joint Chiefs of Staff, Joint Publication 3-60, Joint Targeting (13 April 2007), Appendix C, p. C-4, www.aclu.org/files/dronefoia/dod/drone_dod_jp3_60.pdf.

US Joint Chiefs of Staff, Joint Publication 1-02 2010, available online: US Doctrine, Joint Publication 3-30, the Command and Control of Joint Air Operations, 10 February 2014, www.dtic.mil/doctrine/new_pubs/jp1_02.pdf.

Department of Defense Law of War Manual, DOD Law of War Manual, 2015 and 3rd revised version, December 2016, www.hsdl.org/?view&did=797480.

REPORTS

Amnesty International, 'Lebanon: deliberate destruction or "collateral damage"? Israeli attacks on civilian infrastructure', Report, 22 August 2006, index no. MDE 18/007/2006, www.amnesty.org/en/documents/mde18/007/2006/en/.

Amnesty International, 'Federal Republic of Yugoslavia (FRY) /NATO: "collateral damage" or unlawful killings? Violations of the laws of war by NATO during Operation Allied Force', Report, 5 June 2000, index no. EUR 70/018/2000, www.amnesty.org/en/documents/eur70/018/2000/en/.

Chilcot, J., 'The Iraq Inquiry', the Chilcot Report, The National Archives, 6 July 2016, www.iraqinquiry.org.uk.

Deutscher Bundestag, 'Beschlussempfehlung und Bericht des Verteidigungsausschusses als 1. Untersuchungsausschuss gemäß Artikel 45a Absatz 2 des Grundgesetzes' Report of the German Parliamentary Investigation Committee ('PIC Report'), 20 October 2011, http://dip21.bundestag.de/dip21/btd/17/074/1707400.pdf.

House of Commons, Official Report, 2 April 2003, column 738W as quoted in the Chilcot Report, www.iraqinquiry.org.uk, para. 51 on p. 180.

Human Rights Watch, 'Needless deaths in the Gulf War: civilian casualties during the air campaign and violations of the laws of war', Report, 1 June 1991, www.hrw.org/reports/1991/gulfwar/INTRO.htm

Human Rights Watch, 'Off-target: the conduct of the war and civilian casualties in Iraq', Report, 2003, www.hrw.org/reports/2003/usa1203/4.htm

'Israel and the occupied Palestinian territories: civilians under assault: Hezbollah's rocket attacks on Israel in the 2006 War', Report, August 2007, vol. 19, no. 3(E), www.hrw.org/reports/2007/iopt0807/iopt0807web.pdf.

'Troops in contact, airstrikes and civilian deaths in Afghanistan', Report, 8 September 2008, www.hrw.org/report/2008/09/08/troops-contact/airstrikes-and-civilian-deaths-afghanistan#.

'Up in flames: humanitarian law violations and civilian victims in the conflict over South Ossetia', Report, 23 January 2009, www.hrw.org/en/reports/2009/01/22/flames-o

'Schools and armed conflict: a global survey of domestic laws and state practice protecting schools from attack and military use', Report, 20 July 2011, www.hrw.org/sites/default/files/reports/crd0711webwcover.pdf.

International Crisis Group, 'North Korea: the risks of war in the Yellow Sea, Asia', Report N°198 – 23 December 2010 (ICG Report), www.crisisgroup.org/en/regions/asia/north-east-asia/north-korea/198-north-korea-the-risks-of-war-in-the-yellow-sea.aspx.

International Law Association, 'Final Report of the Study Group on the conduct of hostilities under international humanitarian law – challenges of 21st century warfare' (2011–2017), www.ila-hq.org/en/study-groups/index.cfm/cid/1040. The Final Report of the Study Group, www.ila-hq.org/index.php/study-groups?study-groupsID=58.

International Criminal Court, Office of the Prosecutor, 'Situation in the Republic of Korea, Article 5 Report' (ICC Korea Report), June 2014, www.icc-cpi.int/iccdocs/otp/SAS-KOR-Article-5-Public-Report-ENG-05Jun2014.pdf

International Tribunal for the former Yugoslavia, Office of the Prosecutor, 'Final Report to the Prosecutor by the Committee established to review the NATO bombing campaign against the Federal Republic of Yugoslavia' (ICTY OTP Kosovo Report), 13 June 2000, www.icty.org/en/press/final-report-prosecutor-committee-established-review-nato-bombing-campaign-against-federal.

Israel Ministry of Foreign Affairs, 'The operation in Gaza: cast lead: 27 December 2008 – 18 January 2009, factual and legal aspects', Report, July 2009, , https://reliefweb.int/report/israel/opt-operation-gaza-27-dec-2008-18-jan-2009-factual-and-legal-aspects.

'Findings' Salah Shehadeh-Special Investigatory Commission' (SIC Report), 27 February 2011, https://mfa.gov.il/MFA/AboutIsrael/State/Law/Pages/Salah_Shehadeh-Special_Investigatory_Commission_27-Feb-2011.aspx

'The 2014 Gaza Conflict (7 July–26 August 2014): factual and legal aspects', Report, May 2015, https://mfa.gov.il/ProtectiveEdge/Documents/2014GazaConflictFullReport.pdf.

United Nations General Assembly, 'Human rights in Palestine and other Occupied Arab Territories' Report of the United Nations Fact-Finding Mission on the Gaza Conflict ('Goldstone Report') UN document A/HRC/12/48, 25 September 2009, United Nations Human Rights Council, Twelfth session, Agenda item 7, https://documents-dds-ny.un.org/doc/UNDOC/GEN/G09/158/66/PDF/G0915866.pdf?OpenElement.

'Report of the Independent International Commission of Inquiry on the Syrian Arab Republic concerning the situation in Aleppo', 2 February 2017 (A-HRC-34-64), submitted to the Human Rights Council, Thirty-fourth session, 27 February–24 March 2017, Agenda item 4, https://documents-dds-ny.un.org/doc/UNDOC/GEN/G17/026/63/PDF/G1702663.pdf?OpenElement.

'Report of the Secretary General's Panel of Experts on Accountability in Sri Lanka', 31 March 2011, www.un.org/News/dh/infocus/Sri_Lanka/POE_Report_Full.pdf.

'Report of the Secretary-General's Panel of Inquiry on the 31 May 2010 Flotilla Incident', July 2011 ('Palmer Report'), http://graphics8.nytimes.com/packages/pdf/world/Palmer-Committee-Final-report.pdf.

University Centre for International Humanitarian Law, 'Targeting military objectives', Report, 12 May 2005, Expert Meeting, organized by the University Centre for International Humanitarian Law, Geneva, https://docplayer.net/4077128-Expert-meeting-targeting-military-objectives.html.

OTHER SOURCES

Blank, L. et al., Amicus Curiae brief, 'Application and proposed amicus curiae brief concerning the 15 April 2011 Trial Chamber Judgement and requesting that the Appeals Chamber reconsider the findings of unlawful attacks during Operation Storm', submitted to the ICTY Appeals Chamber, the Prosecutor v. A. Gotovina and M. Markac, Case No. IT-06-90-A, 12 January 2012, http://icr.icty.org/LegalRef/CMSDocStore/Public/English/Application/NotIndexable/IT-06-90-A/MSC7958R0000353013.pdf

Copenhagen process on the handling of detainees in international military operation: principles and guidelines, 2014, www.state.gov/documents/organization/211975.pdf.

Cowie, A. P. (ed.), *Oxford advanced learners dictionary*, 4th edition, Oxford University Press, 1989.

ICRC, Red Cross draft rules for the limitation of the dangers incurred by the civilian population in time of war. *International Review of the Red Cross*, Supplement IX, 1956, p. 164. For the commentary, see *International Review of the Red Cross*, 1956, pp. 623–650 and 695–710.

Mr. I. Mueller, Final record concerning the draft rules for the limitation of the dangers incurred by the civilian population in time of war, third meeting, 30 October 1957, p. 68, www.loc.gov/rr/frd/Military_Law/pdf/RC_Final-record-rules-limitation.pdf.

April 1958, 'Final record concerning the draft rules for the limitation of the dangers incurred by the civilian population in time of war', XIXth International Conference of the Red Cross, New Delhi, October–November 1957, www.loc.gov/rr/frd/Military_Law/pdf/RC_Final-record-rules-limitation.pdf

XXVIII Resolution adopted at the XXth Conference of the Red Cross, published in the IRRC, No. 56, November 1965, www.loc.gov/rr/frd/Military_Law/pdf/RC_Nov-1965.pdf.

Official records of the Diplomatic Conference on the Reaffirmation and Development of International Humanitarian Law Applicable in Armed Conflicts, Volume XV, ICRC, 1974–1977, www.loc.gov/rr/frd/Military_Law/pdf/RC-records_Vol-15.pdf.

'Expert meeting: explosive weapons in populated areas' Report, 15 June 2015, www.icrc.org/en/document/explosive-weapons-populated-areas-humanitarian-legal-technical-and-military-aspects.

Quebec Expert Meeting on the rules governing the conduct of hostilities: the principle of proportionality, Background Document, June 2016, on file with the author.

The report of the International Expert Meeting 22–23 June 2016, Quebec, The principle of proportionality in the rules governing the conduct of hostilities under international humanitarian law, drafted by Laurent Gisel, 3 September 2018, www.icrc.org/en/document/international-expert-meeting-report-principle-proportionality.

NATO/ISAF HQ Kabul, McCrystal Tactical Directive, 6 July 2009, www.nato.int/isaf/docu/official_texts/Tactical_Directive_090706.pdf.

Program on Humanitarian Policy and Conflict Research, Harvard University, *Manual on international law applicable to air and missile warfare*, Bern, 15 May 2009, http://ihlresearch.org/amw/HPCR%20Manual.pdf.

Program on Humanitarian Policy and Conflict Research, Harvard University, *Commentary to the Manual on international law applicable to air and missile warfare*, Bern, 15 May 2009.

San Remo manual on international law applicable to armed conflicts at sea, 1994, in Roberts and Guelff, *Documents on the laws of war*, pp. 573–606.

Schmitt, M. N. et al. (eds.) *Sanremo manual on the law of non-international armed conflicts*, 2006, www.fd.unl.pt/docentes_docs/ma/jc_MA_26125.pdf.

The Tallinn manual 2.0 on the international law applicable to cyber operations, 2nd edition, Cambridge University Press, 2017.

Soanes, C. and Stevenson, A. (eds.), *Concise Oxford English dictionary*, 11th edition revised, Oxford University Press, 2008.

Swiss Federal Department of Foreign Affairs and the ICRC, 'The Montreux Document on pertinent international legal obligations and good practices for States related to operations of private military and security companies during armed conflict', August 2009, www.icrc.org/en/doc/assets/files/other/icrc_002_0996.pdf

Switzerland, 'Status of the Protocols Additional to the Geneva Conventions of 1949 and relating to the protection of victims of armed conflicts, Report for the period 2006–2008', Revocation of declaration to Additional Protocol I, 28 May 2008, www.un.org/en/ga/sixth/63/Addtl_Prot_TEXT/Switzerland.pdf.

United Nations General Assembly, 'Respect for Human Rights in Armed Conflicts' Resolution 2444 (XXIII) of the United Nations General Assembly, 19 December 1968, reprinted in Schindler and Toman, *The Laws of Armed Conflicts*, pp. 345–350.

Index

For EU product safety concerns, contact us at Calle de José Abascal, 56–1°, 28003 Madrid, Spain or eugpsr@cambridge.org.

www.ingramcontent.com/pod-product-compliance
Lightning Source LLC
LaVergne TN
LVHW010341220926
848484LV00004BB/1078
* 9 7 8 1 1 0 8 8 4 5 1 3 7 *